Continuous Delivery in Java

Essential Tools and Best Practices
for Deploying Code to Production

Daniel Bryant and Abraham Marín-Pérez

Beijing · Boston · Farnham · Sebastopol · Tokyo

Continuous Delivery in Java

by Daniel Bryant and Abraham Marín-Pérez

Published by O'Reilly Media, Inc., 1005 Gravenstein Highway North, Sebastopol, CA 95472.

O'Reilly books may be purchased for educational, business, or sales promotional use. Online editions are also available for most titles (*http://oreilly.com/safari*). For more information, contact our corporate/institutional sales department: 800-998-9938 or *corporate@oreilly.com*.

Editor: Virginia Wilson	**Indexer:** Ellen Troutman-Zaig
Production Editor: Nicholas Adams	**Interior Designer:** David Futato
Copyeditor: Sharon Wilkey	**Cover Designer:** Karen Montgomery
Proofreader: Marta Justak	**Illustrator:** Rebecca Demarest

November 2018:   First Edition

Revision History for the First Edition
2018-11-06:   First Release

See *http://oreilly.com/catalog/errata.csp?isbn=9781491986028* for release details.

978-1-491-98602-8

[LSI]

Table of Contents

Forewords

There's been broad agreement in the Continuous Delivery community that tools don't matter ever since Dave Farley and Jez Humble wrote Continuous Delivery. There are plenty of good programming languages out there, and plenty of good tools for building, testing, and deploying your code to production. The wisdom of the crowd has been: it doesn't matter which tools you use, as long as you avoid the really terrible tools.

This year, that wisdom has been augmented by the work of Dr. Nicole Forsgren, Jez Humble, and Gene Kim. Their book Accelerate summarises multiple years of research into Continuous Delivery and IT performance. One of their conclusions is the ability for teams to choose their own tools has a strong, statistical impact on Continuous Delivery. So, now the wisdom of the crowd is: it doesn't matter which tools you use, as long as you're able to choose them yourself and you avoid the really terrible tools.

Take me, for example. The first time I did Continuous Delivery on a team was at Elsevier in 2007. We built a journal website in Java 6, Spring 2, and Tomcat 6 using XP practices like TDD and CI. The pipeline was Ant and Cruise Control. The codebase was always releasable, and once a week we deployed to production.

The first time I did Continuous Delivery across an entire company was at LMAX in 2008. We built a state of the art financial exchange in Java 6, Spring 3, and Resin 3 using XP practices and Domain Driven Design. The pipeline was Ant and Cruise Control, with a lot of custom dashboards. The codebase was always releasable, and once a fortnight we deployed to production.

I'm sure you can see the similarities there. Groups of smart people worked closely together. XP practices and sound design principles were essential. The tools used were deliberately chosen for the task at hand. And in the case of LMAX, it helped that the Head of Development was writing the inaugural book on Continuous Delivery at the time. I think his name was Dafydd, or Dev, or something.

What this all means is you can use Java, or PHP, or .NET, and successfully implement Continuous Delivery. You can use Solaris Zones, or Docker. You can use AWS, Azure, or that on-premises data centre your Head Of Platform keeps saying is cheaper than AWS. Just make sure you choose your tools yourself, for the particular problems you face. And don't use MKS for version control, QTP for testing, or any commercial release management tool. They're terrible.

So, if tools don't matter for Continuous Delivery as long as you choose them yourself and they're not terrible choices, why am I writing this foreword?

There's actually a nuanced answer in here, if we look hard enough. Tools don't matter as much as the principles and practices of Continuous Delivery, but they still matter a great deal. Programming languages can help people to quickly create new features and defect fixes, which reduces the Cost of Delay associated with product development. Programming languages can also encourage a testable, releasable application architecture, which are key enablers of Continuous Delivery. Build, test, and deploy tooling can nudge people in the right direction, towards practices such as TDD and Trunk Based Development.

I was reminded of that nuance recently, when I cleared out my childhood bedroom and found my university copy of Ivor Horton's Understanding Java 2. Java and I married each other in 1999, and now it's been so long we've both forgotten it's our 20 year anniversary very soon. In my opinion, it's a great programming language. Over the years Java, JUnit, Gradle, Spring and many other tools have helped me to build well-tested, releasable applications, and encourage people to adopt Continuous Delivery.

With Cloud, containerization, and Serverless leading our inexorable march towards Skynet, we all need guidance from experienced practitioners on how to use the latest tools and work towards Continuous Delivery. In this book, Daniel and Abraham explain how to use Java and popular tools such as Spring Boot, Kubernetes, and AWS EKS to deliver modern web applications frequently enough to meet market demand. IT practitioners working with Java and any of the other tools mentioned in this book can rely on Daniel and Abraham to explain how to implement a Continuous Delivery toolchain for their applications.

— *Steve Smith*
Continuous Delivery consultant at
Continuous Delivery Consulting

Continuous delivery is one of the key practices that should be at the heart of any engineering team. We have often been asked what are some of the key enablers of success at jClarity and new build farm for OpenJDK/Java at adoptopenjdk.net. The answer is that we can deploy daily with the greatest of confidence, and do this with minimal engineering teams. Ever since Dave Farley's and Jez Humble's seminal *Continuous Delivery: Reliable Software Releases through Build, Test, and Deployment Automation* (Addison-Wesley Signature) came out in 2010, folks have started adopting continuous delivery practices, but there has not been a comprehensive guide on how to do this for the ~10 million Java developers out there. Well, now there is!

Daniel and Abraham are both real-world practitioners and their book contains everything you need as a Java developer on this topic, with in-depth explanations as to "why" you want to follow the practices of continuous delivery; how to architect your application in a way that is amenable to this; how to put together build, test, and deploy pipelines; and also the intricacies of deploying to cloud and container environments.

The impact of "cloud native" technologies on Java cannot be understated—modern applications must now contend with such concerns as connectivity to a larger number of external components (both JVM and not), and a very different approach to handling resources (such as I/O) that had traditionally been provided by the local operating system. Even the life cycle of applications, and their locality to specific machines, is changing, with approaches such as immutable infrastructure and serverless requiring Java developers to shift their thinking to take full advantage of the capabilities of these new ways of delivering applications.

Within this brave new world, techniques such as continuous deployment, the tooling and architectural thinking required to support it, and the requirements of a cloud-centric local development environment, are of paramount importance. Until now, there has been no text that specifically caters to Java developers to guide them on their journey into full adoption of continuous delivery and the benefits it offers.

— Martijn Verburg,
CEO at jClarity and LJC Leader
— Ben Evans,
Author and Consulting CTO

Preface

Why Did We Write This Book?

Both of us have been Java developers long enough to witness, and be part of, several shifts within our chosen profession. Java the language has evolved a long way since we both wrote our first lines of code: Java 1.4 gave us nonblocking I/O, Java 8 gave us streams and lambdas, Java 9 gave us modules, and Java 10 finally gave us local variable type inference. Deployment platforms have also evolved in leaps and bounds, and the emergence of cloud and containers has provided many opportunities and challenges. One thing has not changed, though, and that is the need to deliver value to end users and customers. We have needed to use all of our skills, tools, and practices as best as we could in order to make the delivery of software as effective (and fun) as possible. Perhaps even more importantly, we have needed to work with and lead our teams to share this responsibility.

With an ever-increasing range of "best practices" emerging around software development, architecture, and deployment platforms, there is one thing that developers can generally agree on: the principles of continuous integration and continuous delivery add enormous value to the software delivery life cycle. With the increasing demands from customers on the speed and stability of delivery, you need a framework that provides fast feedback and enables the automation of both quality assurance and the deployment processes. However, the challenges for modern software developers are manifold, and attempting to introduce a methodology like continuous delivery—which touches on all aspect of software design and delivery—means that several new skills must be mastered, and some are typically outside a developer's existing comfort zone.

As our careers have progressed, we've frequently found ourselves working on aspects of a project that used to be handled by other individuals or teams, and as such we've learned the hard way the new three key areas of developer skillsets that are needed to harness the benefits of continuous delivery:

Architectural design
> Correctly implementing the fundamentals of loose coupling and high cohesion can have a dramatic effect on the ability to both continually test and deploy components of a software system in isolation.

Automated quality assurance
> Business requirements for increased velocity, and the associated architecture styles that have co-evolved with this (such as self-contained systems, microservices, Function-as-a-Service, etc.), mean that you are now typically testing distributed and complex adaptive systems. These systems simply cannot be verified and validated repeatedly and effectively using a traditional manual process.

Deploying applications
> The emergence of cloud and container technologies has revolutionized deployment options for Java applications, and new skills are needed for harnessing this and creating automated and safe deployment and release processes.

This book distills our learning and offers guidance for mastering these new skills.

Why You Should Read This Book

If you are a Java developer who wants to learn more about continuous delivery, or are currently struggling with embracing this way of delivering software, then this is the book for you. We have provided not only the "how" and "what" of implementing the various practices and tools associated with continuous delivery, but also the "why." We believe this is important, because if you understand the motivations, you will be well placed to adapt particular practices that don't quite work for you as described. Understanding the reasoning behind an approach also helps build strong foundations, and helps you share and teach these ideas to others. As the Japanese poet Matsuo Bashō said, "Do not seek to follow in the footsteps of the wise; seek what they sought."

We have also written this book as a call to action to you, as a Java developer, to get outside your comfort zone and learn more about architecture, automation, and operations. In the current software development career space, we see increasingly fewer opportunities for pure Java programming roles, with many new roles expecting knowledge of continuous delivery, platforms, and operational tooling. By investing in yourself and increasing your software development knowledge and skills, you will not only be open to more opportunities, but also become a better programmer.

As we wrote this book, we had no single idea of a prototypical reader of this book, other than you being a Java developer, but one of the following target personas may resonate with you:

Traditional enterprise Java developer
> You have most likely been coding Java EE or Spring applications for several years, and now you are realizing that new applications within your organization are being designed around microservice-style architectures, and the sysadmin or operations team is experimenting with the cloud, Docker, and Kubernetes. You are keen to learn more about how all these changes relate to building Java applications, and you want to explore how automation will make testing and deployment less painful.

Java developer looking to embrace DevOps
> You have typically been developing Java applications for a few years, and you have followed along with the blog posts, books, and conference presentations that talk about the cloud, DevOps, and Site Reliability Engineering (SRE). You may have envied the development practices of organizations like Netflix, Google, or Spotify, but you appreciate that not all the things they do are relevant to you and your team. However, you are keen to learn more and understand how you can embrace some of these ideas to increasingly move to a DevOps style of working.

Recently graduated college or univerity student
> You have just started your first professional software development job, and although your time in formal education provided you with many specific programming skills, you realize that you aren't sure how all the practices and tools join up for the effective delivery of software. You want to learn more about the entire software delivery process, filling in gaps in your knowledge, and joining all of your skills together in order to advance to the next level in your career.

What This Book Is Not

This book specifically emphasizes the complete approach to implementing continuous delivery for Java applications, and as such, it doesn't contain a deep dive into everything related to architecture, testing, or cloud technologies. Sure, you'll learn the essentials of all these subjects, but many of the chapter topics could be extended into their own book, and we simply didn't have the time or space to do this. Whereas others have written books that are focused on specific topics, we have attempted to reference and recommend their work.

Conventions Used in This Book

The following typographical conventions are used in this book:

Italic

Indicates new terms, URLs, email addresses, filenames, and file extensions.

`Constant width`

Used for program listings, as well as within paragraphs to refer to program elements such as variable or function names, databases, data types, environment variables, statements, and keywords.

`Constant width bold`

Shows commands or other text that should be typed literally by the user.

`Constant width italic`

Shows text that should be replaced with user-supplied values or by values determined by context.

This element signifies a tip or suggestion.

This element signifies a general note.

This element indicates a warning or caution.

Using Code Examples

Supplemental material (code examples, exercises, etc.) is available for download at *https://github.com/continuous-delivery-in-java*.

This book is here to help you get your job done. In general, if example code is offered with this book, you may use it in your programs and documentation. You do not need to contact us for permission unless you're reproducing a significant portion of the code. For example, writing a program that uses several chunks of code from this book does not require permission. Selling or distributing a CD-ROM of examples from O'Reilly books does require permission. Answering a question by citing this book and quoting example code does not require permission. Incorporating a significant amount of example code from this book into your product's documentation does require permission.

We appreciate, but do not require, attribution. An attribution usually includes the title, author, publisher, and ISBN. For example: "*Continuous Delivery in Java* by Daniel Bryant and Abraham Marín-Pérez (O'Reilly). Copyright 2019 Daniel Bryant and Cosota Team Ltd., 978-1-491-98602-8."

If you feel your use of code examples falls outside fair use or the permission given above, feel free to contact us at *permissions@oreilly.com*.

O'Reilly Safari

 Safari (formerly Safari Books Online) is a membership-based training and reference platform for enterprise, government, educators, and individuals.

Members have access to thousands of books, training videos, Learning Paths, interactive tutorials, and curated playlists from over 250 publishers, including O'Reilly Media, Harvard Business Review, Prentice Hall Professional, Addison-Wesley Professional, Microsoft Press, Sams, Que, Peachpit Press, Adobe, Focal Press, Cisco Press, John Wiley & Sons, Syngress, Morgan Kaufmann, IBM Redbooks, Packt, Adobe Press, FT Press, Apress, Manning, New Riders, McGraw-Hill, Jones & Bartlett, and Course Technology, among others.

For more information, please visit *http://oreilly.com/safari*.

How to Contact Us

Please address comments and questions concerning this book to the publisher:

O'Reilly Media, Inc.
1005 Gravenstein Highway North
Sebastopol, CA 95472
800-998-9938 (in the United States or Canada)
707-829-0515 (international or local)
707-829-0104 (fax)

We have a web page for this book, where we list errata, examples, and any additional information. You can access this page at *http://bit.ly/continuous-delivery-in-java*.

To comment or ask technical questions about this book, send email to *bookquestions@oreilly.com*.

For more information about our books, courses, conferences, and news, see our website at *http://www.oreilly.com*.

Find us on Facebook: *http://facebook.com/oreilly*

Follow us on Twitter: *http://twitter.com/oreillymedia*

Watch us on YouTube: *http://www.youtube.com/oreillymedia*

Acknowledgments

As with almost all technical books, only two names may be listed as authors on the front of this book, but the reality is that many people have contributed, either directly in the form of feedback as the book was written, or indirectly by their teaching and guidance over the years.

Although we can't possibly list everyone who has helped us during this journey, we would like to explicitly thank the people who took time out of their busy schedules to provide extensive discussions, feedback, and support. In particular, we would like to express our gratitude to (in alphabetical order of last name): Tareq Abedrabbo, Alex Blewitt, the Devoxx team, Ben Evans, Trisha Gee, Arun Gupta, Charles Humble, Nic Jackson, James Lewis, Richard Li, Simon Maple, Sam Newman, the SpectoLabs team, Chris Newland, Christian Posta, Chris Richardson, Mani Sarkar, Richard Seroter, Matthew Skelton, Steve Smith, the entire Tomitribe crew (and #usualsuspects), Martijn Verburg, Richard Warburton, and Nicki Watt (and past and present members of the OpenCredo team).

We would also like to express our thanks to the entire O'Reilly team, and although there are surely many people we haven't met behind the scenes who have helped us, we would like to explicitly thank Brian Foster for the opportunity to write this book, Virginia Wilson for providing motivation and a lot of great editorial advice (and for sticking with us when times were tough!), and Susan Conant and Nan Barber for their initial guidance.

Daniel's acknowledgements: I would like to thank my entire famiy for their love and support, both during the writing process and throughout my career. I would also like to thank Abraham for joining me midway through the writing process; there aren't many people who would have accepted and excelled at the challenge quite so quickly. Finally, I would like to thank everyone involved in the London Java Community (LJC), Skills Matter, and the InfoQ/QCon team. These three communities have provided me with access to mentors, guidance, and so many opportunities. I hope to someday pay all of this forward.

Abraham's acknowledgements: It's odd how a city as big and diverse as London can sometimes work in such small circles. The first time that I ever performed a public presentation was next to Daniel, and now it feels only fitting that my first large-scale publication also happens next to him. I was truly excited when I was offered to join this project, and thankful for the support and mentoring that I have received throughout. Other organizations have helped me get to this point, among them the London Java Community, Skills Matter, InfoQ, Equal Experts, and "the usual suspects," who have made learning not just possible, but also incredibly fun. Finally, I need to thank Bea for her patience, for her support, for just being there. Thank you.

## CHAPTER 1

Continuous Delivery: Why and What

In this chapter, you will explore the core concepts of continuous delivery and learn more about the benefits for developers, QA, operations, and business teams. An important question to ask before embarking on any change in the way you work is "Why?" Here you will learn how enabling rapid feedback reduces context switching; how automatic, repeatable, and reliable releases reduce much of the stress and challenges with delivering software to customers; and how codifying the definition of "done" allows rapid verification and facilitates any auditing required. Finally, you will examine what a typical Java continuous delivery build pipeline looks like and learn the fundamentals of each stage in the pipeline.

Setting the Scene

Continuous delivery (CD) is fundamentally a set of practices and disciplines in which software delivery teams produce valuable and robust software in short cycles. Care is taken to ensure that functionality is added in small increments and that the software can be reliably released at any time. This maximizes the opportunity for rapid feedback and learning, both from a business and technical perspective. In 2010, Jez Humble and Dave Farley published their seminal book *Continuous Delivery* (*https://continuousdelivery.com/*) (Addison-Wesley), which collated their experiences of deploying software delivery projects around the world, and this publication is still the go-to reference for CD. The book contains a valuable collection of techniques, methodologies, and advice from the perspective of both technology and organizations.

Much has changed in the world of software development and delivery over the past 20 years. Business requirements and expectations have changed dramatically, with a focus on innovation, speed, and time to market. Architects and developers have reacted accordingly, and new architectures have been designed to support these requirements. New deployment fabrics and platforms have been created and have co-evolved alongside new methodologies like DevOps, Release Engineering, and Site Reliability Engineering (SRE). Alongside these changes, a series of best practices for creating a continuous delivery build pipeline has co-evolved. The core concept is that any candidate change to the software being delivered is built, integrated, tested, and validated before determining that it is ready for deployment to a production environment.

In this book, you will focus on accomplishing the task of creating an effective build pipeline for modern Java-based applications, whether you are creating a monolith, microservices, or "serverless" style function as a service (FaaS) application.

Enabling Developers: The Why

An important questions to ask before undertaking any major task within software development and your approach to this is "Why?" Why, as a Java developer, should you invest your valuable time in embracing continuous delivery and creating a build pipeline?

Rapid Feedback Reduces Context Switching

Feedback is vital when working with complex systems, and nearly all software applications are complex adaptive systems. This is especially true of modern component-based software systems that are deployed to the web, which are essentially distributed systems. A quick review of the IT press publications over the past 20 years reveals that software development issues are often discovered only when large (and costly) failures occur. Continual, rapid, and high-quality feedback provides early opportunities to detect and correct errors. This allows the detection and remediation of problems while they are smaller, cheaper, and easier to fix.

Rapid Feedback Can Provide a Business Competitive Advantage

In their book *Accelerate* (*https://itrevolution.com/book/accelerate/*) (IT Revolution Press), Nicole Forsgren, Jez Humble, and Gene Kim argue that organizations in all industries are moving away from using big projects with long lead times to small teams that work in short cycles and measure feedback from users in order to build products that delight customers and rapidly deliver value. In addition to using metrics for technical concerns, you can also facilitate feedback for the organization by working closely with the business team to identify key performance indicators and metrics that can be implemented within the application.

From a developer's point of view, one of the clear advantages of rapid feedback is the reduced cost in context switching and attempting to remember what you were doing with a piece of code that contains a bug. We don't need to remind you that it is much easier to fix an issue that you were working on five minutes ago, rather than one you were working on five months ago.

Automatic, Repeatable, and Reliable Releases

The build pipeline must provide rapid feedback for the development team in order to be useful within their daily work cycles, and the operation of the pipeline must be highly repeatable and reliable. Accordingly, automation is used extensively, with the goal of 100% automation or as close as you can realistically get to this. The following items should be automated:

- Software compilation and code-quality static analysis
- Functional testing, including unit, component, integration, and end-to-end
- Provisioning of all environments, including the integration of logging, monitoring, and alerting hooks
- Deployment of software artifacts to all environments, including production
- Data store migrations
- System testing, including nonfunctional requirements like fault tolerance, performance, and security
- Tracking and auditing of change history

"Shifting Left" Thinking and Testing

You will often hear people talk about "shifting left" processes like security verification or practices like acceptance testing with continuous delivery. The core idea behind the *shift left* is that you move things that are typically done in later stages earlier, which results in a high-quality implementation or less cost to fix issues that would be discovered only far into the delivery process. In the examples mentioned here, this would mean consulting the InfoSec team or performing some threat modeling when starting to design a new feature, or encouraging developers to implement automated acceptance testing that runs as part of the pipeline test suite. Continuous delivery can be a catalyst for this shift, as not only does the pipeline provide a visualization of all the verification stages involved from code to deployment, but it also provides a framework to implement automated verification and validation.

With the automation of the release process complete (and repeatable and reliable), you, as a developer or operator, have confidence in continually releasing new functionality without causing breakages or regressions. Nothing destroys morale as quickly as having to rely on an unreliable and flaky deployment process. This leads to fear in deploying code, which, in turn, encourages teams to batch large amounts of functionality in a "big bang" release, which ultimately leads to even more problematic releases. This negative feedback loop must be broken, and the adoption of the continuous delivery of functionality in small batch sizes (ideally, with single-piece flow) is a great approach to help encourage this.

Codifying the Definition of "Done"

The fast feedback and automation of the release process is useful for developers in and of itself. However, another clear advantage of creating a build pipeline is that you can codify the definition of "done." When a software component successfully traverses a build pipeline, this should unequivocally indicate that it is ready to go into production, provide the value planned, and function within acceptable operational parameters that include availability, security, and cost. Historically, it has been difficult for teams to ensure a consistent definition of "done," and this can be a friction point between development and business teams within an organization.

Determining Your Goals, Domain Modeling, and User Story Mapping

Although practices like continuous delivery are useful for codifying what "done" means for you and your organization, you must figure out exactly what should be built in order to deliver value to your customers:

- *The Lean Startup* (*http://theleanstartup.com/book*) (Currency) by Eric Reis draws on ideas from design thinking, lean manufacturing, and agile methodologies, and provides guidance on how to continually innovate by generating and testing business ideas and hypotheses.
- *Lean Enterprise* (O'Reilly) by Jez Humble et al. builds on work presented by Eric Reis and many others and presents lean and agile principles and patterns to help organizations move fast at scale.
- *User Story Mapping* (O'Reilly) by Jeff Patton with Peter Economy will help clarify the user journeys within your system, and also help determine the minimal functionality to support them
- *Context mapping* (*http://dddcommunity.org/book/evans_2003/*), as detailed in Eric Evan's *Domain-Driven Design* (Addison-Wesley Professional), is a valuable technique for understanding the (static) domain you are working in, and critically, how to model this domain and the associated interaction within other domains in your codebase.
- *Event Storming* (*http://eventstorming.com/*) (Leanpub) by Alberto Brandolini describes a valuable technique that takes a more dynamic approach to modeling a domain, by determining the business events that flow through a system.

If you are looking to understand the concept of business value in more detail, we recommend *The Art of Business Value* (*https://itrevolution.com/book/the-art-of-business-value/*) (IT Revolution Press) by Mark Schwartz.

As we will show in later chapters, the assertion of many functional and nonfunctional (cross-functional) properties can be codified within a modern Java build pipeline, including fault tolerance, the absence of known security vulnerabilities, and basic performance/load characteristics (which, in turn, can support the calculation of cost).

Exploring a Typical Build Pipeline: The What

It is vital that you understand the "what," or purpose, of each of the core stages within a continuous delivery pipeline, as the goals and principles are often more important than specific implementation details (e.g., whether you use Jenkins or CircleCI, JUnit, or TestNG).

Core Build Pipeline Stages

Figure 1-1 demonstrates a typical continuous delivery build pipeline for a Java-based application. The first step of the process of CD is continuous integration (CI). Code that is created on a developer's laptop is continually committed (integrated) into a shared version-control repository, and is automatically built and packaged into an artifact. After CI, the resulting artifact is submitted to a series of automated acceptance and system quality attribute verification stages, before undergoing manual user acceptance testing and promotion through progressively more production-like environments.

The primary goal of the build pipeline is to prove that any changes to code or configuration are production-ready. A proposed modification can fail at any stage of the pipeline, and this change will accordingly be rejected and not marked as ready for deployment to production. Artifacts that do pass all verification steps can be deployed into production, and this is where both technical and business telemetry can be collected and used to create a positive feedback loop.

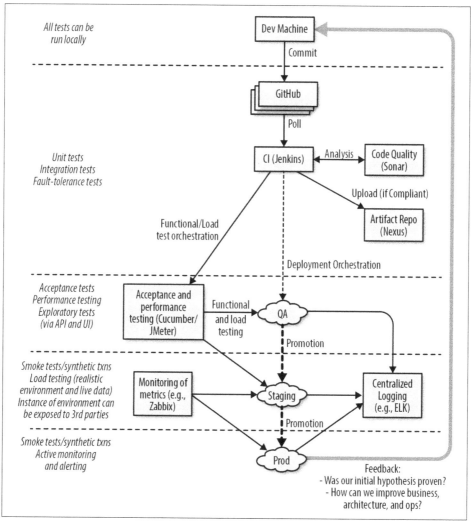

Figure 1-1. A typical Java continuous delivery (CD) build pipeline

Let's look at the purpose of each of the pipeline stages in more depth.

Local development

Initially, a developer or engineer makes a change on their local copy of the code. They may develop new functionality using practices such as behavior-driven development (BDD), test-driven development (TDD), and other extreme programming (XP) practices like pair programming. One of the core goals of this stage is to make the local development environment as production-like as possible; for example, running certain tests in a locally installed virtualization- or container-based environment.

Another goal, one that can be challenging with larger applications, is that a local development should not require all of the system components to be installed and running in order for a developer to work effectively. This is where design principles like loose coupling and high cohesion come into play, to test supporting practices like contract verification, doubles, and service virtualization.

Commit

Developers working locally typically commit their proposed code and configuration changes to a remotely hosted distributed version control system (DVCS) like Git or Mercurial. Depending on the workflow that the team or organization has implemented, this process may require some merging of changes from other branches or the trunk/master, and potentially discussion and collaboration with other developers working in the same area of the codebase.

Continuous integration

At this stage of the pipeline, the software application to which a code or configuration change is being proposed undergoes continuous integration (CI). Using integrated code stored within the trunk or master branch of a version control system (VCS), an artifact is built and tested in isolation, and some form of code quality analysis should be applied, perhaps using tools like PMD, FindBugs, or SonarQube. A successful CI run results in the new artifact being stored within a centralized repository, such as Sonatype Nexus or JFrog Artifactory.

Acceptance tests

Code that successfully passes the initial unit and component tests and the code-quality metrics moves to the right in the pipeline, and is exercised within a larger integrated context. A small number of automated end-to-end tests can be used to verify the core happy paths or user journeys within the application that are essential for the provision of business value. For example, if you are building an e-commerce application, critical user journeys most likely include searching for a product, browsing a product, adding a product to your cart, and checkout and payment.

This is also the stage in which the system quality attributes (also referred to as *nonfunctional requirements*) are validated. Examples of verifications run here include reliability and performance, such as load and soak tests; scalability, such as capacity and autoscaling tests; and security, involving the scanning of code you wrote, the dependencies utilized, and the verification and scanning of associated infrastructure components.

User acceptance tests

At this stage, testers or actual users start preforming exploratory testing. This manual testing should focus on the value of human cognition, and not simply consist of testers following large test scripts. (The repetitive behavior of validating functionality from scripts is ideally suited to computers and should be automated.)

Staging

Once a proposed change has passed acceptance tests and other fundamental quality assurance (QA) tests, the artifact may be deployed into a staging environment. This environment is typically close to the production environment; in fact some organizations do test in a clone of production or the production environment itself. A realistic quantity of representative data should be used for any automated or exploratory tests performed here, and integrations with third-party or external systems should be as realistic as possible; for example, using sandboxes or service virtualization that mimics the characteristics of the associated real service.

Production

Ultimately, code that has been fully validated emerges from the pipeline and is marked as ready for deployment into production. Some organizations automatically deploy applications that have successfully navigated the build pipeline and passed all quality checks—this is known as *continuous deployment*—but this is not an essential practice.

Observing and maintenance

Once code has been deployed to production, you should take care not to forget about observability—monitoring, logging, and alerting—for both the purposes of enabling a positive feedback loop for business and technical hypotheses, and for facilitating potential debugging of issues that occur within production.

Impact of Container Technology

It is increasingly common that software delivery teams are packaging their Java applications within container technology like Docker, and this can alter the way tasks such as local development, artifact packaging, and testing are conducted. Figure 1-2 identifies four key stages where changes occur:

1. Local development now typically requires the ability to provision a containerized environment

2. Packaging of the deployment artifact now focuses on the creation of a container image

3. The mechanism for initializing tests must now interact with and manage the container runtime environment

4. The deployment environments now typically use another layer of abstraction for the dynamic orchestration and scheduling of containers

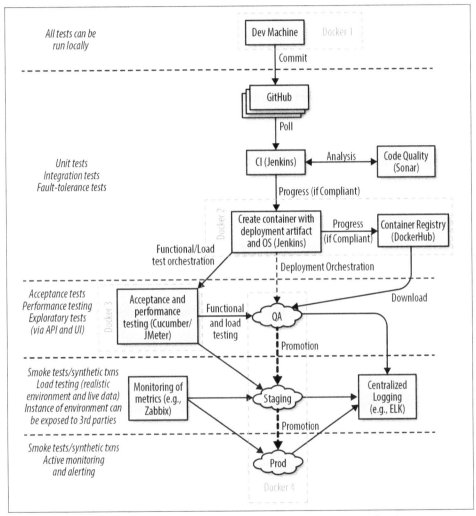

Figure 1-2. A Java continuous delivery pipeline that uses container technology

Changes with Contemporary Architectures

Many teams are now also building applications by using the microservices or FaaS architecture style, and this can require that multiple build pipelines are created, one for each service or function. With these types of architectures, a series of additional integration tests or contract tests are often required in order to ensure that changes to one service do not affect others. Figure 1-3 shows the impact of container technology on the build pipeline steps, as well as the challenges of multiple service integration, as shown by the large shaded arrow.

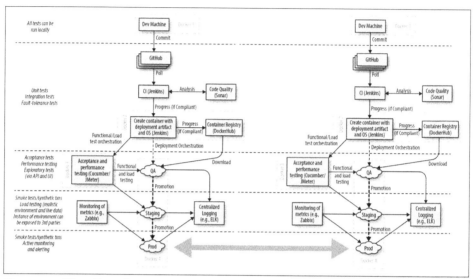

Figure 1-3. The effect of container technology and the microservices architectural style on a typical CD build pipeline

Throughout the book, we will look at creating each stage of these types of pipelines, and share our advice and experience.

Summary

In this introductory chapter, you have learned the core foundations of continuous delivery and explored the associated principles and practices:

- *Continuous delivery* (CD) is fundamentally a set of practices and disciplines in which software delivery teams produce valuable and robust software in short cycles.
- For developers, CD enables rapid feedback (reducing context switching); allows automatic, repeatable, and reliable software releases; and codifies the definition of "done."
- A CD build pipeline consists of local development, commit, build, code quality analysis, packaging, QA and acceptance testing, nonfunctional (system quality attributes) testing, deployment, and observation.

Next you will learn about the evolution of software delivery over the past 20 years, with a focus on how Java application development has changed, and how some of the new challenges and risks introduced can be mitigated with continuous delivery. You will also explore how the ever-changing and evolving requirements, architectural and infrastructure best practices, and shifting roles within IT are increasingly driving changes in the skills required for modern software developers.

## CHAPTER 2

Evolution of Java Development

Since the introduction of Java in 1995, much has changed, and in this chapter you will learn about how this affects your role as a Java developer. Your journey begins with a brief look back in time in order to understand how Java applications and deployment platforms have evolved, with a key focus on the impact this has had on the ability to rapidly and safely deliver new software to production environments. Finally, you will explore the human and "soft skills" aspect of continuous delivery, which focuses on increasing the shared responsibility for the creation and operation of software, such as the approaches of DevOps and Site Reliability Engineering (SRE).

Requirements of Modern Java Applications

Many Java developers have been practicing continuous integration and some form of continuous delivery for the past decade. Innovative books including *Java Power Tools* (O'Reilly) by John Smart provided the guidelines and frameworks to make this possible. Technologies have obviously changed within the last 10 years, and so have associated programming and architectural styles. In particular, business teams within organizations have increasingly demanded that IT teams become more flexible and be capable of rapidly responding to changes in customer preferences and market conditions.

The emergence of dynamic and programmable compute resources and deployment platforms, combined with teams and organizations exposing application programming interfaces (APIs) as products, has resulted in the architectures that Java developers are creating to converge toward component/service/function-based architectures. All of these factors have led to (and, in turn, have been driven by) the emergence of popular movements such as Agile, Lean, DevOps, cloud computing, programmable infrastructure, microservices, and serverless or FaaS.

Need for Business Speed and Stability

During his time as a cloud architect at Netflix, Adrian Cockcroft talked a lot about "time to market" being a competitive advantage, and in many modern markets "speed kills." Uwe Friedrichsen, CTO at codecentric, has also talked extensively about this trend beginning in the 1980s: globalization, market saturation, and the internet led to highly competitive and dynamic ecosystems. The markets became highly demand-driven, and the new biggest challenge of the companies was to adapt to the changing demands of the customers quickly enough. The key driver changed from cost-efficient scaling to responsiveness.

Over the same time period, the move to public commodity infrastructure (the cloud) in combination with increasing transaction value flowing through global computer systems has meant that new failure modes are being discovered, and new attackers are emerging from the shadows. This has caused the need to balance stability and security against the requirement for speed. Often this isn't an easy balance to maintain.

> Continuous delivery is achieved when stability and speed can satisfy business demand.
>
> Discontinuous delivery occurs when stability and speed are insufficient.
>
> —Steve Smith (*@AgileSteveSmith*)

Accordingly, you now need to create applications that support rapid, safe, and stable change, and continually ensure that you are meeting these requirements through automated testing and validation.

Rise of the API Economy

APIs are at the core of the internet and a modern developer's daily life. RESTful services are the de facto way to expose and consume third-party online business services. However, as stated by Jennifer Riggins when attending the 2017 APIDays conference, what people might not realize is how much the API will be at the center of the future technology and part of every connected person's daily life. APIs will continue to play a central role in trends like chatbots and virtual assistants, the Internet of Things (IoT), mobile services, and so much more.

APIs are also being increasingly consumed as "shadow IT" by departments that were traditionally less "tech-savvy," like marketing, sales, finance, and human resources. *Mediated APIs*—APIs that act as bridges between new and old applications—are becoming increasingly popular, as they provide adaptations and opportunities for innovation in businesses that have considerable investment locked within legacy infrastructure. Gartner, the US-based research and advisory firm, suggests that concepts such as the *API marketplace* and the *API economy* are becoming increasingly important within the global economy.

As the API marketplace becomes more sophisticated and widespread, the risks for failure and security issues become more apparent. APIs have made technology more accessible than ever, which means that enterprise architects, the traditional bastions of technology adoption, are no longer the gatekeepers for technical decision-making. Accordingly, this empowers every developer in an organization to innovate, but at the same time can lead to unintended consequences. It is essential to codify not only functional requirements for an API—for example, using BDD and automated testing —but also nonfunctional (or cross-functional) requirements and service-level agreements (SLAs) related to security, performance, and expected cost. These must be continually tested and validated, as this has a direct impact on the product being offered to customers.

Opportunities and Costs of the Cloud

It can be argued that the cloud computing revolution began when Amazon Web Services (AWS) was officially launched in March 2006. Now the cloud computing market includes other big players like Microsoft Azure and Google Cloud Platform, and generates $200+ billion in revenue annually. Cloud computing technologies have brought many advantages—on-demand hardware, rapid scalability and provisioning, and flexible pricing—but have also provided many challenges for developers and architects. These include the requirements to design for the ephemeral nature of cloud computing resources, the need to understand the underlying characteristics of a cloud system (including mechanical sympathy and fault tolerance), and the requirement for an increase in operational and sysadmin knowledge (such as operating systems, configuration management, and networking).

Developers unfamiliar with cloud technologies must be able to experiment and implement continuous testing with these deployment fabrics and platforms, and this must be done in a repeatable and reliable way. Early testing within a build pipeline using applications deployed on infrastructure and platforms that are as like production as possible is essential to ensure that assumptions on performance, fault tolerance, and security are valid.

Modularity Redux: Embracing Small Services

The combination of the need for speed from the business, the adoption of REST-like APIs, and the emergence of cloud computing has provided new opportunities and challenges to software architecture. Core topics in this space include the scaling of both the organizational aspects of developing software (e.g., Conway's law) and the technical aspects (e.g., modularization), as well as the requirement to deploy and operate parts of the codebase independently of each other. Much of this has been incorporated within the emerging architectural pattern known as the *microservices*.

This book discusses the drivers and core concepts of microservices in Chapter 3 and explores how this helps and hinders the implementation of CD. A further introduction to microservices can be found in Christian Posta's *Microservices for Java Developers* (O'Reilly), and a more thorough treatment can be found in Sam Newman's *Building Microservices* (O'Reilly) and Irakli Nadareishvili et al.'s *Microservice Architecture* (O'Reilly). At a high level, the building of Java-based microservices impacts the implementation of CD in several ways:

- Multiple build pipelines (or branches within a single pipeline) must be created and managed.
- Deployment of multiple services to an environment have to be orchestrated, managed, and tracked.
- Component testing may have to mock, stub, or virtualize dependent services.
- End-to-end testing must orchestrate multiple services (and associated state) before and after executing tests.
- Process must be implemented to manage service version control (e.g., the enforcement of allowing the deployment of only compatible, interdependent services).
- Monitoring, metrics, and application performance management (APM) tooling must be adapted to handle multiple services.

Decomposing an existing monolithic application, or creating a new application that provides functionality through a composite of microservices, is a nontrivial task. Techniques such as context mapping, from domain-driven design, can help developers (working alongside stakeholders and the QA team) understand how application/

business functionality should be composed as a series of bounded contexts or focused services. Regardless of how applications are composed, it is still vitally important that both individual components and the system as a whole are continually being integrated and validated. The need for continuous delivery only increases as more and more components are combined, as it becomes nearly impossible to manually reason about their combined interactions and functionality.

Impact on Continuous Delivery

Hopefully, this exploration of the requirements of modern Java applications has highlighted the benefits—and in some cases, the essential need—of continuous delivery to ensure that software systems provide the required functionality. The changing requirements, infrastructure, and architectural styles are just parts of the puzzle, though. At the same time, new platforms have emerged that have either codified several of the architectural best practices or have attempted to help address some of the same problems.

Evolution of Java Deployment Platforms

Java has an amazing history, and not many languages that are still relevant today can claim to have been used for more than 20 years. Obviously, during this time, the language has evolved itself, partly to continually drive improvement and developer productivity, and partly to meet the requirements imposed by new hardware and architectural practices. Because of this long history, there are now a multitude of ways to deploy Java applications into production.

WARs and EARs: The Era of Application Server Dominance

The native packaging format for Java is the Java Application Archive (JAR) file, which can contain library code or a runnable artifact. The initial best-practice approach to deploying Java Enterprise Edition (J2EE) applications was to package code into a series of JARs, often consisting of modules that contain Enterprise JavaBeans (EJB) class files and EJB deployment descriptors. These were further bundled up into another specific type of JAR with a defined directory and structure and required metadata file.

The bundling resulted in either a Web Application Archive (WAR)—which consisted of servlet class files, JSP files, and supporting files—or an Enterprise Application Archive (EAR) file—which contained all the required mix of JAR and WAR files for the deployment of a full J2EE application. As shown in Figure 2-1, this artifact was then deployed into a heavyweight application server (commonly referred to at the time as a "container") such as WebLogic, WebSphere, or JBoss EAP. These application servers offered container-managed enterprise features such as logging, persistence, transaction management, and security.

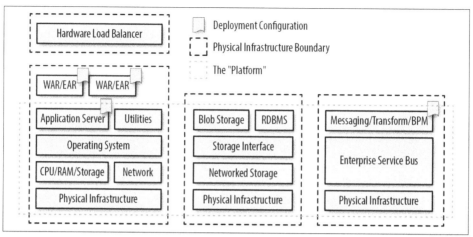

Figure 2-1. The initial configuration of Java applications used WAR and EAR artifacts deployed into an application server that defined access to external platform services via JNDI

Several lightweight application servers also emerged in response to changing developer and operational requirements, such as Apache Tomcat, TomEE, and Red Hat's Wildfly. Classic Java Enterprise applications and service-oriented architecture (SOA) were also typically supported at runtime by the deployment of messaging middleware, such as enterprise service buses (ESBs) and heavyweight message queue (MQ) technologies.

Executable Fat JARs: Emergence of Twelve-Factor Apps

With the emergence of the next generation of cloud-friendly service-based architectures and the introduction of open source and commercial platform-as-a-service (PaaS) platforms like Google App Engine and Cloud Foundry, deploying Java applications by using lightweight and embedded application servers became popular, as shown in Figure 2-2. Technologies that emerged to support this included the in-memory Jetty web server and later editions of Tomcat. Application frameworks such as DropWizard and Spring Boot soon began providing mechanisms through Maven and Gradle to package (for example, using Apache Shade) and embed these application servers into a single deployable unit that can run as a standalone process—the executable *fat JAR* was born.

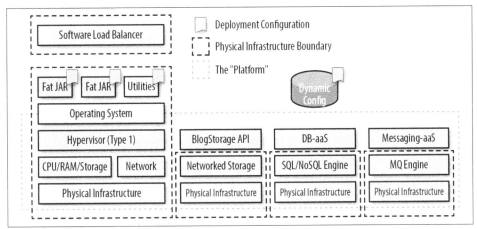

Figure 2-2. The second generation of Java application deployment utilized executable fat JARs and followed the principles of the Twelve-Factor App, such as storing configuration within the environment

The best practices for developing, deploying, and operating this new generation of applications was codified by the team at Heroku as the Twelve-Factor App (*https:// 12factor.net/*).

Container Images: Increasing Portability (and Complexity)

Although Linux container technology had been around for quite some time, the creation of Docker in March 2013 brought this technology to the masses. At the core of containers is Linux technologies like cgroups, namespaces, and a (pivot) root filesystem. If fat JARs extended the scope of traditional Java packaging and deployment mechanisms, containers have taken this to the next level. Now, in addition to packaging your Java application as a fat JAR, you must include an operating system (OS) within your container image.

Because of the complexity and dynamic nature of running containers at scale, the resulting image is typically run on a container orchestration and scheduling platform like Kubernetes, Docker Swarm, or Amazon ECS, as shown in Figure 2-3.

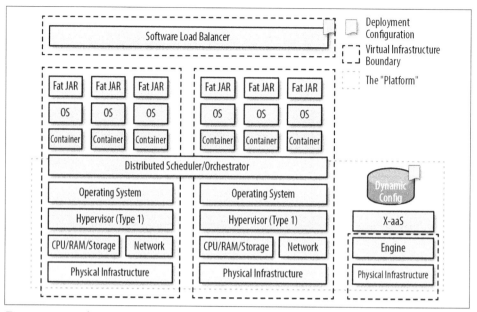

Figure 2-3. Deploying Java applications as fat JARs running within their own name-spaced container (or pod) requires developers to be responsible for packaging an OS within container images

Function as a Service: The Emergence of "Serverless"

In November 2014, Amazon Web Services launched a preview of AWS Lambda at its global re:Invent conference, held annually in Las Vegas. Other vendors followed suit, and in 2016 Azure Functions and Google Cloud Functions were released in preview. As shown in Figure 2-4, these platforms lets developers run code without provisioning or managing servers; this is commonly referred to as "serverless," although FaaS is a more correct term, as serverless offerings are actually a superset of FaaS, which also includes other backend as a service (BaaS) offerings like blob storage and NoSQL data stores. With FaaS, servers are still required to run the functions that make up an application, but the focus is typically on reducing the operational burden of running and maintaining the function's underlying runtime and infrastructure. The development and billing model is also unique in that functions are triggered by external events—which can include a timer, a user request via an attached API gateway, or an object being uploaded into a blobstore—and you pay for only the time your function runs and the memory consumed.

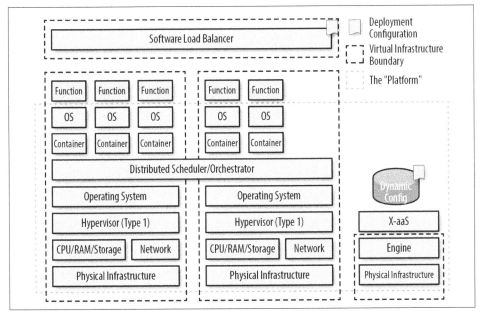

Figure 2-4. Deploying Java applications via the FaaS model. Code is packaged within a JAR or ZIP, which is then deployed and managed via the underlying platform (that typically utilizes containers).

Both AWS Lambda and Azure Functions offer support for Java, and you now return back to the deployment requirement for a JAR or ZIP file containing Java code to be uploaded to the corresponding service.

Impact of Platforms on Continuous Delivery

Developers often ask whether the required platform packaging format of the application artifacts affect the implementation of continuous delivery. Our answer to this question, as with any truly interesting question, is, "It depends." The answer is yes, because the packaging format clearly has an impact on the way an artifact is built, tested, and executed: both from the moving parts involved and the technological implementation of a build pipeline (and potential integration with the target platform). However, the answer is also no, because the core concepts, principles, and assertions of continuously delivering a valid artifact remain unchanged.

Throughout this book, we demonstrate core concepts at an abstract level, but will also provide concrete examples, where appropriate, for each of the three most relevant packaging styles: fat JARs, container images, and FaaS functions.

DevOps, SRE, and Release Engineering

Over the last 10 years, we have seen roles within software development evolve and change, with a particular focus on shared responsibility. We'll now discuss the new approaches and philosophies that have emerged, and share our understanding of how this has impacted continuous delivery, and vice versa.

Development and Operations

At the 2008 Agile Toronto conference, Andrew Shafer and Patrick Debois introduced the term *DevOps* in their talk on Agile infrastructure (*http://www.jedi.be/presenta tions/IEEE-Agile-Infrastructure.pdf*). From 2009, the term has been steadily promoted and brought into more mainstream usage through a series of "devopsdays" events, which started in Belgium and have now spread globally. It can be argued that the compound of "development" and "operations"—DevOps no longer truly captures the spirit of the associated movement or philosophy; potentially, the term "Businss-Development-QA-Security-Operations" (BizDevQaSecOps) captures the components better, but this is far too much of a mouthful.

DevOps at its core is a software development and delivery philosophy that emphasizes communication and collaboration between product management, software development, and operations/sysadmins teams, and close alignment with business objectives. It supports this by automating and monitoring the process of software integration, testing, deployment, and infrastructure changes by establishing a culture (with associated practices) where building, testing, and releasing software can happen rapidly, frequently, and more reliably.

We are sure many of you reading will think this sounds a lot like the principles of continuous delivery—and you would be right! However, continuous delivery is just one tool in the DevOps toolbox. It is an essential and valuable tool, but to truly have success with designing, implementing, and operating a continuous delivery build pipeline, there typically needs to be a certain level of buy-in throughout the organization, and this is where the practices associated with DevOps shine.

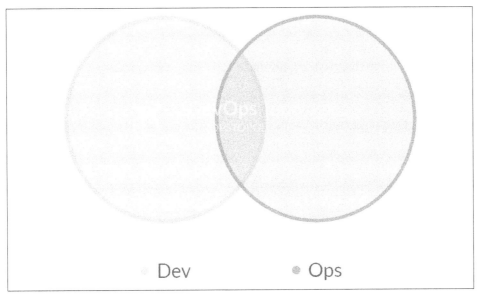

Figure 2-5. DevOps is a combination of development and operations (and more). Image taken from web.devopstopologies.com

---

Keen to Learn More About DevOps?

This book focuses on the technical implementation of continuous delivery. If you are interested in learning more about DevOps and the associated bigger picture, we recommend reading the following:

- *The DevOps Handbook* (*http://itrevolution.com/devops-handbook*) (IT Revolution Press) by Gene Kim et al., provides an excellent overview of all the benefits and challenges of DevOps practices. If you enjoy reading novels, we also recommend the accompanying *The Phoenix Project* (*https://itrevolution.com/book/the-phoenix-project/*) (IT Revolution Press).

- *Lean Enterprise* and *Agile IT Organization Design* (*https://info.thoughtworks.com/download-agile-it-organization-design.html*) (Addison-Wesley Professional) by Sriram Narayan are also excellent references on the organizational and process changes that can drive (and to some degree are required for) continuous delivery.

Site Reliability Engineering

The term Site Reliability Engineering (SRE) (*https://landing.google.com/sre/book.html*) was made popular by the book of the same name that was written by the SRE team at Google. In an interview (*https://landing.google.com/sre/interview/ben-treynor.html*) with Niall Richard Murphy and Benjamin Treynor Sloss, both of whom worked within the engineering division at Google, they stated that fundamentally SRE is what happens when you ask a software engineer to design an operations function: "using engineers with software expertise, and banking on the fact that these engineers are inherently both predisposed to, and have the ability to, substitute automation for human labor."

In general, an SRE team is responsible for availability, latency, performance, efficiency, change management, monitoring, emergency response, and capacity planning. This overlap with DevOps and pure operational concerns can be seen in Figure 2-6. However, a key characteristic of SRE teams at Google is that each engineer should be doing only a maximum of 50% operations work, or "toil" as they refer to it, and the rest of their time should be spent designing and building systems and the supporting tooling. At Google, this split between workloads is continually measured and reviewed regularly. SRE teams at Google are a scarce and valuable resource, and development teams typically have to create a case for SRE support on their projects, particularly in the early proof-of-concept stage with a product.

Google has institutionalized responses to providing SRE support, with processes like the Production Readiness Review (PRR) (*https://landing.google.com/sre/book/chap ters/evolving-sre-engagement-model.html*). The PRR helps to avoid getting into a bad situation where the development teams are not incentivized to create production-ready software with a low operational load by examining both the system and its characteristics before taking it on, and also by having shared responsibility.

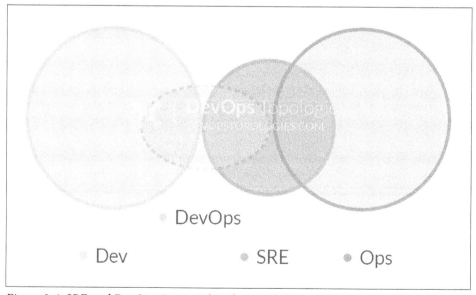

Figure 2-6. SRE and DevOps. Image taken from web.devopstopologies.com

The Google SRE team has also talked extensively about the way it monitors systems. A classic approach to monitoring is to watch a value or a condition, and when the monitoring system observes something interesting, it sends an email. However, email is not the right approach for this; if you are requiring a human to read the email and decide whether something needs to be done, the Google team SRE believes you are making a mistake. Ideally, a human never interprets anything in the alerting domain. Interpretation is done by the software you write. You just get notified when you need to take action. Accordingly, the SRE book states that there are only three kinds of valid monitoring output:

Alerts
These indicate that a human must take action right now. Something is happening or about to happen, and a human needs to take action immediately to improve the situation.

Tickets
A human needs to take action but not immediately. You have maybe hours, typically, days, but some human action is required.

Logging
No one ever needs to look at this information, but it is available for diagnostic or forensic purposes. The expectation is that no one reads it.

This information is important, because as developers, we must implement appropriate logging and metrics within our systems. This also must be tested as part of a continuous delivery pipeline.

Want to Learn More About SRE?

An increasing number of good books are being written that explore the concepts and practices behind SRE. We recommend the following:

- *Site Reliability Engineering* (O'Reilly) by Betsy Beyer et al.
- *The Site Reliability Workbook: Practical Ways to Implement SRE* (O'Reilly) by Betsy Beyer et al.
- *Seeking SRE: Conversations About Running Production Systems at Scale* (O'Reilly) by David Blank-Edelman

---

Release Engineering

Release engineering is a relatively new and fast-growing discipline (*http://bit.ly/ 2QYemAR*) of software engineering that can be described as building and delivering software. Release engineers focus on building a continuous delivery pipeline and have expert understanding of source code management, compilers, automated build tools, package managers, installation, and configuration management. According to the Google SRE book, a release engineer's skill set includes deep knowledge of multiple domains: development, configuration management, test integration, system administration, and customer support.

The Google SRE workbook builds on the required skillset, and presents the basic principles of release engineering as follows:

- Reproducible builds
- Automated builds
- Automated tests
- Automated deployments
- Small deployments

We're sure you can see the similarity between these principles and those of continuous delivery. Even the additional operator-focused principles discussed are understandable to developers: reducing operational load on engineers by removing manual and repetitive tasks; enforcing peer review and version control; and establishing consistent, repeatable, automated processes to minimize mistakes.

The success of release engineering within an organization is highly correlated with the successful implementation of a build pipeline, and typically consists of metrics focused on time taken for a code change to be deployed to production, the number of open bugs, the percentage of successful releases, and the percentage of releases that were abandoned or aborted after they began. Steve Smith has also talked extensively in his book *Measuring Continuous Delivery* (*https://leanpub.com/measuringcontinuous delivery*) (Leanpub) about the need to collect, analyze, and take action based on these metrics.

Shared Responsibility, Metrics, and Observability

If you work within a team at a large enterprise company, the concepts of DevOps, SRE, and release engineering may appear alien at first glance. A common pushback from such teams is that these approaches work for only the "unicorn" companies like Google, Facebook, and Amazon, but in reality these organizations are blazing a trail that many of us are now following. For example, Google was the first to embrace containerization to facilitate rapid deployment and flexible orchestration of services; Facebook promoted the use of a monorepo to store code, and released associated open source build tooling that is now used extensively; and Amazon drove the acceptance of exposing internal service functionality only via well-defined APIs.

Although you should never "cargo cult," or blindly copy only the things or results you can, you can learn much from their approaches and processes. The key trends discussed in the previous sections also have a direct impact on the implementation of continuous delivery:

- Increasing shared responsibility across development, QA, and operations (and arguably the entire organization) is essential for the successful adoption of continuous delivery.
- The definition, capture, and analysis of software build, deployment, and operation metrics are vital to continuous delivery. They help the organization understand where it currently is and what success will look like, and assist in charting and monitoring the journey toward this.
- Automation is essential for reliably building, testing, and deploying software.

Netflix's Full Cycle Developers

Netflix, a rapidly growing, global video-streaming company, has presented at many conferences about the way it builds and operates software based on the concepts of freedom and responsibility. In May 2018, the Netflix Technology Blog described how many Netflix engineers are encouraged to work as full cycle developers (*http://bit.ly/2N6Nzzb*). They are responsible for certain operational aspects of service delivery in addition to the designing and building. Several other organizations have discussed similar ideas, and the blog post is worth reading if you want to understand the challenges and benefits of this approach, as well as the support systems and training required to make this work.

Several luminaries within the Java space have been discussing the need for Java developers to broaden their skillset, and Ben Evan's and Martijn Verburg's *The Well-Grounded Java Developer* (Manning) is a good place to start.

Summary

In this chapter, you have explored the evolution of Java architecture, deployment platforms, and the associated organizational and role changes within IT:

- Modern software architecture must adapt to meet the changing requirements from the business of speed and stability, and implementing an effective continuous delivery pipeline is a core part of delivering and verifying this.
- Java deployment packages and platforms have changed over the years, from WARs and EARs deployed onto application servers, through to fat (runnable) JARs deployed in the cloud or PaaS, and ultimately to container images deployed

into container orchestration or FaaS platforms. A continuous delivery pipeline must be built to support your specific platform.

- The focus on shared responsibility over the last 10 years—through DevOps, SRE, and release engineering—has increased your responsibilities as a developer implementing continuous delivery. You must now implement continual testing and observability within the software you write.

In the next chapter, you will explore how to design and implement an effective software architecture that supports the implementation of continuous delivery.

## CHAPTER 3

Designing Architecture for Continuous Delivery

Now that you have been introduced to the motivations for continuous delivery, you are ready to explore the technical foundations to enable this practice: software architecture. In this chapter, you will learn about the importance of designing systems that are loosely coupled and have high cohesion, and the associated technical and business costs if these guidelines aren't followed. You will be introduced to the importance of designing effective APIs, how cloud computing has impacted software architecture, and why many Java developers are embracing service-oriented development. The key goal of this chapter is for you to understand how to create and cultivate an architecture that supports continuously delivering Java applications.

Fundamentals of Good Architecture

The Software Engineering Institute (SEI) (*http://www.sei.cmu.edu/architecture/*) defines software architecture as "the set of structures needed to reason about the system, which comprises software elements, relations among them, and properties of both." Although this may at first glance appear quite abstract, the mention of structures, elements, and properties is core to what the majority of software engineers think of as architecture. Taking a slightly different perspective, it is quite possible that you can relate to Martin Fowler's (*https://youtu.be/DngAZyWMGR0*) definition that software architecture consists of the "things that people perceive as hard to change." Regardless of which definition you prefer, several properties of a software system are fundamental to creating fit-for-purpose architecture.

Loose Coupling

A *loosely coupled system* is one in which each of its components has, or makes use of, little or no knowledge of the definitions of other separate components. The obvious advantage is that components within a loosely coupled system can be replaced with alternative implementations that provide the same functionality. Loose coupling within programming is often interpreted as encapsulation—or information-hiding—versus nonencapsulation.

Within the Java programming language, this can be seen in primarily two places. First, method signatures utilize interface types versus concrete class types; the former makes extending applications much easier by loosely coupling and deferring the choice of concrete class until runtime. Second, JavaBeans or Plain Old Java Objects (POJOs) getters and setters (accessors and mutators), which enable hiding and controlling the access to internal state, give you much more control in making changes to the internals of the class.

At the application or service level, loose coupling is typically achieved through well-defined and flexible component interfaces; for example, using REST contracts (e.g., Pact or Spring Cloud Contract) with JSON over HTTP/S; using an interface definition language (IDL) such as gRPC, Thrift, or Avro; or messaging via RabbitMQ or Kafka. Examples of tight coupling include Java RMI, where domains objects are exchanged in the native Java serialization format.

High Cohesion

Cohesion refers to the degree to which the elements within a component belong together, and can be thought of within programming as the measure of strength of the relationship between pieces of functionality within a given module or class. Modules with high cohesion tend to be preferable, because high cohesion is associated with several desirable traits of software, including robustness, reliability, reusability, and understandability. In contrast, low cohesion is associated with undesirable traits such as being difficult to maintain, test, reuse, or even understand. A good example in the Java language can be found within the *java.util.concurrent* (*http://bit.ly/2DwCKXB*) package, which contains classes that cohesively offer functions related to concurrency. The classic Java counterexample is the *java.util* (*http://bit.ly/2QbkMey*) package itself, which contains functions that relate to concurrency, collections, and a scanner for reading text input; these functions are clearly not cohesive.

At the application and service level, the level of cohesion is often evident by the interface exposed. For example, if a User service exposed functionality related only to working with application Users, such as add new User, update contact email address, or promote the User's customer loyalty tier, this would be highly cohesive. A counter example would include a User service that also offered functionality to add items to an e-commerce shopping basket, or a payment API that also allowed stock information to be added to the system.

Coupling, Cohesion, and Continuous Delivery

Applications with a loosely coupled and highly cohesive architecture are easier to continuously deliver. Therefore, you should strive to design and evolve systems with this in mind. A good architecture facilitates CD through the following mechanisms:

Design

During the design phase of a new or evolving system, having clear and well-defined interfaces specified throughout the system allows for loose coupling and high cohesion. This, in turn, makes it easier to reason about the system. When given new requirements for a specific area of functionality, a highly cohesive system immediately directs you to where the work should take place, as an alternative to you having to trawl through the code of several multifunctional modules with low cohesion. Loose coupling allows you to change design details of an application (perhaps in order to reduce resource consumption) with a significant reduction in concern that you will impact other components within the overall system.

Build, unit, and integration test

A highly cohesive service or module facilitates dependency management (and the associated testing), as the amount of functionality offered is limited within scope. Unit testing, mocking, and stubbing is also much easier in a loosely coupled system, as you can simply swap configurable synthetic test doubles in for the real thing when testing.

Component test

Components that are highly cohesive lead to easy-to-understand test suites, as the context needed by developers in order to grok the tests and assertions is generally limited. Loose coupling of components allows external dependencies to be easily simulated or virtualized as required.

End-to-end test

Systems that are loosely coupled and highly cohesive are easier to orchestrate when performing end-to-end tests. Highly coupled systems tend to share data sources, which can make the curation of realistic test data fiendishly difficult. When the inevitable issues do occur with end-to-end testing, a highly cohesive system will generally be much easier to diagnose and debug, as functionality is logically grouped in relation to theme.

Deployment

Applications and services that are loosely coupled are generally easy to deploy in a continuous fashion, because each service has little or no knowledge of others. Highly coupled services typically have to be deployed in lockstep (or sequentially) because of the tight integration of functionality, which makes the process time-consuming and error prone. Highly cohesive services typically minimize the number of subsystems that have to be deployed in order to release new functionality, and this results in fewer artifacts being pushed down the pipeline, reducing resource consumption and coordination.

Observability

A cohesive service is easy to observe and comprehend. Imagine you have a service that performs five unrelated tasks, and suddenly your production monitoring tool alerts you to high CPU usage. It will be difficult to understand which functionality is causing the issue. A highly coupled application is often difficult to diagnose when things inevitably go wrong, as failures can cascade throughout the system, which, in turn, obfuscate the underlying causes.

With this foundational guidance in place, let's now take a look at designing applications that provide business value by using modern architectural themes and practices.

Building Maintainable Software

If you are keen to learn more about how these architecture principles relate to creating maintainable code, we recommend reading *Building Maintainable Software, Java Edition* (O'Reilly) by Gijs Wijnholds et al.

Architecture for Business Agility

If you have ever worked on a large-scale software system that is continually being driven by new functional requirements, you will most likely at some point have bumped into a limiting factor imposed by the system architecture. This is almost inevitable because of the increased focus in the business world on short-term gains versus long-term investment, and unforeseen changes in both the business and the development of the technological landscape. Software architecture also tends to evolve over time within many companies, with occasional refactoring sprints being allocated to teams in order to prop up major issues, or in the worst case, little attention being paid until a "big bang" rewrite is forced. Continuous delivery can be used to monitor and enforce certain architectural properties, but you have to understand the principles of how architecture relates to business value, and then design applications and process accordingly.

Bad Architecture Limits Business Velocity

If a business has no well-defined architecture to its systems, it is much harder to properly assess the cost of doing something in a well-defined time frame. The "mess" of your architecture creates excessive costs and missed opportunities. This can have really bad competitive consequences, as the overhead incurred can increase dramatically, depending on the number of systems and overall complexity. Often developers and architects find it difficult to convince nontechnical management of these issues. Although empathy must be developed by both sides, one analogy that spans disciplines is building a house from a complete plan with the intended usage versus starting from an empty plot of land and adding rooms and floors as you go along and watching how the building is being used. Just as it would be much easier to design and build a house with the intended usage in mind from day one, the same conclusion can be drawn for designing and building software.

The other hidden cost with a lack of architectural quality is that an inordinate amount of time is spent patching systems rather than innovating. If more time is spent playing software bug whack-a-mole than actually creating new features, you know you have a rotten architecture. Good software architectures encourage the production of bug-free software and guard against the negative consequences of a bug; well-architected systems "contain" the error, and through their structure provide mechanisms to overcome any problems caused with minimal cost. Good architecture also encourages greater innovation, as it is clearer what needs doing to support innovation on top of it. In addition, good architecture in itself can be a catalyst for innovation. You might see gaps or opportunities that would have otherwise been hidden.

Although the continual monitoring and analysis of architectural qualities in relation to business value is somewhat orthogonal to the implementation of continuous delivery, the creation of a build pipeline can be an effective way to introduce the capture of relevant metrics. Tools such as SonarQube can be woven into the build process and used to show cohesion, coupling, and complexity hotspots within the code and also report high-level complexity metrics such as cyclomatic complexity (the quantitative measure of the number of linearly independent paths through a program's source code) and the design structure quality index (DSQI) (an architectural design metric used to evaluate a computer program's design structure and the efficiency of its modules).

Additional tooling, such as Adam Tornhill's Code Maat, can also mine and analyze data from version-control systems, and show areas of the codebase that are regularly churning. This can demonstrate to the business that spending time and money on improving the architecture will facilitate understanding within these high-churn areas of the code, and, in turn, provide a high return on investment.

Complexity and Cost of Change

A typical mature or legacy architecture usually consists of a mix of technologies, often based on frameworks that were popular at the time of construction and the experiences of the engineers involved. This is where such a lack of structure (or an overly complex structure) in the architecture can greatly impact an organization; instead of having to consider just one technology when making changes, you end with a forest of interconnecting technologies in which no one person or team is the subject-matter expert. Making any change is a risky undertaking with a lot of inherent cost. If you compare this to an organization that has been careful to keep its architectural complexity under control, its costs of change could be a fraction of that experienced by its "complex" competitor.

Some organizations have fine-tuned management of their technical complexity and architecture to such a point that they are able, with complete confidence, to ship live multiple updates each day. The end result is that the organization with a complex architecture cannot keep pace with its more technically lean rival; this can result in a "death by a thousand paper cuts" with many delayed and failed features and bug fixes.

A well-defined software architecture assists the management of complexity by showing and tracking the following:

- The real interdependencies between systems
- What system holds which data and when
- The overall technical complexity in terms of operating systems, frameworks, libraries, and programming languages used

Many of these properties can be verified and monitored within a good continuous delivery pipeline.

Best Practices for API-Driven Applications

All software applications expose APIs somewhere within the system, from the internal classes, packages, and modules, to the external systems interface. Since 2008, there has been an increase in APIs being seen as software products themselves: just look at the prevalence of SaaS-based API offerings like Google Maps, Stripe payments, and the Auth0 authentication API. From a programmer's perspective, an API that is easy to work with must be highly cohesive and loosely coupled, and the same applies for integrating API-based services into the CD pipeline.

Build APIs "Outside-In"

A good API is typically designed outside-in, as this is the best way to meet user requirements without overly exposing internal implementation details. One of the challenges with classical SOA was that APIs were often designed inside-out, which meant that the interface presented "leaked" details on the internal entities and functions provided. This broke the principle of encapsulating data, and, in turn, meant that services integrating with other services were highly coupled as they relied on internal implementation details.

Many teams attempt to define a service API up front, but in reality the design process will be iterative. A useful technique to enable this iterative approach is the BDD technique named *The Three Amigos*, where any requirement should be defined with at least one developer, one QA specialist, and one project stakeholder present. The typical outputs from this stage of the service design process include a series of BDD-style acceptance tests that assert component-level (single microservice) requirements, such as Cucumber Gherkin syntax acceptance test scripts; and an API specification, such as a Swagger or RAML file, which the test scripts will operate against.

We also recommend that each service has basic (happy path) performance test scripts created (for example, using Gatling or JMeter) and security tests (for example, using *bdd-security* (*https://www.continuumsecurity.net/bdd-security/*)). These service-level component tests can then be run continuously within the build pipeline, and will validate local microservice functional and nonfunctional requirements. Additional internal resource API endpoints can be added to each service, which can be used to manipulate the internal state for test purposes or to expose metrics.

Good APIs Assist Continuous Testing and Delivery

The benefits to the CD process of exposing application or service functionality via a well-defined API include the following:

- Easier automation of test fixture setup and teardown via internal resource endpoints (and this limits or removes the need to manipulate state via filesystem or data store access).

- Easier automation of specification tests (e.g., REST Assured). Triggering functionality through a fragile UI is no longer required for every test.

- API contracts can be validated automatically, potentially using techniques like consumer contracts and consumer-driven contracts (e.g., Pact-JVM).

- Dependent services that expose functionality through an API can be efficiently mocked (e.g., WireMock), stubbed (e.g., stubby4j), or virtualized (e.g., Hoverfly).

- Easier access to metrics and monitoring data via internal resource endpoints (e.g., Codahale Metrics or Spring Boot Actuator).

The popularity of APIs has increased exponentially in recent history, but with good reason, and embracing good architectural practices around this clearly makes implementing continuous delivery much easier.

Deployment Platforms and Architecture

In 2003, the deployment options for enterprise Java applications were relatively limited, consisting of mostly heavyweight application servers that attempted to provide cross-cutting platform concerns such as application life cycle management, configuration, logging, and transaction management. With the emergence of cloud computing from Amazon Web Services (AWS), Google Cloud Platform (GCP), and Microsoft Azure; platform-as-a-service (PaaS) offerings, such as Heroku, Google App Engine, and Cloud Foundry; and container-as-a-service (CaaS) offerings like Kubernetes, Mesos, and Docker Swarm, there are now a lot more choices for Java developers. As the underlying deployment fabrics and platforms have changed, so too have the associated architectural best practices.

Designing Cloud-Native "Twelve-Factor" Applications

In early 2012, PaaS pioneer Heroku developed the Twelve-Factor App (*https://12factor.net/*), a series of rules and guidance for helping developers build cloud-ready PaaS applications that:

- Use declarative formats for setup automation, to minimize time and cost for new developers joining the project
- Have a clean contract with the underlying operating system, offering maximum portability between execution environments
- Are suitable for deployment on modern cloud platforms, minimizing the need for servers and systems administration
- Minimize divergence between development and production, enabling continuous deployment for maximum agility
- Can scale up without significant changes to tooling, architecture, or development practices

---

Independent Systems Architecture Principles

Closely related to the Twelve-Factor App, but with more focus on architecture, are the Independent Systems Architecture Principles (*https://isa-principles.org*). These are a collection of best practices based on experience with microservices and self-contained systems (SCS) in particular and the challenges faced in those projects.

Let's look briefly at each of the factors now, and see how they map to continuously deploying Java applications:

1. *Codebase: one codebase tracked in revision control, many deploys*
   Each Java application (or service) should be tracked in a single, shared code repository. Deployment configuration files, such as scripts, Dockerfiles, and Jenkinsfiles, should be stored alongside the application code.

2. Dependencies: explicitly declare and isolate dependencies

Dependencies are commonly managed within Java applications by using build tooling such as Maven or Gradle, and OS-level dependencies should be clearly specified in the associated virtual machine (VM) image manifest, Dockerfile, or serverless configuration files.

3. Config: store config in the environment

The Twelve-Factor App guidelines suggest that configuration data should be injected into an application via environment variables. In practice, many Java developers prefer to use configuration files to manage these variables, and there can be potential security issues with exposing secrets via environment variables, particularly when building VMs or containers that contain secrets.

Storing nonsensitive configuration data in a remote service like Spring Cloud Config (backed by Git or Consul) and secrets in a service like HashiCorp's Vault can be a good compromise between the Twelve-Factor recommendations and current best practices.

4. Backing services: treat backing services as attached resources (typically consumed over the network)

Java developers are accustomed to treating data stores and middleware in this fashion, and in-memory substitutes (e.g., HSQLDB, Apache Qpid, and Stubbed Cassandra) or service virtualization (e.g., Hoverfly and WireMock) can be used for in-process component testing within the build pipeline.

5. Build, release, run: strictly separate build and run stages

For a compiled language such as Java, this guideline comes as no surprise (and with little choice of implementation). It is worth mentioning that the flexibility provided by VM and container technology means that separate artifacts can be used to build, test, and run the application, each configured as appropriate. For example, a deployment artifact can be created for build and test with a full OS, JDK, and diagnostic tools; and an artifact can be built for running an application in production with only a minimal OS and JRE.

However, we see this as an anti-pattern, as there should be only one artifact created that is the "single source of truth" that is pushed along the build pipeline. Using multiple artifacts can easily lead to configuration drift, in which the development and production artifacts have a subtly different configuration that can cause issues and make debugging challenging.

6. Processes: execute the app as one or more stateless processes

Building and running a Java application as a series of microservices can be made easier by using VM images, container images, or serverless functions.

7. Port binding: export services via port binding
Java developers are used to exposing application services via ports (e.g., running an application on Jetty or Apache Tomcat).

8. Concurrency: scale out via the process model
Traditional Java applications typically take the opposite approach to scaling, as the JVM runs as a giant "uberprocess" that is often vertically scaled by adding more heap memory, or horizontally scaled by cloning and load-balancing across multiple running instances. However, the combination of decomposing Java applications into microservices and running these components within VMs, containers, or serverless runtimes can enable this approach to scalability. Regardless of the approach taken to implement scalability, this should be tested within the build pipeline.

9. Disposability: maximize robustness with fast startup and graceful shutdown
This can require a mindset shift with developers who are used to creating a traditional long-running Java application, where much of the expense of application configuration and initialization was front-loaded in the JVM/application startup process. Modern, container-ready applications should utilize more just-in-time (JIT) configuration, and ensure that best efforts are taken to clean up resource and state during shutdown.

10. Dev/prod parity: keep development, staging, and production as similar as possible
The use of VM or container technology in combination with orchestration technologies like VMware, Kubernetes, and Mesos can make this easier in comparison with traditional bare-metal deployments in which the underlying hardware and OS configuration is often significantly different from that of developer or test machines.

As an application artifact moves through the build pipeline, it should be exposed to more and more realistic environments (e.g., unit testing can run in-memory on a build box). However, exploratory end-to-end testing should be conducted in a production-like environment.

11. Logs: treat logs as event streams
Java has had a long and sometimes arduous relationship with logging frameworks, but modern frameworks like Logback and Log4j 2 can be configured to stream to standard output or streamed to disk.

12. Admin processes: run admin/management tasks as one-off processes
The ability to create simple Java applications that can be run within a container or as a serverless function allows administrative tasks to be run as one-off processes. However, these processes must be tested within (or as part of) the build pipeline.

The principles of the Twelve-Factor App have hinted at designing systems that not only embrace the properties of the underlying deployment fabric, but also actively exploit it. Closely related is a topic known as *mechanical sympathy*.

Cultivating Mechanical Sympathy

Martin Thompson and Dave Farley have talked about the concept of mechanical sympathy in software development for several years. They were inspired by the Formula One racing driver Jackie Stewart's famous quote, "You don't have to be an engineer to be a racing driver, but you do have to have mechanical sympathy." Understanding how a car works will make you a better driver, and it has been argued that this is analogous to programmers understanding how computer hardware works. You don't necessarily need a degree in computer science or to be a hardware engineer, but you do need to understand how hardware works and take that into consideration when you design software.

The days of architects sitting in ivory towers and drawing UML diagrams is over. Architects and developers must continue to develop practical and operational experience from working with the new technologies. Using PaaS, CaaS, and functions can fundamentally change the way your software interacts with the hardware it is running on. In fact, many modern PaaS and function-based solutions use container technology behind the scenes in order to provide process isolation, and it is beneficial to be aware of these changes:

- PaaS and container technology can limit access to system resources because of developer/operator specifications, or resource contention.

- Container technology can (incidentally) expose incorrect resource availability to the JVM (e.g., the number of processor cores typically exposed to a containerized JVM application is based on the underlying host hardware properties, not the restrictions applied to a running container).

- When running a PaaS, additional layers of abstraction often are applied over the operating system (e.g., orchestration framework, container technology itself, and an additional OS).

- PaaS and container orchestration and scheduling frameworks often stop, start, and move containers (and applications) much more often in comparison to traditional deployment platforms.

- The hardware fabric upon which public cloud PaaS and container platform applications are run is typically more ephemeral in nature.
- Containerized and serverless applications can expose new security attack vectors that must be understood and mitigated.

These changes to the properties of the deployment fabric should not be a surprise to developers, as the use of many new technologies introduce some form of change (e.g., upgrading the JVM version on which an application is running, deploying Java applications within an application container, and running Java applications in the cloud). The vast majority of these potential issues can be mitigated by augmenting the testing processes within the CD build pipeline.

Design and Continually Test for Failure

Cloud computing has provided amazing opportunities for developers; a decade ago, we could only dream of the hardware that can now be spun up at the touch of a button. But the nature of this type of infrastructure has also introduced new challenges. Because of the networked implementation, commodity costing, and scale of modern cloud computing, performance issues and failures within the platform are inevitable.

The vast majority of I/O operations within a cloud-based platform are going over the wire. For example, elastic block storage that can appear local is typically provided by a storage area network (SAN), and the performance characteristics are considerably different. If you develop an application on your local development machine that consists of three chatty services with intensive access to a database, you can be sure that the network performance of the localhost loopback adapter and direct access to an SSD-based block store will be markedly different than the corresponding cloud operations. This can make or break a project.

Most cloud computing infrastructure is ephemeral in nature, and you are also exposed to failure with much more regularity in comparison with on-premises hardware. Combine this with the fact that many of us are designing inherently distributed systems, and you must design systems that tolerate services disappearing or being redeployed. When many developers think of testing this type of failure, the Netflix Simian Army and Chaos Monkeys jump to mind; however, this type of testing is typically conducted within production. When you are developing a CD build pipeline, you need to also implement a limited (but equally) valuable form of this type of chaos testing, but provided in a more controlled and deterministic fashion.

> ## Release It! Essential Reading for Developers
>
> Now in it's second edition, Michael Nygard's *Release It!* (*https://pragprog.com/book/mnee2/release-it-second-edition*) (Pragmatic Bookshelf) is still sometimes ignored by developers, as they don't realize what the topic is. However, this is the go-to reference for designing and deploying highly available and fault-tolerant production-ready software. In our opinion, this is essential reading for any Java developer building modern service-based applications or deploying into a (distributed) cloud computing environment.

Systems that are designed with loose coupling are typically easier to test, as you can isolate components more readily, and high cohesion helps with the mental effort needed to understand what is happening when fixing bugs. The key takeaway from this section is that a continuous delivery pipeline must allow deployment and testing on a realistic production-like environment as soon as possible, and performance and failure scenarios must be simulated and tested.

The Move Toward Small Services

It would appear that every other software development article published today mentions microservices, and so much so that it is often difficult to remember that other architectural styles do exist. Behind the popularity of this architecture, there are, of course, many benefits of decomposing large and complex applications into smaller interconnected services. However, there are also several challenges.

Challenges for Delivering Monolithic Applications

Despite what the software development press may say, nothing is inherently wrong with designing and building a monolithic application. It is simply an architectural style, and as with any architectural approach, it has trade-offs. The increase in adoption and rise in popularity of building service-based applications is primarily due to three constraints imposed with working on a single monolithic application:

- Scaling development efforts on the codebase and system
- Isolating subsystems for independent deployability
- Operationally scaling subsystems within the application (independently, elastically, and on demand)

Let's examine each of these issues in turn, and discuss how this impacts the implementation of continuous delivery.

Scaling development

When working with a monolithic application, all the developers have to "crowd around" the same codebase. This can lead to developers having to develop an understanding of the entire codebase in order to cultivate the appropriate domain context. During implementation, code merge conflicts are almost inevitable, which leads to rework and lost time. If a monolithic codebase is designed and implemented well—for example, embracing the principles of high cohesion, loose coupling, and modularity—then this shouldn't be a problem. However, the reality with long-running systems is that they are incrementally evolved, and either by accident or on purpose, the modularity breaks down over time.

Extracting modules from a monolithic codebase and building these as independent subsystem services can lead to clearer domain boundaries and interfaces, which, in turn, facilitates the ability of developers to understand the context. The independent nature of these services also facilitates the distribution of labor over the codebase.

Differing change cadence: Independent deployability

An application that is designed as a single artifact has limited options for independent deployability, and this can be a problem if functionality within the application requires differing change cadence. At a basic level, every time a new piece of functionality is developed within the codebase, the entire application must be deployed. If releasing the application is resource-intensive, on-demand resources may not be practical. Worse still is if the application is highly coupled, as this means that a change in a supposed isolated area of the codebase will require intensive testing to ensure that no hidden dependencies have caused regressions.

By dividing the codebase into independently deployable modules or services, you can schedule the release of functionality independently.

Subsystem scalability and elasticity

An application that is run as a single process (or tightly coupled group of processes) has limited options for scaling. Typically, the only approach is to replicate the entire runnable application instance and load-balance requests across the multiple instances. If you design an application as a series of cohesive subsystems that are loosely coupled, you have many more options for scaling. A subsystem that is under high load can be scaled independently from the rest of the application.

Microservices: SOA Meets Domain-Driven Design

Building small services that follow the Unix *single responsibility principle* has clear benefits. If you design services and tools that do one thing and do it well, it is easy to compose these systems to provide more-complicated functionality, and it is also easier to deploy and maintain such systems. Large organizations like Netflix, eBay, and

Spotify have also talked publicly about how they are building smaller service-based architectures.

The topic of Domain-Driven Design (DDD) is frequently mentioned alongside discussions of microservices, and although the founding work by Eric Evans in this space was published in 2003 in *Domain-Driven Design: Tackling Complexity in the Heart of Software* (*https://domainlanguage.com/ddd/*) (Addison-Wesley Professional), the technique gained traction only when supporting technologies and methodologies converged: i.e., the combination of the evolution of architectural practices, the emergence of cloud platforms that allowed dynamic provisioning and configuration, and the rise of the DevOps movement that encouraged more collaboration throughout the build and operation of software.

Exploring Microservices and DDD Further

The term microservices (*https://martinfowler.com/articles/microservices.html*) first emerged during a talk by James Lewis in 2012, "Micro Services: Java the Unix Way" (*https://www.infoq.com/presentations/Micro-Services*), and was also talked about by Fred George and Martin Fowler around a similar time. Covering microservices or DDD in much depth is beyond the scope of this book; instead, an introduction to the topic can be found in *Microservices for Java Developers* (O'Reilly), and a more thorough treatment can be found in *Microservice Architecture* (O'Reilly) and Sam Newman's *Building Microservices* (O'Reilly).

A core concept of microservices revolves around creating services that follow the single-responsibility principle and have one reason to change. This is closely related to designing effective domain models, or bounded contexts, within DDD.

Building Java-based microservices impacts the implementation of CD in several ways:

- Multiple build pipelines (or branches within a single pipeline) must be created and managed.

- Deployment of multiple services to an environment now have to be orchestrated, managed, and tracked.

- Component testing may now have to mock, stub, or virtualize dependent services.

- End-to-end testing must now orchestrate multiple services (and associated state) before and after executing tests.

- Processes must be implemented to manage service version control (e.g., the enforcement of allowing the deployment of only compatible interdependent services).

- Monitoring, metrics, and APM tooling must be adapted to handle multiple services.

Decomposing an existing monolithic application, or creating a new application that provides functionality through a composite of microservices, is a nontrivial task. Techniques such as context mapping, from DDD, can help developers (working alongside stakeholders and the QA team) understand how application/business functionality should be composed as a series of bounded contexts or focused services.

Functions, Lambdas, and Nanoservices

As stated by Mike Roberts (*https://martinfowler.com/articles/serverless.html*) on the Martin Fowler blog, there is no one clear view of what *serverless* is, and this is not helped by people talking about it in regards to two different but overlapping areas:

- *Serverless* was first used to describe applications that significantly or fully depend on third-party applications or cloud services to manage server-side logic and state. These are typically thick client applications (think single-page web apps or mobile apps) that use the vast ecosystems of cloud-accessible databases (like Parse, Firebase), authentication services (Auth0, AWS Cognito), etc. These types of services have been previously described as *backend as a service (BaaS)*.

- *Serverless* can also mean applications for which some amount of server-side logic is still written by an application developer, but unlike traditional architectures, the code is run in stateless compute containers that are event-triggered, ephemeral (may last for only one invocation), and fully managed by a third party. One way to think of this is as *functions as a service (FaaS)*.

This book focuses on the second type of serverless applications. The challenges of continuously delivering serverless and FaaS applications are much the same as with microservices, although not getting access to the underlying platform can provide additional challenges when testing nonfunctional requirements.

Architecture: "The Stuff That's Hard to Change"

Fundamentally, architecture can be thought of as the "stuff that is hard to change." Getting a software system's architecture correct is a key enabler to facilitating continuous delivery. Following the key principles of designing systems with loose coupling and high cohesion facilitates testing and continuous deployment by allowing services to easily be understood and to be worked with and validated in isolation before being assembled as part of the large systems.

Designing APIs outside-in (and with supporting internal APIs) also facilitates continuous testing of functional and nonfunctional requirements. Developers must now be aware of cloud, PaaS, and container runtimes, and the impact this has on continuous delivery. It can be a fundamental benefit, allowing the dynamic provisioning of resources for testing, but it also changes the characteristics of the underlying infrastructure fabric, and this must be continually tested and assumptions validated.

Diagramming and Modeling Architecture: Daniel's Experience

Regardless of your approach to architecture, you can benefit a lot from attempting to diagram and model your architecture. When working as a consultant, my team and I joined many software development teams, and it was expected by clients that I would understand the software system and become productive working with it as soon as possible.

One of the first things I did on any new project was ask the current team to provide an overview of the architecture. I use the analogy of software architecture as a map (with high-level components, structure, and interactions) of the underlying terrain (code and deployment config). Most of the time, the team had to draw the architecture on a whiteboard because they didn't maintain any kind of diagram or model. Frequently, the team doing the drawing had big arguments, as they couldn't agree on the components, structure, and connections, and they often learned several things from each other. A few teams even realized that they were building the wrong components, or that they were duplicating effort across teams.

I strongly recommend that you diagram and model your architecture outside the code and regularly maintain this. My go-to reference for doing this is the C4 model (*https://c4model.com/*) by Simon Brown, which he covers extensively in *Software Architecture for Developers* (*https://leanpub.com/u/simonbrown*) (Leanpub).

Summary

In this chapter, you have learned about the considerable effect that architecture has on your ability to continuously deliver a software system:

- The fundamentals of creating an effective and maintainable architecture consist of designing systems that are highly cohesive and loosely coupled.

- High cohesion and loose coupling affect the entire CD process: at design time, a cohesive system is easier to reason about; when testing, a loosely coupled system allows the easy substitution of mocks to isolate the functionality being verified; modules or services within a loosely coupled system can be deployed in isolation; and a cohesive system is generally a more observable and understandable system.

- Bad or casually designed architecture limits both technical and business velocity, and will reduce the effectiveness of a CD pipeline.

- Designing effective APIs, which are built outside-in, assist with effective testing and CD as they provide an interface for automation.
- The architectural principles captured within Heroku's Twelve-Factor App assist with implementing systems that can be continuously delivered.
- Cultivating mechanical sympathy (learning about the application platform and deployment fabric, alongside designing for failure) are essential skills for a modern Java developer.
- There is a trend within software development to design systems consisting of small and independently deployable (micro)services. Because of high cohesion and loose coupling, these systems lend themselves to being continuously delivered. These systems also require continuous delivery to ensure that both functional and nonfunctional system-level requirements are met, and to avoid an explosion of complexity.
- Architecture is "the stuff that is hard to change." Continuous delivery allows you to codify, test, and monitor core system-quality attributes throughout the lifetime of software systems.

Now that you have a good understanding of the principles of architecture, in the next chapter you will learn about how to effectively build and test Java applications that embody these properties.

## CHAPTER 4

Deployment Platforms, Infrastructure, and Continuous Delivery of Java Apps

In this chapter, you will explore the various deployment options available to you for continuously delivering web-based Java applications. Along the way, you will learn about each platform's components, its various strengths and weaknesses, and the core areas of focus in relation to Java and continuous delivery. Upon completion of this chapter, you should have the knowledge and tools to choose a platform for your next project, and be aware of the best practices and pitfalls.

Functionality Provided by a Platform

In the context of modern web-based Java applications, or distributed Java applications (based on the microservices architectural style), a platform provides the following functionality:

- A physical (or virtual) location to host your applications from, which is accessible to your users
- A Java runtime
- Persistent storage—either a block store or database
- Access to (or the ability to install) required middleware, such as ESBs or message queues
- Self-healing or resilience—automated restart of failed applications
- Service discovery—a mechanism to locate your additional application services and third-party services

- Fundamental security—hardened machine images, restricted ports, and strong authentication required to access any control plane
- A clear mechanism to understand costs incurred from operation

The emergence of the cloud, containers, and DevOps has been empowering for software developers. You can now create and manage custom platforms at a scale that was only dreamed of 10 years ago. However, with this power comes great responsibility. It is all too tempting for Java development teams to build their own custom platform. Not only does this take time and resources away from coding the application that was going to deliver the actual functionality required by the business, but often these platforms are poorly designed, fragile, and cost-ineffective.

The Dangers of Building Your Own Platform

Sure, it may initially be a lot of fun assembling your own platform. In addition, teams often (incorrectly) assume that their project is somehow "special" and needs a custom platform. But before starting to build your own custom platform, always ask yourself the following:

- Have you clearly identified that the most important and urgent problem for your team to be working on is building a bespoke platform to deploy software?
- Have you discussed the impact of the decision to build a custom platform with core stakeholders?
- Do you (and your team) have the appropriate knowledge and skillset to build an effective and maintainable platform?
- Have you assessed existing (open source and commercial) platforms and determined that there is no clear long-term cost/benefit trade-off in using or buying an existing platform?

Designing and operating a platform for Java applications is a specialist skill, and the engineers behind platforms like AWS ECS, Google App Engine, Azure App Service, and Cloud Foundry have a lot of expertise that you can leverage by using their offerings.

Essential Development Processes

Regardless of what platform you ultimately deploy your Java application to, you and your team must implement a series of fundamental first steps when starting your journey with continuous delivery:

- Ensure that all application code and associated configuration is under version control, and that this is the single source of truth.

- Create a continuous delivery pipeline that takes code from version control, builds and tests the application, and deploys this onto a test (or, ideally, a production) environment.

- Encode any manual deployment steps, such as changing configuration or upgrading a database into the automated deployment process that is triggered by the CD pipeline.

- Package your applications as standard Java artifacts (e.g., a WAR or fat JAR) and remove any nonstandard deployment process (e.g., manual patching of class files). This allows standard deployment mechanisms to be used (e.g., uploading a WAR via an application server API or copying a fat JAR onto the filesystem) and will facilitate further migration to additional or new platforms in the future.

The Value of Developer Experience: Daniel's Perspective

The topic of developer experience, sometimes referred to as *DevEx* or *DX*, is a rapidly emerging area of development for open source and commercial tooling. The topic focuses on the workflow and tooling that is required to convert an idea into code, and ultimately through to delivering value to users in production. DevEx is fundamentally about minimizing friction for engineers and making tasks such as debugging and observability easier. Many people, including me, are currently working in this space, and some early thoughts can be found in my July 2018 CNCF webinar "Creating an Effective Developer Experience on Kubernetes" (*http://bit.ly/2zwtqi4*).

Traditional Infrastructure Platforms

Many of you have undoubtedly deployed Java applications on what can now be referred to as *traditional infrastructure*—application servers running within an on-premises data center that is managed by a separate sysadmin team. Many teams are also undoubtedly still deploying here. Although this book focuses on continuously delivering Java applications onto modern platforms, there is still much here that can be learned that is directly transferable to traditional environments.

Traditional Platform Components

Within traditional infrastructure, you (as a Java developer of web applications) typically interact with the following components:

Application server

A software framework that provides facilities to create web applications and a server environment to run them. For example, JBoss Application Server, Glass-Fish, or Tomcat.

Middleware

Software that sits "in the middle" between application software that may be working on different operating systems, with the goal of supporting and simplifying complex distributed applications. Examples include ESB technology, like IBM WebSphere ESB, and MQ offerings, like ActiveMQ.

Database

An organized collection of data, which typically in a traditional infrastructure stack is a relational database management system (RDBMS). For example, Oracle RDBMS, Microsoft SQL Server, or IBM DB2.

Challenges with Traditional Infrastructure Platforms

The core challenge with traditional infrastructure is that there is no standardized or broadly accepted continuous delivery out-of-the-box complete solution. This is because the platform and deployment procedures are typically bespoke, and the underlying infrastructure is not programmable. This can make the life of a developer deploying onto this platform quite challenging. Often the deployment and operation of these platforms is captured via "tribal knowledge"; the constantly evolving customized processes and mechanisms are not captured formally, but are instead shared through stories and partially correct wiki pages.

Platform Automation Is Useful for Continuous Delivery

One of the biggest technical challenges with implementing CD by using a traditional infrastructure stack is the difficulty in automating the creation of infrastructure configuration. You should strive to make your tests and deployments as deterministic and reliable as possible, and you must therefore work closely with the sysadmin team to explain the need for consistent and reproducible infrastructure environments and deployment mechanisms.

Typically, deploying an application onto traditional infrastructure requires some form of artifact "hand-off" that may or may not include deployment instructions—potentially, a text file with a few snippets of SQL that are required to be run against the associated database. The lack of codification and repeatability of these instructions can lead to errors and friction between dev and ops. Another core challenge with this type of platform is that it can fall into disrepair over time (particularly if the sysadmin or operator who created the platform leaves the organization), and generally speak-

---

ing, when something major goes wrong, it quickly becomes a murder-mystery-style debugging adventure, which is not fun.

Benefits of Being Traditional

The benefits of running traditional infrastructure is that the sysadmin and operational teams responsible for management typically have full control (unless, of course, a third-party is maintaining the platform!). This full control allows rapid changes and configuration—sometimes for better or worse—as well as full visibility into the underlying hardware. Knowledge and skills are required for understanding these inner workings, but this ability to look "behind the curtain" can save many hours of debugging in comparison with using a blackbox third-party service.

Sysadmins—Even Developers Need Heroes

Although the relationship between dev and ops can sometimes be like that of cats and dogs, we can't stress enough the benefits of increased collaboration between these two teams. As it states on the T-shirt, "sysadmins: even developers need heroes." Over our careers, we have learned so much from sysadmins and operations teams, and this has helped us to understand more about infrastructure, and ultimately to become a better developer.

CI/CD on Traditional Infrastructure Platforms

Introducing continuous delivery to this type of platform typically provides many benefits, such as improved build reliability and faster deployment times. Here is what you should focus on:

- Once an application is being built and deployed via a pipeline, this is a great opportunity to begin augmenting the application test suite with assertions that test for well-known (and repeated) issues. This is also a good opportunity to include nonfunctional testing services within the pipeline, such as code quality analysis, code test coverage, and security testing. You may not be able to fix it all straight away, but you will have a baseline from which to demonstrate continual improvement.

- Creation of a pipeline can also trigger the discussion with the ops team as to characteristics of the underlying infrastructure, and can lead to the formulation of SLAs. The creation of SLAs allows all parties—developers, QA, and ops—to agree on what the platform should provide, and, in turn, what operational functionality the application should have (i.e., should the app boot within 30 seconds, or be tolerant of disk failures, or handle intermittent network failures?).

- Once the pipeline is in place, you will also be able to gain more visibility into areas of your workflow that require improvement. For example, code merge conflicts may indicate a need to change commit policies or implement something like Gitflow, slow test runs may indicate the need to parallelize tests, or repeated failed deployments may mean extra effort should be invested within the deployment scripts.

Cloud (IaaS) Platform

Infrastructure-as-a-service (IaaS) cloud infrastructure and platforms currently come in many forms:

Private cloud

This is an evolution from traditional infrastructure, and, in essence, is virtualized hardware that is managed on premises or within a private data center. The line can be drawn between traditional infrastructure and private cloud by requiring that the private cloud must be manageable via an API or SDK—e.g., VMware vSphere, OpenStack, Cisco Open Network Environment (ONE), and Scality RING storage.

Public cloud

Technology that the majority of people reference when they talk about the cloud, which is typically provided by vendors like AWS, Microsoft Azure, GCP, and others.

Hybrid cloud

This is a blend of traditional private virtualized infrastructure with public cloud offerings. Major cloud vendors are starting to offer products that will allow organizations to run hybrid clouds (or help with migration), such as Azure's Stack (and AWS's VM Import/Export and Direct Connect).

Looking Inside the Cloud

The cloud is different from traditional infrastructure in that you, as a developer, are exposed to more fundamental infrastructure components:

Compute

A machine, VM, or other type of computing instance. This is directly analogous to your desktop or laptop computer, and examples include AWS EC2, vSphere VM, and OpenStack Nova.

Storage

Storage for your application data. This can be block storage that can be used to boot a machine and host application binaries, much like the hard drive on your local machine, or object storage that is not usable for booting a machine and can be used to store binary or other style data objects. Examples of block storage include AWS EBS, GCP Persistent Disk, and VMware local storage. Examples of object storage include Amazon S3, Azure Storage Blobs, and OpenStack Swift.

Network

Connections, routers, firewalls, and other communication infrastructure. Examples include Amazon VPC, security groups/firewall rules, and OpenStack Neutron.

Services

Database and external middleware services that are directly analogous to that of traditional infrastructure, but these are typically fully managed services offered by the cloud vendor (e.g., Amazon RDS, Google Cloud Spanner, or Azure Service Bus).

Continuous delivery services

Increasingly, you will see that virtualization and cloud vendors are providing out-of-the-box CD solutions, such as an integrated Jenkins solution or a bespoke solution such as VMware vRealize Code Stream or Amazon CodePipeline.

Additional Resources for Cloud Best Practices

If you are completely new to cloud technologies, we recommend reading *The Practice of Cloud System Administration: Designing and Operating Large Distributed Systems* (*http://bit.ly/2xSQoOC*) (Addison-Wesley Professional) by Thomas Limoncelli et al.

The public cloud can be a brave new world for many engineers, so the majority of cloud vendors have created best-practice documentation, which discusses everything from recommended architecture principles, security practices, and approaches to managing infrastructure. Many engineers we talk to on our consulting travels believe that vendor-created content can often be biased, but this is becoming less of an issue. The current vendor-driven cloud best practices are very much recommended reading if you are working within their ecosystem:

- Amazon Web Services (*https://aws.amazon.com/whitepapers/*) white papers, including "AWS Well-Architected Framework" (*http://bit.ly/2R2kyrf*) and "Architecting for the Cloud: AWS Best Practices" (*https://amzn.to/2xP3Hj2*)
- "Azure Architecture Center" (*http://bit.ly/2ORxizz*) and "Azure Security Best Practices" (*http://bit.ly/2xNhoig*)
- "How to Use Google Cloud Platform" (*https://cloud.google.com/docs/tutorials*) and "Best Practices for Enterprise Organizations" (*http://bit.ly/2OS3Olj*)

Cloud Challenges

The core challenge for you, as a developer moving to cloud technologies, is dealing with the learning curve needed to understand not only the new infrastructure building blocks, but also the characteristics and performance of these technologies. You will need to spend time understanding the impact of being exposed to networked computers; you will nearly always be building a distributed system. You also will need to ensure that you design your applications to perform as well within a networked environment as they do on your local development machine.

Mechanical Sympathy: Daniel's First Cloud Experiences

When I first started using cloud technologies, this was one of the biggest learning hurdles for me, as it means that the characteristics and performance of infrastructure on your local machine may not match that of production—in a big way! For one particular project in the earlier 2010s, I spent a week building a product feed parsing application that wrote high volumes of temporary data to local storage. This worked great on my development machine (with a locally connected SSD drive), but as soon as I deployed this code to production, the performance dropped by nearly two orders of magnitude as the block storage on the cloud instance communicated over the network, which had very different performance characteristics!

Because of the nature (and scale) of the hardware used within IaaS platforms, there is a relatively high probability that individual components will fail. Therefore, you will need to design, build, and test resilient applications that can handle known failure modes; for example, most cloud compute instances are ephemeral and can stop unexpectedly, and your application must handle this gracefully. Werner Vogels, CTO at Amazon, is famous for saying that "everything fails all of the time in the cloud." Initially, this might appear a strange thing for the CTO of a cloud vendor to say, but he was referring to the benefits of the public cloud—on-demand and cost-effective access to incredible infrastructure that can run at large scale—coming at a cost, and this cost is the reliability of individual components.

The Ephemeral Nature of the Cloud: Daniel's Experience

Another one of my core learning experiences when I started developing Java applications for the cloud was the ephemeral nature of the compute instances. My applications would randomly stop when an instance was terminated, and because I was using elastic configurations to ensure that I always had a set number of instances running, a new instance would be started. I was used to creating Java applications that were started only once a month, or even less often, and so I didn't worry about long startup times (and the JVM and Java applications are almost famous for their long initialization times!). I was also used to applications rarely being terminated in an uncontrolled fashion, and so wrote only basic graceful restart or cleanup functionality. This all had to change!

The benefit of applying continuous delivery when deploying Java applications onto cloud infrastructure is that you can capture what you've learned in the build pipeline. For example, if you discover strange performance characteristics that affect your application negatively, you can create an integration test that simulates this and asserts the correct handling. This test can be run on every build in order to prevent regression from future modifications.

Many cloud vendors provide options to choose and provision infrastructure that has low levels of baseline CPU, network, and disk performance, but has "credits" to allow time-limited burstable performance that is considerably over the baseline. An initial allowance of credits is given, and credits can be accumulated when the infrastructure is being used below the baseline. This allows for the creation of cost-effective systems; the starting credit balance allows the infrastructure to initialize rapidly, and if the system usage patterns truly are burstable, then a healthy level of credit can be maintained to burst as required. However, if the usage patterns of an application are not burstable, the credit balance can soon become depleted, and the corresponding application's performance will drop, or potentially the application may fail.

Watch for the Effects of "Burstable" Infrastructure

Short development and test runs of an application deployed onto this type of infrastructure can lead to the development team believing that longer-term performance will be better than it actually is. Accordingly, the baseline performance of such infrastructure must be understood, and simulations created within a build pipeline that test for system performance when running at the baseline infrastructure performance.

Benefits of the Cloud

The core benefit for developers working with cloud infrastructure is that everything is programmable: you can now apply all of your programming know-how and skills to infrastructure. The cloud technologies are generally more standardized than traditional infrastructure, too, and although a lot of variation exists across public cloud vendors, it is possible to transfer your infrastructure knowledge as you move teams or even organizations.

Immutable Infrastructure

Cloud computing (or, really, the introduction of programmable virtualization) made the vision of immutable infrastructure possible. Immutable infrastructure is not modifiable after creation. Instead of updating, you re-create the infrastructure, either by using the same template (guaranteeing that it is identical to the infrastructure being replaced) or using a new "updated" template. This generally makes your life as a developer much easier, as you can provide stronger guarantees of a packaged deployment artifact that works in QA, and staging will work in production.

Another core benefit with the cloud is the flexibility of instantiating infrastructure. The cloud makes it possible for potentially each developer to create their own test environment, or to run large-scale tests (but watch the cost!).

Developers Can't (or Shouldn't) Do Everything with the Cloud

As the cloud allows most infrastructure to be manipulated programmatically, it can be tempting for developers to take on more and more responsibility for the operational side of delivering software. For small-scale organizations or startups, this can be useful, allowing a small development team to be self-sufficient and move fast. However, this can also mean that developers become overworked, or must learn increasing amounts of new skills (sometimes outside their expertise or comfort zone), or become blind to the inherent trade-offs and friction between the dev and ops roles. This can lead to individual or team burnout, or lots of operational issues with applications in production. This should be avoided at all costs.

Continuously Delivering into the Cloud

Introducing CD within a cloud environment is generally easier in comparison to a traditional infrastructure platform, as CD practices largely co-evolved with cloud technologies (and vice versa). The introduction of APIs and SDKs by virtualization and public cloud vendors meant that codifying and reproducing environments (for testing and QA, etc.) became much easier. In addition to the steps mentioned previously for practicing CD with traditional infrastructure, the following guidelines also apply to the cloud:

- Conduct analysis on which type of cloud deployment paradigm your current project will fit best. Large cloud vendors like AWS, GCP, and Azure offer many forms of cloud platform, from containers (covered later) like AWS ECS, and Azure AKS, to PaaS-style offerings like AWS Elastic Beanstalk and Azure App Service, in addition to the IaaS building blocks of compute, storage, and networking.

- Focus on the creation of a CD pipeline that delivers your application (or even a proof-of-concept application) from your local development environment to production. This will highlight any technical or organizational issues with using cloud platforms.

- Codify as much of the cloud platform as possible (ideally, everything) by using tools like HashiCorp Terraform, Ansible, or Puppet.

- Codify what you've learned (and your mistakes) into the pipeline—for example, load testing, security testing, and chaos/resilience testing.

The cloud offers many possibilities for deploying Java applications at a rapid pace, but speed is nothing without control, and control in the sense of CD is the ability to repeatedly and reliably verify that your application is fit for production usage.

Platform as a Service

Platform as a service (PaaS) has a longer history than most people realize. The JavaScript-supporting Zimki was the first recognized PaaS released in 2005. Within the Java space, the launch of Google's App Engine and Cloud Foundry have been the most influential events.

Diving Deeper into PaaS Platforms

Many of the core takeaways from this book can be directly applied to PaaS technologies, but because they often provide an opinionated (preset) workflow, we also recommend consulting specific PaaS-flavored books if you are deploying here. For example, if you are deploying applications on Google App Engine, *Programming Google App Engine with Java* (O'Reilly) by Dan Sanderson is an interesting read. If you are working with Cloud Foundry (specifically, Pivotal Cloud Foundry), then *Cloud Native Java* (O'Reilly) by Josh Long and Kenny Bastani provides a comprehensive guide.

Peeking Inside a PaaS

PaaSs generally have similar primitives to cloud computing, although some of the abstractions might be at a slightly higher level. For example, within Cloud Foundry, you don't directly spin up an instance to deploy your code onto, and instead you focus on creating a "droplet" application artifact:

Compute
> A machine, VM, or container environment.

Storage
> Storage for your application data. This can be block storage that can be used to boot a machine and host application binaries, much like the hard drive on your local machine, or object storage that is not usable for booting a machine and can be used to store binary or other style data objects.

Network
> Connections, routers, firewalls, and other communication infrastructure.

Services
> Database and external middleware services that are directly analogous to that of traditional infrastructure, but these are typically fully managed services offered by the PaaS vendor.

Continuous delivery services
> Many PaaS vendors provide a complete solution for taking code from a local development environment all the way through to production. For example, Cloud Foundry has the integrated cf CLI tool and Concourse CD platform, and Red Hat's OpenShift has an integrated Jenkins solution.

PaaS Challenges

Many of the challenges revolving around the use of PaaS are concerned with the learning curve and usage models. Generally speaking, most PaaSs are quite opinionated in regards to both developer workflow and deployment models. Some projects will not fit into the models provided by a PaaS, and this is where it can become challenging to bend the PaaS to work with your application. Having said this, if you are building relatively typical web-based applications, then this should not be a problem.

Don't Automatically Assume That PaaS Is Over-Opinionated

Many developers assume a PaaS like Cloud Foundry is over-opinionated in regards to workflow, or that the project they are working on is "special" or unique in some way, and won't be deployable onto a PaaS. Generally speaking, if you are creating a web application for an e-commerce business, then this shouldn't require a bespoke developer workflow. In fact, we even know of many large-scale banking and data processing organizations that use (for example) Cloud Foundry very successfully.

Another possible challenge imposed by a PaaS is the potentially constrained Java JDK or runtime environment. If you don't know about these differences between your local JDK and development environment, or you are relatively inexperienced with Java development, this can be a steep learning curve! Examples of PaaS JDK modifications include only whitelisted access to the JDK (i.e., some APIs within the standard OpenJDK may be unavailable); the use of a Java security manager to restrict operations available; the use of a sandbox that restricts access to resources like the Java threads, the network, or filesystem; and differing class-loading strategies. Some PaaS providers also encourage (or force) you to use their proprietary SDKs for accessing databases or middleware.

Understand How Your PaaS Implements and Exposes the JDK: Daniel's Experience

If your PaaS provider provides a native Java environment (you don't have to install a Java runtime), please take time to understand how the JDK and associated runtime have been implemented. This was a big learning curve when I created my first Java application on Google App Engine. The platform offered many great things (particularly in relation to operation and scaling), but the sandboxed Java runtime environment took away a lot of the tools I was used to working with. Ultimately, the application I created met the business requirements, but my estimation was way off, as I didn't budget for the learning curve!

The runtime and OS exposed via a PaaS can also be modified or restricted. In addition to the access restriction to resources like the network and filesystems (which can be implemented within the Java runtime or the OS), resources can also be throttled or controlled—for example, CPU and usage are common targets for this—and the platform instances (and other infrastructure such as network routers or IP addresses) can often be ephemeral. Once this has been identified, the learning can be codified into the build pipeline; for example, asserting that your application does not produce

`OutOfMemoryExceptions` when under heavy load, or that your application gracefully handles forced restarts.

Modern PaaS Documentation Is (Generally Speaking) Excellent

In my experience, most popular Java-friendly PaaSs provide great documentation, both about the developer workflow and about the runtime environment and any caveats or limitations. For example, the Google App Engine team has written extensive notes about its (now deprecated) Java 7 runtime (*http://bit.ly/2OSuQZy*) as well as its Java 8 runtime (*http://bit.ly/2xEx5JF*). The Cloud Foundry team has created similar notes about the corresponding Java build packs and runtime (*http://bit.ly/2OTAmeL*), and each CF commercial vendor usually provides additional documentation on any details unique to their environment.

If you do decide that a hosted PaaS is the best fit for your project, one final thing to be aware of is how hosted offerings are priced. Most of the Java PaaSs are priced based on memory per application instance, and the number of application instances, and other resources (such as CPU speed and cores and network bandwidth) are scaled proportionally. This can mean that some CPU- or memory-intensive applications can be expensive to run, and you often cannot pack applications on infrastructure to accommodate this. With traditional or cloud infrastructure, you can run two resource-intensive applications—one CPU-bound and one memory-bound—side by side on the same hardware, and this way, you are not "wasting" (or being charged for wasting) the resources that may go unused if just one application were running here.

Benefits of PaaS

Once you have taken the time to learn the core principles (and let's be honest: every new technology requires some learning), you can often become very productive, and your knowledge is directly transferable to the next project that uses PaaS. This leads to a (potentially massive) increase in developer productivity. If you are using a PaaS that is based on open standards, such as Cloud Foundry, you also can operate your PaaS across multiple infrastructures—for example, a hybrid of on-premises Cloud Foundry, public-cloud-operated Pivotal Cloud Foundry, and public-cloud-operated IBM Bluemix. Transitioning from one infrastructure/vendor to another should not impact you greatly as a developer, because the platform provides all the core abstractions you care about.

In addition, if your team decides to use a hosted PaaS offering, the operational burden of running the platform, and maintaining and patching the underlying infrastructure, is removed. This can free up time for other value-adding development activities!

CI/CD and PaaS

Introducing continuous delivery with applications deployed into a PaaS environment is usually a no-brainer, and often it is not optional; the only way to deploy your application is via a build pipeline. The following list highlights several areas you should prioritize investing your time in when implementing CD with a PaaS:

- Focus on the creation of a CD pipeline that delivers your application (or even a proof-of-concept application) from your local development environment to production. This will highlight any technical or organizational issues with using the PaaS you have chosen to deploy to.

- Store all PaaS and application configuration and metadata within version control; for example, any service discovery configuration or custom build packs you have created.

- Codify your learning (and mistakes) into the pipeline—for example, load testing, security testing, and chaos/resilience testing.

Containers (Docker)

Many developers use the words "container" and "Docker" interchangeably. This isn't strictly correct; a *container* is an abstract concept of OS-level virtualization or process isolation, and *Docker* is an implementation of this technology by the company Docker, Inc. Container technology existed before the emergence of Docker in Linux Containers (LXC), but Docker provided the missing user experience and mechanism to centrally share, pull, and push container images. There are many other container technologies such as CoreOS's rkt, Microsoft's Hyper-V containers (and Windows containers), and Canonical's LXD.

Learning More About Docker

Because the container technology space is currently still evolving (and often changes at a rapid pace), the best resources can often be found online. For engineers who like to get the basics of a technology from a book, we recommend *Docker Deep Dive* by Nigel Poulton.

Container Platform Components

A typical container-based deployment platform has multiple components:

The container technology

Fundamentally, a container provides OS-level virtualization, and although all of the running containers on a single machine share an OS kernel, they each have separate namespaces for processes and networking, control groups (cgroups) for allocating and controlling resources like CPU and memory, and a root filesystem (rootfs) that is not the same as the underlying host's rootfs.

Container scheduler/orchestrator

This component is responsible for starting, stopping, and managing the container processes. This technology is often referred to as container infastructure as a service (CIaaS), and in the Docker ecosystems this is typically provided by Docker Swarm or Kubernetes.

Storage

Storage for your application data. This can be block storage that can be mapped into a container, or object storage that can be used to store binary or other style data objects. This is often managed by the CIaaS component.

Network

Connections, routers, firewalls, and other communication infrastructure. This is often managed by the CIaaS component.

Services

Database and external middleware services that are directly analogous to that of traditional infrastructure, but these are typically fully managed services offered by the container platform vendor.

Continuous delivery services

Many container platform vendors provide a complete solution for taking code from a local development environment all the way through to production. For example, Docker Enterprise provides a solution integrated with its Docker Hub, Azure provides Azure Pipelines, and AWS ECS provides CodeBuild and CodePipeline.

In Chapter 10, you will learn how to deploy Docker containers onto AWS's ECS.

Container Challenges

The biggest challenge with container technology is the learning curve. Not only is the technology quite different from that of the cloud or PaaS, but it is very much an emerging and evolving technology. It can sometimes be almost a full-time job keeping up-to-date with the latest container innovations! Another core challenge is that older technologies (including the JVM itself) may not always work correctly or as expected when running within a container, and you will often require (at least basic) operational knowledge to identify, understand, and fix issues.

Running Java Within Docker: Common Gotchas Daniel Experienced

I've worked on several projects with Java and Docker, and my team and I had to overcome quite a few issues. Steve Poole, Developer Advocate for IBM Cloud Runtimes, and I talked about "Debugging Java Apps In Containers: No Heavy Welding Gear Required" (*http://bit.ly/2DxYdzm*) at JavaOne in 2015, and here is a summary of some of the challenges and issues:

- Any Java runtime pre Java 9 is not control group (cgroup) aware. A call to obtain the number of CPU cores available to an application will return the underlying host CPU resource information, which, in reality, may be shared across multiple containers running on the same host. This also affects several Java runtime properties, as the fork-join pool and garbage-collection parameters are configured based on this information. This can be overcome by specifying resource limits as command-line flags when starting the JVM.

- Containers typically share a single source of entropy (*/dev/random*) on the host machine, and this can be quickly exhausted. This manifests itself with Java applications unexpectedly stalling/blocking during cryptographic operations such as token generation on the initialization of security functionality. It is often beneficial to use the JVM option `-Djava.security.egd=file:/dev/urandom`, but be aware that this may have security implications (*http://bit.ly/2R40yof*).

It is also appropriate to remember that not all developers are operationally aware, nor do they want to be; they simply want to write code that solves business problems. For this reason, it can be beneficial to hide some of the container technology from developers and provide them with a CD process that manages the building and deploying of Java applications within this space. As we've mentioned earlier, this still does not remove the requirement for developers to at least understand the operational characteristics and impact of running their applications by using this technology; always think about mechanical sympathy!

Container Technology Is Still Rapidly Evolving

Although the speed of innovation has slowed somewhat over the past year, the container technology ecosystem is still very much a pioneering space. Technologies are evolving rapidly, tooling is emerging, and a better understanding of development practices is also occurring. However, the trade-off with access to new (better) ways of packaging and deploying applications means that there can be a steep learning curve—involving much experimentation—and things change rapidly. Be sure that you and your team are happy to commit to this trade-off before embracing container technology!

Container Benefits

The core benefits of container technology are the standardization of deployment packaging—the container image—and the flexibility of execution. The standardization of deployment packaging makes it easier to deploy and operate a platform because the container image becomes the new abstraction/interface between dev and ops. As long as you can package your code within a container, ops can run this on a platform; they don't have to worry (to some degree) exactly how you have configured the application.

Containers Enable Easier Immutable Infrastructure

We mentioned that virtualization and cloud technologies enabled the creation and deployment of immutable artifacts (and infrastructure), and containers really are an extension of this. It is generally easier and quicker to create an immutable container image artifact than a full VM image, and this allows you to iterate and deploy faster.

Continuously Delivering Containers

Introducing continuous delivery with applications deployed into a container platform is usually relatively easy:

- Focus on the creation of a CD pipeline that packages your application (or even a proof-of-concept application) as a container image and takes this from your local development environment to production. This will highlight any technical or organizational issues with using the platform you have chosen to deploy to.

- If you are running your own container platform, capture all configuration within version control, and automate all installation and upgrading via infrastructure as code (IaC) tooling like Terraform or Ansible.

- Store any application configuration and metadata within version control; for example, any service discovery configuration or custom build containers you have created.

- Codify your learning (and mistakes) into the pipeline—for example, load testing, security testing, and chaos/resilience testing.

Kubernetes

Kubernetes is an open source orchestrator for deploying containerized applications that was originally developed by Google. Google has been running containerized applications for many years, and this led to the creation of the Borg container orchestrator (*http://bit.ly/2zwQ5v3*) that is used internally within Google and was the source of inspiration for Kubernetes.

If you are not familiar with this technology, a few core concepts may appear alien at first glance, but they hide great power. The first is that Kubernetes embraces the principles of immutable infrastructure. Once a container is deployed, the contents (i.e., the application) are not updated by logging into the container and making changes. Instead, a new version is deployed. Second, everything in Kubernetes is declaratively configured. The developer or operator specifies the desired state of the system through deployment descriptors and configuration files, and Kubernetes is responsible for making this happen; you don't need to provide imperative, step-by-step instructions.

These principles of immutable infrastructure and declarative configuration have several benefits: it is easier to prevent configuration drift, or "snowflake" application instances; declarative deployment configuration can be stored within version control, alongside the code; and Kubernetes can be largely self-healing, so if the system experiences failure like an underlying compute node failure, the system can rebuild and rebalance the applications according to the state specified in the declarative configuration.

Core Concepts of Kubernetes

Kubernetes provides several abstractions and APIs that make it easier to build these distributed applications, such as those based on the microservice architectural style:

Pods (http://bit.ly/2xFXGG1)
> This is the lowest unit of deployment within Kubernetes, and is essentially a group of containers. A pod allows a microservice application container to be grouped with other "sidecar" containers that may provide system services like logging, monitoring, or communication management. Containers within a pod

share a filesystem and network namespace. Note that a single container can be deployed, but it is always deployed within a pod

Services (http://bit.ly/2q7AbUD)
Kubernetes services provide load balancing, naming, and discovery to isolate one microservice from another. Services are backed by Deployments (*http://bit.ly/2q7vR7Y*), which, in turn, are responsible for details associated with maintaining the desired number of instances of a pod to be running within the system. Services, deployments, and pods are connected together in Kubernetes through the use of labels (*http://bit.ly/2NKpuD8*), both for naming and selecting.

In Chapter 10, you will learn how to deploy Docker containers into a Kubernetes cluster.

Kubernetes: Up and Running

The container and Kubernetes space is rapidly evolving, and therefore the best learning resources are often online. In fact, the Kubernetes online documentation is generally excellent. If you are looking for a book to bootstrap your learning, we recommend *Kubernetes: Up and Running* (O'Reilly), which is written by Kelsey Hightower et al., a group of Kubernetes creators and experts.

Kubernetes Challenges

As with container technology in general, the biggest challenge for developers using Kubernetes is the learning curve. Not only do you have to understand Docker (or another container technology), but you also have to come to grips with concepts like scheduling, orchestration, and service discovery. On top of this, many development teams like the idea of running their own Kubernetes cluster, perhaps within on-premises infrastructure, and the operational learning curve for this can be steep—particularly if you do not have experience in running distributed or container-based platforms.

Don't Run Your Own Kubernetes Cluster (Unless Essential)

All of the major cloud vendors now offer a hosted and fully managed Kubernetes offering, and so we strongly recommend against running your own Kubernetes cluster—particularly if you are a relatively small team, say, under 100 developers. The cloud vendors have much more expertise and operational experience of running the platform, taking on the burden of the platform SLA, and handling issues with Kubernetes or the underlying infrastructure when they (inevitably) go wrong. In our opinion, running your own Kubernetes cluster is viable only if you have a dedicated operations team or strong compliance and governance requirements.

The core concepts of Kubernetes are all learnable, but it will take time, and not every developer wants to deep-dive into the operational side of a technology like Kubernetes. They simply want to code applications that deliver business value.

Although the speed of innovation has slowed somewhat over the past few months, the Kubernetes ecosystem (much like the container ecosystem in general) is still very much an evolving space. Technologies are evolving rapidly, tooling is emerging, and a better understanding of development practices is also occurring. However, the trade-off with access to new (better) ways of packaging and deploying applications means that there can be a steep learning curve—involving much experimentation—and things change rapidly.

Kubernetes Is Still Evolving (into a PaaS?)

Kubernetes is increasingly being thought of as a lower-level platform component, as vendors like Red Hat and Apprenda are building PaaS offerings on top of this technology. The core idea here is to encapsulate and hide some of the more operationally focused aspects of Kubernetes, and to expose abstractions that will be more useful to developers. Be sure that you and your team are happy to commit to the trade-off of using the raw (and evolving) Kubernetes offering before building an associated platform.

Benefits of Kubernetes

Kubernetes offers many benefits, and the technology encompasses many thousands of hours learning how to run applications at scale within a company like Google. The core benefit is that many of the difficult challenges with running applications within containers are handled for you: you simply specify in a declarative manner how your application is composed of services, the resources that you want your service components to have (CPU, memory, storage, etc.), and the number of service instances that should be running at any given time. Kubernetes provides a framework for you to specify resource and security boundaries (using network policies and ACLs, etc.), creates and manages a cluster from underlying infrastructure resources that handles the allocation of resources, and starts and stops instances according to infrastructure failure or some other issues.

Continuous Delivery on Kubernetes

Introducing continuous delivery with applications deployed into a container platform is usually relatively easy:

- Focus on the creation of a CD pipeline that packages your application (or even a proof-of-concept application) as a container image and then takes this from your local development environment to a production Kubernetes cluster. This will highlight any technical or organizational issues with using the platform you have chosen to deploy to.

- If you are running your own Kubernetes platform, capture all configuration within version control, and automate all installation and upgrading via IaC tooling like Terraform or Ansible. However, generally it is most likely more cost-effective (and requires less learning) to not run your own Kubernetes platform, and instead use a hosted offering from one of the cloud vendors.

- Store any application configuration and metadata within version control; for example, any service discovery configuration or custom build containers you have created.

- Store any sensitive configuration and metadata within security and key management applications like HashiCorp's Vault.

- Codify your learning (and mistakes) into the pipeline—for example, handling service failures gracefully, load testing, security testing, and chaos/resilience testing.

- Ensure that you load-test not only your applications, but also the ability of the underlying platform to scale on demand.

Function-as-a-Service/Serverless Functions

FaaS is a compute service that lets you run code without provisioning or managing servers. FaaS platforms executes your code only when needed and scales automatically, from a few requests per day to thousands per second. You pay only for the compute time you consume. There is no charge when your code is not running. With FaaS, you can run code for virtually any type of application or backend service—all with zero administration. FaaS vendors run your code on a high-availability compute infrastructure and perform all the administration of the compute resources, including server and operating system maintenance, capacity provisioning and automatic scaling, code monitoring, and logging. All you need to do is supply your code in one of the languages that the platform supports.

Additional Learning

The topics of FaaS and serverless are evolving crazy fast, but for those who are looking for a general introduction to the core principles and associated architectural requirements, we recommend *Serverless Architectures on AWS* (Manning) by Peter Sbarski.

FaaS Concepts

You can use FaaS to run your code in response to events, such as changes to data in an blob storage bucket or a managed NoSQL database table, or to run your code in response to HTTP requests using an API Gateway. You can also invoke your code by using API calls made using vendor-specific SDKs. With these capabilities, you can use functions to easily create comprehensive data processing pipelines or reactive event-driven applications that can scale on demand, and you are charged only when a function is running.

Eventing-All-the-Things: A Completely New Paradigm

Don't underestimate the learning curve for adapting to the event-driven model imposed by FaaS serverless platforms, as this can be completely new to many developers. We have seen several developers creating applications by chaining functions together with synchronous (blocking) calls, much as they would with traditional procedural development, and this causes the creation of fragile and inflexible applications. We definitely recommend learning more about event-driven architecture, asynchronous programming, and designing reactive systems.

When using FaaS, you are responsible only for your code. The FaaS platform manages the compute (server) fleet that offers a balance of memory, CPU, network, and other resources. This is in exchange for flexibility, which means you cannot log in to compute instances, or customize the operating system or language runtime. These constraints enable FaaS platforms to perform operational and administrative activities on your behalf, including provisioning capacity, monitoring fleet health, applying security patches, deploying your code, and monitoring and logging your Lambda functions.

Challenges of FaaS

As with many of the other modern deployment platforms, the biggest challenge with FaaS technologies is the learning curve. Not only is the platform and Java runtime often restricted (in much the same way as PaaS), but the development paradigm is skewed toward event-driven architecture (EDA). FaaS applications are generally composed of *reactive* functions; the application functions are triggered by events like the arrival of a message in an MQ or a file upload notification from the object store, and the execution of the function may result in side effects (persistence of data in a database, etc.) and the generation of additional events.

FaaS platforms are available to run on your own infrastructure, often on top of an orchestration system like Kubernetes (e.g., kubeless (*http://kubeless.io/*), fission (*http://fission.io/*), and OpenFaaS (*https://www.openfaas.com/*)), standalone (like Apache OpenWhisk (*https://openwhisk.apache.org/faq.html*)), or as a hosted service (such as AWS Lambda (*https://aws.amazon.com/lambda/*), Azure Functions (*https://azure.microsoft.com/en-gb/services/functions/*), or Google Cloud Functions (*https://cloud.google.com/functions/*)). If you choose to use a hosted offering—and generally speaking, this is the best option because of the reduction in operational burden and close integration with the vendor's other services—then you must be aware of how resources are provided and the control you have over this. For example, with AWS Lambda and Azure Functions, you specify the required memory, and the CPU resources available are scaled in relation to this.

Understand the FaaS Java Runtime

In much the same way with PaaS, the Java runtime that is made available in FaaS platforms can be a modified version of the JRE. Common restrictions imposed by running the JRE in a sandbox include limited access to filesystem and network. The functions also typically have a time limit for execution, and this means that the code within your function will be forcefully terminated if this limit is exceeded.

In addition, although FaaS functions are modeled as ephemeral deployment units that are instantiated and terminated on demand, the reality of the implementation details (typically, the function is executed within an OS container) may leak, and this means a function executed twice sequentially may use the same instantiation of the function. This can be bad—for example, if you have left global state like a public class variable set incorrectly, this will persist between executions. Alternatively, it can be good—allowing you to avoid repeated resource instantiation costs by opening a database connection or prewarming a cache within a static initializer and storing the result in a public variable.

Testing FaaS applications can also be challenging, both from a functional and non-functional perspective, as events must be created to trigger functionality, and often many functions have to be composed together to provide a meaningful unit of functionality. For functional testing, this means that triggering test events have to be curated, and a variety of functions (of a specific version) instantiated. For nonfunctional tests, you typically have to run the tests on the platform itself (perhaps in a "staging" environment) with the same caveats applying in regard to curating events and composing applications.

Be Aware of (Account-Wide) FaaS Limits

If you are using a fully managed hosted FaaS environment, be aware of various limits that may apply; for example, the maximum number of simultaneous concurrent executions of a function. These limits can also apply account-wide, so if you have a runaway function, this may impact your entire organization's systems!

FaaS Benefits

The core benefit of FaaS is that the model allows the rapid creation and deployment of new features. Applications with low-volume and spiky usage patterns can also be operated at low cost.

Worth-Based Development: A Powerful Concept

Simon Wardley has written much about the powerful model that FaaS provides, and a core theme is *worth-based development*. The essence of this concept is that design choices are made to maximize the value provided by these systems in relation to their costs. This implies that you, as a developer, will need to understand how "value" is defined within your organization and for the component you are working on (for example, it may be revenue generated, or the number of sign-ups), as well as the costing model of the underlying platform and infrastructure.

Hosted FaaS platforms make the second part of this challenge much easier as you are billed per function execution, and you have limited (or no) fixed costs of maintaining infrastructure if your application is not used.

CI/CD and FaaS

Introducing continuous delivery with applications deployed within a FaaS platform is usually a no-brainer, and may even be enforced by the vendor:

- Focus on the creation of a CD pipeline that packages your application (or even a proof-of-concept application) as an artifact and takes this from your local development environment through to a production FaaS environment. This will high-light any technical or organizational issues with using FaaS technologies.

- If you are running your own FaaS platform, capture all configuration within ver-sion control, and automate all installation and upgrading via IaC tooling like Terraform or Ansible. However, generally it will be more cost-effective to not operate your own platform and instead use a hosted offering from one of the cloud vendors.

- Store any application configuration and metadata within version control; for example, any service discovery configuration or custom build containers you have created. This metadata should also include the current version of the func-tion that is considered "master" or the most current.

- Ensure that you are exposing and capturing core metrics for each function deployed, such as memory used and execution time.

- It may be beneficial to conduct "right-sizing" experiments as part of the load test-ing within your pipeline: you deploy your function to a variety of container/instance/runtime sizes and evaluate throughput and latency. Load testing FaaS applications is generally challenging, as the underlying platform typically auto-scales based on load, but the size (CPU and memory) of the container/instance/runtime will impact the individual and aggregate execution speed.

- Codify your learning (and mistakes) into the pipeline—for example, handling service failures gracefully, security testing, and chaos/resilience testing.

- Although FaaS platforms abstract away the servers (and associated security patching), don't forget that you are responsible for identifying and resolving security issues with your code and all of your dependencies.

- Don't forget to decommission or delete old functions. It is all too easy to forget about an old unused function, or to create a new replacement function and leave the existing one. However, this can not only be confusing for other engineers (wondering which functions are actively used), but also increase the attack sur-face from a security perspective.

Working with Infrastructure as Code

If you are creating your own platform or working closely with an operations team that is doing this, we recommend learning more about programmable infrastructure and infrastructure as code (IaC). This will not only allow you to create or customize your own infrastructure, but also help you to cultivate mechanical sympathy for the platform.

> ### Infrastructure as Code: Learning More from Kief Morris
>
> This book focuses on Java development, so IaC is not covered in much detail because of space limitations. However, if you are interested in learning more, then *Infrastructure as Code* by Kief Morris (O'Reilly) is highly recommended.

Our preferred tooling in this space is HashiCorp's Terraform for specifying cloud environments and related configuration (block storage, networking, additional cloud vendor services, etc.), and Red Hat's Ansible for configuration management and machine instance installation.

Summary

In this chapter, you learned about the functionality that is provided by platforms for deployment of Java-based web applications, and how the choice of platform affects CI/CD.

- A platform provides an entry point for your users to access your application; a Java runtime (which you may have to manage); access to CPU, memory, and block storage; access to middleware or data stores; resilience (e.g., restarts of failed applications); service discovery; security; and cost management.

- Regardless of the platform used, all code and configuration must be stored within version control, and a continuous delivery build pipeline created that can take code from a local machine, build and test, and deploy.

- Packaging and deploying Java applications as standard Java artifacts, such as the JAR or WAR, provides more flexibility and safety than using a bespoke process (e.g., zipping code artifacts or class patching).

- The four main platform types—traditional infrastructure platforms, cloud (IaaS), PaaS, and FaaS—all have differing benefits and challenges for implementing CI/CD for your application.

- You can augment your skills as a Java developer by learning more about infrastructure as code (IaC) and using tools like Terraform and Ansible. This will allow you to create test environments and to cultivate a better understanding of the underlying platform you are using.

Now that you have a good understanding of Java deployment platforms, let's look into building Java applications in more detail.

## CHAPTER 5

Building Java Applications

In this chapter, you will learn about how Java applications are built and explore the typical life cycle of a build process. You will also learn about the value of automating the build by using specialized tools (rather than just your IDE's out-of-the box build tool), the benefits of which allow the easy translation of the build to a continuous integration build server. Finally, you'll review the good, bad, and ugly of the most popular build tools, with the goal of being able to make the best choice for your next Java project.

Breaking Down the Build Process

Nearly all software has to be built (or at least packaged), and Java applications are no exception. At the most basic level, the Java code you write has to be compiled into Java bytecode before it is executed on the Java Virtual Machine (JVM). However, any Java application of sufficient complexity will require the inclusion of additional external dependencies. This includes the libraries you use so often that you can forget they are third-party code, like SLF4J and Apache Commons Lang. With this in mind, a typical series of build steps for a Java application would look something like this (and the Maven users among you might recognize this):

Validate
Validate that the project is correct and all necessary information is available.

Compile
Compile the source code of the project.

Test
Test the compiled source code by using a suitable unit-testing framework. These tests should not require the code to be packaged or deployed.

Package

Take the compiled code and package it in its distributable format, such as a JAR.

Verify

Run any checks on results of integration tests to ensure that quality criteria are met.

Install

Install the package into the local repository, for use as a dependency in other projects locally.

Deploy

Done in the build environment, copies the final package to the remote repository for sharing with other developers and projects.

All of these steps can be done manually, and indeed it is recommended that every developer undertakes all of these steps manually at least once in their career. Much can be learned by going back to basics and working with the fundamental processes and tooling.

Experimenting with javac, java, and the Classpath

A lot can be learned from utilizing the `javac` and `java` command-line utilities for compiling and executing simple Java applications, and particular attention should be paid to managing class path issues. It is our belief that every Java developer should learn the fundamentals of `javac`, the working directory, the challenges of managing a class path, and the core JVM `java` command-line flags.

Although there is value in manually exploring build steps to learn, there is little to be gained from continually doing this. Not only can your (valuable) time as a developer be better used elsewhere, but automating a process makes it much more repeatable and reliable. Build tooling automates the compilation, dependency management, testing, and packaging of software applications.

Automating the Build

Many Java application frameworks, IDEs, and platforms provide build tooling functionality out of the box, and it is often seemlessly integrated into the developer workflow; sometimes using bespoke implementations, and sometimes by using a specialized build tool. Although there are always exceptions, it is generally advantageous to utilize a specialialized build tool, as this allows all developers working on a project to successfully build the application, regardless of the operating system, IDE, or framework they are using. In the modern Java world, this is typically implemented with Maven or Gradle, but other options do exist, as you'll explore later in this chapter.

According to the RebelLabs' Ultimate Java Build Tool Comparison (*http://bit.ly/ 2NL4PPp*) guide, a good build tool should provide the following features:

- Managing dependencies
- Incremental compilation
- Properly handling compilation and resource management tasks across multiple modules or applications
- Handling different profiles (development versus production)
- Adapting to changing product requirements
- Build automation

Build tools have evolved over the years, becoming progressively more sophisticated and feature rich. This provides developers with useful additions, such as the ability to manage project dependencies as well as automate tasks beyond compiling and packaging. Typically, build tools require two major components: a build script and an executable that processes the build script. Build scripts should be platform agnostic: they must be executable without modification on Windows, Linux, and Mac, and only the build tool binaries change. Within the build script, the concept of dependency management is vital, as is the structure (modularity) of the associated projects and the build process itself. Modern build tools address these concepts though the management of the following:

- Build dependencies
- External dependencies
- Multimodule projects
- Repositories
- Plugins
- Releasing and publishing artifacts

Before exploring several popular build tools, you first will need to be familiar with what each of the preceding concepts encompasses.

Build Dependencies

Before build tooling provided dependency management, the management of a Java application's supporting libraries was typically done by manually copying around folders of class files and JARs! As you can imagine, this was not only time-consuming and error-prone, but critically it made a developer's job much harder, as time and energy were needed to form a mental model of all the components (and the corresponding versions) within a codebase when assembling an application or debugging.

The majority of build tools have their own ways of handling code dependencies, as well as their differences. However, one thing is consistent: each dependency or library has a unique identity that consists of a group of some kind, a name, and a version. In Maven and Gradle, this is commonly referred to as the *GAV* coordinates of a dependency: group ID, artifact ID, and version. The dependencies required for your application are specified using this format, rather than the filename or URI of the external library. Your build tool is expected to know how to locate the dependency identified by the unique coordinates, and will typically download these from a centralized source, such as Maven Central (*https://search.maven.org/*) or Repo@JFrog (*https:// repo.jfrog.org/artifactory/*).

Take Care to Avoid "Dependency Hell"

In the world of software development, there exists a dreaded place called *dependency hell*. The bigger your system grows and the more dependencies you integrate into your software, the more likely you are to find yourself languishing in this nightmare. With an application that has many dependencies, releasing new package versions can quickly become challenging, as changing one dependency may have a cascading effect.

You'll explore the concept of semantic versioning (semver) in the next section of this chapter, but a core takeaway from this warning is that if dependency specifications are too rigid, you are in danger of version lock—the inability to upgrade a package without having to release new versions of every dependent package. However, approaching this problem from another perspective shows that if dependencies are specified too loosely, you will inevitably be affected by version promiscuity—assuming compatibility with more future versions than is reasonable. Dependency hell is where version lock and/or version promiscuity prevent you from easily and safely moving your project forward.

The majority of dependency management tooling allows you to specify a version range for your dependencies instead of a specific version if required. This allows you to find a common version of a dependency across multiple modules that have requirements. These can be extremely useful and equally dangerous if not used sensibly. Ideally, software builds should be deterministic; the resulting artifact from two identical builds (even those built some time apart) should be identical. You will explore some of the challenges with this shortly, but first let's look into the possible ranges that you can specify. If you have used version ranges before, you will likely have used a similar, if not identical, syntax in the past. The following is the typical version range taken from the RebelLabs Java Build Tools crash course mentioned previously:

$[x,y]$
    From version x up to version y inclusive

(x,y)
    From version x up to version y exclusive

$[x,y)$
    From version x inclusive, up to version y exclusive

$(x,y]$
    From version x exclusive, up to version y inclusive

$[x,)$
    From version x inclusive and all greater versions

$(,x]$
    From version x inclusive and all lesser versions

$[x,y),(y,)$
    From version x inclusive and all greater versions, but specifically excluding version y

If you are using Maven to manage your dependencies, you might use something like Example 5-1 when importing the Twitter4J API.

Example 5-1. Specifying dependency ranges by using Maven

```
<dependency>
    <groupId>org.twitter4j</groupId>
    <artifactId>twitter4j-core</artifactId>
    <version>[4.0,)</version>
</dependency>
```

The preceding example uses semantic versioning (explained in more detail later), and essentially states that you want to import version 4.0.0 and up for the minor version of the dependency. If you initially create the project when the Twitter4J API is available at 4.0.0, this is the version you will include within your artifact. If a new 4.0.1 version is released, a new build of your artifact will include this version—and the same for the versions in this range, such as 4.0.2 and 4.0.15. However, if a new 4.1.0 or 5.0.0 version is released, this would not be included within your artifact, because this is outside the range specified. The theory behind using ranges like this is that patch upgrades will not change the API or semantic behavior of the dependency, but will include any security and nonbreaking bug fixes.

If you are regularly building and deploying your applications, any new minor upgrade will automatically get pulled in to your project without you having to manually modify any build configuration. However, the trade-off is that any updated version of the dependency may break your project—perhaps the authors of the patch did not realize that they must not break the API with a patch update, or maybe you were relying on an incorrectly functioning API. Because of this, it may be best to specify exact dependency versions, and only manually update them.

Many build tools provide plugins to ensure that you are using the most recent versions of all of your dependencies, and will warn you or fail the build if you are not. You will, of course, need a good suite of tests within your application to ensure that upgrading the libraries does not cause any unexpected failures; a compilation failure is the easiest to spot, but often not the most damaging.

Administrating Build Dependencies Is Your Responsibility!

Build tooling can detect and warn if you are using out-of-date build dependencies. Some even detect if a library has known security issues, which can be invaluable. But you are responsible for making sure this functionality is enabled and that you take action on any warnings. Increasingly, many of our projects are assembled from a vast array of third-party libraries and frameworks, and the applications you are building are handling data that is critical to your organization. This only increases your responsibility as a developer.

If you are working on a project that consists of multiple applications, it can be challenging to coordinate using the same dependencies across them. Sometimes this isn't needed. For example, one of the key tenets with microservice-style systems is the independent evolvability of each of the services, and therefore you don't want a mechanism that enforces dependencies to be upgraded in lockstep. In this case, the services should be loosely coupled, and tests or contracts used to assert that an upgrade of a component in one service does not break another.

In other situations, this coupling can be useful. Perhaps you have a group of (deliberately designed) high-coupled applications that must use the same serialization library, and all applications must be upgraded at the same time. Most modern Java dependency management tools have a concept of a *parent* build descriptor—for example, the Parent project object model (POM) in Maven—that allows the specification of dependencies that will be inherited via *child* build descriptors (for example, the dependency Management section within a Maven POM).

High-Coupling and Dependency Management: Daniel's Experience

The use of parent build descriptors is powerful, but it can be abused, particularly with microservice projects. In one of my first microservice projects in 2012, my team and I decided to separate our entity classes into a separate Maven artifact that would be built and released separately from the other services that would import this. However, I soon discovered that any change and new release in the entity artifact meant that we had to build, release, and deploy all of our microservices because we were using the classes for serialization when sharing data across service boundaries. I had accidentally created a highly coupled application.

External Dependencies

External dependencies include everything else that your project requires in order to be built successfully. This includes external executables—perhaps a JavaScript code minifier or an embedded driver—and access to any external resources—for example, a centralized security scanner. A build tool must allow you to package, execute, or specify a connection to an external resource.

Packaging Client-Side JavaScript Libraries as WebJars

For any of us who create Java applications that require a web frontend, you will know that manually adding and managing client-side dependencies often results in codebases that are difficult to maintain. WebJars provide an alternative approach, as they are client-side dependencies packaged into JAR archive files and are made available via Maven Central. They work with most JVM containers and web frameworks, such as Twitter Bootstrap, Angular JS, and Jasmine.

Advantages of using WebJars, rather than packaging your own frontend resources, include the following:

- Explicitly and easily manage the client-side dependencies in JVM-based web applications
- Use JVM-based build tools (e.g., Maven, Gradle) to download your client-side dependencies
- Know which client-side dependencies you are using
- Transitive dependencies are automatically resolved and optionally loaded via RequireJS

More information, including the current WebJars available, can be found on the WebJars (*https://www.webjars.org/*) website.

Multimodule Projects

Although multimodule projects are some of the least understood (and perhaps anecdotally, most abused) concepts, they can be powerful when deployed properly. Multimodule builds are effective when there are clearly defined components within an application that, although they have well-defined interfaces and clear boundaries, perhaps do not provide much value outside some large scope—in this case, the parent project. Accordingly, a multimodule project allows you to group together such components, along with the user-facing components, such as a GUI or web application, and build the entire system with a single command. The build system should be capable of determining the build order for such applications, and the resulting components and applications are all versioned with the same identifier.

Less Is Typically More with Multimodule Projects

In our anecdotal experience (also backed up by a quick search on Stack Overflow), multimodule projects add more complexity to a typical application. Before you begin to divide your application this way, do yourself a favor and really think about the trade-offs involved with organizing your code this way: is the added complexity and increased potential lock-in to a build tool-specific methodology worth the benefits of this style of modularization?

Multiple Repositories (or a Monorepo)?

The choice of how to organize your code has many implications, but your build tool should be able to build the project regardless. With the rise in popularity of the microservices architectural style, there has been increasing interest in the debate of using a single (mono)repo or multiple repositories to store your code. Although the concept sounds similar to the previously discussed ideas around multimodule projects, a multimodule project should always be stored within a single repository; this is because the modules are effectively coupled (in a positive way). However, if you are creating an application consisting of several (or many) microservices, the choice is not so clear-cut. If you have a large number of small, independently versioned code repositories, each project will have a small, manageable codebase, but what about all the code it depends on?

Questions for the Multi Versus Monorepo Debate

Several great resources online can help with making the decision between using multiple repositories or a monorepo, but at the core of this, you need to ask yourself the following questions:

- How do you find and modify the code your project depends on?

- If you are a library developer, how and when will applications adopt your most recent changes?
- If you are a product developer, how and when will you upgrade your library dependencies?
- Whose job is it to verify that changes don't break other projects that depend on them?

Several large engineering organizations prefer to keep their codebase in a single, large repository. Such a codebase is sometimes referred to as a *monorepo*. Monorepos have various advantages when it comes to scaling a codebase in a growing engineering organization. Having all the code in one place:

- Allows a single lint, build, test, and release process.
- Increases code reuse, and enables easy collaboration among many authors.
- Encourages a cohesive codebase in which problems are refactored, not worked around. Tests across modules are run together, which finds bugs that touch multiple modules easier.
- Simplifies dependency management within the codebase. All of the code you run with is visible at a single commit in the repo.
- Provides a single place to report issues.
- Makes it easier to set up a development environment.

As with many things within software development, there are always trade-offs. The negatives with using a single repository include the following:

- The codebase looks more intimidating, and the cognitive load of understanding the system is typically much higher (especially if the system has low cohesion and high coupling).
- The repository is typically (much) bigger in size, and there can be lots of feature branches if the team working on the codebase is large.
- Loss of version information can occur; if all you have is a Git hash, how can you map this to version numbers of dependencies?
- Forking dependencies into the monorepo can lead to modifications being made into this codebase that prevent upgrading of the library.

In regards to a build tool, having a large codebase in a single repository can present challenges, too. In particular, it requires a scalable version-control system and a build system that can perform fine-grained dependency management among many thousands of code modules in a single source tree. Compiling with tools that have arbitrary recursively evaluated logic becomes painfully slow. Build tools like Blaze, Pants, and Buck were designed for this type of usage in a way that other popular build tools, such as Ant, Maven, and SBT, were not.

Plugins

Often, steps within a build, although not core to the build tool's functionality, are nevertheless vital for a successful build. You often find yourself needing the same functionality over and over again, and you want to avoid copy/pasting hacks or quick fixes. This is where build tooling plugins can be useful. Plugins provide a way to package common build functionality that can be created by you or a third-party for reuse.

Provenance, and Avoiding "Not Invented Here"

As we mentioned in the previous build dependency section, you are responsible for all libraries and dependencies that you bring into your application, and this also includes plugins. Be sure to research the quality of a plugin before using it, and ideally examine the associated source code. On a related note, this should not be an excuse for writing every plugin yourself. Please avoid *Not Invented Here (NIH)*, as the developers of a well-built and maintained plugin will have done a lot of the difficult design work and edge-case handling for you.

Releasing and Publishing Artifacts

Every build tool must be able to publish artifacts ready for deployment or consumption by a downstream dependency. Most build tools have the concept of *releasing* a module or code artifact. This process assigns a unique version number to a specific build, and ensures that this coordinate is also tagged appropriately in your VCS.

Semantic Versioning

Semantic versioning, or *semver*, is a simple set of rules and requirements that dictate the way version numbers are assigned and incremented. These rules are based on pre-existing widespread common practices in use in both closed and open source software. Once you identify your public API—which in the Java development world could be an interface at the code level or a REST-like API at the application level— you communicate changes to it with specific increments to your version number. Semver uses a version format of X.Y.Z (Major.Minor.Patch). Bug fixes not affecting the API increment the patch version, backward-compatible API additions/changes increment the minor version, and backward-incompatible API changes increment the major version. Under this scheme, version numbers and the way they change convey

---

meaning about the underlying code and what has been modified from one version to the next. Additional information can be found on the Semantic Versioning 2.0.0 (*https://semver.org/*) website.

Java Build Tooling Overview

This section presents several of the popular Java build tools, and highlights strengths and weaknesses, with the goal of helping you decide which is best for your current project.

Ant

One of the first popular build tools in the Java space was Apache Ant. For many of us who were previously used to manually building Java applications via a combination of `javac` and Bash scripts, Ant was heaven sent. Ant takes an imperative approach: developers specify a series of tasks that contain instructions on how exactly to build a project. Ant was written in Java, and users of Ant could develop their own *antlibs* containing Ant tasks and types. A large number of ready-made commercial or open source antlibs provided useful functionality. Ant was extremely flexible and did not impose coding conventions or directory layouts to the Java projects that adopt it as a build tool. However, this flexibility was also its downfall.

The range of possible directory structures and layouts meant that nearly every project (even within the same organizations) were subtly different from each other. The flexibility of how artifacts were built also meant that developers could not rely on the availability of key life cycle events within a build, such as cleaning the workspace, verifying the build, packaging, releasing, and deploying. Developers attempted to compensate for this by writing accompanying build documentation, but this was difficult to maintain as a project evolved, and was particularly challenging for large projects consisting of many artifacts. Another challenge presented by Ant was although it followed the good design principle of single responsibility, it didn't assist developers with managing dependencies. To address these shortcomings, Maven emerged from the Apache Turbine project as a competitor against Ant.

Installation

You can download Apache Ant from *ant.apache.org*. Extract the ZIP file into a directory structure of your choice. Set the `ANT_HOME` environment variable to this location and include the *ANT_HOME/bin* directory in your path. Make sure that the `JAVA_HOME` environment variable is set to the JDK. This is required for running Ant.

You can also install Ant by using your favorite package manager; for example:

```
$ apt-get install ant
```

```
$ brew install ant
```

Check your installation by opening a command line and typing ant -version into the command line:

```
$ ant -version
Apache Ant(TM) version 1.10.1 compiled on February 2 2017
```

The system should find the command ant and show the version number of your installed Ant version.

Build example

You can see an example *build.xml* build script in Example 5-2.

Example 5-2. Ant build.xml

```xml
<project name="MyProject" default="dist" basedir=".">
  <description>
    simple example build file
  </description>
  <!-- set global properties for this build -->
  <property name="src" location="src"/>
  <property name="build" location="build"/>
  <property name="dist" location="dist"/>
  <property name="version" value="1.0"/>

  <target name="init">
    <!-- Create the time stamp -->
    <tstamp/>
    <!-- Create the build directory structure used by compile -->
    <mkdir dir="${build}"/>
  </target>

  <target name="compile" depends="init"
        description="compile the source">
    <!-- Compile the java code from ${src} into ${build} -->
    <javac srcdir="${src}" destdir="${build}"/>
  </target>

  <target name="dist" depends="compile"
        description="generate the distribution">
    <buildnumber/>
    <!-- Create the distribution directory -->
    <mkdir dir="${dist}/lib"/>

    <!-- Put everything in ${build} into the
    MyProject-${version}.${build.number}.jar -->
    <jar destfile="${dist}/lib/MyProject-${version}.${build.number}.jar"
    basedir="${build}"/>
  </target>
```

```
<target name="clean"
        description="clean up">
    <!-- Delete the ${build} and ${dist} directory trees -->
    <delete dir="${build}"/>
    <delete dir="${dist}"/>
</target>
</project>
```

Assuming that you have packaged the Java source files in the directory structure as specified in the build script, you can build this project by using the following command:

```
$ ant -f build.xml
```

Releasing and publishing

The simplest way to release and version your build artifacts with Apache Ant is to use the buildnumber task. In the dist target in the preceding *build.xml*, you can see the use of the <buildnumber/> declaration tag. You can also see that the build artifact destination file—shown as destfile="${dist}/lib/MyProject-${version}.${build.number}.jar"—is named as a concatenation of the string MyProject, a version variable set within the global properties and the build.number variable that is generated by the buildnumber task. This is a number that increases with each build, which ensures uniqueness.

You can also release artifacts built by Ant (and manage dependencies) by using the companion project Apache Ivy (*http://ant.apache.org/ivy/*).

Maven

The Apache Maven build tool focuses on "convention over configuration," and the primary goal is to allow a developer to comprehend the complete state of a development effort in the shortest period of time. To attain this goal, that Maven attempts to deal with several areas of concern:

- Making the build process easy
- Providing a uniform build system
- Providing quality project information
- Providing guidelines for best-practices development
- Allowing transparent migration to new features

Maven allows a project to build by using its POM and a set of plugins that are shared by all projects using Maven, providing a uniform build system. Once you familiarize yourself with how one Maven project builds, you automatically know how all Maven projects build, saving you immense amounts of time when trying to navigate many projects. Maven aims to gather current principles for best-practices development, and make it easy to guide a project in that direction. For example, specification, execution, and reporting of unit tests are part of the normal build cycle using Maven. Current unit-testing best practices were used as guidelines:

- Keeping your test source code in a separate, but parallel source tree
- Using test case naming conventions to locate and execute tests
- Have test cases set up their environment and don't rely on customizing the build for test preparation.
- Maven also aims to assist in project workflow such as release management and issue tracking.

Maven also suggests some guidelines on how to lay out your project's directory structure so that after you learn the layout, you can easily navigate any other project that uses Maven and the same defaults. There are three built-in build life cycles: default, clean, and site. The default life cycle handles your project deployment, the clean life cycle handles project cleaning, and the site life cycle handles the creation of your project's site documentation. Each of these build life cycles is defined by a different list of build phases, wherein a build phase represents a stage in the life cycle.

These life cycle phases (plus the other life cycle phases not noted here) are executed sequentially to complete the default life cycle. Given the preceding life cycle phases, this means that when the default life cycle is used, Maven will first validate the project, then will try to compile the sources, run those against the tests, package the binaries (e.g., JAR), run integration tests against that package, verify the integration tests, install the verified package to the local repository, and then deploy the installed package to a remote repository.

Installation

You can download Maven from the Apache Maven project web page (*https://maven.apache.org/download.cgi*). Ensure that the JAVA_HOME environment variable is set and points to your JDK installation, and then extract the ZIP file into a directory structure of your choice. Add the bin directory of the created directory *apache-maven-3.5.2* to the PATH environment variable.

You can also install Maven by using your favorite package manager; for example:

```
$ apt-get install maven
$ brew install maven
```

Confirm everything is working:

```
$ mvn -v
```

```
Maven home: /usr/local/Cellar/maven/3.5.2/libexec
Java version: 9.0.1, vendor: Oracle Corporation
Java home: /Library/Java/JavaVirtualMachines/jdk-9.0.1.jdk/Contents/Home
Default locale: en_GB, platform encoding: UTF-8
OS name: "mac os x", version: "10.12.6", arch: "x86_64", family: "mac"
```

Build example

You can see an example *pom.xml* build script in Example 5-3.

Example 5-3. pom.xml of a simple Spring Boot application

```xml
<?xml version="1.0" encoding="UTF-8"?>
<project xmlns="http://maven.apache.org/POM/4.0.0"
    xmlns:xsi="http://www.w3.org/2001/XMLSchema-instance"
    xsi:schemaLocation="http://maven.apache.org/POM/
    4.0.0 http://maven.apache.org/xsd/maven-4.0.0.xsd">
    <modelVersion>4.0.0</modelVersion>

    <groupId>uk.co.danielbryant.oreilly.cdjava</groupId>
    <artifactId>conference</artifactId>
    <version>${revision}</version>
    <packaging>jar</packaging>

    <name>conference</name>
    <description>Project for Daniel Bryant's
    O'Reilly Continuous Delivery with Java</description>

    <parent>
        <groupId>org.springframework.boot</groupId>
        <artifactId>spring-boot-starter-parent</artifactId>
        <version>1.5.6.RELEASE</version>
        <relativePath/> <!-- lookup parent from repository -->
    </parent>

    <properties>
        <project.build.sourceEncoding>UTF-8</project.build.sourceEncoding>
        <project.reporting.outputEncoding>UTF-8</project.reporting.outputEncoding>
        <java.version>1.8</java.version>
        <!-- Sane default when no revision property
        is passed in from the commandline -->
        <revision>0-SNAPSHOT</revision>
    </properties>

    <scm>
        <connection>scm:git:https://github.com/danielbryantuk/
        oreilly-docker-java-shopping</connection>
    </scm>

    <distributionManagement>
        <repository>
            <id>artifact-repository</id>
```

```
                <url>http://mojo.codehaus.org/oreilly-docker-java-shopping</url>
            </repository>
    </distributionManagement>

    <dependencies>
        <dependency>
            <groupId>org.springframework.boot</groupId>
            <artifactId>spring-boot-starter-web</artifactId>
        </dependency>
        <dependency>
            <groupId>org.springframework.boot</groupId>
            <artifactId>spring-boot-starter-actuator</artifactId>
        </dependency>
        <dependency>
            <groupId>org.springframework.boot</groupId>
            <artifactId>spring-boot-starter-data-jpa</artifactId>
        </dependency>

        <!-- Utils -->
        <dependency>
            <groupId>net.rakugakibox.spring.boot</groupId>
            <artifactId>orika-spring-boot-starter</artifactId>
            <version>1.4.0</version>
        </dependency>
        <dependency>
            <groupId>org.apache.commons</groupId>
            <artifactId>commons-lang3</artifactId>
            <version>3.6</version>
        </dependency>

        <!-- Test -->
        <dependency>
            <groupId>org.springframework.boot</groupId>
            <artifactId>spring-boot-starter-test</artifactId>
            <scope>test</scope>
        </dependency>
    </dependencies>

    <build>
        <plugins>
            <plugin>
                <groupId>org.springframework.boot</groupId>
                <artifactId>spring-boot-maven-plugin</artifactId>
            </plugin>
            <plugin>
                <artifactId>maven-scm-plugin</artifactId>
                <version>1.9.4</version>
                <configuration>
                    <tag>${project.artifactId}-${project.version}</tag>
                </configuration>
            </plugin>
        </plugins>
```

```
    </build>
</project>
```

Assuming that all the Java code files are present and in the correct directory structure, you can build the application:

```
$ mvn clean install
```

Releasing and publishing

Historically, releasing and versioning in Maven was conducted with the Maven Release plugin, but this had issues, particularly around the plugin doing lots of operations for each release: multiple clean and package cycles, POM transformations, commits, and source code management (SCM) revisions. Importantly for you, the Maven Release plugin does not support continuous delivery effectively.

Maven Release Plugin: Dead and Buried

Axel Fontaine has written a popular blog series (*https://axelfontaine.com/blog/dead-burried.html*) on the problems with the Maven Release plugin over the last six years. If you want to learn more about the issues and your options for releasing via Maven, we highly recommend you have a look at this series.

Inspired by Axel Fontaine's blog series about more-effective releasing with Maven (post-Maven 3.2.1), many developers favor using the Versions Maven plugin. At its core, the purpose of producing a release is nothing more than being able to link a version of the software as deployed onto a machine back to the matching revision of the source code in SCM. To accomplish this, you have to go through multiple steps, the minimum of which include the following:

- Checking out the application code as it is
- Specifying a version number so it can be uniquely identified
- Building, testing, and packaging the application
- Deploying the application artifact to an artifact repository where it can be deployed from
- Tagging this state in the SCM so it can be associated with the matching artifact

The preceding POM has been configured to enable Fontaine's releasing methodology. You'll notice the `<version>${revision}</version>` and associated property that can be set via a command-line argument (and would typically be set as an environment variable via your continuous integration server). The `<scm>` and `<distribution Management>` sections of the POM remain unchanged from the standard Maven approach. You can now produce releases on your CI server by invoking the following:

```
$ mvn deploy scm:tag -Drevision=$BUILD_NUMBER
```

BUILD_NUMBER is the environment variable provided by your CI server to identify the current build number for the project. For services and deliverables consumed by other teams and external parties, you can also easily combine this technique with semantic versioning by prefixing the version tag in your POM with the correct semantic version. You can then automatically produce releases internally and manually update this semantic version before each external delivery.

Using Gitflow? There Is Another Plugin for You

You will explore Gitflow in Chapter 9, but if you are using this Git-based branching workflow, there is another plugin you should look at: JGit-Flow (*https://bitbucket.org/atlassian/jgit-flow/*). The Maven JGit-Flow plugin is based on and is a replacement for the Maven Release plugin, and enables support for Gitflow-style releases via Maven. While this plugin is primarily used to perform releases, it also provides full Gitflow functionality, including the following:

Starting a release
    Creates a release branch and updates POM(s) with release versions

Finishing a release
    Runs a Maven build (deploy or install), merges the release branch, and updates POM(s) with development versions

Starting a hotfix
    Creates a hotfix branch and updates POM(s) with hotfix versions

Finishing a hotfix
    Runs a Maven build (deploy or install), merges the hotfix branch, and updates pom(s) with previous versions

Starting a feature
    Creates a feature branch

Finishing a feature
    Merges the feature branch

Maven was influential within the Java build ecosystem, but a new community emerged that believed that Maven, and the build process, was inflexible and overly opinionated. Accordingly, Gradle emerged as a potential competitor that was not only a lot more flexible, but also less verbose.

Gradle

Gradle is an open source build automation system that builds upon the concepts of Apache Ant and Apache Maven and introduces a Groovy-based domain-specific language (DSL) instead of the XML form used by Apache Maven for declaring the project configuration. Gradle was designed for multiproject builds that could grow to be quite large, and it supports incremental builds by intelligently determining which parts of the build tree are up-to-date, so that any task dependent upon those parts will not need to be reexecuted. The initial plugins are primarily focused around Java, Groovy, and Scala development and deployment, but more languages and project workflows are on the roadmap.

Gradle and Maven have fundamentally different views on how to build a project. Gradle is based on a graph of task dependencies, where the tasks do the work. Maven uses a model of fixed, linear phases to which you can attach goals (the things that do the work). Despite this, migrations can be surprisingly easy because Gradle follows many of the same conventions as Maven, and dependency management works in a similar way.

Installation

You can download Gradle from the project's installation page (*https://gradle.org/ install/*). You must have Java 7 or later installed in order to run the latest version of Gradle. Ensure that the JAVA_HOME environment variable is set and points to your JDK installation, and then extract the ZIP file into a directory structure of your choice. Add the bin directory of the created directory *apache-maven-3.5.2* to the PATH environment variable.

You can also install Gradle by using your favorite package manager; for example:

```
$ apt-get install gradle
$ brew install gradle
```

Once you have everything installed, you can check that everything is working by executing the gradle binary with the v flag. You should see something similar to the following output:

```
~ $ gradle -v
------------------------------------------------------------
Gradle 4.3.1
------------------------------------------------------------

Build time:   2017-11-08 08:59:45 UTC
Revision:     e4f4804807ef7c2829da51877861ff06e07e006d
Groovy:       2.4.12
Ant:          Apache Ant(TM) version 1.9.6 compiled on June 29 2015
JVM:          9.0.1 (Oracle Corporation 9.0.1+11)
OS:           Mac OS X 10.12.6 x86_64
```

Build example

You can see an example *build.gradle* build script in Example 5-4.

Example 5-4. build.gradle of a simple Spring Boot application

```
buildscript {
    ext {
        springBootVersion = '1.5.3.RELEASE'
    }
    repositories {
        mavenCentral()
    }
    dependencies {
        classpath("org.springframework.boot:↵
            spring-boot-gradle-plugin:${springBootVersion}")
        classpath("net.researchgate:gradle-release:2.6.0")
    }
}

apply plugin: 'java'
apply plugin: 'eclipse'
apply plugin: 'org.springframework.boot'
apply plugin: 'net.researchgate.release'

version = '0.0.1-SNAPSHOT'
sourceCompatibility = 1.8

repositories {
    mavenCentral()
}

dependencies {
    compile('org.springframework.boot:spring-boot-starter')
    compile('org.springframework.boot:spring-boot-starter-web')
    compile('com.google.guava:guava:21.0')
    compile 'com.fasterxml.jackson.datatype:jackson-datatype-jsr310:2.8.6'

    testCompile('org.springframework.boot:spring-boot-starter-test')
}
```

Assuming that all of the code is included in the expected directory structure, you can build the project by executing the following command:

```
$ gradle build
```

Releasing and publishing

There are several popular options for releasing and publishing Gradle artifacts, but here you'll focus on the ResearchGate gradle-release (*https://github.com/researchgate/ gradle-release*) plugin, which is for providing Maven-like Gradle releases.

But Wait, You Said the Maven Release Plugin Was Dead and Buried?

Yes, yes, we did. However, the most common approach to releasing Gradle artifacts in the wild is through the gradle-release plugin, and so we were keen to demonstrate it. There is a plugin—the Intershop Communications AG scmversion-gradle-plugin (*http://bit.ly/2xH14R8*)—that will allow you to perform the same steps that we have documented from Axel Fontaine's effective Maven release process. Another popular Gradle release mechanism uses the Gradle Artifactory plugin (*http://bit.ly/2R48Gp1*), but this is appropriate only if you are managing your dependencies and release artifacts via JFrog's Artifactory repository.

The preceding *build.gradle* script includes the dependencies for the gradle-release plugin, and also activates this within the `apply plugin` section of the script. You can begin an interactive release by issuing the `gradle release` command. This will trigger the following default series of events:

1. The plugin checks for any uncommitted files (added, modified, removed, or unversioned).

2. Checks for any incoming or outgoing changes.

3. Removes the `SNAPSHOT` flag on your project's version (if used).

4. Prompts you for the release version.

5. Checks if your project is using any `SNAPSHOT` dependencies.

6. Will build your project.

7. Commits the project if `SNAPSHOT` was being used.

8. Creates a release tag with the current version.

9. Prompts you for the next version.

10. Commits the project with the new version.

You can also release artifacts not using the interact process (which will be essential when you begin releasing from a continuous integration build server), by executing the release command with the `release.useAutomaticVersion` flag set to `true`, with the essential arguments passed as additional command-line flags. Full details, including all of the command-line options, can be found within the project's documentation (*http://bit.ly/2NHDw8x*). Here is the command:

```
$ gradle release -Prelease.useAutomaticVersion=true
-Prelease.releaseVersion=1.0.0 -Prelease.newVersion=1.1.0-SNAPSHOT
```

Bazel, Pants, and Buck

Bazel is an open source tool that allows for the automation of building and testing of software. Google uses the build tool Blaze internally and released an open source part of the Blaze tool as Bazel, named as an anagram of Blaze. The Bazel extension language allows it to work with source files written in any language, with native support for Java, C, C++, and Python. Bazel produces builds and runs tests for multiple platforms. Bazel's BUILD files describe how Bazel should build your project. They have a declarative structure and use a language similar to Python. BUILD files allow you to work at a high level of the system by listing rules and their attributes.

The complexity of the build process is handled by these preexisting rules. You can modify rules to tweak the build process, or write new rules to extend Bazel to work with any language or platform. Hermetic rules and sandboxing allow Bazel to produce correct, reproducible artifacts and test results. Caching allows reuse of build artifacts and test results. Bazel's builds are fast. Incremental builds allow Bazel to do the minimum required work for a rebuild or retest. Correct and reproducible builds allow Bazel to reuse cached artifacts for whatever is not changed. If you change a library, Bazel will not rebuild your entire source.

Build systems most similar to Bazel are Pants and Buck. Pants' development and feature set were informed by the needs and processes of many prominent software engineering organizations, including those at Twitter, Foursquare, Square, Medium, and others. But it can also be used in smaller projects. Pants supports Java, Scala, Python, C/C++, Go, Thrift, Protobuf, and Android code. Support for other languages, frameworks, and code generators can be added by third-party developers by authoring plugins through a well-defined module interface.

Buck is a build system developed and used by Facebook. It encourages the creation of small, reusable modules consisting of code and resources, and supports a variety of languages on many platforms. Buck is designed for building multiple deliverables from a single repository (a monorepo) rather than across multiple repositories. It has been Facebook's experience that maintaining dependencies in the same repository makes it easier to ensure that all developers have the correct version of all the code, and simplifies the process of making atomic commits.

As these tools are not as popular as Ant, Maven, and Gradle, and because of the limited scope of this book, a full installation and release guide will not be included here. However, all of these details can be found on the respective project websites. An example Bazel BUILD file can be seen in Example 5-5, and you can see that the structure is not dissimilar to the Gradle build script that you examined earlier.

Example 5-5. Bazel BUILD file

```
package(default_visibility = ["//visibility:public"])

java_binary(
    name = "hello-world",
    main_class = "com.example.myproject.Greeter",
    runtime_deps = [":hello-lib"],
)

java_library(
    name = "hello-lib",
    srcs = glob(
        ["*.java"],
        exclude = ["HelloErrorProne.java"],
    ),
)

java_binary(
    name = "hello-resources",
    main_class = "com.example.myproject.Greeter",
    runtime_deps = [":custom-greeting"],
)

java_library(
    name = "custom-greeting",
    srcs = ["Greeter.java"],
    resources = ["//examples/java-native/src/main/resources:greeting"],
)

java_library(
    name = "hello-error-prone",
    srcs = ["HelloErrorProne.java"],
)

filegroup(
    name = "srcs",
    srcs = ["BUILD"] + glob(["**/*.java"]),
)
```

These new style of build tools can be useful if you are working with a large monorepo-based codebase, and we will explore this in more detail in Chapter 9.

Other JVM Build Tools: SBT and Leiningen

Many more open source JVM-based build tools could have been mentioned in this book, although we have tried to focus on the tools that are popular or provide novel functionality. This book focuses primarily on Java within the JVM space, but it is also worth mentioning that if you are working with Scala or Clojure, the Simple Build Tool (SBT) (*http://www.scala-sbt.org/index.html*) or Leiningen (*https://leiningen.org/*)

build tools are worth considering. Even if you are not working with other languages, these tools can still be useful when working with other projects. You will see the use of SBT later in the book when you will learn about load testing with the Gatling tool. Before wrapping up our tour of Java build tools, let's look quickly at one final classic build tool: Make.

Make

GNU Make is a tool that controls the generation of executables and other nonsource files of a program from the program's source files. As shown in Example 5-6, Make gets its knowledge of how to build your program from a file called the *makefile*, which lists each of the nonsource files and how to compute it from other files. When you write a program, you should write a makefile for it, so that it is possible to use Make to build and install the program.

When you run Make, you can specify particular targets to update; otherwise, Make updates the first target listed in the makefile. Of course, any other target files needed as input for generating these targets must be updated first. Make uses the makefile to figure out which target files ought to be brought up-to-date, and then determines which of them actually need to be updated. If a target file is newer than all of its dependencies, it is already up-to-date, and it does not need to be regenerated. The other target files do need to be updated, but in the right order: each target file must be regenerated before it is used in regenerating other targets.

Example 5-6. makefile for simple Java project

```
JFLAGS = -g
JC = javac
.SUFFIXES: .java .class
.java.class:
        $(JC) $(JFLAGS) $*.java

CLASSES = \
        Foo.java \
        Blah.java \
        Library.java \
        Main.java

default: classes

classes: $(CLASSES:.java=.class)

clean:
        $(RM) *.class
```

Make may appear verbose to many Java developers, but it is worth learning about for simple build environments that are resource constrained and cannot run Maven of Gradle, or for building multilanguage projects.

Choosing a Build Tool

Maven has long been the default Java build tool, primarily because of its standardized build process and structure. If you know how to build one Maven project, you know how to build them all. However, Gradle has seen an increase in popularity in the past several years, most likely because of the concise nature of the *build.gradle* build script. If you have ever had to wade through a large Maven project, you will remember only too well the challenges of navigating large XML files. Choosing a build tool is often an important first step in a new Java project, and this can be a life-long commitment, as migrating from one build tool to another is not a pleasant experience. So, which tool should you choose?

Ant + Ivy

- A good choice if your organization has heavy investment in this tool, or you are migrating/upgrading a project that already uses this tool.

- You are in complete control of the project directory structure, build tooling, and build life cycle.

- Not a good choice if your organization likes things to be standardized, as the flexibility provided by Ant means that build scripts will often diverge in layout and process.

- Generally not recommended for starting a new project that uses modern frameworks like Dropwizard or Spring Boot.

Maven

- A good de facto choice for building Java applications, especially if your organization already has good skills or an investment in this build tool.

- The lack of flexibility and challenge of writing custom plugins mean that this tool is not appropriate for projects that require a custom build process (but do check that you *really* need a custom build process!).

- Not recommended if you are building a simple project with many dependencies; navigating a 500+ line *pom.xml* can be challenging.

Gradle

- A good choice for building projects that require more flexibility in the life cycle or process than Maven can provide.

- Great integration with the Groovy language and associated test frameworks like Spock and Geb.

- The combination of the Gradle DSL and Groovy enable you to write custom and complex build logic.

- Good for Spring Boot and other microservice frameworks, and has useful integration with, for example, contract-based testing tools.

- The learning curve (and reliance on Groovy) could make this a bad choice if your organization works exclusively with Java.

- Not a good choice if your organization likes things to be standardized, as there are many ways to write a *build.gradle*.

Bazel, Buck, Pants, etc.
- Good if working with a large monorepo-based application.

- No real benefit over other tooling if working with many small (microservice-style) code repositories.

- Can be challenging to learn if your team is familiar with only existing Java build tooling.

Make
- A good choice if your project consists of multiple non-JVM languages, and/or requires the use of several command-line tools for the build.

- Can be challenging to learn if your team is familiar with only existing Java build tooling, or not comfortable working with the command line.

It really is worth spending some time at the beginning of a project to make sure you are using the most appropriate build tool, as this is something you will interact with every day.

Summary

You have covered a lot of ground on how Java applications are built within this chapter, and explored the benefits of automating the build process. Your new knowledge of the strengths and weaknesses of popular Java build tools will be useful when starting your next project, whether this is a large monorepo-based project or a series of independently built microservice-style code repositories. In summary:

- All Java applications must be built—compiled to Java byte code—before they can be executed on the JVM.

- Java applications of sufficient complexity will require the inclusion of additional external dependencies or libraries; these must be managed effectively.

- You should package client-side JavaScript libraries as WebJars.

- Although there is value in manually exploring build steps in order to learn more about this process, there is little to be gained from continually doing this.

- Build tooling automates the compilation, dependency management, testing, and packaging of software applications.

- It is generally advantageous to utilize a specialized build tool, such as Maven or Gradle, as this allows all developers working on a project to successfully build the application, regardless of the operating system, IDE, or framework they are using.

- Build tooling can often detect and warn if you are using out-of-date (or insecure) build dependencies, but you are responsible for making sure this functionality is enabled and that you take action on any warnings.

- Application code can be structured within a single version-controlled monorepo, or multiple independent repositories. The choice of structure will affect the build process and determine which build tool to use.

- Semantic versioning, or semver, is a simple set of rules and requirements that dictate how version numbers are assigned and incremented. This is useful for releasing and managing your own dependencies, and is essential for avoiding "dependency hell."

- Choosing a build tool is often an important first step in a new Java project, and it can be a life-long commitment, because migrating from one build tool to another is generally not a pleasant experience.

Before learning about packaging Java applications for deployment, you will explore several additional build tools and associated skills that can be useful in the next chapter.

## CHAPTER 6

Additional Build Tooling and Skills

Because of the increase in popularity of ideas like DevOps and Site Reliability Engineering (SRE), the modern Java developer can rarely rely on coding exclusively in Java in order to accomplish tasks, particularly in relation to building, testing, and deploying code. In this chapter, you will learn more about operating systems and associated tooling for building and running diagnostics on Java applications.

Linux, Bash, and Basic CLI Commands

Linux, Bash, and command-line skills are essential for installing development tools, configuring external build steps, and understanding and managing the underlying operating system environment. Even if you work on a Microsoft Windows development machine, which has excellent PowerShell support as an alternative to Bash, it is useful to understand the Linux OS because many platforms utilize this. Knowledge acquired from learning core Bash skills can often be easily transferred to the Windows environment.

Further Learning Resources

You will learn the core skills required with the command line, JSON manipulation, basic scripting, and provisioning infrastructure in this chapter. However, space limitations prevent this from being a complete reference. For more information, we refer to *Bash Pocket Reference* by Arnold Robbins (O'Reilly), *Classic Shell Scripting* by Arnold Robbins and Nelson Beebe (O'Reilly), and *Infrastructure as Code* by Kief Morris (O'Reilly).

Users, Permissions, and Groups

Linux operating systems (OSs) have the ability to multitask in a manner similar to other operating systems, and from its inception Linux was designed to allow more than one user to have access to the system at the same time. In order for this multiuser design to work properly, there needs to be a method to protect users from each other. Understanding this concept of users is vital for implementing CD, as you will often be creating build pipelines that run as multiple, different users. Often, developers run applications in all environments as the root user—an all-powerful user that by default has access to all files and commands on a Linux OS—when running Java applications (perhaps because they are used to doing this locally). But you really should be using a specific user with minimal permissions for running applications in production.

Users and the Principle of Least Privilege

In IT and computer science, the *principle of least privilege* (also known as the *principle of minimal privilege* or the *principle of least authority*) requires that in a particular abstraction layer of a computing environment, every module—such as a user, process, or program, depending on the subject—must be able to access only the information and resources that are necessary for its legitimate purpose. When you are running Java applications, the principle means giving a user account only those privileges that are essential to perform its intended function. For example, the OS user running a typical Java application should be able to access the required parts of the local filesystem and network, but not be capable of installing new software.

Benefits of the principle of least privilege include the following:

Better system stability
> When code is limited in the scope of changes it can make to a system, it is easier to test its possible actions and interactions with other applications.

Better system security
> When code is limited in the systemwide actions it may perform, vulnerabilities in one application cannot be used to exploit the rest of the machine.

Ease of deployment
> In general, the fewer privileges an application requires, the easier it is to deploy within a larger environment.

Users and permissions

To create a new standard user, use the `useradd` command: `useradd <name>`. The `user add` command utilizes a variety of variables:

-d *<home_dir>*
> *home_dir* will be used as the value for the user's login directory.

-e *<date>*
> The date when the account will expire.

-f *<inactive>*
> The number of days before the account expires.

-s *<shell>*
> Sets the default shell type.

You will need to set a password for the new user by using the `passwd` command (note that you will need root privileges to change a user's password): `passwd <username>`. The user will be able to change their password at any time by using the `passwd` command without specifying a username. A user account and associated password will allow authentication, but you will need to use permissions in order to authorize a user's activities to manipulate files. Permissions are the "rights" to act on a file or directory. The basic rights are read, write, and execute:

Read
> A readable permission allows the contents of the file to be viewed. A read permission on a directory allows you to list the contents of a directory.

Write
> A write permission on a file allows you to modify the contents of that file. For a directory, the write permission allows you to edit the contents of a directory (e.g., add/delete files).

Execute
> For a file, the executable permission allows you to run the file and execute a program or script. For a directory, the execute permission allows you to change to a different directory and make it your current working directory. Users usually have a default group, but they may belong to several additional groups.

To view the permissions on a file or directory, issue the command `ls -l <direc tory/file>`, as shown in Example 6-1.

Example 6-1. Examining file permissions

```
(master *+) conferencemono $ ls -l
total 32
-rw-r--r--  1 danielbryant  staff  9798 31 Oct 16:17 conferencemono.iml
-rw-r--r--  1 danielbryant  staff  2735 31 Oct 16:16 pom.xml
drwxr-xr-x  4 danielbryant  staff   136 31 Oct 09:16 src
drwxr-xr-x  6 danielbryant  staff   204 31 Oct 09:37 target
```

The first 10 characters show the access permissions. The first dash (-) indicates the type of file (d for directory, s for special file, and - for a regular file). The next three characters (rw-) define the owner's permission to the file. In the preceding example, for the *pom.xml* file, the file owner danielbryant has read and write permissions only. The next three characters (r--) are the permissions for the members of the same staff group as the file owner, which in this example is read-only. The last three characters (r--) show the permissions for all other users, and in this example it is read-only.

You can change a file's permissions and ownership with the chmod and chown commands, respectively. The command chmod is short for *change mode*, and can be used to change permissions on files and directories. By default, all files are "owned" by the user who creates them and by that user's default group. To change the ownership of a file, use the chown command in the chown user:group /path/to/file format. To change the ownership of a directory and all the files contained inside, you can use the recursive option with the -R flag: chown -R danielbryant:staff /opt/applica tion/config/. If a file is not owned by you, you will need root account access in order to change permissions or ownership; however, you don't necessarily need to log in as root in order to achieve this.

Self-Help: Using man and help

Linux has many *man* manuals that provide more information on all of the commands mentioned in this chapter, and many command and applications also have associated help. If you want to learn more about a command, try typing **man <command>** or **<command> --help**.

Understanding sudo—superuser do

The root user acccount is the super user and has the ability to do anything on a system. Therefore, in order to have protection against potential damage, the sudo command is often used in place of root. sudo allows users and groups access to commands they normally would not be able to use, and allows a user to have administration privileges without logging in as root, from which it is all too easy to accidentally do all kinds of damage to the underlying OS and configuration.

A common example of the sudo command used within continuous delivery is when installing software into a virtual machine or container: sudo apt-get install *<package>* for Ubuntu or Debian, and sudo yum install *<package>* for Red Hat or CentOS distributions. To provide a user with sudo ability, their name will need to be added to the *sudoers* file. This file is important and should not be edited directly with a text editor; if the *sudoers* file is edited incorrectly, it could result in preventing access to the system. Accordingly, the visudo command should be used to edit the *sudoers* file. If you are initializing a system, you will need to log in as root and enter the command visudo. As soon as your user has sudo privileges, you can use sudo with visudo. Example 6-2 shows an example of a *sudoers* file.

Example 6-2. Portion of the sudoers file that shows the users with sudo access.

```
# User privilege specification
root     ALL=(ALL:ALL) ALL
danielbryant  ALL=(ALL:ALL) ALL
ashleybryant  ALL=(ALL:ALL) ALL
```

Working with groups

Groups in Linux are simply a (potentially) empty collection of users, which can be used to manage several users at once or allow multiple independent user accounts to collaborate and share files. Every user has a default or primary group, and control of group membership is administered through the */etc/group* file, which shows a list of groups and its members. When a user logs in, the group membership is set for their primary group. This means that when a user launches a program or creates a file, both the file and the running program will be associated with the user's current group membership. This is an important concept within continuous delivery, as it means that if your user starts a process (a Java application, a build server, test execution, or indeed any process), this process inherits your permissions. If you are running with generous permissions, it can mean that the process you started can do a lot of damage!

A user may access other files in other groups, as long as they are also a member of that group and the access permissions are set. To run programs or create a file in a different group, you must run the newgrp command to switch your current group (e.g., newgrp *<group_name>*). If you are a member of the *group_name* in the */etc/group* file, the current group membership will change. It is important to note that any files created will now be associated with the new group rather than your primary group. You can also change your group by using the chgrp command: chgrp *<newgroup>*.

Working with the Filesystem

The most fundamental skills you need to master are moving around the filesystem and getting an idea of what is around you. When you log into your server (for example, a new build server), you are typically dropped into your user account's home directory.

Navigating directories

A *home directory* is a directory set aside for your user to store files and create directories. To find out where your home directory is in relationship to the rest of the filesystem, you can use the `pwd` command. This command displays the directory that you are currently in, as shown in Example 6-3.

Example 6-3. Using pwd to see the location of your current directory in the filesystem

```
(master *+) conferencemono $ pwd
/Users/danielbryant/Documents/dev/daniel-bryant-uk/
oreilly-book-support/conferencemono
```

You can view the contents of the current directory with the `ls` command. The `ls` command has many useful flags, and it is common to use `ls -lsa` in order to view more details about the file (`lsa` lists files in *long* format, file *sizes*, and showing *all* files).

Example 6-4. Using ls in order to see the contents of the current directory

```
(master *+) conferencemono $ ls
conferencemono.iml pom.xml              src                 target
(master *+) conferencemono $ ls -lsa
total 32
 0 drwxr-xr-x   7 danielbryant  staff   238 31 Oct 16:17 .
 0 drwxr-xr-x   8 danielbryant  staff   272 31 Oct 09:48 ..
 0 drwxr-xr-x  11 danielbryant  staff   374  3 Jan 09:30 .idea
24 -rw-r--r--   1 danielbryant  staff  9798 31 Oct 16:17 conferencemono.iml
 8 -rw-r--r--   1 danielbryant  staff  2735 31 Oct 16:16 pom.xml
 0 drwxr-xr-x   4 danielbryant  staff   136 31 Oct 09:16 src
 0 drwxr-xr-x   6 danielbryant  staff   204 31 Oct 09:37 target
(master *+) conferencemono $
```

You can navigate directories by using the `cd <directory name>` command, as shown in Example 6-5. `cd ..` moves you up one directory, and by combining the usage of this `ls` and `pwd`, you can easily view files and not get lost.

Example 6-5. Navigating the filesystem

```
(master *+) conferencemono $ pwd
/Users/danielbryant/Documents/dev/daniel-bryant-uk/ ↵
oreilly-book-support/conferencemono
(master *+) conferencemono $ cd target/
(master *+) target $ ls
classes                 generated-sources       generated-test-sources test-classes
(master *+) target $ cd classes/
(master *+) classes $ pwd
/Users/danielbryant/Documents/dev/daniel-bryant-uk/ ↵
oreilly-book-support/conferencemono/target/classes
(master *+) classes $ ls -lsa
total 0
0 drwxr-xr-x  4 danielbryant  staff   136 31 Oct 16:21 .
0 drwxr-xr-x  6 danielbryant  staff   204 31 Oct 09:37 ..
0 drwxr-xr-x  4 danielbryant  staff   136 31 Oct 16:21 templates
0 drwxr-xr-x  3 danielbryant  staff   102 31 Oct 10:20 uk
(master *+) classes $ cd ..
(master *+) target $ cd ..
(master *+) conferencemono $ pwd
/Users/danielbryant/Documents/dev/daniel-bryant-uk/ ↵
oreilly-book-support/conferencemono
```

Creating and manipulating files

The most basic method of creating a file is with the touch command. This creates an empty file using the name and location specified: touch `<file_name>`. You will need to have write permissions for the directory in which you are currently located for this to succeed. You can also "touch" an existing file, and this will simply update the last accessed and last modified times of the file to the current time. Many operations within continuous delivery monitor the last modified date and use any change as a trigger for an arbitrary operation, and using touch can short-circuit the check and cause the operation to run. Similar to the touch command, you can use the mkdir command to create empty directories: mkdir example You can also create a nested directory structure by using the -p flag (otherwise, you will get an error, as mkdir can create a directory only within a directory that already exists): mkdir -p deep/ nested/directories.

You can move a file to a new location by using the mv command mv file ./some/ existing_dir. (This command succeeds only if the */some/existing_dir* directories already exist.) Perhaps somewhat confusingly, mv can also be used to rename files: mv original_name new_name. You are responsible for ensuring that these operations will not do anything destructive—for example, mv can be used to overwrite existing files, which cannot be recovered! In a similar fashion, you can copy files by using the cp command: cp original_file new_copy_file. To copy directories, you must include the -r option to the command. This stands for *recursive*, as it copies the directory, plus all of the directory's contents. This option is necessary with directories, regardless of whether the directory is empty: `cp -r existing_directory location_for_deep_copy`. To delete a file, you can use the `rm` command. If you want to remove a non-empty directory, you will have to use the `-r` flag, which removes all of the directory's contents recursively, plus the directory itself.

There Is Often No Undo on the CLI

Please be extremely careful when using any destructive command like `rm`, and potentially `mv` and `cp`. There is no "undo" command for these actions, so it is possible for you to accidentally destroy important files permanently. If you're anything like us, you'll do this a few times before you fully learn your lesson! One tactic we use now is to list files we want to delete/move/replace before actually issuing the command. For example, if we want to delete all the files with a *.ini* extension, but leave everything else intact, we will navigate to the appropriate directory and list (by using `ls *.ini`) and check the resulting files before issuing the remove command: `rm *.ini`.

Viewing and Editing Text

In contrast to some operating systems, Linux and other Unix-like operating systems rely on plain-text files for vast portions of the system, so it is important that you learn how to view text files via the command line. The basic mechanism to view a file's contents on your terminal is by using the cat application (e.g., `cat /etc/hosts`). This doesn't work well with large files, or files with text you want to search, and therefore it is common to also use a *pager* like `less` (e.g., `less /etc/hosts`). This opens the less program with the contents of the */etc/hosts* file. You can navigate through the pages in the file with Ctrl-F and Ctrl-B (think forward and back). To search for text in the document, you can type a forward slash, /, followed by the search term (e.g., `/local host`). If the file contains more than one instance of the string being searched for, you can press N to move to the next search, and Shift-N to move back to the previous result. When you wish to exit the less program, you can type Q to quit.

When attempting to use continuous delivery or build tools, it is a common requirement to be either able to view the first few lines or the last few lines of a large file—this is especially common when looking at the first few lines of a configuration file, or the last few lines of a log file (and you might want to follow along as more lines are appended to the log file). The `head` and `tail` commands, respectively, can help a lot here: e.g., `head /etc/hosts` or `tail server.log`.

Programs like cat, less, head, and tail allow you only view or read-only access to a file's contents. If you need to edit a text file by using the command line, you can use the vi, vim, emacs, or nano programs. Each Linux distribution provides different tools by default, although you can usually install your favorite via a package manager (providing your user has appropriate permissions).

Joining Everything Together: Redirects, Pipes, and Filters

Linux also has a powerful concept of redirects, pipes, and filters that allow you to combine simple command-line programs to perform complicated processing and filter the output (and text contents within the files) at any point within the processing steps. More information on this can be found in the *Linux Pocket Guide* (O'Reilly) by Daniel Barrett, but several examples are included here to demonstrate the power:

```
ls > output.log
```
Redirects (saves) the contents of the ls command to the text file *output.log*, overwriting any content that exists in this file.

```
ls >> output.log
```
Redirects (saves) the contents of the ls command to the text file *output.log*, appending the new text to the existing contents of the file.

```
ls | less
```
Pipes the output of the `ls` command to the less pager, allowing you to page up and down through long directory listings, as well as search the content.

```
ls | head -3
```
Pipes the output of the `ls` command to the `head` command (showing the top three lines only).

```
ls | head -3 | tail -1 > output.log
```
Pipes the output of the `ls` command to `head`, which takes the top three lines and pipes this to `tail`, which takes the bottom one line and redirects (saves) this to the *output.log* file.

```
cat < input.log
```
Redirects (loads) the contents on *input.log* into cat. This example appears trivial, as you don't need to redirect the contents of a file into cat for it to be displayed, but the program can be more complicated than cat. For example, this command can be used to redirect (load) a database dump file into the MySQL command-line program.

Searching and Manipulating Text: grep, awk, and sed

Some of the most basic—but also the most powerful—tooling in Linux searches and manipulates text. *grep* is a command-line utility for searching plain-text data sets for lines that match a regular expression. *awk* is a programming language designed for text processing and typically used as a data extraction and reporting tool. *sed* is a stream editor utility that parses and transforms text, using a simple, compact programming language. These tools are extremely useful when building continuous delivery pipelines or diagnosing issues on Linux machines. The following are examples:

```
grep "literal_string" filename
```
Searches for the exact match of `literal_string` in the file specified by `filename`.

```
grep "REGEX" filename
```
Searches for the regular expression `REGEX` in the file specified by `filename`.

```
grep -iw "is" demo_file
```
A case-insensitive search (`-i`) for the exact match of the word (`-w`) *is*. The word must have space or punctuation on either side of it to match, in the file specified by *demo_file*.

```
awk '{print $3 "\t" $4}' data_in_rows.txt
```
Prints to the terminal the third and fourth columns, separated by a tab (`\t`), of all rows of data within the file specified.

```
sed 's/regexp/replacement/g' inputFileName > outputFileName
```
Globally (/g) replaces (s/) the regular expression (regex) with the (replace
ment) string in the *inputFileName* file and redirects—or saves—the results in the
outputFileName.

The Power of Regular Expressions

There is an old joke within IT that if you try to solve one problem with regular
expressions (regex), all you end up with is two problems. There is probably some
truth to this joke, but regex is a powerful tool when used correctly. We highly recommend that you learn more about the principles of regex, and at least become profi-
cient in the basics, because lots of build and deployment tools employ regex for
matching configuration or metadata.

Diagnostic Tooling: top, ps, netstat, and iostat

The following list should be good to get you started diagnosing issues with Linux
machines, and all of these tools should be available on a standard Linux distro (or
easily installed via a package manager). You can find more details of each command
in the Linux Pocket Reference of by using the man tool to view the corresponding
manuals:

top
> Allows you to view all processes running on the (virtual) machine.

ps
> Lists all of the processes running on the (virtual) machine.

netstat
> Allows you to view all network connections on the (virtual) machine.

iostat
> Lists all of the I/O statistics of block devices (disk drives) connected to the (vir-
> tual) machine.

dig or nslookup
> Provides information on DNS address.

ping
> Checks whether an IP or domain names can be reached over the network.

tracert
> Allows you to trace the route of an IP packet within the network (both an inter-
> nal network and the internet).

tcpdump
> Allows you to spy on TCP network traffic. This is typically an advanced tool, but can be useful in cloud environments where much of the communication occurs via TCP.

strace
> Allows you to trace system calls. This is typically an advanced tool, but can be invaluable for debugging container or security issues.

Become Familiar with Your OS Package Manager

You will often find that the diagnostic tooling that you require is not available on a machine you are working on, and therefore it is beneficial to become familiar with how to install these tools via a package manager. For example, on many Ubuntu (or Debian) OSs, you will have to install the sysstat package (`sudo apt-get install -y sysstat`) in order to run iostat. Don't forget that you will require the appropriate permissions to be able to install them on the machine you are working on!

If you are working a lot with containers, you may require additional tooling, as some of the preceding programs (and additional diagnostic tooling) do not work correctly with container technology. The following list includes several tools that we have found useful for understanding container runtimes:

sysdig (https://www.sysdig.org/install/)
> A useful container-aware diagnostic tool

systemd-cgtop (http://bit.ly/2xFaFaX)
> A systemd-specific tool to view top-like data within cgroups (containers)

atomic top and docker top (http://bit.ly/2Dxz3kd)
> Useful utilities by Red Hat and Docker, respectively, that allow you to examine processes running within containers

Several Older Diagnostic Tools Are Not Container Friendly!

Several of the popular diagnostic tools were created before container technology like Docker was created (or became popular), and therefore they don't work as you might expect. For example, containers run as a process, and then the programs within each container namespace also run as a process. Some tools may have to be able to distinguish that all of the programs running within the OS are separated via namespaces.

HTTP Calls and JSON Manipulation

Many of the third-party services you interact with use HTTP/S as the transport protocol and JSON as the data format. Therefore, it makes sense to become comfortable working with these technologies, and also to develop skills that allow you to quickly experiment and test ideas without needing to build an entire application in Java.

curl

The Linux curl command is a useful command for testing web-based REST-like APIs. Example 6-6 shows usage of curl against the GitHub API.

Example 6-6. curl making a request against the GitHub API repos endpoint

```
$ curl 'https://api.github.com/repos/danielbryantuk/
oreilly-docker-java-shopping/commits?per_page=1'
[
  {
    "sha": "3182a8a5fc73d2125022bf317ac68c3b1f4a3879",
    "commit": {
      "author": {
        "name": "Daniel Bryant",
        "email": "daniel.bryant@tai-dev.co.uk",
        "date": "2017-01-26T19:48:46Z"
      },
      "committer": {
        "name": "Daniel Bryant",
        "email": "daniel.bryant@tai-dev.co.uk",
        "date": "2017-01-26T19:48:46Z"
      },
      "message": "Update Vagrant Box Ubuntu and Docker Compose. Remove sudo usage",
      "tree": {
        "sha": "24eb583bd834734ae9b6c8133c99e4791a7387e8",
        "url": "https://api.github.com/repos/danielbryantuk/↵
        oreilly-docker-java-shopping/git/trees/↵
        24eb583bd834734ae9b6c8133c99e4791a7387e8"
      },
      "url": "https://api.github.com/repos/danielbryantuk/↵
      oreilly-docker-java-shopping/git/commits/↵
      3182a8a5fc73d2125022bf317ac68c3b1f4a3879",
      "comment_count": 0
    },
    "url": "https://api.github.com/repos/danielbryantuk/↵
    oreilly-docker-java-shopping/commits/↵
    3182a8a5fc73d2125022bf317ac68c3b1f4a3879",
    "html_url": "https://github.com/danielbryantuk/↵
    oreilly-docker-java-shopping/commit/↵
    3182a8a5fc73d2125022bf317ac68c3b1f4a3879",
    "comments_url": "https://api.github.com/repos/danielbryantuk/↵
    oreilly-docker-java-shopping/commits/↵
```

```
  3182a8a5fc73d2125022bf317ac68c3b1f4a3879/comments",
  "author": {
    "login": "danielbryantuk",
    ...
  },
  "committer": {
    "login": "danielbryantuk",
    ...
  },
  "parents": [
    {
      "sha": "05b73d1f0c9904e6904d3f1bb8f13384e65e7840",
      "url": "https://api.github.com/repos/danielbryantuk/↵
      oreilly-docker-java-shopping/commits/↵
      05b73d1f0c9904e6904d3f1bb8f13384e65e7840",
      "html_url": "https://github.com/danielbryantuk/↵
      oreilly-docker-java-shopping/commit/↵
      05b73d1f0c9904e6904d3f1bb8f13384e65e7840"
    }
  ]
  }
]
```

The preceding example made a GET request to the repos endpoint and displayed the JSON response. You can also use curl to get more detail from the endpoint response, such as the HTTP status code, the content length, and any additional header information like rate-limiting. The -I flag makes a HEAD request against the specified URI and displays the response, as shown in Example 6-7.

Example 6-7. Using curl to obtain additional information about an endpoint response (by making a HEAD request)

```
$ curl -I 'https://api.github.com/repos/danielbryantuk/↵
oreilly-docker-java-shopping/commits?per_page=1'
HTTP/1.1 200 OK
Server: GitHub.com
Date: Thu, 21 Sep 2017 08:28:06 GMT
Content-Type: application/json; charset=utf-8
Content-Length: 3861
Status: 200 OK
X-RateLimit-Limit: 60
X-RateLimit-Remaining: 51
X-RateLimit-Reset: 1505983279
Cache-Control: public, max-age=60, s-maxage=60
Vary: Accept
ETag: "4ce9e0d9cf4e2339bbc1f0fd028904c4"
Last-Modified: Thu, 26 Jan 2017 19:48:46 GMT
X-GitHub-Media-Type: github.v3; format=json
Link: <https://api.github.com/repositories/67352921/↵
commits?per_page=1&page=2>;
```

```
rel="next", <https://api.github.com/repositories/67352921/↵
commits?per_page=1&page=43>; rel="last"
Access-Control-Expose-Headers: ETag, Link, X-GitHub-OTP,↵
 X-RateLimit-Limit,
X-RateLimit-Remaining, X-RateLimit-Reset, X-OAuth-Scopes,↵
 X-Accepted-OAuth-Scopes, X-Poll-Interval
Access-Control-Allow-Origin: *
Content-Security-Policy: default-src 'none'
Strict-Transport-Security: max-age=31536000;↵
 includeSubdomains; preload
X-Content-Type-Options: nosniff
X-Frame-Options: deny
X-XSS-Protection: 1; mode=block
X-Runtime-rack: 0.037989
X-GitHub-Request-Id: FC09:1342:19A449:37EA9C:59C37816
```

If you want additional information about an endpoint's response, but don't want to make a HEAD request, you can also use the verbose mode of curl via the -v flag. This uses the HTTP method specified (the default of which is GET), but provides much more detail in the response in addition to the JSON payload, as shown in Example 6-8.

Example 6-8. Using curl with the verbose flag set

```
$ curl -v 'https://api.github.com/repos/danielbryantuk/↵
oreilly-docker-java-shopping/commits?per_page=1'
*   Trying 192.30.253.117...
* TCP_NODELAY set
* Connected to api.github.com (192.30.253.117) port 443 (#0)
* TLS 1.2 connection using TLS_ECDHE_RSA_WITH_AES_128_GCM_SHA256
* Server certificate: *.github.com
* Server certificate: DigiCert SHA2 High Assurance Server CA
* Server certificate: DigiCert High Assurance EV Root CA
> GET /repos/danielbryantuk/oreilly-docker-java-shopping/↵
commits?per_page=1 HTTP/1.1
> Host: api.github.com
> User-Agent: curl/7.54.0
> Accept: */*
>
< HTTP/1.1 200 OK
< Server: GitHub.com
```

Finally, you can also use curl to download files over HTTP/S and FTP, as shown in Example 6-9.

Example 6-9. Using curl to download a file over HTTPS and FTP

```
curl -O https://domain.com/file.zip
```

```
curl -O ftp://ftp.uk.debian.org/debian/pool/main/alpha.zip
```

The `curl` command also supports ranges. Example 6-10 demonstrates how you would list files via FTP in the *debian/pool/main* directory whose filename starts with the letters *a* to *c*.

Example 6-10. Listing files via FTP

```
$ curl ftp://ftp.uk.debian.org/debian/pool/main/[a-c]/
```

The `curl` command is a powerful tool. It is available on all modern Linux and macOS distributions by default, and also installable on Windows (*https://curl.haxx.se/down load.html*). However, there is a newer tool that can be much more intuitive to use: HTTPie.

HTTPie

HTTPie is a command-line HTTP client with an intuitive UI, JSON support, syntax highlighting, wget-like downloads, plugins, and more. It can be installed (*https:// httpie.org/doc#installation*) on macOS, Linux, or Windows and provides an `http` command that provides expressive and intuitive command syntax and sensible defaults, as shown in Example 6-11.

Example 6-11. Using HTTPie to curl the GitHub API

```
$ http 'https://api.github.com/repos/danielbryantuk/↵
oreilly-docker-java-shopping/commits?per_page=1'
HTTP/1.1 200 OK
Access-Control-Allow-Origin: *
Access-Control-Expose-Headers: ETag, Link, X-GitHub-OTP,↵
 X-RateLimit-Limit,
X-RateLimit-Remaining, X-RateLimit-Reset, X-OAuth-Scopes,↵
 X-Accepted-OAuth-Scopes, X-Poll-Interval
Cache-Control: public, max-age=60, s-maxage=60
Content-Encoding: gzip
Content-Security-Policy: default-src 'none'
Content-Type: application/json; charset=utf-8
Date: Thu, 21 Sep 2017 08:03:10 GMT
ETag: W/"4ce9e0d9cf4e2339bbc1f0fd028904c4"
Last-Modified: Thu, 26 Jan 2017 19:48:46 GMT
Link: <https://api.github.com/repositories/67352921/↵
commits?per_page=1&page=2>;
rel="next", <https://api.github.com/repositories/67352921/↵
commits?per_page=1&page=43>; rel="last"
Server: GitHub.com
Status: 200 OK
Strict-Transport-Security: max-age=31536000;↵
 includeSubdomains; preload
Transfer-Encoding: chunked
Vary: Accept
```

```
X-Content-Type-Options: nosniff
X-Frame-Options: deny
X-GitHub-Media-Type: github.v3; format=json
X-GitHub-Request-Id: F159:1345:23A3CA:4C9FC3:59C3723E
X-RateLimit-Limit: 60
X-RateLimit-Remaining: 54
X-RateLimit-Reset: 1505983279
X-Runtime-rack: 0.029789
X-XSS-Protection: 1; mode=block

[
    {
        "author": {
            "avatar_url": "https://avatars2.githubusercontent.com/u/2379163?v=4",
            "events_url": "https://api.github.com/users/danielbryantuk/↵
                            events{/privacy}",
            "followers_url": "https://api.github.com/users/danielbryantuk/↵
                            followers",
            "following_url": "https://api.github.com/users/danielbryantuk/↵
                            following{/other_user}",
            "gists_url": "https://api.github.com/users/danielbryantuk/↵
                        gists{/gist_id}",
            "gravatar_id": "",
            "html_url": "https://github.com/danielbryantuk",
            "id": 2379163,
            "login": "danielbryantuk",
            "organizations_url": "https://api.github.com/users/danielbryantuk/orgs",
            "received_events_url": "https://api.github.com/users/danielbryantuk/↵
                                    received_events",
            "repos_url": "https://api.github.com/users/danielbryantuk/repos",
            "site_admin": false,
            "starred_url": "https://api.github.com/users/danielbryantuk/↵
                            starred{/owner}{/repo}",
            "subscriptions_url": "https://api.github.com/users/danielbryantuk/↵
                                subscriptions",
            "type": "User",
            "url": "https://api.github.com/users/danielbryantuk"
        },
        "comments_url": "https://api.github.com/repos/danielbryantuk/↵
                        oreilly-docker-java-shopping/commits/↵
                        3182a8a5fc73d2125022bf317ac68c3b1f4a3879/comments",
        "commit": {
            "author": {
                "date": "2017-01-26T19:48:46Z",
                "email": "daniel.bryant@tai-dev.co.uk",
                "name": "Daniel Bryant"
            },
            "comment_count": 0,
            "committer": {
                "date": "2017-01-26T19:48:46Z",
                "email": "daniel.bryant@tai-dev.co.uk",
                "name": "Daniel Bryant"
```

```
            },
            "message":↵
            "Update Vagrant Box Ubuntu and Docker Compose. Remove sudo usage",
            "tree": {
                "sha": "24eb583bd834734ae9b6c8133c99e4791a7387e8",
                "url": "https://api.github.com/repos/danielbryantuk/↵
                oreilly-docker-java-shopping/git/trees/↵
                24eb583bd834734ae9b6c8133c99e4791a7387e8"
            },
            "url": "https://api.github.com/repos/danielbryantuk/↵
            oreilly-docker-java-shopping/git/commits/↵
            3182a8a5fc73d2125022bf317ac68c3b1f4a3879"
        },
        "committer": {
            "avatar_url": "https://avatars2.githubusercontent.com/u/2379163?v=4",
            "events_url": "https://api.github.com/users/danielbryantuk/↵
                        events{/privacy}",
            "followers_url": "https://api.github.com/users/danielbryantuk/↵
                            followers",
            "following_url": "https://api.github.com/users/danielbryantuk/↵
                            following{/other_user}",
            "gists_url": "https://api.github.com/users/danielbryantuk/↵
                        gists{/gist_id}",
            "gravatar_id": "",
            "html_url": "https://github.com/danielbryantuk",
            "id": 2379163,
            "login": "danielbryantuk",
            "organizations_url": "https://api.github.com/users/danielbryantuk/orgs",
            "received_events_url": "https://api.github.com/users/danielbryantuk/↵
                                received_events",
            "repos_url": "https://api.github.com/users/danielbryantuk/repos",
            "site_admin": false,
            "starred_url": "https://api.github.com/users/danielbryantuk/↵
                        starred{/owner}{/repo}",
            "subscriptions_url": "https://api.github.com/users/danielbryantuk/↵
                                subscriptions",
            "type": "User",
            "url": "https://api.github.com/users/danielbryantuk"
        },
        "html_url": "https://github.com/danielbryantuk/↵
        oreilly-docker-java-shopping/commit/↵
        3182a8a5fc73d2125022bf317ac68c3b1f4a3879",
        "parents": [
            {
                "html_url": "https://github.com/danielbryantuk/↵
                oreilly-docker-java-shopping/commit/↵
                05b73d1f0c9904e6904d3f1bb8f13384e65e7840",
                "sha": "05b73d1f0c9904e6904d3f1bb8f13384e65e7840",
                "url": "https://api.github.com/repos/danielbryantuk/↵
                oreilly-docker-java-shopping/commits/↵
                05b73d1f0c9904e6904d3f1bb8f13384e65e7840"
            }
```

```
    ],
    "sha": "3182a8a5fc73d2125022bf317ac68c3b1f4a3879",
    "url": "https://api.github.com/repos/danielbryantuk/↵
    oreilly-docker-java-shopping/↵
    commits/3182a8a5fc73d2125022bf317ac68c3b1f4a3879"
  }
]
```

HTTPie also supports making requests against an authenticated endpoint, as shown in Example 6-12 (additional Auth plugins (*https://httpie.org/doc#auth-plugins*) can be found on the website).

Example 6-12. Using HTTPie with basic authentication

```
$ http -a USERNAME:PASSWORD POST https://api.github.com/repos/danielbryantuk/↵
oreilly-docker-java-shopping/issues/1/comments body='HTTPie is awesome! :heart:'
```

Sending headers in a request is also much easier to manage using HTTPie than with curl, as shown in Example 6-13.

Example 6-13. Sending headers in a request using HTTPie

```
$ http example.org User-Agent:Bacon/1.0 'Cookie:valued-visitor=yes;foo=bar'↵
X-Foo:Bar Referer:http://httpie.org/
```

Proxies can also be specified for both HTTP and HTTPS, as shown in Example 6-14.

Example 6-14. Using a proxy for HTTP and HTTPS

```
$ http --proxy=http:http://10.10.1.10:3128↵
--proxy=https:https://10.10.1.10:1080 example.org
```

Now that you are familiar with two tools for making requests against HTTP REST-like APIs, let's look at a tool for manipulating JSON data: jq.

jq

jq is like sed for JSON data: you can use it to slice, filter, map, and transform structured data with the same ease that sed, awk, and grep let you manipulate with text. Example 6-15 queries the GitHub API for details on commits, but displays only the first (0-indexed) result. Note that all of the response data will be sent over the wire, as the `jq` command filters the data on the client side; this may be important when dealing with responses with a large payload.

Example 6-15. Piping the output of curl to jq and displaying on the first result

```
$ curl 'https://api.github.com/repos/danielbryantuk/↵
oreilly-docker-java-shopping/commits?per_page=1'| jq '.[0]'
{
  "sha": "9f3e6514a55011c26ca18a1a69111c0a418e6dea",
  "commit": {
    "author": {
      "name": "Daniel Bryant",
      "email": "daniel.bryant@tai-dev.co.uk",
      "date": "2017-09-30T10:18:58Z"
    },
    "committer": {
      "name": "Daniel Bryant",
      "email": "daniel.bryant@tai-dev.co.uk",
      "date": "2017-09-30T10:18:58Z"
    },
    "message": "Add first version of Kubernetes deployment config",
    "tree": {
      "sha": "7568df5f6bfe6725ad9fb82ac8cf8a0c0c4661ec",
      "url": "https://api.github.com/repos/danielbryantuk/↵
      oreilly-docker-java-shopping/git/trees/↵
      7568df5f6bfe6725ad9fb82ac8cf8a0c0c4661ec"
    },
    "url": "https://api.github.com/repos/danielbryantuk/↵
    oreilly-docker-java-shopping/git/commits/↵
    9f3e6514a55011c26ca18a1a69111c0a418e6dea",
    "comment_count": 0,
    "verification": {
      "verified": false,
      "reason": "unsigned",
      "signature": null,
      "payload": null
    }
  },
  "url": "https://api.github.com/repos/danielbryantuk/↵
  oreilly-docker-java-shopping/commits/9f3e6514a55011c26ca18a1a69111c0a418e6dea",
  "html_url": "https://github.com/danielbryantuk/↵
  oreilly-docker-java-shopping/commit/9f3e6514a55011c26ca18a1a69111c0a418e6dea",
  "comments_url": "https://api.github.com/repos/danielbryantuk/↵
  oreilly-docker-java-shopping/commits/9f3e6514a55011c26ca18a1a69111c0a418e6dea/↵
  comments",
  "author": {
  ...
```

jq can also be used to filter the JSON objects displayed. Example 6-16 builds on the preceding jq query by displaying only a few select fields within the first commit resource.

Example 6-16. curl against the GitHub API with jq filtering

```
$ curl 'https://api.github.com/repos/danielbryantuk/↵
oreilly-docker-java-shopping/commits?per_page=1'| jq '.[0] |↵
 {message: .commit.message, name: .commit.committer.name}'
{
  "message": "Update Vagrant Box Ubuntu and Docker Compose. Remove sudo usage",
  "name": "Daniel Bryant"
}
```

Using curl, HTTPie, and jq can allow for quick experimentation and prototyping against a REST-like API, which can be an invaluable skill for a Java developer working with this technology.

Basic Scripting

Learning the basics of Bash scripting can be a useful skill for a Java developer. This knowledge can often be combined with tools like curl and jq to expand on and automate basic experimentation, testing, and build processes. The *Classic Shell Scripting* book elaborates on this concept in much more detail, but let's take a closer look at several useful examples.

xargs

The xargs command can be used to build and execute command lines from standard input. This can be used to download a list of URLs that is contained within a text file named *urls.txt*, as shown in Example 6-17.

Example 6-17. Using xargs to download multiple files as specified within the urls.txt file

```
$ xargs -n 1 curl -O < urls.txt
```

Pipes and Filters

Using pipes and filters can be a great way to chain simple commands to performance complicated processes. Example 6-18 shows how to use the curl command to make a silent HEAD request against *http://www.twitter.com* with the -L follow flag, which shows all of the steps within the HTTP flow of getting a response from the Twitter home page. The output of this command is then piped to grep in order to search for the pattern HTTP/.

Example 6-18. Using curl with grep to find the steps in the HTTP flow when accessing Twitter

```
$ curl -Is https://www.twitter.com -L | grep HTTP/
HTTP/1.1 301 Moved Permanently
HTTP/1.1 200 OK
```

The script in Example 6-19 can be used to extract the location of a shortened URL.

Example 6-19. Unfurling a URL from a shortened form

```
$ $ curl -sIL buff.ly/2xrgUwi | grep ^Location;
Location: https://skillsmatter.com/↵
skillscasts/10668-looking-forward-to-daniel-bryant-talk?↵
utm_content=buffer887ce&utm_medium=social&utm_source=twitter.com&utm_campaign=buffer
```

Loops

Simple loops using for within Bash can be used to repeatedly test an API quickly, perhaps confirming that the response is identical across multiple requests, or determining which status code is indicated when the API is broken. See Example 6-20.

Example 6-20. Using a loop in Bash to repeatedly curl a URI

```
#!/bin/bash

for i in `seq 1 10`; do
    curl -I http://www.example.com
done
```

Conditionals

You can also add in conditional logic; for example, to check the status code returned from an API. Example 6-21 uses HTTPie and a simple Bash case check to display to the terminal more details on the HTTP status code returned from the call to the *example.com* URI.

Example 6-21. Simple Bash script using HTTPie and case to display additional information based on the HTTP response code

```
#!/bin/bash

if http --check-status --ignore-stdin
--timeout=2.5 HEAD example.org/health &> /dev/null; then
    echo 'OK!'
else
    case $? in
        2) echo 'Request timed out!' ;;
```

```
        3) echo 'Unexpected HTTP 3xx Redirection!' ;;
        4) echo 'HTTP 4xx Client Error!' ;;
        5) echo 'HTTP 5xx Server Error!' ;;
        6) echo 'Exceeded --max-redirects=<n> redirects!' ;;
        *) echo 'Other Error!' ;;
    esac
fi
```

Keep Your Own Bash Scripts Library: Abraham's Experience

One of the benefits of consulting work is that I get to experience an array of technologies. In the last few years, I have worked on Java, Scala, PHP, .NET, Ruby, and even some VBA (although I'm not particularly proud of the last one). One thing has remained constant, though: wherever I have been, I have always found it useful to keep a set of small scripts to execute common tasks.

I advise that you do this, too, and even that you share your scripts with your team. Over the years, I have built my own little library of scripts, and recently I decided to make it publicly available at bash-utils (*https://github.com/quiram/bash-utils*) in case someone else found it useful. Even if your particular needs are not exactly the same as mine, maybe my scripts can serve as an inspiration to make your day-to-day work easier.

Summary

In this chapter, you have learned the fundamentals of additional skills and build tooling that will benefit your work as a modern Java developer:

- Linux, Bash, and command-line skills are essential for installing development tools, configuring external build steps, and understanding and managing the underlying operating system environment.

- Learning the basics of OS diagnostics tooling like top, ps, and netstat allow you to debug applications more effectively in test and production.

- The curl, jq, and HTTPie tools are essential for viewing, manipulating, and debugging REST-like APIs.

Now that you have a good understanding of build tooling and skills, you can learn more about how Java applications are packaged for deployment across a range of platforms: from traditional infrastructure, to cloud, to containers and serverless.

## CHAPTER 7

Packaging Applications for Deployment

You can deploy modern Java applications across a variety of platforms, and therefore it is beneficial to understand the fundamentals of how to best package applications using recommended artifact formats and practices. This chapter will walk you through building a JAR step-by-step, and along the way explore issues such as creating manifests, packaging dependencies (and classloading), and making a JAR executable. This information is fundamental for building artifacts for all platforms, even modern serverless ones. After this, you will explore other packaging options, such as fat JARs, skinny JARs, and WARs, and also lower-level OS artifacts like RPMs, DEBS, machine images, and container images.

Building a JAR: Step-by-Step

This chapter will be much easier to understand if you work through several concrete examples, and to help with this, a simple example project has been created with one dependency: the popular Logback logging framework. Maven will be used in the examples, but we will also mention how similar practices can be applied to other build tools. The example *pom.xml* for the project can be seen in Example 7-1.

Example 7-1. The super-simple example project pom.xml

```xml
<?xml version="1.0" encoding="UTF-8"?>
<project xmlns="http://maven.apache.org/POM/4.0.0"
        xmlns:xsi="http://www.w3.org/2001/XMLSchema-instance"
        xsi:schemaLocation="http://maven.apache.org/POM/4.0.0
        http://maven.apache.org/xsd/maven-4.0.0.xsd">
    <modelVersion>4.0.0</modelVersion>

    <groupId>uk.co.danielbryant.oreillyexamples</groupId>
    <artifactId>builddemo</artifactId>
```

```
<version>0.1.0-SNAPSHOT</version>

<properties>
    <project.build.sourceEncoding>UTF-8</project.build.sourceEncoding>
    <project.reporting.outputEncoding>UTF-8</project.reporting.outputEncoding>
    <maven.compiler.source>1.8</maven.compiler.source>
    <maven.compiler.target>1.8</maven.compiler.target>
</properties>

<dependencies>
    <dependency>
        <groupId>ch.qos.logback</groupId>
        <artifactId>logback-classic</artifactId>
        <version>1.2.3</version>
    </dependency>
</dependencies>

</project>
```

All this project will do is output a log message to the console. You can see the main class in Example 7-2.

Example 7-2. LoggingDemo class, which logs a statement to the console using Logback and SLF4J

```
package uk.co.danielbryant.oreillyexamples.builddemo;

import org.slf4j.Logger;
import org.slf4j.LoggerFactory;

public class LoggingDemo {

    public static final Logger LOGGER = LoggerFactory.getLogger(LoggingDemo.class);

    public static void main(String[] args) {
        LOGGER.info("Hello, (Logging) World!");
    }
}
```

The directory of this project follows the standard Maven project structure. Before you issue any build command, a tree of the root directory will look like Example 7-3.

Example 7-3. Using the tree command to view the directory structure

```
builddemo $ tree
.
├── builddemo.iml
├── pom.xml
└── src
    ├── main
```

```
|   ├── java
|   |   └── uk
|   |       └── co
|   |           └── danielbryant
|   |               └── oreillyexamples
|   |                   └── builddemo
|   |                       └── LoggingDemo.java
|   └── resources
└── test
    └── java

11 directories, 3 files
```

If you build and package the Maven project, as shown in Example 7-4, you will see that a JAR file is created and stored within *target/builddemo-0.1.0-SNAPSHOT.jar*.

Example 7-4. Packaging the Maven application

```
builddemo $ mvn package
[INFO] Scanning for projects...
[INFO]
[INFO] ------------------------------------------------------------------------
[INFO] Building builddemo 0.1.0-SNAPSHOT
[INFO] ------------------------------------------------------------------------
[INFO]
[INFO] --- maven-resources-plugin:2.6:resources (default-resources) @ builddemo ---
[INFO] Using 'UTF-8' encoding to copy filtered resources.
[INFO] Copying 0 resource
[INFO]
[INFO] --- maven-compiler-plugin:3.1:compile (default-compile) @ builddemo ---
[INFO] Changes detected - recompiling the module!
[INFO] Compiling 1 source file to /Users/danielbryant/Documents/↵
dev/daniel-bryant-uk/builddemo/target/classes
[INFO]
[INFO] --- maven-resources-plugin:2.6:testResources↵
(default-testResources) @ builddemo ---
[INFO] Using 'UTF-8' encoding to copy filtered resources.
[INFO] skip non existing resourceDirectory /Users/danielbryant/Documents/↵
dev/daniel-bryant-uk/builddemo/src/test/resources
[INFO]
[INFO] --- maven-compiler-plugin:3.1:testCompile↵
(default-testCompile) @ builddemo ---
[INFO] Nothing to compile - all classes are up-to-date
[INFO]
[INFO] --- maven-surefire-plugin:2.12.4:test (default-test) @ builddemo ---
[INFO] No tests to run.
[INFO]
[INFO] --- maven-jar-plugin:2.4:jar (default-jar) @ builddemo ---
[INFO] Building jar: /Users/danielbryant/Documents/↵
dev/daniel-bryant-uk/builddemo/target/builddemo-0.1.0-SNAPSHOT.jar
```

```
[INFO] ------------------------------------------------------------------------
[INFO] BUILD SUCCESS
[INFO] ------------------------------------------------------------------------
[INFO] Total time: 1.412 s
[INFO] Finished at: 2017-12-04T15:11:22-06:00
[INFO] Final Memory: 14M/48M
[INFO] ------------------------------------------------------------------------
```

If you try to execute the JAR by using the `java -jar` command, you will see the following error message:

```
builddemo $ java -jar target/builddemo-0.1.0-SNAPSHOT.jar
no main manifest attribute, in target/builddemo-0.1.0-SNAPSHOT.jar
```

In order for a JAR to be a runnable JAR, there must be a manifest. You could easily correct this now by adding such a file, using *maven-jar-plugin*, as shown in Example 7-5.

Example 7-5. Adding maven-jar-plugin to the pom.xml

```
<?xml version="1.0" encoding="UTF-8"?>
<project xmlns="http://maven.apache.org/POM/4.0.0"
        xmlns:xsi="http://www.w3.org/2001/XMLSchema-instance"
        xsi:schemaLocation="http://maven.apache.org/POM/4.0.0
        http://maven.apache.org/xsd/maven-4.0.0.xsd">

...

    <build>
        <plugins>
            <plugin>
                <groupId>org.apache.maven.plugins</groupId>
                <artifactId>maven-jar-plugin</artifactId>
                <version>2.6</version>
                <configuration>
                    <archive>
                        <manifest>
                            <addClasspath>true</addClasspath>
                            <mainClass>uk.co.danielbryant.
                            oreillyexamples.builddemo.LoggingDemo</mainClass>
                        </manifest>
                    </archive>
                </configuration>
            </plugin>
        </plugins>
    </build>
</project>
```

However, if you package the project and attempt to run the JAR, you will still receive an error:

```
builddemo $ java -jar target/builddemo-0.1.0-SNAPSHOT.jar
Exception in thread "main" java.lang.NoClassDefFoundError:↵
 org/slf4j/LoggerFactory at uk.co.danielbryant.oreillyexamples.builddemo.
LoggingDemo.<clinit>(LoggingDemo.java:8)
Caused by: java.lang.ClassNotFoundException:↵
 org.slf4j.LoggerFactory at java.base/jdk.internal.loader.BuiltinClassLoader.↵
 loadClass(BuiltinClassLoader.java:582)
at java.base/jdk.internal.loader.ClassLoaders$AppClassLoader.↵
loadClass(ClassLoaders.java:185)
at java.base/java.lang.ClassLoader.loadClass(ClassLoader.java:496)
... 1 more
```

This error message is quite helpful, and you can see by the `NoClassDefFoundError`
that the Logback dependencies that are required to run have not been included
within the JAR. You can see this by looking into the JAR file:

```
builddemo $ jar tf target/builddemo-0.1.0-SNAPSHOT.jar
META-INF/
META-INF/MANIFEST.MF
uk/
uk/co/
uk/co/danielbryant/
uk/co/danielbryant/oreillyexamples/
uk/co/danielbryant/oreillyexamples/builddemo/
uk/co/danielbryant/oreillyexamples/builddemo/LoggingDemo.class
META-INF/maven/
META-INF/maven/uk.co.danielbryant.oreillyexamples/
META-INF/maven/uk.co.danielbryant.oreillyexamples/builddemo/
META-INF/maven/uk.co.danielbryant.oreillyexamples/builddemo/pom.xml
META-INF/maven/uk.co.danielbryant.oreillyexamples/builddemo/pom.properties
```

The *LoggingDemo.class* file is present, as is your *META-INF/MANIFEST.MF* file
(which was missing earlier), but there are no other Java class files, such as your
dependencies.

Building a Fat Executable "Uber" JAR

You can create an executable JAR, most commonly referred to as a *fat JAR* or *uber
JAR*, by using plugins, but the most effective is typically the Maven Shade Plugin
(*http://bit.ly/2NI7eKM*). Many modern Java web application frameworks, such as
Spring, now include this plugin (or something offering equivalent functionality) by
default, and you may not even by aware you are using it. However, it is worth peeking
under the covers of how a fat JAR is built, as this can often provide hints as to how to
solve bizarre classpath issues!

> ## Other Options: Maven Jar Plugin and Maven Assembly Plugin
>
> You explored using the Maven Jar plugin earlier in this chapter, and although this plugin can build executable JAR files, it cannot package dependencies in with the corresponding JAR (i.e., this plugin cannot make fat JARs). Another plugin that is often used is the Maven Assembly plugin, and this plugin can create fat JARs. However, because of the way this plugin assembles the JAR, it can cause name-conflict issues.
>
> This generally isn't an issue with small projects like our example, but can cause lots of problems when dealing with projects with a lot of dependencies—which is usually the case when using modern Java application frameworks. If you are interested in the technical details of how the Maven Shade plugin overcomes the issues of class name conflicts, you can read more about class relocating (*http://bit.ly/2Q7vDGn*) on the project's website.

Maven Shade Plugin

The Maven Shade plugin (*http://bit.ly/1kEDuZk*) can be added to your project *pom.xml*, as shown in Example 7-6.

Example 7-6. pom.xml with the Maven Shade plugin

```
<?xml version="1.0" encoding="UTF-8"?>
<project xmlns="http://maven.apache.org/POM/4.0.0"
        xmlns:xsi="http://www.w3.org/2001/XMLSchema-instance"
        xsi:schemaLocation="http://maven.apache.org/POM/4.0.0
        http://maven.apache.org/xsd/maven-4.0.0.xsd">

...
    <build>
        <plugins>
            <plugin>
                <groupId>org.apache.maven.plugins</groupId>
                <artifactId>maven-shade-plugin</artifactId>
                <version>3.1.0</version>
                <executions>
                    <execution>
                        <phase>package</phase>
                        <goals>
                            <goal>shade</goal>
                        </goals>
                        <configuration>
                            <transformers>
                                <transformer implementation=↵
    "org.apache.maven.plugins.shade.resource.ManifestResourceTransformer">
                                    <mainClass>
                        uk.co.danielbryant.oreillyexamples.builddemo.LoggingDemo
```

```
                    </mainClass>
                  </transformer>
                </transformers>
              </configuration>
            </execution>
          </executions>
        </plugin>
      </plugins>
    </build>
</project>
```

The key points to note in the plugin are contained within the `execution` tag. The phase specifies in which part of the life cycle this plugin should be executed (which in this case is the package phase), and the goal specifies that the "shade" functionality should be executed. The preceding configuration includes a `ManifestResourceTrans former` resource transformer that specifies a main class to include within the JAR manifest.

Maven Shade Plugin Resource Transformers

Aggregating classes and resources from several artifacts into one uber JAR is straight-forward as long as there is no overlap. Otherwise, some kind of logic to merge resources from several JARs is required. This is where resource transformers (*http://bit.ly/ 2zwYTAP*) can help. Various default resource transformers are included within the `org.apache.maven.plugins.shade.resource` package of the Maven Shade plugin, and it is well worth reviewing this package in order to know the options you have available to you!

If you now package your project, you will see additional details from the Maven Shade plugin as it explains how the uber JAR is being assembled; see Example 7-7.

Example 7-7. Packaging the application with the Maven Shade plugin

```
builddemo $ mvn clean package
[INFO] Scanning for projects...
[INFO]
[INFO] ------------------------------------------------------------------------
[INFO] Building builddemo 0.1.0-SNAPSHOT
[INFO] ------------------------------------------------------------------------
[INFO]
...
[INFO]
[INFO] --- maven-jar-plugin:2.4:jar (default-jar) @ builddemo ---
[INFO] Building jar: /Users/danielbryant/Documents/dev/daniel-bryant-uk/↵
builddemo/target/builddemo-0.1.0-SNAPSHOT.jar
[INFO]
```

```
[INFO] --- maven-shade-plugin:3.1.0:shade (default) @ builddemo ---
[INFO] Including ch.qos.logback:logback-classic:jar:1.2.3 in the shaded jar.
[INFO] Including ch.qos.logback:logback-core:jar:1.2.3 in the shaded jar.
[INFO] Including org.slf4j:slf4j-api:jar:1.7.25 in the shaded jar.
[INFO] Replacing original artifact with shaded artifact.
[INFO] Replacing /Users/danielbryant/Documents/dev/daniel-bryant-uk/↵
builddemo/target/builddemo-0.1.0-SNAPSHOT.jar with /Users/danielbryant/↵
Documents/dev/daniel-bryant-uk/builddemo/target/builddemo-0.1.0-SNAPSHOT-shaded.jar
[INFO] Dependency-reduced POM written at: /Users/danielbryant/↵
Documents/dev/daniel-bryant-uk/builddemo/dependency-reduced-pom.xml
[INFO] ------------------------------------------------------------------------
[INFO] BUILD SUCCESS
[INFO] ------------------------------------------------------------------------
[INFO] Total time: 2.402 s
[INFO] Finished at: 2018-01-03T16:28:25Z
[INFO] Final Memory: 19M/65M
[INFO] ------------------------------------------------------------------------
```

This all looks great, so now you can try to execute the resulting fat JAR, as shown in Example 7-8.

Example 7-8. Running the fat JAR from the Maven Shade build

```
builddemo $ java -jar target/builddemo-0.1.0-SNAPSHOT.jar
16:28:38.198 [main] INFO uk.co.danielbryant.oreillyexamples↵
.builddemo.LoggingDemo - Hello, (Logging) World!
```

Success! You can now look into the resulting fat JAR to see all of the dependency class files that have been included by the Maven Shade plugin; see Example 7-9.

Example 7-9. Partial list of dependency class files included in the shaded fat JAR

```
builddemo $ jar tf target/builddemo-0.1.0-SNAPSHOT.jar
META-INF/MANIFEST.MF
META-INF/
uk/
uk/co/
uk/co/danielbryant/
uk/co/danielbryant/oreillyexamples/
uk/co/danielbryant/oreillyexamples/builddemo/
uk/co/danielbryant/oreillyexamples/builddemo/LoggingDemo.class
META-INF/maven/
META-INF/maven/uk.co.danielbryant.oreillyexamples/
META-INF/maven/uk.co.danielbryant.oreillyexamples/builddemo/
META-INF/maven/uk.co.danielbryant.oreillyexamples/builddemo/pom.xml
META-INF/maven/uk.co.danielbryant.oreillyexamples/builddemo/pom.properties
ch/
ch/qos/
ch/qos/logback/
ch/qos/logback/classic/
```

```
ch/qos/logback/classic/AsyncAppender.class
ch/qos/logback/classic/BasicConfigurator.class
...
org/slf4j/impl/StaticMarkerBinder.class
org/slf4j/impl/StaticMDCBinder.class
META-INF/maven/ch.qos.logback/
META-INF/maven/ch.qos.logback/logback-classic/
META-INF/maven/ch.qos.logback/logback-classic/pom.xml
META-INF/maven/ch.qos.logback/logback-classic/pom.properties
ch/qos/logback/core/
...
META-INF/maven/org.slf4j/slf4j-api/pom.xml
META-INF/maven/org.slf4j/slf4j-api/pom.properties
```

As you can see, a lot of extra files are included as a result of shading the dependencies into the fat JAR (and we've deliberately omitted 600 other classes from the preceding example list). Hopefully, you are starting to understand some of the challenges with managing dependencies with large applications.

Maven dependency:tree

It is quite common to get dependency clashes when initially using the Shade plugin to package an artifact. A useful Maven command to know is `mvn dependency:tree`. Executing this command on a project will show you a tree of all of your dependencies. You can also use the `-Dverbose` flag to add more details about conflicts, and the `-Dincludes=<dependency-name>` flag to target specific dependencies. For example:

```
mvn dependency:tree -Dverbose -Dincludes=commons-collections
```

Building Spring Boot Uber JARs

If you are using Spring Boot, you have the option of using the Spring Boot Maven plugin in order to create fat JARs rather than the Maven Shade plugin. Including the plugin into your project is super simple; see Example 7-10.

Example 7-10. Including the Spring Boot Maven plugin into a pom.xml

```
<?xml version="1.0" encoding="UTF-8"?>
<project xmlns="http://maven.apache.org/POM/4.0.0"
        xmlns:xsi="http://www.w3.org/2001/XMLSchema-instance"
        xsi:schemaLocation="http://maven.apache.org/POM/4.0.0
        http://maven.apache.org/xsd/maven-4.0.0.xsd">

...

    <build>
        <plugins>
            <plugin>
```

```
            <groupId>org.springframework.boot</groupId>
            <artifactId>spring-boot-maven-plugin</artifactId>
        </plugin>
      </plugins>
   </build>
</project>
```

The Spring Boot Maven plugin will repackage a JAR or WAR that is built during the package phase of the Maven life cycle. All you need to do is trigger a regular Maven build.

Using the Maven Shade Plugin with Spring Boot

You can build Spring Boot applications by using the Maven Shade plugin, but you may run into problems, particularly in regards to application entry points and controllers not functioning correctly (*http://bit.ly/2R1m6li*). We're sure all these problems can be solved (with enough time and effort), but our advice is that if you are working with Spring Boot, stick to using the Spring Boot Maven plugin unless you have a very good reason not to. Otherwise, you could be exposing yourself to more pain than necessary.

Bill of Materials: BOM

When working with Spring dependencies, you may encounter the acronym *BOM* used alongside the traditional Maven *POM*. A *bill of materials* (BOM) is a special type of POM that can be used to manage the versions of a project's dependencies and provide a central location to define and update these versions. The use of a BOM makes managing complicated and interdependent libraries within the Spring framework much easier, but there generally isn't much reason for you to build your own BOMs.

Skinny JARs—Deciding Not to Build Fat JARs

In modern Java web development, the thought of packaging and running applications in anything other that a fat JAR is almost becoming heretical. However, there can be distinct disadvantages to building and deploying these large files. The HubSpot engineering team has created a fantastic blog post (*http://bit.ly/2N469rA*) that explains some of the challenges they were having when deploying large fat JARs continuously to the AWS cloud.

The blog explains how the team initially used the Maven Shade plugin to build and package applications, but this was turning an application with 70 class files—which totalled 210 KB in the original JAR containing no dependencies—into a 150+ MB-sized fat JAR. Using Shade to combine 100,000+ files into a single archive was also a slow process, and then as the build server copied and deployed the resulting JAR to and from the AWS S3 storage service, this consumed both time and network resources. This was magnified by the fact that the HubSpot team has 100 engineers that were constantly committing and triggering 1,000–2,000 builds per day; they were generating 50–100 GB of build artifacts per day!

The HubSpot team ultimately created a new Maven plugin: SlimFast (*https://github.com/HubSpot/slimfast*). This plugin differs from the Shade plugin, in that it separates the application code from the associated dependencies, and accordingly builds and uploads two separate artifacts. It may sound inefficient to build and upload the application dependencies separately, but this step occurs only if the dependencies have changed. As the dependencies change infrequently, the HubSpot team states that this step is often a no-op; the package dependencies' JAR file is uploaded to S3 only once.

The HubSpot blog post and corresponding GitHub repository provide comprehensive details, but, in essence, the SlimFast plugin uses the Maven JAR plugin to add a Class-Path manifest entry to the Skinny JAR that points to the dependencies JAR file, and generates a JSON file with information about all of the dependency artifacts in S3 so that these can downloaded later. At deploy time, the HubSpot team downloads all of the application's dependencies, but then caches these artifacts on each of the application servers, so this step is usually a no-op as well. The net result is that at build time only the application's skinny JAR is uploaded, which is only a few hundred kilobytes. At deploy time, only this same thin JAR needs to be downloaded, which takes a fraction of a second.

The SlimFast plugin is currently tied to AWS S3 for the storage of artifacts, but the code is available on GitHub, and the principles can be adapted for any type of external storage (see the following sidebar for other plugin options).

Looking to Create Skinny Spring Boot JARs?

Although the SlimFast plugin can be used to create Skinny Spring Boot JARs, it is easier to use Dave Syer's Spring Boot Thin Launcher (*https://github.com/dsyer/spring-boot-thin-launcher*) plugin. This is a completely separate project (using similar concepts) that has been built with Spring Boot support from the ground up. Dave's plugin also uses the local Maven repository for the caching of the "launcher" dependencies JAR file, so there is no tie-in to AWS like there is with the SlimFast plugin. The Spring Boot Thin Launcher is well-documented, offers good Gradle support, and is also highly configurable.

Building WAR Files

If you are deploying your code to an application server (or potentially some serverless platforms), you may need to package your code as a WAR file. A *WAR file* is much like a JAR file: it is a zipped collection of files. However, in addition to class files, a WAR file contains files needed to serve a web application, such as JSP, HTML, and image files, and a *WEB-INF* folder is required that requires web application metadata. If you have been following along in this chapter, you are probably thinking that you could build your own WAR by using any one of the previously mentioned techniques—and you would be correct. However, there exists the even more convenient Maven WAR plugin (*http://maven.apache.org/plugins/maven-war-plugin/*), shown in Example 7-11.

Example 7-11. Including the Maven WAR plugin within a pom.xml

```
<project xmlns="http://maven.apache.org/POM/4.0.0"
         xmlns:xsi="http://www.w3.org/2001/XMLSchema-instance"
         xsi:schemaLocation="http://maven.apache.org/POM/4.0.0
         http://maven.apache.org/xsd/maven-4.0.0.xsd">

  <groupId>uk.co.danielbryant.oreillyexamples</groupId>
  <artifactId>builddemo</artifactId>
  <version>0.1.0-SNAPSHOT</version>
  <packaging>war</packaging>
...
  <build>
    <plugins>
      <plugin>
        <groupId>org.apache.maven.plugins</groupId>
        <artifactId>maven-war-plugin</artifactId>
        <version>3.2.0</version>
        <configuration>
          <archive>
            <manifest>
              <addClasspath>true</addClasspath>
            </manifest>
          </archive>
        </configuration>
      </plugin>
      ...
    </plugins>
  </build>
</project>
```

You simply need to use Maven to package the application, and a resulting WAR file will be generated within the target folder.

Building a WAR file with Spring Boot

If you include the Spring Boot Maven plugin within your project, you can easily build WAR files, as this plugin automatically includes (and configures) the Maven WAR plugin. You will need to change the packaging to war (as you saw in the standalone Maven WAR plugin) and you will also need to explicitly specify (*http://bit.ly/2QcrOLn*) the spring-boot-starter-tomcat dependency within the dependencies section of the POM and indicate that the scope is provided in order to ensure that the embedded servlet container doesn't interfere with the servlet container to which the WAR file will be deployed.

The Maven WAR plugin is highly configurable. It is relatively easy to include and exclude specific (*http://bit.ly/2IhEoLa*) Java class files (or other files), create Skinny WARs (*http://bit.ly/2NGZybQ*), or quickly spin up the built WAR (*http://bit.ly/2NICvgD*) for testing by using the Jetty embedded application server plugin.

Escaping JAR (and WAR) Hell

Earlier we discussed how you could use the mvn dependency:tree command to view dependency information in a project. When building and deploying a WAR to an application server like GlassFish or WildFly, additional JAR files might be loaded onto the classpath by the server itself, and these can also cause conflicts with dependencies that you have included within your artifact.

A useful tool in this situation is JHades (*http://jhades.github.io/*), which allows you to troubleshoot classpath issues, even if the application won't start.

Packaging for the Cloud

When deploying Java applications to the cloud, it can be advantageous to package the resulting build artifacts in OS or VM native artifacts, as this allows you to specify more fine-grained configuration and deployment instructions, and also include additional metadata. For example, by building a Red Hat RPM Package Manager artifact (an RPM) or a Debian Software Package file (a DEB file), you can specify where your fat JAR file can be deployed within the filesystem, create a user to run this, and specify configuration. This provides much more scope for automated installs, and it helps developers and operators to collaborate and capture the required installation instructions and process.

Moving down another layer of abstraction into the machine or VM image, if you build this type of artifact, then in addition to all of the previously mentioned controls, you also have complete control of the entire OS installation and configuration. Netflix popularized the approach to deploying Java applications as complete AWS VM images—referred to as *Amazon Machine Images* (AMIs)—with its Aminator tooling before the introduction of container technology, which also allows a similar approach.

Cooking Configuration: Baking or Frying Machines

Creating and deploying an application as a machine or VM image is often referred to as *baking* an image. Using a cooking analogy, you are effectively putting all of the application deployment ingredients together and baking this as a single action before the food is ready. You will often hear that that the counterapproach to this deployment style is *frying*, and although this abuses the coking analogy slightly, the key idea is that application deployment ingredients are added gradually, perhaps in layers. Deploying a Java application by using an RPM or DEB (or even a basic JAR or WAR file) is part of a frying deployment, whereas deploying an application using a machine VM image is baking.

The advantage of baking is that you are creating immutable deployment artifacts, and therefore it is easier to understand what was deployed, and much more difficult to see configuration drift (i.e., with frying, it is possible that each application could be installed in subtly different ways across a large fleet of machines). The disadvantages are that this process generally takes longer than frying a machine, and the resulting deployment artifacts can be large, which can, in turn, cause storage and network issues. The advantages of frying are that this is generally quicker and more flexible to deploy an application using a prebuilt base image that uses something like configuration management tooling (Chef, Ansible, Puppet, SaltStack, etc.) to deploy the smaller application layer. Although config management tools attempt to minimize configuration drift, this is still one of the main disadvantages with the frying approach.

Building RPMs and DEBs OS Packages

The construction of RPM and DEB packages is relatively easy because of the Maven plugins available. The core challenges you may experience are the configuration of the installation process within the package (which requires operational/sysadmin knowledge) and how you will test the Java application outside the OS package.

Packaging OS Artifacts Requires Operational Knowledge

When you are creating OS artifacts, you will be modifying the OS during installation of the application, and with this comes greater responsibility than simply packaging a JAR artifact. Depending on how the underlying OS is configured, you may (at worst) be able to irreparably damage the OS or render the machine unbootable. Your organization may also have a specific method or configuration for installing software, perhaps for compliance or governance reasons. Because of this, it is always advisable to consult with your organization's operations or sysadmin team.

In general, it is recommended that you build and deploy your Java application locally as you always have done (e.g., as a fat JAR or WAR). However, all build servers and remote environments (QA, staging, and production) build and deploy using the OS package. This provides choice minimal hassle (and tool changes) locally, but will catch any configuration issues early within the build pipeline.

Building OS Artifacts Takes Time!

It is generally inadvisable to configure your local build process to build the OS package on every build (*mvn* package). For a project of medium size or complexity, this will soon start to consume your time waiting for builds to complete, or your system resources such as CPU and storage. This advice does somewhat go against the general principle of making your local development environment as similar to production as possible, but as with everything in software development, this is a trade-off.

An RPM can be built using the RPM Maven plugin (*http://www.mojohaus.org/rpm-maven-plugin/*), and it is recommend that the RPM is either built on demand (see the preceding warning) or built as a side effect within the Maven life cycle.

Example 7-12. Example pom.xml that uses the RPM Maven plugin to create RPM deployment artifacts

```
<project xmlns="http://maven.apache.org/POM/4.0.0"
         xmlns:xsi="http://www.w3.org/2001/XMLSchema-instance"
         xsi:schemaLocation="http://maven.apache.org/POM/4.0.0
         http://maven.apache.org/xsd/maven-4.0.0.xsd">

  <groupId>uk.co.danielbryant.oreillyexamples</groupId>
  <artifactId>builddemo</artifactId>
  <version>0.1.0-SNAPSHOT</version>
  <packaging>jar</packaging>
...
    <build>
```

```
    <plugins>
      <plugin>
        <groupId>org.codehaus.mojo</groupId>
        <artifactId>rpm-maven-plugin</artifactId>
        <version>2.1.5</version>
        <executions>
          <execution>
            <id>generate-rpm</id>
            <goals>
              <goal>rpm</goal>
            </goals>
          </execution>
        </executions>
      </plugin>
    </plugins>
  </build>
</project>
```

You will often find yourself creating quite complicated application deployment procedures, and the plugin is generally well equipped to handle common use cases. A snippet of a typical plugin configuration (taken from the samples section (*http://bit.ly/2N4ZwVZ*) of the plugin website) is shown in Example 7-13.

Example 7-13. Sample RPM Maven plugin configuration for installation of a Java application

```
<configuration>
  <license>GPL (c) 2005, SWWDC</license>
  <distribution>Trash 2005</distribution>
  <group>Application/Collectors</group>
  <icon>src/main/resources/icon.gif</icon>
  <packager>SWWDC</packager>
  <prefix>/usr/local</prefix>
  <changelogFile>src/changelog</changelogFile>
  <defineStatements>
    <defineStatement>_unpackaged_files_terminate_build 0</defineStatement>
  </defineStatements>
  <mappings>
    <mapping>
      <directory>/usr/local/bin/landfill</directory>
      <filemode>440</filemode>
      <username>dumper</username>
      <groupname>dumpgroup</groupname>
      <sources>
        <source>
          <location>target/classes</location>
        </source>
      </sources>
    </mapping>
...

    <mapping>
```

```
              <directory>/usr/local/lib</directory>
              <filemode>750</filemode>
              <username>dumper</username>
              <groupname>dumpgroup</groupname>
              <dependency>
                <includes>
                  <include>jmock:jmock</include>
                  <include>javax.servlet:servlet-api:2.4</include>
                </includes>
                <excludes>
                  <exclude>junit:junit</exclude>
                </excludes>
              </dependency>
            </mapping>
...

            <mapping>
              <directory>/usr/local/oldbin</directory>
              <filemode>750</filemode>
              <username>dumper</username>
              <groupname>dumpgroup</groupname>
              <sources>
                <softlinkSource>
                  <location>/usr/local/bin</location>
                </softlinkSource>
              </sources>
            </mapping>
            ...
          </mappings>
          <preinstallScriptlet>
            <script>echo "installing now"</script>
          </preinstallScriptlet>
          <postinstallScriptlet>
            <scriptFile>src/main/scripts/postinstall</scriptFile>
            <fileEncoding>utf-8</fileEncoding>
          </postinstallScriptlet>
          <preremoveScriptlet>
            <scriptFile>src/main/scripts/preremove</scriptFile>
            <fileEncoding>utf-8</fileEncoding>
          </preremoveScript>
        </configuration>
```

The Debian Maven plugin (*http://debian-maven.sourceforge.net/*) allows the simple artifact creation for DEB files, as shown in Example 7-14.

Example 7-14. Creating DEB artifacts using the Maven plugin

```
<project xmlns="http://maven.apache.org/POM/4.0.0"
        xmlns:xsi="http://www.w3.org/2001/XMLSchema-instance"
        xsi:schemaLocation="http://maven.apache.org/POM/4.0.0
        http://maven.apache.org/xsd/maven-4.0.0.xsd">
```

```
    <groupId>uk.co.danielbryant.oreillyexamples</groupId>
    <artifactId>builddemo</artifactId>
    <version>0.1.0-SNAPSHOT</version>
    <packaging>jar</packaging>
...
  <build>
    <plugins>
      <plugin>
        <groupId>net.sf.debian-maven</groupId>
        <artifactId>debian-maven-plugin</artifactId>
        <version>1.0.6</version>
        <configuration>
          <packageName>my-package</packageName>
          <packageVersion>1.0.0</packageVersion>
        </configuration>
      </plugin>
    </plugins>
  </build>
</project>
```

As with the RPM Maven plugin, the DEB Maven plugin also allows lots of configuration options (*http://debian-maven.sourceforge.net/usage.html*) for installing and configuring your application.

Additional OS Package Build Tools (with Windows Support)

As an alternative to RPMs and DEBs, there exist other mechanisms for creating OS artifacts in order to deploy Java applications. The first is IzPack (*http://izpack.org/*), which allows you to create installers that can deploy applications to Linux and Solaris, as well as to Microsoft Windows and macOS. The deployment and configuration of a Java application is codified in IzPack by the creation of an installation description XML file; Example 7-15 shows a sample file. This is then read in by an IzPack compiler (*http://bit.ly/2zvLCZt*) (which can be invoked via the command line, Maven, or Ant), and an OS-specific runnable installer is created. The installer can run interactively using a Swing GUI or text console, or more usefully for continuous delivery, noninteractively using records of previous sessions of properties file.

Example 7-15. IzPack installation description file

```
<izpack:installation version="5.0"
                xmlns:izpack="http://izpack.org/schema/installation"
                xmlns:xsi="http://www.w3.org/2001/XMLSchema-instance"
                xsi:schemaLocation="http://izpack.org/schema/installation
                http://izpack.org/schema/5.0/izpack-installation-5.0.xsd">

  <info>
    <appname>Test</appname>
    <appversion>0.0</appversion>
```

```
      <appsubpath>myapp</appsubpath>
      <javaversion>1.6</javaversion>
   </info>

   <locale>
      <langpack iso3="eng"/>
   </locale>

   <guiprefs width="800" height="600" resizable="no">
      <splash>images/peas_load.gif</splash>
      <laf name="substance">
         <os family="windows" />
         <os family="unix" />
         <param name="variant" value="mist-silver" />
      </laf>
      <laf name="substance">
         <os family="mac" />
         <param name="variant" value="mist-aqua" />
      </laf>
      <modifier key="useHeadingPanel" value="yes" />
   </guiprefs>

   <panels>
      <panel classname="TargetPanel"/>
      <panel classname="PacksPanel"/>
      <panel classname="InstallPanel"/>
      <panel classname="FinishPanel"/>
   </panels>

   <packs>
      <pack name="Test Core" required="yes">
         <description>The core files needed for the application</description>
         <fileset dir="plain" targetdir="${INSTALL_PATH}" override="true"/>
         <parsable targetfile="${INSTALL_PATH}/test.properties"/>
      </pack>
   </packs>

</izpack:installation>
```

Additional open source tooling in this space includes Launch4j (*http://launch4j.source forge.net/*) and (Windows-specific) Nullsoft Scriptable Install System (NSIS) (*http://nsis.sourceforge.net/Main_Page*). Many commercial tools are also available that can be found from a web search.

Creating Machine Images for Multiple Clouds with Packer

Packer (*https://www.packer.io/*) is an open source tool from HashiCorp for creating identical machine images for multiple platforms from a single source configuration. Packer is lightweight, command-line driven, runs on every major operating system, and is highly performant, creating machine images for multiple platforms in parallel.

Packer can provision images by using shell scripts or configuration management tooling like Ansible, Chef, or Puppet. Packer defines a machine image as a single static unit that contains a preconfigured operating system and installed software that is used to quickly create new running machines. Machine image formats change for each platform, and some examples include AMIs for EC2, VMDK/VMX files for VMware, and OVF exports for VirtualBox.

Striving for Dev/Prod Parity with Packer

Packer can be used to help keep development, staging, and production environments as similar as possible, which is a decidedly good thing. You can be much more confident that your tests running in development and staging are much more indicative of the behavior in the production environment.

A useful feature of Packer is that it can be used to generate images for multiple platforms at the same time. So if you use AWS for production and VirtualBox (perhaps with Vagrant) for development, you can generate both an AMI and a VBox machine by using Packer at the same time from the same template. If this is utilized within a continuous delivery pipeline, you have a good system for consistent work environments from development all the way through to production.

Packer can be installed through most operating system installers, or by visiting the Install Packer (*https://www.packer.io/intro/getting-started/install.html*) web page. The Packer Getting Started web page provides a fantastic introduction to the tool. A sample configuration file in Example 7-16 demonstrates the metadata required in order to build an AWS AMI using provisioners that copy files from a local directory to the image, and run a series of scripts. These commands could be the copying of a JAR file and a simple *init* script to run this application.

Example 7-16. Packer firstimage.json build config file

```json
{
    "variables": {
        "aws_access_key": "{{env `AWS_ACCESS_KEY_ID`}}",
        "aws_secret_key": "{{env `AWS_SECRET_ACCESS_KEY`}}",
        "region":         "us-east-1"
    },
    "builders": [
        {
            "access_key": "{{user `aws_access_key`}}",
            "ami_name": "packer-linux-aws-demo-{{timestamp}}",
            "instance_type": "t2.micro",
            "region": "us-east-1",
            "secret_key": "{{user `aws_secret_key`}}",
            "source_ami_filter": {
```

```
            "filters": {
            "virtualization-type": "hvm",
            "name": "ubuntu/images/*ubuntu-xenial-16.04-amd64-server-*",
            "root-device-type": "ebs"
            },
            "owners": ["099720109477"],
            "most_recent": true
        },
        "ssh_username": "ubuntu",
        "type": "amazon-ebs"
    }
],
"provisioners": [
    {
        "type": "file",
        "source": "./welcome.txt",
        "destination": "/home/ubuntu/"
    },
    {
        "type": "shell",
        "inline":[
            "ls -al /home/ubuntu",
            "cat /home/ubuntu/welcome.txt"
        ]
    },
    {
        "type": "shell",
        "script": "./example.sh"
    }
]
}
```

A Packer configuration can include multiple builders, so you can easily specify a local VirtualBox build in addition to the AWS builder. Packer is run via the `packer` command-line tool, and properties can be loaded in via flags or a properties file. An example run of the `packer build` command is shown in Example 7-17.

Example 7-17. Output from a Packer execution of the firstimage.json build file

```
$ export AWS_ACCESS_KEY_ID=MYACCESSKEYID
$ export AWS_SECRET_ACCESS_KEY=MYSECRETACCESSKEY
$ packer build firstimage.json
amazon-ebs output will be in this color.

==> amazon-ebs: Prevalidating AMI Name: packer-linux-aws-demo-1507231105
    amazon-ebs: Found Image ID: ami-fce3c696
==> amazon-ebs: Creating temporary keypair:↵
packer_59d68581-e3e6-eb35-4ae3-c98d55cfa04f
==> amazon-ebs: Creating temporary security group for this instance:↵
packer_59d68584-cf8a-d0af-ad82-e058593945ea
==> amazon-ebs: Authorizing access to port 22 on the temporary security group...
```

```
==> amazon-ebs: Launching a source AWS instance...
==> amazon-ebs: Adding tags to source instance
    amazon-ebs: Adding tag: "Name": "Packer Builder"
    amazon-ebs: Instance ID: i-013e8fb2ced4d714c
==> amazon-ebs: Waiting for instance (i-013e8fb2ced4d714c) to become ready...
==> amazon-ebs: Waiting for SSH to become available...
==> amazon-ebs: Connected to SSH!
==> amazon-ebs: Uploading ./scripts/welcome.txt => /home/ubuntu/
==> amazon-ebs: Provisioning with shell script:↵
/var/folders/8t/0yb5q0_x6mb2jldqq_vjn3lr0000gn/T/packer-shell661094204
    amazon-ebs: total 32
    amazon-ebs: drwxr-xr-x 4 ubuntu ubuntu 4096 Oct  5 19:19 .
    amazon-ebs: drwxr-xr-x 3 root   root   4096 Oct  5 19:19 ..
    amazon-ebs: -rw-r--r-- 1 ubuntu ubuntu  220 Apr  9 2014 .bash_logout
    amazon-ebs: -rw-r--r-- 1 ubuntu ubuntu 3637 Apr  9 2014 .bashrc
    amazon-ebs: drwx------ 2 ubuntu ubuntu 4096 Oct  5 19:19 .cache
    amazon-ebs: -rw-r--r-- 1 ubuntu ubuntu  675 Apr  9 2014 .profile
    amazon-ebs: drwx------ 2 ubuntu ubuntu 4096 Oct  5 19:19 .ssh
    amazon-ebs: -rw-r--r-- 1 ubuntu ubuntu   18 Oct  5 19:19 welcome.txt
    amazon-ebs: WELCOME TO PACKER!
==> amazon-ebs: Provisioning with shell script: ./example.sh
    amazon-ebs: hello
==> amazon-ebs: Stopping the source instance...
    amazon-ebs: Stopping instance, attempt 1
==> amazon-ebs: Waiting for the instance to stop...
==> amazon-ebs: Creating the AMI: packer-linux-aws-demo-1507231105
    amazon-ebs: AMI: ami-f76ea98d
==> amazon-ebs: Waiting for AMI to become ready...
```

Packer can create images for Microsoft Windows machines and the corresponding cloud instances, and there is also open source support, such as osx-vm-templates (*https://github.com/timsutton/osx-vm-templates*), for creating macOS images.

Additional Tools for Creating Machine Images

Several additional open source image creation solutions do exist, such as Netflix's aminator (*https://github.com/Netflix/aminator*) (a tool for creating AWS AMIs) and Veewee (a tool for creating Vagrant base boxes, kernel-based virtual machines, and VMs). However, Aminator is AWS specific and requires that your Java application is packaged as an RPM or DEB before installation, and Veewee doesn't support the majority of the main cloud vendor image formats and requires Ruby to be installed.

You can also use open source multicloud Java toolkits like jclouds (*https://jclouds.apache.org*) to create machine images, but the scope of doing this is outside this book. If you are interested in this, you can explore the jclouds ImageApi (*http://bit.ly/2xIdFmW*) JavaDoc. Finally, commercial machine-image creation tools are also available; for example, Boxfuse (*https://boxfuse.com*), which can create AWS AMIs for deploying JVM, Node.js, and Go applications. There is comprehensive support (*https://boxfuse.com/getstarted/*) for a range of Java web frameworks, such as Spring

Boot, Dropwizard, and Play, and images are built using a simple (automatable) command-line tool.

The Trade-offs with Commercial Image-Creation Tools

If you want to package and deploy applications as machine images, we recommend using HashiCorp Packer, as described in the previous section of this chapter. Packer is a fully open source tool that is configurable and supports multiple platforms. This allows you to look into the internals to see what is happening during a build, tweak the build steps and configuration, and change the output format (with minimal changes) if you move to deploying to a new platform.

The main trade-off with using Packer in comparison with a commercial tool like Boxfuse is user experience. In our opinion, the HashiCorp tools are generally awesome, but they do assume a certain level of operational awareness, which not all developers have.

Building Containers

Deploying Java applications to containers like Docker requires that not only the Java application artifact be created, but also a container image be built.

Managing the Operational Complexity of Containers

By packaging your Java artifact within a container image, you will be exposed to potentially new operational concerns. For example, you will have to specify a base image with an operating system and associated tooling to be used as a foundation for your image (or use a Google Distroless (*https://github.com/GoogleContainerTools/distro less*) base image), and also configure ports to be exposed and the execution method of the JVM and Java application. We recommend consulting your operations or platform team if this is the first time you are doing this, or if you are unsure as to what the values should be.

Creating Container Images with Docker

Building a Docker image requires the creation of a Dockerfile, which is essentially an image manifest that specifies the base operating system, the application artifacts to be added, and associated runtime configuration; see Example 7-18.

Example 7-18. Example Dockerfile

```
FROM openjdk:8-jre
ADD target/productcatalogue-0.0.1-SNAPSHOT.jar app.jar
ADD product-catalogue.yml app-config.yml
EXPOSE 8020
ENTRYPOINT ["java","-Djava.security.egd=file:/dev/./urandom","-jar","app.jar",↵
"server", "app-config.yml"]
```

Once you have your Dockerfile, you can build and tag a Docker image by using the commands in Example 7-19.

Example 7-19. Building and tagging a new Docker image using a Dockerfile

```
$ docker build -t danielbryantuk/productcatalogue:1.1 .
Sending build context to Docker daemon  15.56MB
Step 1/5 : FROM openjdk:8-jre
 ---> 8363d7ceb7b7
Step 2/5 : ADD target/productcatalogue-0.0.1-SNAPSHOT.jar app.jar
 ---> 664d4edcb774
Step 3/5 : ADD product-catalogue.yml app-config.yml
 ---> 8c732b560055
Step 4/5 : EXPOSE 8020
 ---> Running in 3955d790a531
 ---> 738157101d64
Removing intermediate container 3955d790a531
Step 5/5 : ENTRYPOINT java -Djava.security.egd=file:/dev/./urandom -jar app.jar
server app-config.yml
 ---> Running in 374eb13492e7
 ---> e504828640df
Removing intermediate container 374eb13492e7
Successfully built e504828640df
Successfully tagged danielbryantuk/productcatalogue:1.1
```

The Importance of Metadata

Regardless of the format, it is important to add build and packaging metadata to an artifact, such as build date, base image identification (and core OS library version numbers), and testing/verification signatures. This allows everyone to quickly understand what is in the artifact, and can also help with auditing or determining whether an artifact is exposed to a new security vulnerability. Docker allows the use of labels to add key-value information to a Dockerfile, and we recommend that you use this to add key information. You can also store additional metadata about artifacts within your artifact repository.

Fabricating Docker Images with fabric8

fabric8 (*https://fabric8.io/*) is an open source project stewarded by Red Hat that aims to provide an end-to-end development platform from development to production for the creation of cloud-native applications and microservices. You can build, test, and deploy your applications via continuous delivery pipelines and then run and manage them with ChatOps tooling. You will explore fabric8 in more detail later in the book, but in this chapter, you will learn about a relevant useful feature: fabric8 provides a Maven plugin that makes building Docker images easy. The Docker Maven plugin not only allows container images to be built, but you can also run containers, perhaps during an integration test. Example 7-20 shows how the plugin can be used to build a container.

Example 7-20. Project using the Docker Maven plugin

```
<project xmlns="http://maven.apache.org/POM/4.0.0"
        xmlns:xsi="http://www.w3.org/2001/XMLSchema-instance"
        xsi:schemaLocation="http://maven.apache.org/POM/4.0.0
        http://maven.apache.org/xsd/maven-4.0.0.xsd">

  <groupId>uk.co.danielbryant.oreillyexamples</groupId>
  <artifactId>builddemo</artifactId>
  <version>0.1.0-SNAPSHOT</version>
  <packaging>jar</packaging>
...
  <build>
    <plugins>
      <plugin>
        <groupId>io.fabric8</groupId>
        <artifactId>docker-maven-plugin</artifactId>
        <configuration>
          <images>
            <image>
              <alias>service</alias>
              <name>fabric8/docker-demo:${project.version}</name>
              <build>
                <from>java:8</from>
                <assembly>
                  <descriptor>docker-assembly.xml</descriptor>
                </assembly>
                <cmd>
                    <shell>java -jar /maven/service.jar</shell>
                </cmd>
              </build>
            </image>
          </images>
        </configuration>
      </plugin>
    </plugins>
```

```
    </build>
</project>
```

Additional Java-Specific Container Build Tooling

In addition to writing your own Dockerfile or using the Fabric8 plugin, there are a range of options for building container images as part of a standard Java build process, which may suite your workflow better:

- Spotify docker-maven-plugin (*https://github.com/spotify/docker-maven-plugin*), and its latest incarnation dockerfile-maven (*https://github.com/spotify/dockerfile-maven*). These plugins allow a range of image build configuration options to be specified within the POM, and also provide hooks for running containers during the integration-test phases of the build life cycle.
- Google's Jib (*https://github.com/GoogleContainerTools/jib*), which provides both Maven and Gradle plugins for building OCI-compatible container images. This tools provides a fast build due to its clever use of image layering (in combination with the Distroless base images), and also does not require the Docker daemon to be running locally.

Packaging FaaS Java Applications

A FaaS Java application code can typically be uploaded to the service by using either a fat JAR (which shouldn't be executable) or a ZIP file.

When building a fat JAR, the AWS Lambda guide recommends using the Maven Shade plugin. If you look at the example *pom.xml* file in Example 7-21, you will see the `aws-lambda-java-core` dependency that you can reference within your source code (and does not affect the build life cycle), and you can also see the Shade plugin with the `createDependencyReducedPom` configuration being declared as `false`. This is because a FaaS Java application that is uploaded to the AWS Lambda service must include all of their dependencies.

Example 7-21. Example pom.xml for an AWS Lambda FaaS Java application

```
<project xmlns="http://maven.apache.org/POM/4.0.0"
xmlns:xsi="http://www.w3.org/2001/XMLSchema-instance"
xsi:schemaLocation="http://maven.apache.org/POM/4.0.0
http://maven.apache.org/maven-v4_0_0.xsd">
  <modelVersion>4.0.0</modelVersion>

  <groupId>doc-examples</groupId>
  <artifactId>lambda-java-example</artifactId>
  <packaging>jar</packaging>
```

```
<version>1.0-SNAPSHOT</version>
<name>lambda-java-example</name>

<dependencies>
  <dependency>
    <groupId>com.amazonaws</groupId>
    <artifactId>aws-lambda-java-core</artifactId>
    <version>1.1.0</version>
  </dependency>
</dependencies>

<build>
  <plugins>
    <plugin>
      <groupId>org.apache.maven.plugins</groupId>
      <artifactId>maven-shade-plugin</artifactId>
      <version>2.3</version>
      <configuration>
        <createDependencyReducedPom>false</createDependencyReducedPom>
      </configuration>
      <executions>
        <execution>
          <phase>package</phase>
          <goals>
            <goal>shade</goal>
          </goals>
        </execution>
      </executions>
    </plugin>
  </plugins>
</build>
</project>
```

The Azure Functions documentation recommends using the maven-dependency-plugin (*https://maven.apache.org/plugins/maven-dependency-plugin/*) to package all of the relevant class and configuration files appropriately, and this can be seen in the *pom.xml* file generated by the Maven artefact generator, as shown in Example 7-22.

Example 7-22. Example pom.xml for Azure Function Java FaaS application

```
<?xml version="1.0" encoding="UTF-8"?>
<project xmlns="http://maven.apache.org/POM/4.0.0"
    xmlns:xsi="http://www.w3.org/2001/XMLSchema-instance"
    xsi:schemaLocation="http://maven.apache.org/POM/4.0.0
    http://maven.apache.org/xsd/maven-4.0.0.xsd">
    <modelVersion>4.0.0</modelVersion>

    <groupId>helloworld</groupId>
    <artifactId>ProductCatalogue</artifactId>
    <version>1.0-SNAPSHOT</version>
    <packaging>jar</packaging>
```

```xml
<name>Azure Java Functions</name>

<dependencyManagement>
    <dependencies>
        ...
    </dependencies>
</dependencyManagement>

<dependencies>
    <dependency>
        <groupId>com.microsoft.azure.functions</groupId>
        <artifactId>azure-functions-java-library</artifactId>
    </dependency>
    ...
</dependencies>

<build>
    <pluginManagement>
        <plugins>
            ...
        </plugins>
    </pluginManagement>

    <plugins>
      ...
      <plugin>
            <groupId>org.apache.maven.plugins</groupId>
            <artifactId>maven-dependency-plugin</artifactId>
            <executions>
                <execution>
                    <id>copy-dependencies</id>
                    <phase>prepare-package</phase>
                    <goals>
                      <goal>copy-dependencies</goal>
                    </goals>
                    <configuration>
                      <outputDirectory>${stagingDirectory}/lib</outputDirectory>
                      <overWriteReleases>false</overWriteReleases>
                      <overWriteSnapshots>false</overWriteSnapshots>
                      <overWriteIfNewer>true</overWriteIfNewer>
                      <includeScope>runtime</includeScope>
                      <excludeArtifactIds>
                        azure-functions-java-library
                      </excludeArtifactIds>
                    </configuration>
                </execution>
            </executions>
      </plugin>
    </plugins>
</build>
</project>
```

Creating an AWS Lambda or Azure Function artifact is as simple as running `mvn package`.

In Chapter 8, you will learn how to work locally with AWS Lambda and Azure Functions and how to deploy locally and test a FaaS-based Java application.

Summary

In this chapter, you have learned all you need to know about building JAR files. You have also learned about other packaging options that are available, and explored the creation of lower-level deployment artifacts like machine and container images:

- Understanding (in-depth) how a JAR file is built is essential. You can use this knowledge when creating artifacts for any platform and when you are debugging build issues like class-loading problems.

- You can create executable fat JARs or skinny JARs, depending on your requirements and constraints.

- There are Maven (and other build tool) plugins for creating OS artifacts like DEBs and RPMs, and for creating container images.

- You can use a tool like HashiCorp's Packer to create and package Java applications into a variety of machine images for test and production deployment across OS hypervisors like VirtualBox and cloud platforms like AWS or Azure.

- FaaS applications are typically packaged in the same way as traditional Java applications, by using JARs and tooling like the Maven Shade or Maven Dependency plugin for managing dependencies.

Now that you have developed a good understanding of building and packaging Java applications, it is time to work on ensuring that your pre-pipeline local development process is as effective as possible. This is the topic of the next chapter.

## CHAPTER 8

Working Locally (Like It Was Production)

Before you can begin to construct a continuous delivery pipeline, you must first ensure that you can work efficiently and effectively with code and systems on a local development machine. In this chapter, you will explore several of the inherent challenges with this—particularly when working with modern distributed systems and service-based architectures—and then discusses techniques like mocking, service virtualization, infrastructure virtualization (both VM and container-based), and local development of FaaS applications.

Challenges with Local Development

As a Java developer, you will typically be used to configuring a simple local work environment for working with a traditional monolithic web application. This often involves installing an operating system, a Java Development Kit (JDK), a build tool (Maven or Gradle), and an integrated development environment (IDE), like IntelliJ IDEA or Eclipse. Sometimes you may also need to install middleware or a database, and perhaps an application server. This local development configuration works fine for a single Java application, but what happens when you are developing a system with multiple services that will be deployed into a cloud environment, a container orchestration framework, or a serverless platform?

When you start working with an application with multiple services, the most logical initial approach is to simply attempt to replicate your local development practices for each new service. However, as with many things within computing—manual replication gets you only so far. The biggest problem with this style of working is the integration costs of testing. Even if each service has integration/component-level testing, it can be difficult to coordinate test configuration and initialization once you develop more than a few services. You'll often find yourself spinning up an external service locally (by cloning the code repository from VCS, building, and running), fiddling around with the state, running tests on the service code in which you are developing, and finally verifying the state of the external service.

The Dangers of Custom Local Development Config Scripts

In the past, we have seen many developers attempt to overcome the local initialization problem by creating simple scripts (bash, Groovy, etc.) that wire everything together and initialize data for tests. In our experience, these scripts quickly become a nightmare to maintain, and therefore this isn't a recommended approach. We include a mention of this here only as a start for the discussion.

Mocking, Stubbing, and Service Virtualization

The first approach that you can use to scale the local working environment is a technique familiar to many—mocking. In this section, you will explore how best to use this approach, and you will also examine a technique that is not so widely used but nonetheless is useful when working with a large number of services or external APIs: service virtualization.

Pattern #1: Profiles, Mocks, and Stubs

If you are familiar with developing code using the JVM-based Spring framework (or the Maven build tool), you will instantly recognize the concept of profiles. Essentially, *profiles* allow multiple configurations to be developed and switched at build or runtime. This will allow you to develop mock or stub implementations of external service interfaces for a local development profile and switch this version to the actual production implementation as required. For example, this technique could be used when developing a Java-based e-commerce *shop-front* service that is dependent on a *product-search* service. The interface for the *product-service* is well-defined, and therefore you can develop several profiles for use when running automated tests via Maven:

no-search
> This profile can simply mock the *product-search* service as a no-op (using Mockito) and return empty results. This is useful when the locally developed code is interacting with the *product-search* service, but you don't care about the results coming back from a call.

parameterized-search
> This profile can contain a stub implementation of the *product-search* service that you can parametrize in your tests to return various search results (e.g., one product, two products, a product with a specific property, an invalid product, etc.). The stub implementation can simply be created as a Java class, and the precanned

search results can be loaded from an external JSON data file. This is a useful pattern, but if the stub begins to become complex (with lots of conditionals), it may be time to look at the *service virtualization* pattern.

production

This is the production implementation of the *product-search* interface that will communicate to a real instance of the service and undertake appropriate object marshalling and error-handling, etc.

Although not exactly stubbing or mocking, you can also include the use of embedded or in-process data stores and middleware within this pattern. Running an embedded process will typically allow you to interact with this component as if you were running a full out-of-process instance, but with much less initialization overhead or the need to externally configure the process.

The Benefits of Running Embedded Databases and Middleware

Mocking and stubbing are effective techniques for creating tests, but when working with data stores and middleware, you will sometimes find yourself either creating complicated mocks or needing to simulate complex behavior. If you notice these issues, we recommend exploring whether your data store or middleware applications can be run in an "embedded" or in-process/memory mode. This gives all the benefits of running the real thing, but with a reduced resource footprint compared to running the full application.

Running an application in this mode typically means that the startup time is reduced, along with the response times (as everything is running in memory and doesn't require disk access), and you apply configuration upon each start of the process. The disadvantage of running in this mode is that you can typically use only small datasets (that can fit into memory) and the data mutations are not persistent across test runs.

We have had much success using the following embedded applications during testing and the creation of automated test suites:

- H2 or HSQL as a test replacement for MySQL (be aware there are some differences between the implementations).
- Stubbed Cassandra for Apache Cassandra.
- ElasticSearch can be run as a single embedded node.
- Apache Qpid as an embedded alternative for RabbitMQ or ActiveMQ.
- The Localstack project contains an embedded/in-process version of many of the AWS data store services, like DynamoDB and Kinesis.

For any data store or middleware that does not provide an embedded or in-memory mode, or you require large amounts of data for testing, the testcontainers project *(https://www.testcontainers.org/)* can be used to containerize these systems and execute them via JUnit.

Mocking with Mockito

One of the most popular mocking libraries within the Java ecosystem is Mockito. The latest version of the library, version 2.0+, provides a flexible framework to allow the verification of interactions with dependencies, or the stubbing of method calls.

Verifying interactions

Often when you are developing against a third-party dependency, you want to verify that the application you are developing interacts correctly with this external system, particularly when given certain use cases (either happy path or edge/problem cases). An example of this is shown in Example 8-1.

Example 8-1. Verifying interactions with the mocked List class, using Mockito

```
import static org.mockito.Mockito.*;

// mock creation
List mockedList = mock(List.class);

// using mock object - it does not throw any "unexpected interaction" exception
mockedList.add("one");
mockedList.clear();

// selective, explicit, highly readable verification
verify(mockedList).add("one");
verify(mockedList).clear();
```

The assertions within your test are focused on the behavior of your application (i.e., did it behave correctly given a certain use case or precondition).

Stubbing method calls

In addition to verifying the behavior of your application, you may often want to verify output or state, or return precanned data from an external service during the execution of a method under development or test. Often, this is the case when you have created a complicated algorithm, or you are interacting with several external services and the individual interactions are not as important as the end result. Example 8-2 illustrates.

Example 8-2. Stubbing the mocked LinkedList class to return a value

```
// you can mock concrete classes, not only interfaces
LinkedList mockedList = mock(LinkedList.class);

// stubbing appears before the actual execution
when(mockedList.get(0)).thenReturn("first");

// the following is true
assertThat(mockedList.get(0), is("first"));

// the following prints "null" because get(999) was not stubbed
System.out.println(mockedList.get(999));
```

This simple test shows how you can assert on the value (which happens to come directly from the mock in this trivial example), rather than on the interactions.

Watch for Mock Complexity

If you find that your mocks are continually drifting from the real application or service that you are mocking/stubbing, or you find yourself spending a large amount of time maintaining the mocks, then this may be a sign that your mocks contain too much complexity, and you should use another tool or technique. Always remember that your tools should work for you, not the other way around!

The Mockito framework is a powerful library, and we have presented only a limited demonstration of functionality within this chapter.

Pattern #2: Service Virtualization and API Simulation

When mocking or stubbing external (third-party) services becomes complex, this can be the signal that it would be more appropriate to virtualize the service. If your stubs start to contain lots of conditional logic, are becoming a point of contention with people changing precanned data and breaking lots of tests, or are becoming a maintenance issue, this can be a sign of too much complexity. Service virtualization is a technique that allows you to create an application that will emulate the behavior of an external service without actually running or connecting to the service. This differs from running an actual service in an embedded or in-process mode, as a virtual service is typically not the real thing, and can behave only in ways that you have either defined or recorded from previous interactions with the real thing.

The service virtualization technique allows for the more manageable implementation of complex service behavior than mocking or stubbing alone. You can use this technique successfully in multiple scenarios; for example, when a dependent service returns complex (or large amounts of) data, when you don't have access to the external service (for example, it may be owned by a third-party or is run as a SaaS), or when many additional services will interact with this dependency and it will be easier to share the virtual service than a mock or stub code.

Tooling in this area includes the following:

Mountebank

This tool is a JavaScript/Node.js application that provides "cross-platform, multi-protocol test doubles over the wire," and can be used to virtualize services that speak HTTP/HTTPS and TCP (it also supports SMTP). The API is easy to use, and although some of the code you may write may look verbose, it is easy to craft complicated virtualized responses.

WireMock

This tool is similar to Mountebank in that it works by creating an actual server (HTTP in this case) that can be configured to respond with a range of virtualized responses. WireMock is written in Java and is well supported by its creator, Tom Akehurst.

Stubby4j

This is a Java-focused tool that shares a lot of similarity with Mountebank and WireMock. This is an older service virtualization tool, but it can be used to emulate complicated SOAP and WSDL messages when interacting with external legacy service.

VCR/Betamax

These are both useful implementations of applications that allow you to record and replay network traffic. These tools can be particularly useful when you don't have access to the code of the external dependent services (and therefore can only observe a response from a request), when the service returns a large amount of data (which can be captured in an external "cassette"), or when making a call to the service is restricted or expensive.

Hoverfly

This is a new service virtualization tool that provides additional configuration options over WireMock and VCR, and you can emulate responses for complicated legacy applications, as well as complex microservice architectures with many interdependent services. You can also use Hoverfly when performing load testing that interacts with third-party services. For example, where an external SaaS-based application test sandbox is on the critical path and it won't allow you to ramp up the number of test requests without becoming the bottleneck itself. The fact that Hoverfly is written in Go means that it is lightweight and highly performant: you can easily get thousands of request/responses per second when running on a small AWS EC2 node.

Service virtualization is not that common to many Java developers, so let's explore the uses and configuration a little more.

Virtualizing Services with Hoverfly

In this section, you will explore how to virtualize services for your local development environment by using the Hoverfly API simulation tool.

Installing Hoverfly

Hoverfly can be installed via the macOS brew package manager, and can also be downloaded and installed for Windows and Linux systems by following the instructions on the Hoverfly website (*http://bit.ly/2Q8dhVC*).

You can also download the simple Spring Boot–powered flight service API that we will use to explore the concept of service virtualization from here.

Capturing and simulating a request with Hoverfly

First, start an instance of Hoverfly, as shown in Example 8-3.

Example 8-3. Start Hoverfly

```
$ hoverctl start
Hoverfly is now running

+------------+------+
| admin-port | 8888 |
| proxy-port | 8500 |
+------------+------+
```

At any time, you can check whether Hoverfly is running and which ports it is listening on by issuing the `hoverctl status` command, as shown in Example 8-4.

Example 8-4. Hoverctl

```
$ hoverctl status

+------------+----------+
| Hoverfly   | running  |
| Admin port |     8888 |
| Proxy port |     8500 |
| Mode       | capture  |
| Middleware | disabled |
+------------+----------+
```

Start the flights service, and make a request to it to validate that it is running. Here we are just searching for all the flights that are available tomorrow (note that your results from the curl may appear different from the results shown in Example 8-5, as the flight service returns a random set of flight data!):

Example 8-5. Running the sample flight service

```
$ ./run-flights-service.sh
waiting for service to start
waiting for service to start
waiting for service to start
service started

$ curl localhost:8081/api/v1/flights?plusDays=1 | jq
[
  {
    "origin": "Berlin",
    "destination": "New York",
    "cost": "617.31",
    "when": "03:45"
  },
  {
    "origin": "Amsterdam",
    "destination": "Dubai",
    "cost": "3895.49",
    "when": "21:20"
  },
  {
    "origin": "Milan",
    "destination": "New York",
    "cost": "4950.31",
    "when": "08:49"
  }
]
```

Now move Hoverfly into capture mode, as shown in Example 8-6. During this mode, any request that is intercepted by Hoverfly will be captured.

Example 8-6. Hoverctl capture

```
$ hoverctl mode capture
Hoverfly has been set to capture mode
```

Once in capture mode, make a request to the flights API, but this time specify Hoverfly as a proxy, as shown in Example 8-7 (note that your curled flight results may look different from those shown here).

Example 8-7. Capturing API responses with Hoverfly

```
$ curl localhost:8081/api/v1/flights?plusDays=1 --proxy localhost:8500 | jq
[
```

```
{
  "origin": "Berlin",
  "destination": "Dubai",
  "cost": "3103.56",
  "when": "20:53"
},
{
  "origin": "Amsterdam",
  "destination": "Boston",
  "cost": "2999.69",
  "when": "19:45"
}
]
```

By specifying the proxy flag, the request will first go to the proxy (Hoverfly) and then be forwarded onto the real flights API afterward. The reverse is true for the response, and this is how Hoverfly is able intercept network traffic. The Hoverfly logs can be consulted at any time that you are unsure of what has occurred (e.g., was a request/response proxied), an example of which can be seen in Example 8-8.

Example 8-8. Viewing Hoverfly logs

```
$ hoverctl logs
INFO[2017-09-20T11:38:48+01:00] Mode has been changed
mode=capture
INFO[2017-09-20T11:40:28+01:00] request and response captured↵
mode=capture request=&map[headers:map[Accept:[*/*]↵
Proxy-Connection:[Keep-Alive] User-Agent:[curl/7.54.0]]↵
body: method:GET scheme:http destination:localhost:8081↵
path:/api/v1/flights query:map[plusDays:[1]]]↵
response=&map[error:nil response]
...
```

Now, let's take a look at the simulation that we have produced, by exporting it and then opening it in a text editor. In Example 8-9, we use atom, but feel free to substitute your favorite (like vim or emacs) in the command.

Example 8-9. Exporting Hoverfly simulation data

```
$ hoverctl export module-two-simulation.json
Successfully exported simulation to module-two-simulation.json
$ atom module-two-simulation.json
```

Take a look at the simulation file, and see if you recognize your recorded data. The request you captured should correspond to a single element in the pairs array. Now, we can use our simulation to simulate the flights API. First, stop the flights service to make sure we are unable to communicate with it, as shown in Example 8-10.

Example 8-10. Stop the flight service

```
$ ./stop-flights-service.sh
service successfully shut down
$ curl localhost:8081/api/v1/flights?plusDays=1
curl: (7) Failed to connect to localhost port 8081: Connection refused
```

Now, put Hoverfly into simulate mode, as shown in Example 8-11.

Example 8-11. Putting Hoverfly into simulate mode

```
$ hoverctl mode simulate
Hoverfly has been set to simulate mode with a matching strategy of 'strongest'
```

During simulate mode, instead of forwarding the traffic to the real API, Hoverfly will immediately respond to the client with our recorded request. Now we can repeat our request, only this time using Hoverfly as a proxy. We should now receive our recorded response rather than an error, as shown in Example 8-12.

Example 8-12. Making a request against Hoverfly as a proxy

```
$ curl localhost:8081/api/v1/flights?plusDays=1 --proxy localhost:8500 | jq
[
  {
    "origin": "Berlin",
    "destination": "Dubai",
    "cost": "3103.56",
    "when": "20:53"
  },
  {
    "origin": "Amsterdam",
    "destination": "Boston",
    "cost": "2999.69",
    "when": "19:45"
  }
]
```

That's it: we have successfully simulated our first API endpoint! Although you used curl for this demonstration, in a real test, this would typically be the application under test making these requests against Hoverfly. Once request and response data have been stored within Hoverfly, we no longer need access to the service we recorded the data from, and we can also control the exact response given by Hoverfly. One of the major benefits of using a service virtualization tool like Hoverfly is that the tool has a lightweight resource footprint and initializes fast. Therefore, you can virtualize many more services on your laptop than you could run real services, and you can also include the use of Hoverfly within fast integration tests.

Don't Reimplement Your Service "Virtually"

If you find that your virtual services are continually drifting from the functionality of the real application, you may be tempted to add more logic or conditional responses; this can be an antipattern! Although tempting at times, you should definitely not reimplement a service as a virtual copy. Service virtualization is ideal for acting like an intelligent mock or stub for a service that has complex internal logic but a well-defined interface and relatively simple data output (i.e., you should aim to virtualize [encapsulate] behavior, not state, within a virtual service).

If you find yourself modifying virtual services with lots of conditional logic for determining what state should be returned from interactions, or your virtual service logic begins to look similar to the real service workflow, this is an antipattern, and the user of another technique could be more appropriate.

VMs: Vagrant and Packer

Often when working with or deploying to cloud platforms, you will want to package your Java applications within VM images. If you have a small number of services (and a reasonably powerful development machine), this may also allow you to spin up several dependent services when building and testing an application. You will now explore how to use the HashiCorp Vagrant tool for building and initalizing VMs on your local development machine.

Installing Vagrant

Vagrant can be downloaded and installed from the Vagrant website (*https://www.vagrantup.com/downloads.html*), and there are installers for macOS, Linux, and Windows. You will also need to install a VM hypervisor application such as Oracle's VirtualBox (*https://www.virtualbox.org/wiki/Downloads*) or VMware Fusion (*https://www.vmware.com/uk/products/fusion.html*), upon which the Vagrant VMs will run.

Creating a Vagrantfile

All VMs that will be part of your local Vagrant development environment will be defined in a Vagrantfile. This file allows you to specify the number of VMs, their allotted compute resources, and networking configuration. You can also specify installation and provisioning scripts that will configure the VM and install the required OS dependencies. An example Vagrantfile is shown in Example 8-13.

Example 8-13. Vagrantfile that configures a single VM with Ubuntu and installs the Jenkins build server via a simple sets of Bash CLI commands

```
# -*- mode: ruby -*-
# vi: set ft=ruby :

# All Vagrant configuration is done below. The "2" in Vagrant.configure
# configures the configuration version (we support older styles for
# backward compatibility). Please don't change it unless you know what
# you're doing.
Vagrant.configure("2") do |config|
  # The most common configuration options are documented and commented below.
  # For a complete reference, please see the online documentation at
  # https://docs.vagrantup.com.

  # Every Vagrant development environment requires a box. You can search for
  # boxes at https://atlas.hashicorp.com/search.
  config.vm.box = "ubuntu/xenial64"
  config.vm.box_version = "20170922.0.0"

  config.vm.network "forwarded_port", guest: 8080, host: 8080
  config.vm.provider "virtualbox" do |v|
    v.memory = 2048
  end

  # Enable provisioning with a shell script. Additional provisioners such as
  # Puppet, Chef, Ansible, Salt, and Docker are also available. Please see the
  # documentation for more information about their specific syntax and use.
  config.vm.provision "shell", inline: <<-SHELL
    apt-get update

    # Install OpenJDK Java JDK and Maven
    apt-get install -y openjdk-8-jdk
    apt-get install -y maven

    # Install sbt
    echo "deb https://dl.bintray.com/sbt/debian /" |
    tee -a /etc/apt/sources.list.d/sbt.list
    apt-key adv --keyserver hkp://keyserver.ubuntu.com:80
    --recv 2EE0EA64E40A89B84B2DF73499E82A75642AC823
    apt-get update
    apt-get install sbt

    # Install Docker (made slightly more complex by the need
    # to use specific Docker package repos)
    apt-get install -y apt-transport-https ca-certificates
    apt-key adv --keyserver hkp://p80.pool.sks-keyservers.net:80
    --recv-keys 58118E89F3A912897C070ADBF76221572C52609D
    echo deb https://apt.dockerproject.org/repo ubuntu-xenial main >>
    /etc/apt/sources.list.d/docker.list
    apt-get update
    apt-get purge lxc-docker
```

```
    apt-get install -y linux-image-extra-$(uname -r) linux-image-extra-virtual
    apt-get install -y docker-engine

    # Install Jenkins
    wget -q -O - https://pkg.jenkins.io/debian/jenkins-ci.org.key | apt-key add -
    echo deb http://pkg.jenkins-ci.org/debian binary/ >
    /etc/apt/sources.list.d/jenkins.list
    apt-get update
    apt-get install -y jenkins
    # Echo the Jenkins security key that is required upon initialization
    printf "\n\nJENKINS KEY\n*******************************"
    # Add the Jenkins user to the Docker group
    usermod -aG docker jenkins
    # Wait until the initialAdminPassword file is generated via Jenkins startup
    while [ ! -f /var/lib/jenkins/secrets/initialAdminPassword ]
    do
        sleep 2
    done
    cat /var/lib/jenkins/secrets/initialAdminPassword
    printf "*******************************"
    # restart the Jenkins service so that the usermod command above takes effect
    service jenkins restart

    # Install Docker Compose
    curl -s -L https://github.com/docker/compose/releases/
    download/1.10.0/docker-compose-`uname -s`-`uname -m` >↵
    /usr/local/bin/docker-compose
    chmod +x /usr/local/bin/docker-compose
  SHELL
end
```

The VMs defined in the Vagrantfile can be initialized with the vagrant up command,
as shown in Example 8-14, and stopped and deleted with vagrant halt and vagrant
destroy, respectively.

Example 8-14. Vagrant booting a VM

```
$ vagrant up
Bringing machine 'default' up with 'virtualbox' provider...
==> default: Checking if box 'ubuntu/xenial64' is up-to-date...
==> default: Clearing any previously set forwarded ports...
==> default: Clearing any previously set network interfaces...
==> default: Preparing network interfaces based on configuration...
    default: Adapter 1: nat
==> default: Forwarding ports...
    default: 8080 (guest) => 8080 (host) (adapter 1)
    default: 22 (guest) => 2222 (host) (adapter 1)
==> default: Running 'pre-boot' VM customizations...
==> default: Booting VM...
==> default: Waiting for machine to boot. This may take a few minutes...
```

```
         default: SSH address: 127.0.0.1:2222
         default: SSH username: ubuntu
         default: SSH auth method: password
==> default: Machine booted and ready!
```

If you examine the preceding Vagrantfile, you will notice the line `config.vm.network`
`"forwarded_port"`, `guest: 8080`, `host: 8080`, which maps port 8080 in the VM to
port 8080 on the localhost development machine. This means that we can view *http://
localhost:8080* in a web browser and view our Jenkins installation running on the VM
provisioned via Vagrant.

You have learned about Packer in "Creating Machine Images for Multiple Clouds
with Packer" on page 147, and you can use this tool to create images that can be initialized via Vagrant using the `config.vm.box` property in the Vagrant box configuration.

Pattern #3: Production-in-a-Box

The use of environment virtualization tools like HashiCorp's Vagrant enables you to
download precanned images of services to a local machine that can be easily executed
when developing an application or running automated tests. This technology also
allows you to build a production-in-a-box—a replicated (smaller version) of your
production environment that can be shared around a team for a consistent development experience. To implement this, you create (for example) a preconfigured VBox
image that contains an application's code/binaries alongside an OS, configuration,
and associated data stores.

Is the "Production-in-a-Box" an Antipattern?

The production-in-a-box is most useful for teams with a small
number of services operating in a relatively simple and stable production environment. As soon as an application grows to involve
more than three to five services or involves complicated infrastructure or configuration, it can become impractical to attempt to replicate a production environment locally or it can become too
time-consuming to maintain parity between production and development. If you notice that the local production replica is not
behaving as the real production environment, or you are spending
large amounts of effort and resources to maintain this, then it may
be that this pattern is becoming an antipattern for you.

The arrival of HashiCorp Packer has made the image creation process even easier,
and it gives you the ability to specify application packaging once and reuse this across
environments (e.g., Azure in production, OpenStack for QA, and VirtualBox for local
development). Arguably, the arrival of Docker (explored next) pushed this style of

application packaging and sharing into the mainstream, and the Fig composition tool was the icing on the cake. Fig has since evolved into Docker Compose, and now allows the declarative specification of applications/services and associated dependencies and data stores. This pattern does allow for the flexible execution of a collection of dependent services on a local development machine, and the main limiting factor in our experience is machine resources (particularly when running on hypervisor-based virtual platforms).

The production-in-box pattern can allow you to keep a much cleaner local developer environment and remove potential configuration clashes by encapsulating a service and its dependencies and configuration (e.g., different requirements of Java versions). You can also parametrize the images (through initialization params or environment variables), much as you saw with the profiles pattern previously, and it allows services to behave as you require. You can also use Docker plugins for Maven, which enable the integration of container life cycles with test runs. A potential extension to this pattern is developing within the actual images themselves; for example, by mounting local source code into the running instance of an image. If done correctly, this can remove the need for the installation of practically all tooling on the local development machine (except perhaps your favorite editor or IDE), and it greatly simplifies the build toolchain.

Cloud-Based Development (with Production-in-a-Large-Box)?

Several cloud-based IDEs are emerging on the market, such as Eclipse Che and Amazon's Cloud9 platforms, and some industry analysts are suggesting that the future of development could be conducted using these tools rather than local installs. Time will tell, but you will often see that the online IDEs allow you to spin up a replica (or a subset) of a production environment that is then attached to your "local" cloud development environment; this is particularly the case for serverless FaaS applications. Regardless of whether you want to work locally like this, this is a good pattern to explore in order to understand future developer workflows.

Containers: Kubernetes, minikube, and Telepresence

In this section, you will explore working locally with Docker containers and the Kubernetes orchestration platform.

Introducing the "Docker Java Shop" Sample App

Running containers at any real-world scale requires a container orchestration and scheduling platform, and although many exist (i.e., Docker Swarm, Apache Mesos, and AWS ECS), the most popular is Kubernetes (*https://kubernetes.io/*). Kubernetes is used in production at many organizations, and is now hosted by the Cloud Native

Computing Foundation (CNCF) (*https://www.cncf.io/*). Here you will take a simple Java-based, e-commerce shop and package this within Docker containers and run this on Kubernetes.

The architecture of the Docker Java Shopfront application that we will package into containers and deploy onto Kubernetes is shown in Figure 8-1.

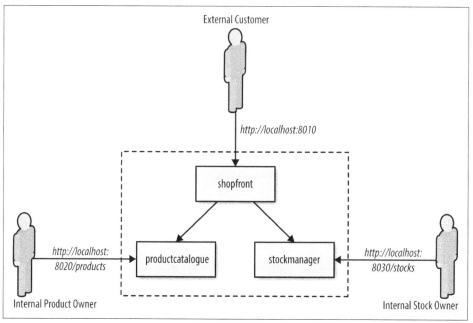

Figure 8-1. Docker Java Shopfront application architecture

Building Java Applications and Container Images

Before we create a container and the associated Kubernetes deployment configuration, we must ensure that we have installed the following prerequisites:

Docker for Mac (https://dockr.ly/2zwBIqz)/Windows (https://dockr.ly/2NL7dWn)/Linux (https://dockr.ly/2xUSIV5)
> This allows us to build, run, and test Docker containers outside Kubernetes on our local development machine.

minikube (http://bit.ly/2xNk8w4)
> This is a tool that makes it easy to run a single-node Kubernetes test cluster on our local development machine via a virtual machine.

A GitHub (https://github.com/) account and Git (https://git-scm.com/) installed locally
> The code examples are stored on GitHub, and by using Git locally, you can fork the repository and commit changes to your own personal copy of the application.

Docker Hub (https://hub.docker.com/) account
> If you would like to follow along with this tutorial, you will need a Docker Hub account in order to push and store your copies of the container images that we will build next.

Java 8 (http://bit.ly/2xO16pw) (or 9) SDK and Maven (https://maven.apache.org/)
> We will be building code with the Maven build and dependency tool that uses Java 8 features.

Clone the project repository from GitHub (optionally, you can fork this repository and clone your personal copy), as shown in Example 8-15. Locate the Shopfront microservice application (*http://bit.ly/2Og0JOP*).

Example 8-15. Clone the example repository

```
$ git clone git@github.com:danielbryantuk/oreilly-docker-java-shopping.git
$ cd oreilly-docker-java-shopping/shopfront
```

Feel free to load the Shopfront code into your editor of choice, such as IntelliJ IDEA or Eclipse, and have a look around. Let's build the application using Maven, as shown in Example 8-16. The resulting runnable JAR file that contains the application will be located in the *./target* directory.

Example 8-16. Building the Spring Boot application

```
$ mvn clean install
…
[INFO] ------------------------------------------------------------------------
[INFO] BUILD SUCCESS
[INFO] ------------------------------------------------------------------------
[INFO] Total time: 17.210 s
[INFO] Finished at: 2017-09-30T11:28:37+01:00
[INFO] Final Memory: 41M/328M
[INFO] ------------------------------------------------------------------------
```

Now you will build the Docker container image. The operating system choice, configuration, and build steps for a Docker image are typically specified via a Dockerfile. Let's look at the example Dockerfile that is located in the *shopfront* directory; see Example 8-17.

Example 8-17. Sample Dockerfile for Spring Boot Java application

```
FROM openjdk:8-jre
ADD target/shopfront-0.0.1-SNAPSHOT.jar app.jar
EXPOSE 8010
ENTRYPOINT ["java","-Djava.security.egd=file:/dev/./urandom","-jar","/app.jar"]
```

The first line specifies that your container image should be created *from* the *openjdk:8-jre* base image. The *openjdk:8-jre* (*https://hub.docker.com/_/openjdk/*) image is maintained by the OpenJDK team, and contains everything we need to run a Java 8 application within a Docker container (such as an operating system with the OpenJDK 8 JRE installed and configured). The second line takes the runnable JAR and *adds* this to the image. The third line specifies that port 8010, which your application will listen on, must be *exposed* as externally accessible, and the fourth line specifies the entrypoint, or command to run, when the container is initialized. Let's build the container; see Example 8-18.

Example 8-18. Docker build

```
$ docker build -t danielbryantuk/djshopfront:1.0 .
Successfully built 87b8c5aa5260
Successfully tagged danielbryantuk/djshopfront:1.0
```

Now let's push this to Docker Hub, as shown in Example 8-19. If you haven't logged into the Docker Hub via your command line, you must do this now and enter your username and password.

Example 8-19. Pushing to Docker Hub

```
$ docker login
Login with your Docker ID to push and pull images from Docker Hub.
If you don't have a Docker ID, head over to https://hub.docker.com to create one.
Username:
Password:
Login Succeeded
$
$ docker push danielbryantuk/djshopfront:1.0
The push refers to a repository [docker.io/danielbryantuk/djshopfront]
9b19f75e8748: Pushed
...
cf4ecb492384: Pushed
1.0: digest: sha256:8a6b459b0210409e67bee29d25bb512344045bd84a262ede80777edfcff3d9a0
size: 2210
```

Deploying into Kubernetes

Now let's run this container within Kubernetes. First, change the *kubernetes* directory in the root of the project:

```
$ cd ../kubernetes
```

Open the *shopfront-service.yaml* Kubernetes deployment file and have a look at the contents, shown in Example 8-20.

Example 8-20. Sample Kubernetes deployment.yaml file for the Shopfront service

```
---
apiVersion: v1
kind: Service
metadata:
  name: shopfront
  labels:
    app: shopfront
spec:
  type: ClusterIP
  selector:
    app: shopfront
  ports:
  - protocol: TCP
    port: 8010
    name: http

---
apiVersion: apps/v1beta2
kind: Deployment
metadata:
  name: shopfront
  labels:
    app: shopfront
spec:
  replicas: 1
  selector:
    matchLabels:
      app: shopfront
  template:
    metadata:
      labels:
        app: shopfront
    spec:
      containers:
      - name: djshopfront
        image: danielbryantuk/djshopfront:1.0
        ports:
        - containerPort: 8010
        livenessProbe:
          httpGet:
            path: /health
            port: 8010
          initialDelaySeconds: 30
          timeoutSeconds: 1
```

The first section of the YAML file creates a Service named shopfront that will route
TCP traffic targeting this service on port 8010 to pods with the label app: shopfront.
The second section of the configuration file creates a Deployment that specifies
Kubernetes should run one replica (instance) of your Shopfront container, which you

have declared as part of the spec (specification) labeled as app: shopfront. You will also specify that the 8010 application traffic port we exposed in your Docker container is open and declared a livenessProbe, or healthcheck, that Kubernetes can use to determine whether your containerized application is running correctly and is ready to accept traffic. Let's start minikube and deploy this service (note that you may need to change the specified minikube CPU and memory requirements depending on the resources available on your development machine); see Example 8-21.

Example 8-21. Starting minikube

```
$ minikube start --cpus 2 --memory 4096
Starting local Kubernetes v1.7.5 cluster...
Starting VM...
Getting VM IP address...
Moving files into cluster...
Setting up certs...
Connecting to cluster...
Setting up kubeconfig...
Starting cluster components...
Kubectl is now configured to use the cluster.
$ kubectl apply -f shopfront-service.yaml
service "shopfront" created
deployment "shopfront" created
```

You can view all services within Kubernetes by using the kubectl get svc command, as shown in Example 8-22. You can also view all associated pods by using the kubectl get pods command. (Note that the first time you issue the get pods command, the container may not have finished creating, and is marked as not yet ready).

Example 8-22. kubectl get svc

```
$ kubectl get svc
NAME            CLUSTER-IP    EXTERNAL-IP    PORT(S)          AGE
kubernetes      10.0.0.1      <none>         443/TCP          18h
shopfront       10.0.0.216    <nodes>        8010:31208/TCP   12s
$ kubectl get pods
NAME             READY     STATUS                  RESTARTS   AGE
shopfront-0w1js  0/1       ContainerCreating       0          18s
$ kubectl get pods
NAME             READY     STATUS     RESTARTS   AGE
shopfront-0w1js  1/1       Running    0          2m
```

You have now successfully deployed our first service into Kubernetes!

Simple Smoke Test

You can use curl to attempt to get data from the shopfront application's healthcheck endpoint, as shown in Example 8-23. This is a simple way to check whether everything is working as it should be.

Example 8-23. Simple smoke test in minikube

```
$ curl $(minikube service shopfront --url)/health
{"status":"UP"}
```

You can see from the results of the curl against the *application/health* endpoint that the application is up and running, but you will need to deploy the remaining microservice application containers before the application will function as required.

Building the Remaining Applications

Now that you have one container up and running, let's build the remaining two supporting microservice applications and containers, as shown in Example 8-24.

Example 8-24. Building the remaining applications

```
$ cd ..
$ cd productcatalogue/
$ mvn clean install
…
$ docker build -t danielbryantuk/djproductcatalogue:1.0 .
...
$ docker push danielbryantuk/djproductcatalogue:1.0
...
$ cd ..
$ cd stockmanager/
$ mvn clean install
...
$ docker build -t danielbryantuk/djstockmanager:1.0 .
...
$ docker push danielbryantuk/djstockmanager:1.0
```

At this point, you have built all of your microservices and the associated Docker images, and pushed the images to Docker Hub. Let's now deploy the productcatalogue and stockmanager services to Kubernetes.

Deploying the Entire Java Application in Kubernetes

In a similar fashion to the process you used previously to deploy the Shopfront service, you can now deploy the remaining two microservices within your application to Kubernetes; see Example 8-25.

Example 8-25. Deploying the entire Java application in Kubernetes

```
$ cd ..
$ cd kubernetes/
$ kubectl apply -f productcatalogue-service.yaml
service "productcatalogue" created
deployment "productcatalogue" created
$ kubectl apply -f stockmanager-service.yaml
service "stockmanager" created
deployment "stockmanager" created
$ kubectl get svc
NAME               CLUSTER-IP     EXTERNAL-IP    PORT(S)          AGE
kubernetes         10.0.0.1       <none>         443/TCP          19h
productcatalogue   10.0.0.37      <nodes>        8020:31803/TCP   42s
shopfront          10.0.0.216     <nodes>        8010:31208/TCP   13m
stockmanager       10.0.0.149     <nodes>        8030:30723/TCP   16s
$ kubectl get pods
NAME                   READY     STATUS    RESTARTS   AGE
productcatalogue-79qn4 1/1       Running   0          55s
shopfront-0w1js        1/1       Running   0          13m
stockmanager-lmgj9     1/1       Running   0          29s
```

Depending on how quickly you issue the `kubectl get pods` command, you may see that all the pods are not yet running. Before moving on to the next section, wait until the command shows that all of the pods are running (maybe this is a good time to brew a cup of tea!)

Viewing the Deployed Application

With all services deployed and all associated pods running, you now should be able to access your completed application via the Shopfront service GUI. You can open the service in your default browser by issuing the following command in minikube:

```
$ minikube service shopfront
```

If everything is working correctly, you should see the page shown in Figure 8-2 in your browser.

In addition to running minikube locally, it is also possible to provision a remote Kubernetes cluster and develop locally against this by using tooling like Datawire's Telepresence. Let's explore this pattern now.

Figure 8-2. Simple UI of Docker Java Shopfront

Telepresence: Working Remotely, Locally

Telepresence is an open source tool that lets you run a single service locally, while connecting that service to a remote Kubernetes cluster. This lets developers working on multiservice applications do the following:

- Do fast local development of a single service, even if that service depends on other services in your cluster. Make a change to your service and save, and you can immediately see the new service in action.

- Use any tool installed locally to test/debug/edit your service. For example, you can use a debugger or IDE!

- Make your local development machine operate as if it's part of your Kubernetes cluster. If you have an application on your machine that you want to run against a service in the cluster, it's easy to do.

First, you need to install Telepresence (*http://bit.ly/2N6wAwJ*). This is easy if you are using a Mac or Linux machine to develop software locally, and full instructions for all platforms can be found on the Telepresence website. Example 8-26 details installation on a Mac.

Technical Details of Telepresence

Telepresence deploys a two-way network proxy in a pod running in your Kubernetes cluster. This pod proxies data from your Kubernetes environment (e.g., TCP connections, environment variables, volumes) to the local process. The local process has its networking transparently overridden so that DNS calls and TCP connections are routed over the proxy to the remote Kubernetes cluster.

This approach gives the following:

- Your local service full access to other services in the remote cluster
- Your local service full access to Kubernetes environment variables, secrets, and ConfigMap
- Your remote services full access to your local service

How Telepresence works is discussed in more detail here (*http://bit.ly/2IkkXl7*).

Example 8-26. Installing Telepresence on a Mac local development machine

```
$ brew cask install osxfuse
$ brew install socat datawire/blackbird/telepresence
...
$ telepresence --version
0.77
```

Now you can create a remote Kubernetes cluster. Example 8-27 uses the Google Cloud Platform (GCP) GKE service to deploy a fully managed cluster. If you want to follow along, you need to sign up for a GCP account and install the gclouds command-line tool. Don't forget that after you have installed the gclouds tool locally, you must configure the tool to use the credentials of the account you have just created (full details can be found on the Google Cloud SDK (*http://bit.ly/2NKqjfm*) web page). At the time of writing, you will also need to install the beta components of the gcloud tool. (Instructions can be found on the gcloud install web page (*http://bit.ly/2OTEknF*).)

The cluster will be created with slightly bigger compute instances than the default, n1-standard-2, as some of the Java applications' memory requirements can be too large for the smaller instances. To keep costs low, you can also specify that the Kubernetes cluster is created using *preemptible* instances. These instances are a lot less expensive than the standard instances, but the risk is they might be preempted, or reclaimed, if Google needs the extra compute capacity. Typically, this doesn't happen often, and if it does, then Kubernetes self-heals and redeploys the affected applications.

Example 8-27. Creating a preemptible Kubernetes cluster on GCP GKE

```
$ gcloud container clusters create telepresence-demo
--machine-type n1-standard-2 --preemptible
Creating cluster telepresence-demo...done.
Created [https://container.googleapis.com/v1beta1/projects/↵
k8s-leap-forward/zones/us-central1-a/clusters/telepresence-demo].

To inspect the contents of your cluster, go to:
https://console.cloud.google.com/kubernetes/workload_/gcloud/↵
us-central1-a/telepresence-demo?project=k8s-leap-forward

kubeconfig entry generated for telepresence-demo.
NAME  LOCATION  MASTER_VERSION  MASTER_IP  MACHINE_TYPE  NUM_NODES  STATUS
telepresence-demo  us-central1-a 1.8.8-gke.0 35.193.55.23 n1-standard-2  3 RUNNING
```

With your cluster built, you can now deploy the example services onto this remote cluster. You'll notice that once Telepresence has initialized, you can curl the shop front healthendpoint as if you were located in the cluster; you don't need to use the external IP address (or even expose this service to the internet).

Example 8-28. Curling a remote service healthcheck endpoint as if it were local

```
$ cd oreilly-docker-java-shopping/kubernetes
$ kubectl apply -f .
service "productcatalogue" created
deployment "productcatalogue" created
service "shopfront" created
deployment "shopfront" created
service "stockmanager" created
deployment "stockmanager" created
$
$ telepresence
Starting proxy with method 'vpn-tcp', which has the following limitations:
All processes are affected, only one telepresence can run per machine,↵
 and you can't use other VPNs. You may need to add cloud hosts with↵
 --also-proxy. For a full list of method limitations↵
 see https://telepresence.io/reference/methods.html
Volumes are rooted at $TELEPRESENCE_ROOT.↵
 See https://telepresence.io/howto/volumes.html for details.

No traffic is being forwarded from the remote Deployment to your local machine.
You can use the --expose option to specify which ports you want to forward.

Password:
Guessing that Services IP range is 10.63.240.0/20. Services started after
this point will be inaccessible if are outside this range; restart↵
 telepresence if you can't access a new Service.

@gke_k8s-leap-forward_us-central1-a_demo| $ curl shopfront:8010/health
```

```
{"status":"UP"}
@gke_k8s-leap-forward_us-central1-a_demo| kubernetes $ exit
```

This is only scratching the surface with what Telepresence can do, and the most exciting thing is debugging a local service (*http://bit.ly/2OjmPQg*) that is communicating with other services located in the remote cluster. The Telepresence website has full details on how to do this.

Cleaning Up Your GKE Cluster

Don't forget to delete your cluster, or else you could end up with an unexpected bill at the end of the month! You can delete your cluster by running the following command:

```
$ gcloud container clusters delete telepresence-demo
```

Pattern #4: Environment Leasing

In a nutshell, the environment leasing pattern is implemented by allowing each developer to create and automatically provision their own remote environment that can contain an arbitrary configuration of services and data. This pattern is somewhat similar to the production-in-a-box pattern, but instead of running a replica of production locally, you are running this in the cloud. The services and data (and associated infrastructure components and glue) must be specified programmatically via an infrastructure as code (IaC) tool (like Terraform (*https://terraform.io/*)) or one of the automated provisioning and configuration management tools (like Ansible (*http://www.ansible.com/*)). The configuration and operational knowledge must also be shared across the team for this approach to be viable, and therefore you must be embracing a DevOps mindset.

After an environment is specified and initialized, it is then "leased" by an individual developer. Each developer's local machine is then configured to communicate with services and dependencies installed into the remote environment as if all the services were running locally. You can use this pattern when deploying applications to cloud-based platforms, as it allows you to spin up and shut down environments on demand and rapidly.

Platform Leasing Requires Programmable Infra and DevOps

The platform-leasing pattern is an advanced pattern, and does rely on both the ability to provision platform environments on demand (e.g., private/public cloud with elastic scaling) and that the development team has a reasonable awareness of operational characteristics of the production platform. The pattern also requires that a developer's machine has a stable network connection to this environment. Running a local proxy, such as Datawire's Telepresence, NGINX, or HAProxy in combination with HashiCorp's Consul (*https://www.consul.io/*) and consul-template (*https://github.com/hashicorp/consul-template*), or a framework such as Spring Cloud (*http://bit.ly/2Q76njB*) in combination with Netflix's Eureka (*https://github.com/Netflix/eureka*), is useful in order to automate the storage and updating of each developer's environment location.

FaaS: AWS Lamba and SAM Local

AWS introduced *Serverless Application Model* (SAM) in 2016 in order to make it easier for developers to deploy FaaS serverless applications. At its core, SAM is an open source specification built on AWS CloudFormation that makes it easy to specify and maintain your serverless infrastructure as code.

SAM Local takes all the useful parts of SAM and brings them to your local machine:

- It lets you develop and test your AWS Lambda functions locally with SAM Local and Docker.

- It lets you simulate function invocations from known event sources like Amazon Simple Storage Service (S3), Amazon DynamoDB, Amazon Kinesis, Amazon Simple Notification Service (SNS), and nearly all of the other Amazon services offered.

- It lets you start a local Amazon API Gateway from a SAM template, and quickly iterate on your functions with hot-reloading.

- It lets you quickly validate your SAM template and even integrate that validation with linters or IDEs.

- It provides interactive debugging support for your Lambda functions.

Let's take AWS SAM Local for a spin.

Installing SAM Local

There are several ways to install SAM Local, but the easiest is through the pip (*https://pypi.org/project/pip/*) Python package management tool. A discussion of installing pip and Python is outside the scope of this book, but both the SAM Local (*https://github.com/awslabs/aws-sam-cli*) and pip websites provide more information.

Once pip is installed locally, SAM Local can be installed using the command shown in Example 8-29 in the terminal.

Example 8-29. Installing SAM Local

```
$ pip install aws-sam-cli
```

The latest version can also be installed from the source if you have Go installed on your local development machine: `go get github.com/awslabs/aws-sam-local`.

AWS Lambda Scaffolding

You can use the simple Java function in Example 8-30 that is a basic implementation of the Product Catalogue service you explored earlier in the Shopping demonstration application. The full code can be found in the book's GitHub repo (*https://github.com/continuous-delivery-in-java/product-catalogue-aws-lambda*). The main handler function class can be seen in Example 8-30.

Example 8-30. Simple Java "Hello World" AWS Lambda function

```
package uk.co.danielbryant.djshoppingserverless.productcatalogue;

import com.amazonaws.services.lambda.runtime.Context;
import com.amazonaws.services.lambda.runtime.RequestHandler;
import com.google.gson.Gson;
import uk.co.danielbryant.djshoppingserverless.productcatalogue.↵
services.ProductService;

import java.util.HashMap;
import java.util.Map;

/**
 * Handler for requests to Lambda function.
 */
public class ProductCatalogueFunction implements RequestHandler<Map<String, Object>,
GatewayResponse> {

    private static final int HTTP_OK = 200;
    private static final int HTTP_INTERNAL_SERVER_ERROR = 500;

    private ProductService productService = new ProductService();
    private Gson gson = new Gson();

    public GatewayResponse handleRequest(final Map<String, Object> input,
    final Context context) {
        Map<String, String> headers = new HashMap<>();
```

```
        headers.put("Content-Type", "application/json");

        String output = gson.toJson(productService.getAllProducts());
        return new GatewayResponse(output, headers, HTTP_OK);
    }
}
```

The handleRequest method will be called by the AWS Lambda framework when you run the function locally or remotely (in production). Several predefined RequestHan dler (*https://amzn.to/2QbAgiF*) interfaces and associated handleRequest methods are available in the aws-lambda-java-core library that you can import via Maven. This example uses RequestHandler<Map<String, Object>, GatewayResponse> that allows you to capture the JSON map of data that is passed to the function (and contains details such as the HTTP method, headers, and request param/body) and return a GatewayResponse object, which ultimately gets sent to the requesting service or user.

The project's *pom.xml* can be seen in Example 8-31, and notice also that the function JAR is being packaged for deployment using the Maven Shade plugin that you learned about earlier.

Example 8-31. ProductCatalogue AWS Lambda pom.xml

```
<project xmlns="http://maven.apache.org/POM/4.0.0"
    xmlns:xsi="http://www.w3.org/2001/XMLSchema-instance"
    xsi:schemaLocation="http://maven.apache.org/POM/4.0.0
    http://maven.apache.org/maven-v4_0_0.xsd">
    <modelVersion>4.0.0</modelVersion>
    <groupId>uk.co.danielbryant.djshoppingserverless</groupId>
    <artifactId>ProductCatalogue</artifactId>
    <version>1.0</version>
    <packaging>jar</packaging>
    <name>A simple Product Catalogue demo created by the SAM CLI sam-init.</name>
    <properties>
        <maven.compiler.source>1.8</maven.compiler.source>
        <maven.compiler.target>1.8</maven.compiler.target>
    </properties>

    <dependencies>
        <dependency>
            <groupId>com.amazonaws</groupId>
            <artifactId>aws-lambda-java-core</artifactId>
            <version>1.1.0</version>
        </dependency>
        <dependency>
            <groupId>com.google.code.gson</groupId>
            <artifactId>gson</artifactId>
            <version>2.8.5</version>
        </dependency>
```

```
    <dependency>
      <groupId>junit</groupId>
      <artifactId>junit</artifactId>
      <version>4.12</version>
      <scope>test</scope>
    </dependency>
  </dependencies>

  <build>
    <plugins>
      <plugin>
        <groupId>org.apache.maven.plugins</groupId>
        <artifactId>maven-shade-plugin</artifactId>
        <version>3.1.1</version>
        <configuration>
        </configuration>
        <executions>
          <execution>
            <phase>package</phase>
            <goals>
              <goal>shade</goal>
            </goals>
          </execution>
        </executions>
      </plugin>
    </plugins>
  </build>
</project>
```

To build and test this locally, you also need a *template.yaml* manifest file, which specifies the Lambda configuration and wires up a simple API Gateway to allow us to test our function; see Example 8-32.

Example 8-32. AWS Lambda template.yaml

```
AWSTemplateFormatVersion: '2010-09-09'
Transform: AWS::Serverless-2016-10-31
Description: >
    Product Catalogue Lambda Function

    (based on the sample SAM Template for sam-app)

Globals:
    Function:
        Timeout: 20


Resources:

    ProductCatalogueFunction:
        Type: AWS::Serverless::Function
```

```
    Properties:
        CodeUri: target/ProductCatalogue-1.0.jar
        Handler: uk.co.danielbryant.djshoppingserverless.↵
        productcatalogue.ProductCatalogueFunction::handleRequest
        Runtime: java8
        Environment: # More info about Env Vars: https://github.com/awslabs/↵
         serverless-application-model/blob/master/versions/↵
        2016-10-31.md#environment-object
            Variables:
                PARAM1: VALUE
        Events:
            HelloWorld:
                Type: Api # More info about API Event Source:
                https://github.com/awslabs/serverless-application-model/↵
                 blob/master/versions/2016-10-31.md#api
                Properties:
                    Path: /products
                    Method: get

Outputs:

    HelloWorldApi:
      Description: "API Gateway endpoint URL for Prod stage for
      Product Catalogue Lambda "
      Value: !Sub "https://${ServerlessRestApi}.execute-api
      .${AWS::Region}.amazonaws.com/prod/products/"

    HelloWorldFunction:
      Description: "Product Catalogue Lambda Function ARN"
      Value: !GetAtt ProductCatalogueFunction.Arn

    HelloWorldFunctionIamRole:
      Description: "Implicit IAM Role created for Product Catalogue Lambda function"
      Value: !GetAtt ProductCatalogueFunction.Arn
```

Testing AWS Lambda Event Handling

The SAM Local tooling allows you to generate test events through the `sam local generate-event` command. You can learn more about the event generation options available to you by using the `--help` argument at various locations within the CLI commands. In this example, you need to generate an example API gateway event. This is effectively a synthetic version of the JSON object that will be sent when a service or user makes a request against the Amazon API Gateway that is fronting your function. Let's explore in Example 8-33.

Example 8-33. Generating test events using SAM Local

```
$ sam local generate-event --help
Usage: sam local generate-event [OPTIONS] COMMAND [ARGS]...
```

```
   Generate an event

Options:
  --help  Show this message and exit.

Commands:
  api       Generates a sample Amazon API Gateway event
  dynamodb  Generates a sample Amazon DynamoDB event
  kinesis   Generates a sample Amazon Kinesis event
  s3        Generates a sample Amazon S3 event
  schedule  Generates a sample scheduled event
  sns       Generates a sample Amazon SNS event
$
$ sam local generate-event api --help
Usage: sam local generate-event api [OPTIONS]

Options:
  -m, --method TEXT    HTTP method (default: "POST")
  -b, --body TEXT      HTTP body (default: "{ "test": "body"}")
  -r, --resource TEXT  API Gateway resource name (default: "/{proxy+}")
  -p, --path TEXT      HTTP path (default: "/examplepath")
  --debug              Turn on debug logging
  --help               Show this message and exit.
$
$ sam local generate-event api -m GET -b "" -p "/products"
{
    "body": null,
    "httpMethod": "GET",
    "resource": "/{proxy+}",
    "queryStringParameters": {
        "foo": "bar"
    },
    "requestContext": {
        "httpMethod": "GET",
        "requestId": "c6af9ac6-7b61-11e6-9a41-93e8deadbeef",
        "path": "/{proxy+}",
        "extendedRequestId": null,
        "resourceId": "123456",
        "apiId": "1234567890",
        "stage": "prod",
        "resourcePath": "/{proxy+}",
        "identity": {
            "accountId": null,
            "apiKey": null,
            "userArn": null,
            "cognitoAuthenticationProvider": null,
            "cognitoIdentityPoolId": null,
            "userAgent": "Custom User Agent String",
            "caller": null,
            "cognitoAuthenticationType": null,
            "sourceIp": "127.0.0.1",
```

```
            "user": null
        },
        "accountId": "123456789012"
    },
    "headers": {
        "Accept-Language": "en-US,en;q=0.8",
        "Accept-Encoding": "gzip, deflate, sdch",
        "X-Forwarded-Port": "443",
        "CloudFront-Viewer-Country": "US",
        "X-Amz-Cf-Id": "aaaaaaaaaae3VYQb9jd-nvCd-de396Uhbp027Y2JvkCPNLmGJHqlaA==",
        "CloudFront-Is-Tablet-Viewer": "false",
        "User-Agent": "Custom User Agent String",
        "Via": "1.1 08f323deadbeefa7af34d5feb414ce27.cloudfront.net (CloudFront)",
        "CloudFront-Is-Desktop-Viewer": "true",
        "CloudFront-Is-SmartTV-Viewer": "false",
        "CloudFront-Is-Mobile-Viewer": "false",
        "X-Forwarded-For": "127.0.0.1, 127.0.0.2",
        "Accept": "text/html,application/xhtml+xml,application/xml;q=0.9,
        image/webp,*/*;q=0.8",
        "Upgrade-Insecure-Requests": "1",
        "Host": "1234567890.execute-api.us-east-1.amazonaws.com",
        "X-Forwarded-Proto": "https",
        "Cache-Control": "max-age=0",
        "CloudFront-Forwarded-Proto": "https"
    },
    "stageVariables": null,
    "path": "/products",
    "pathParameters": {
        "proxy": "/products"
    },
    "isBase64Encoded": false
}
```

You can use this generated event to test your function in several ways. The simplest method is to simply pipe the results of the event generation through a local invocation of your function, which is triggered via sam local invoke *<function_name>*; see Example 8-34.

Example 8-34. Generating an Amazon API Gateway event and sending this to a local invocation of a Lambda function

```
$ sam local generate-event api -m GET -b "" -p "/products" | ↵
 sam local invoke ProductCatalogueFunction
2018-06-10 14:06:04 Reading invoke payload from stdin (you can also↵
 pass it from file with --event)
2018-06-10 14:06:05 Invoking uk.co.danielbryant.djshoppingserverless.↵
productcatalogue.ProductCatalogueFunction::handleRequest (java8)
2018-06-10 14:06:05 Found credentials in shared credentials file:↵
 ~/.aws/credentials
2018-06-10 14:06:05 Decompressing /Users/danielbryant/Documents/↵
dev/daniel-bryant-uk/tmp/aws-sam-java/sam-app/target/↵
```

```
ProductCatalogue-1.0.jar


Fetching lambci/lambda:java8 Docker container image......
2018-06-10 14:06:06 Mounting /private/var/folders/1x/↵
81f0qg_50vl6c4gntmt008w40000gn/T/tmp1kC9fo as↵
 /var/task:ro inside runtime container
START RequestId: 054d0a81-1fa9-41b9-870c-18394e6f6ea9↵
 Version: $LATEST
END RequestId: 054d0a81-1fa9-41b9-870c-18394e6f6ea9
REPORT RequestId: 054d0a81-1fa9-41b9-870c-18394e6f6ea9↵
 Duration: 82.60 ms Billed Duration: 100 ms↵
 Memory Size: 128 MB Max Memory Used: 19 MB
```

```
{"body":"[{\"id\":\"1\",\"name\":\"Widget\",↵
\"description\":\"Premium ACME Widgets\",↵
\"price\":1.19},{\"id\":\"2\",\"name\":\"Sprocket\",↵
\"description\":\"Grade B sprockets\",↵
\"price\":4.09},{\"id\":\"3\",\"name\":\"Anvil\",↵
\"description\":\"Large Anvils\",\"price\":45.5},↵
{\"id\":\"4\",\"name\":\"Cogs\",↵
\"description\":\"Grade Y cogs\",\"price\":1.80},↵
{\"id\":\"5\",\"name\":\"Multitool\",↵
\"description\":\"Multitools\",\"price\":154.09}]",↵
"headers":{"Content-Type":"application/json"},"statusCode":200}
```

If you want to customize the generated event in more detail, you can pipe the generated results to a file, modify the contents or the file, and then cat this into an invocation, as shown in Example 8-35.

Example 8-35. Piping a generated event to a file, modifying it, and then using cat to pipe the file content to SAM Local

```
$ sam local generate-event api -m GET -b "" -p "/products" > api_event.json
$ # modify the api_event.json file with your favourite editor and then save
$ cat api_event.json | sam local invoke ProductCatalogueFunction
...
```

You can also debug the function that is being invoking via Docker by specifying the `--debug-port` *<port_number>* and attaching a remote debugger to the specified port (for example, using an IDE like IntelliJ). You can then invoke the function, and the SAM Local framework will pause until you attach a debugging process. You can then set breakpoints and variable watches as you would typically when debugging, and simply allow the Lambda function call to complete in order to see the data returned via the terminal invocation.

Smoke Testing with SAM Local

SAM Local also allows you to simulate the running of an Amazon API Gateway locally, which can integrate with your function. The gateway and function can be started via SAM Local by typing `sam local start-api` in the directory with the *template.yaml* file. You can now curl the local endpoints to smoke test the Lambda function, as shown in Example 8-36.

Example 8-36. Using SAM Local to start the function and API gateway, and then curling the API

```
$ sam local start-api
2018-06-10 14:56:03 Mounting ProductCatalogueFunction
at http://127.0.0.1:3000/products [GET]
2018-06-10 14:56:03 You can now browse to the above
endpoints to invoke your functions. You do not need to restart/reload SAM CLI↵
 while working on your functions changes will be reflected↵
 instantly/automatically. You only need to restart SAM CLI if you update your↵
 AWS SAM template
2018-06-10 14:56:03  * Running on http://127.0.0.1:3000/ (Press CTRL+C to quit)

[Open new terminal]

$ curl http://127.0.0.1:3000/products
[{"id":"1","name":"Widget","description":"Premium ACME Widgets","price":1.19},↵
...]
```

If you switch back to the first terminal session in which you started the API, you will notice that additional information is echoed to the screen, which can be useful for viewing not only all of your logging statements, but also data on how long the function ran and how much memory it consumed. Although this data is unique to the configuration (and CPU and RAM) of your machine, it can be useful to attempt an approximate calculation of how much running your function will cost in production.

Example 8-37. Viewing the terminal output of SAM Local running a simulated local Amazon API Gateway

```
$ sam local start-api
2018-06-10 14:56:03 Mounting ProductCatalogueFunction
at http://127.0.0.1:3000/products [GET]
2018-06-10 14:56:03 You can now browse to the above
endpoints to invoke your functions. You do not need to restart/reload SAM CLI↵
 while working on your functions changes will be reflected↵
 instantly/automatically. You only need to restart SAM CLI if you update↵
 your AWS SAM template
2018-06-10 14:56:03  * Running on http://127.0.0.1:3000/ (Press CTRL+C to quit)
2018-06-10 14:56:37 Invoking uk.co.danielbryant.djshoppingserverless.
productcatalogue.ProductCatalogueFunction::handleRequest (java8)
```

```
2018-06-10 14:56:37 Found credentials in shared credentials file:↵
~/.aws/credentials
2018-06-10 14:56:37 Decompressing /Users/danielbryant/Documents/
dev/daniel-bryant-uk/tmp/aws-sam-java/sam-app/target/ProductCatalogue-1.0.jar


Fetching lambci/lambda:java8 Docker container image......
2018-06-10 14:56:38 Mounting /private/var/folders/↵
1x/81f0qg_50vl6c4gntmt008w40000gn/
T/tmp9BwMmf as /var/task:ro inside runtime container
START RequestId: b5afd403-2fb9-4b95-a887-9a8ea5874641 Version: $LATEST
END RequestId: b5afd403-2fb9-4b95-a887-9a8ea5874641
REPORT RequestId: b5afd403-2fb9-4b95-a887-9a8ea5874641 Duration: 94.77 ms
Billed Duration: 100 ms Memory Size: 128 MB Max Memory Used: 19 MB
2018-06-10 14:56:40 127.0.0.1 - - [10/Jun/2018 14:56:40]↵
 "GET /products HTTP/1.1" 200 -
```

Often when testing Lambda functions locally, your code will integrate with another service within Amazon, such as S3 or DynamoDB. This can cause difficulties with testing, and the solution is often to mock or virtualize dependencies by using the techniques presented within this chapter. Rather than creating your own solutions, it is wise to explore current community options (although care must be taken when downloading and executing any code or application locally, particularly if this will ultimately be run as root or within a build pipeline with access to staging or production). One particular community solution within the domain of AWS is LocalStack (*https://github.com/localstack/localstack*)—a fully functional local AWS cloud stack.

Running AWS Services Locally with LocalStack

The LocalStack testing utilities provide useful tools for integration testing, as they allow you to spin up a local version (on a development machine or within the pipeline) of many of the AWS services, such as DynamoDB, Kinesis, and S3. These local services look and behave like the real thing—typically exposing REST-like APIs and service-specific protocols—and can be configured with appropriate data or behavior for your test. You can even inject cloud- or service-specific errors that you may see in production, and test against these.

FaaS: Azure Functions and VS Code

In 2016 Azure introduced Azure Functions, with support for Java applications being added to the FaaS platform in 2017. There isn't a direct analogy to AWS SAM for specifying the infrastructure associated with Azure Functions, but the Microsoft team have focused on creating an effective set of configuration files and associated tooling in order to make it easy to build and test functions both locally and remotely. You can perform all of the necessary tasks via the command line, although in general we have found it much easier to use the excellent integrations with Microsoft's VS Code editor (*https://code.visualstudio.com/*).

Installing Azure Function Core Tools

In order to develop Azure Function-based applications with Java, you must have the following installed on your local development machine:

- Java Developer Kit, version 8
- Apache Maven, version 3.0 or above
- Azure CLI (*http://bit.ly/2xH4raK*)
- Azure Functions Core Tools (*http://bit.ly/2OdOuSR*) (which also requires the .NET Core 2.1 SDK)
- VS Code (*optional*)

You can easily create Java functions using the Maven archetype generator. Example 8-38 demonstrates the initial parameters required for the `mvn arche type:generate` command and also the questions asked as part of the generation process:

Example 8-38. Creating a Java Azure Function using Maven

```
$ mvn archetype:generate -DarchetypeGroupId=com.microsoft.azure ↵
    -DarchetypeArtifactId=azure-functions-archetype
[INFO] Scanning for projects...
Downloading from central: https://repo.maven.apache.org/maven2/org/apache/↵
maven/plugins/maven-release-plugin/2.5.3/maven-release-plugin-2.5.3.pom
Downloaded from central: https://repo.maven.apache.org/maven2/org/apache/↵
maven/plugins/maven-release-plugin/2.5.3/maven-release-plugin-2.5.3.pom↵
 (11 kB at 24 kB/s)
...
Define value for property 'groupId'↵
 (should match expression '[A-Za-z0-9_\-\.]+'): helloworld
[INFO] Using property: groupId = helloworld
Define value for property 'artifactId'↵
 (should match expression '[A-Za-z0-9_\-\.]+'): ProductCatalogue
[INFO] Using property: artifactId = ProductCatalogue
Define value for property 'version' 1.0-SNAPSHOT: :
Define value for property 'package' helloworld: :↵
 uk.co.danielbryant.helloworldserverless.productcatalogue
Define value for property 'appName' productcatalogue-20180923111807725: :
Define value for property 'appRegion' westus: :
Define value for property 'resourceGroup' java-functions-group: :
Confirm properties configuration:
groupId: helloworld
```

```
groupId: helloworld
artifactId: ProductCatalogue
artifactId: ProductCatalogue
version: 1.0-SNAPSHOT
package: uk.co.danielbryant.helloworldserverless.productcatalogue
appName: productcatalogue-20180923111807725
appRegion: westus
resourceGroup: java-functions-group
 Y: : Y
...
[INFO] Project created from Archetype in dir: /Users/danielbryant/Documents/dev/↵
daniel-bryant-uk/tmp/ProductCatalogue
[INFO] ------------------------------------------------------------------------
[INFO] BUILD SUCCESS
[INFO] ------------------------------------------------------------------------
[INFO] Total time: 03:25 min
[INFO] Finished at: 2018-09-23T11:19:12+01:00
[INFO] ------------------------------------------------------------------------
```

As part of the generation process, a simple Java Function class is created, which contains an HttpTrigger Java function method that can be invoked with an HTTP GET request. Example 8-39 shows the contents of this class, and you can use this sample to learn how to work locally and debug an Azure Function.

Example 8-39. The sample Function class generated by the Maven archetype

```java
public class Function {
    @FunctionName("HttpTrigger-Java")
    public HttpResponseMessage HttpTriggerJava(
    @HttpTrigger(name = "req",
                methods = {HttpMethod.GET, HttpMethod.POST},
                authLevel = AuthorizationLevel.ANONYMOUS)↵
                  HttpRequestMessage<Optional<String>> request,
                final ExecutionContext context) {
        context.getLogger().info("Java HTTP trigger processed a request.");

        // Parse query parameter
        String query = request.getQueryParameters().get("name");
        String name = request.getBody().orElse(query);

        if (name == null) {
            return request.createResponseBuilder(HttpStatus.BAD_REQUEST)
                        .body("Please pass a name on the query string↵
                        or in the request body").build();
        } else {
            return request.createResponseBuilder(HttpStatus.OK)
                    .body("Hello, " + name).build();
        }
    }
}
```

In the root of the generated Java project you can see the configuration files *local.settings.json* and *host.json*. The file *local.settings.json* stores application settings, connection strings, and settings for the Azure Functions Core Tools. The *host.json* metadata file contains global configuration options that affect all functions for a function app. The default *host.json* is typically simple, but as Example 8-40 shows, you can configure HTTP API and endpoint properties, health checks, and logging for more advanced use cases.

Example 8-40. A more complicated host.json Azure Function configuration file

```
{
    "version": "2.0",
    "extensions": {
        "http": {
            "routePrefix": "api",
            "maxConcurrentRequests": 5,
            "maxOutstandingRequests": 30
            "dynamicThrottlesEnabled": false
        }
    },
    "healthMonitor": {
        "enabled": true,
        "healthCheckInterval": "00:00:10",
        "healthCheckWindow": "00:02:00",
        "healthCheckThreshold": 6,
        "counterThreshold": 0.80
    },
    "id": "9f4ea53c5136457d883d685e57164f08",
    "logging": {
        "fileLoggingMode": "debugOnly",
        "logLevel": {
          "Function.MyFunction": "Information",
          "default": "None"
        },
        "applicationInsights": {
            "sampling": {
              "isEnabled": true,
              "maxTelemetryItemsPerSecond" : 5
            }
        }
    },
    "watchDirectories": [ "Shared", "Test" ]
}
```

You can treat the project like any other Maven project, and you can build the artifact ready for upload to the Azure Function service via the `mvn clean package` command.

Building and Testing Locally

You can use Azure Function Core Tools to initialize your function ready for local testing by running the Azure-Function Maven plugin using the `mvn` `azure-
functions:run` command, as demonstrated in Example 8-41.

Example 8-41. Using the Azure Maven plugin to run a Java function locally

```
$ mvn azure-functions:run
[INFO] Scanning for projects...
[INFO]
[INFO] --------------------< helloworld:ProductCatalogue >--------------------
[INFO] Building Azure Java Functions 1.0-SNAPSHOT
[INFO] -----------------------------[ jar ]-----------------------------
[INFO]
[INFO] --- azure-functions-maven-plugin:1.0.0-beta-6:run↵
 (default-cli) @ ProductCatalogue ---
AI: INFO 1: Configuration file has been successfully found as resource
AI: INFO 1: Configuration file has been successfully found as resource
[INFO] Azure Function App's staging directory found at:↵
 /Users/danielbryant/Documents/dev/daniel-bryant-uk/↵
tmp/ProductCatalogue/target/azure-functions/↵
productcatalogue-20180923111807725
[INFO] Azure Functions Core Tools found.
```

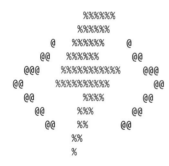

```
Azure Functions Core Tools (2.0.3)
Function Runtime Version: 2.0.12115.0


...


Now listening on: http://0.0.0.0:7071
Application started. Press Ctrl+C to shut down.
Listening on http://0.0.0.0:7071/
Hit CTRL-C to exit...
```

```
Http Functions:


HttpTrigger-Java: http://localhost:7071/api/HttpTrigger-Java


[23/09/2018 10:25:24] [INFO] {MessageHandler.handle}:↵
 Message generated by "StartStream.Builder"
[23/09/2018 10:25:24] Worker initialized
[23/09/2018 10:25:25] "HttpTrigger-Java" loaded
 (ID: 7115f6e7-f5de-475c-b196-089e6a6a2a89,
 Reflection: "/Users/danielbryant/Documents/dev/
 daniel-bryant-uk/tmp/ProductCatalogue/target/
 azure-functions/productcatalogue-20180923111807725/
 ProductCatalogue-1.0-SNAPSHOT.jar"::
 "uk.co.danielbryant.helloworldserverless.productcatalogue.Function.run")
[23/09/2018 10:25:28] Host lock lease acquired by
 instance ID '0000000000000000000000000826B7EEE'.
```

All of the HTTP functions that are available to call are displayed in the final stages of the `mvn azure-functions:run` output, along with the associated URL, e.g., "`HttpTrigger-Java: http://localhost:7071/api/HttpTrigger-Java`". You can call the locally running function using another terminal session and a tool like `curl`, as shown in Example 8-42. Note how the function accepts the data payload of `Local FunctionTest` as a parameter the `HttpTriggerJava` function, and returns this prefixed with the string `Hello`.

Example 8-42. Using curl to call the local Azure Function endpoint

```
$ curl -w '\n' -d LocalFunctionTest http://localhost:7071/api/HttpTrigger-Java
Hello, LocalFunctionTest
```

You can press Ctrl-C in the terminal session that is running the local function in order to stop the function executing.

If you have installed the VS Code editor you can also install the Azure Functions Extension (*http://bit.ly/2DwMwsH*) and Java Extension Pack (*http://bit.ly/2xR580l*), and run functions directly from the editor by pressing F5, as shown in Figure 8-3.

If you chose to run your functions using VS Code, you can also take advantage of the integrated debugging functionality. You do this by simply specifying break points in the margin of the appropriate line of Java code and calling the function endpoint via curl or another testing tool.

Figure 8-3. Running a Java Azure Function using the VS Code editor

Testing Remotely, Locally Using VS Code

In certain situations it can be very difficult to test your function locally. For example, you may have a dependency on a service running within the cloud that is challenging to stub or mock in a realistic way. Azure Functions make it relatively easy to debug a Java function running remotely in a cloud deployment.

To follow along with this guide you will need to have signed up for an Azure account, and also have a valid subscription, free or otherwise. To log into Azure from VS Code you will have select "Sign In" from the Command Palette, and follow the device login flow (which is typically achieved by opening your default browser and directing you to the the Azure login page).

After signing in, click the "Deploy to Function App" button on the Azure panel or select this option from the Command Palette. After this, select the folder of the project you would like to deploy, and follow the prompts to configure your function project. Once the function is deployed you will see the associated endpoint displayed in the output window. You can then `curl` this endpoint as you did with the locally running function, as shown in Example 8-43.

Example 8-43. Curling an Azure Function deployed into the Azure cloud

```
$ curl -w '\n' https://product-catalogue-5438231.azurewebsites.net/↵
api/httptrigger-java -d AzureFunctionsRemote
Hello, AzureFunctionsRemote
```

In order to debug this function running remotely you will need to install the cloud-debug-tools utility via the Node Package Manager (NPM), as shown in Example 8-44.

Example 8-44. Installing the cloud-debug-tools via NPM

```
$ npm install -g cloud-debug-tools
```

Once this tool is installed, you can run the debug proxy tool in order to attach to the running Function on Azure, specifying the remote base URL for the function. Example 8-45 shows an example of this.

Example 8-45. Using the cloud-debug-tools dbgproxy

```
$ dbgproxy product-catalogue-5438231.azurewebsites.net
Function App:              "product-catalogue-5438231.azurewebsites.net"
Subscription:             "Pay-As-You-Go" (ID = "xxxx")
Resource Group:           "new-java-function-group"
Fetch debug settings:     done
done
done
Set JAVA_OPTS:            done
Set HTTP_PLATFORM_DEBUG_PORT: done
Remote debugging is enabled on "product-catalogue-5438231.azurewebsites.net"
[Server] listening on 127.0.0.1:8898

Now you should be able to debug using "jdb -connect com.sun.jdi.SocketAttach:↵
hostname=127.0.0.1,port=8898"
```

Once the proxy is connected to the running function, you can add a new debugging configuration in VS Code (specified within the *.vscode/launch.json* file) to attach to the local port opened by it.

Example 8-46. Example debug launch configuration for VS Code

```
{
    "name": "Attach to Azure Functions on Cloud",
    "type": "java",
    "request": "attach",
    "hostName": "localhost",
    "port": 8898
}
```

Now you can set a break point within VS Code and attach to your cloud function using the editor's debug panel functionality. When you call the remote function with the debugger attached you will be able to debug locally as is you were working in the cloud.

Summary

This chapter has explored how to best configure a local development environment for building and testing systems locally. You have explored the following techniques:

- Mocking, stubbing, and service virtualization to simulate dependencies that you may not have access to (e.g., for connectivity or resource reasons).

- The use of tooling like Vagrant to instantiate consistent and re-creatable VMs for local development.

- The use of container-focused tooling like minikube and Telepresence for creating consistent and easily debuggable environments for local and remote development.

- The use of support utilities included within AWS SAM Local to facilitate developing FaaS code and support infrastructure locally.

- Using the Azure cloud-debug-tools to run locally debug a remotely executing Azure Function Java application.

In the next chapter, you will learn about continuous integration and the first stages of creating a continuous delivery pipeline.

## CHAPTER 9

Continuous Integration: The First Steps in Creating a Build Pipeline

In this chapter, you will learn how to implement continuous integration (CI). You will learn why CI is important, and then explore the fundamental topic of version control systems (VCSs). You will also learn the basics of the Git-distributed VCS, and how best to organize your team to work with this tool. The topic of code reviewing can be challenging, but you will also explore some of the core benefits of doing this, along with a guide on how to get started. The final topic you will explore in this chapter is automating CI builds.

Why Continuous Integration?

Continuous integration (CI) is the practice of frequently integrating your new or changed code with the existing code repository, merging all working copies to a shared mainline or trunk regularly. The use of the word "regularly" here is open to interpretation, but to truly practice CI, this should be several times a day. A well-accepted best practice is to trigger code builds upon every commit made to a shared code repository, and to schedule a regular "nightly" build in order to catch any integration issues within externally modified systems or issues outside our control (e.g., a new security vulnerability being found within one of your dependencies).

The main aim of CI is to prevent integration problems, referred to as *integration hell* in early descriptions of extreme programming (XP), which is recognizable to many developers. In XP, CI was intended to be used in combination with automated unit tests written through the practice of test-driven development (TDD). After a series of local red-green-refactor coding loops were complete, you would typically run all unit tests within your local environment and verify that they had all passed before committing your new work to the mainline. By committing regularly, every developer can reduce the number of conflicting changes, and this helps to avoid the situation where your current work-in-progress unintentionally breaks another developer's work.

In modern CI, a development team typically uses a build server to implement the continuous processes of building and running automated tests and verification processes. In addition to executing unit and integration tests, a build server can also run static and dynamic code-quality validation, measure and profile performance, perform basic security verification, and extract and format documentation from the source code.

The CI process, along with this continuous application of quality control, aims to improve the repeatability and stability of software, and the velocity at which it can be delivered. In comparison with traditional approaches to software delivery, where the testing and quality assurance (much of it manual) is completed after the majority of the coding efforts, CI has the potential to find defects and help guide best practices much earlier in the application development life cycle.

Implementing CI

As discussed in Humble and Farley's *Continuous Delivery* book, several prerequisites must be met before you can practice CD:

Version control
> Everything must be committed to a single version-control repository: code, config, tests, data store scripts, build files, etc.

An automated build
> You need to be able to run your build process in an automated way from a local command line and remote continuous integration environment (build server).

Agreement of the team
> CI is a practice, and not a set of specific tools. Everyone on your team needs to be on board with the process, or this will not work.

In the remainder of this chapter, you will learn about each of these steps.

Centralized Versus Distributed Version-Control Systems

In the late 1990s and early 2000s, the use of centralized-version control systems (VCS), such as Concurrent Versions System (CVS) (*https://www.nongnu.org/cvs/*) and Apache Subversion (SVN) (*https://subversion.apache.org/*), became popular. Before the adoption of VCS, the storage of source code and the ability for multiple developers to collaborate on the same codebase was often implemented using bespoke solutions, and it was not uncommon to see an FTP repository with multiple gzipped files in the format of *source_v1.gz.tar*, *source_v2.gz.tar*, *source_v1_patch1.gz.tar*, etc.

Understandably, the operation and management of these systems were fraught with danger, and developers could not easily transfer their knowledge of working with source code management systems between different projects or organizations.

In 2005, Linus Torvalds, creator of Linux, released Git (*https://git-scm.com/*), a distributed version-control system (DVCS). Inspiration for Git was taken from Bit-Keeper and other earlier DVCSs, which although initially used to store source code for Linux kernel development, could not be used from April 2005 because of a change in licensing. Other DVCSs emerged at the same time as Git, including Mercurial (hg) (*https://www.mercurial-scm.org/*) and DCVS, with each being written in different languages and supporting subtly different design goals. However, the release of Git under the GNU v2 open source license and the choice of the Linux kernel development team to adopt this to manage their source code ultimately led to Git now being the DVCS tool of choice for the majority of developers.

Git repositories can be stored remotely; for example, on popular hosting sites like GitHub (*https://github.com/*) and Atlassian Bitbucket (*https://bitbucket.org/*). Each developer can clone a repository to their personal development machine, and this gives them a local copy of the full development history. Changes can be copied from one such repository to another, and these changes imported as added development branches that can be merged in the same way as a locally developed branch. Git supports rapid branching and merging, and includes specific tools for visualizing and navigating a nonlinear development history. In Git, a core assumption is that a change will be merged more often than it is written, because newly committed code will be passed around to various reviewers.

Compared to older VCS technologies, branches in Git are lightweight, and a branch is simply a reference to one commit. However, the flip side of this "cheapness" of branch creation is that it can be tempting for developers working on larger features to create long-lived branches that may diverge away from the mainline, or trunk, branch.

Many open source and commercial projects use hosting sites like GitHub to not only provide a canonical copy of the source code for continuous integration and delivery, but also to act as a central hub for contributor management, documentation, and issue tracking. You'll be getting a firsthand tour of GitHub when using the examples throughout this book. However, don't worry if you choose to use another hosted platform, as the core concepts of version control and project collaboration should apply to all DVCS hosting sites.

Stuck with a Centralized VCS? Consider Upgrading

If you are stuck using a centralized version control system like VCS or SVN, we highly recommend experimenting with a decentralized system like Git. Many great tutorials are on the internet, such as Code School's Git tutorial (*https://try.github.io/levels/1/challenges/1*) (sponsored by GitHub), and the benefits are numerous. There are also many comprehensive guides and tools for migrating an existing code repository to Git, such as the official Git documentation's guide Migrating to Git (*https://git-scm.com/book/en/v2/Git-and-Other-Systems-Migrating-to-Git*), for SVN and Perforce repositories (alongside several other more esoteric VCSs), and Git for CVS Users (*https://git-scm.com/docs/gitcvs-migration*), which contains an overview of migrating from CVS alongside several example commands.

Git Primer

You will be using Git a lot within the examples in this book, and therefore it makes sense to learn the basics of operating the tool. The Git system itself is extremely flexible and powerful. Much like the game of chess, it is easy to learn but difficult to master.

Additional Resources

Because of the space limitations (and scope) of this book, you will learn only the very basics of Git. If you would like to learn more, we recommend *Version Control with Git, 2nd Edition* (O'Reilly) by Jon Loeliger and Matthew McCullough. The Git documentation (*https://git-scm.com/doc*) is also excellent, with a complete reference site, as well as a full online copy of *Pro Git* (Apress) by Scott Chacon and Ben Straub.

Core Git CLI Commands

You will need to make sure you have Git installed on your local development machine, either via your favorite package manager, or by downloading a binary from the Git website (*https://git-scm.com/book/en/v2/Getting-Started-Installing-Git*).

Initializing and working with a repo (history)

You can initialize a new Git repo within a new (or current) directory like so:

```
$ git init
```

This creates a hidden directory within the current directory that contains all the repo data. You can also add a *.gitignore* file at this point, which will configure Git to ignore, or not track, changes to certain files.

Don't Include Secret Files or Local Config

It is vitally important that you do not commit secrets, such as database access passwords or cloud vendor credentials, within Git—even if this is a private repository. This is a dangerous security vulnerability, and it can easily be exploited if the repo is ever made public or a bad actor gains access to the repo. It is also important not to include local configuration files that are unique to you, and this includes your IDE config files. You filesystem path details may be different from those of other developers (along with other information), which can cause merge conflicts when your teammates attempt to commit code.

An example Java *.gitignore* file is shown in Example 9-1. This file is commonly used to avoid tracking unwanted Java and Maven files in addition to IntelliJ project files.

Example 9-1. Java .gitignore file

```
### Java ###
# Compiled class file
*.class

# Package Files #
*.jar
*.war
*.ear
*.zip
*.tar.gz
*.rar

# Log file
*.log

### Maven ###
target/

# IntelliJ-specific stuff:
.idea
*.iml
/out/
```

The *.gitignore* file you will want to use may vary between projects, but always make sure you have at least a skeleton file, as you will rarely want to track every single file within a repository.

Generating .gitignore Files

You can generate comprehensive *.gitignore* files via gitignore.io (*https://www.gitignore.io/*). This website allows you to specify all the platforms and tooling within your project (e.g., Java, Maven, IntelliJ) and create a ready-to-use *.gitignore* file!

If you are working with a remote repository, you can clone the repo like so:

```
$ git clone <repo_name>
```

By default, this will create a directory with the name of the repo within the current directory.

You can attempt to update your local copy of this repo at any time by issuing a pull against the repo:

```
$ git pull origin <branch_name>
```

Once you have your local copy of a Git repo, you can add files to the staging area before committing them, like so:

```
$ git add . #add all files recursively within the current directory
```

```
$ git add <specific_file_or_dir>
```

To see what files have been added to the staging area, as well as what changes have been made within locally tracked files, you query for the status, like so:

```
$ git status
```

You can remove files that have been added to the staging area:

```
$ git rm <specific_file_or_dir> --cached # keep the local copy of the file or dir
```

```
$ git rm <specific_file_or_dir> -f # force removal of the local file or dir
```

You can commit new or updated files that are located within the staging area:

```
$ git commit -m "Add meaningful commit message"
```

If this repo is tracking a remote repository, you can attempt to push your commits like so (you'll learn more about potential merge conflicts in the following subsection):

```
$ git push origin master
```

Finally, you can also view the log or history of commits within a repo:

```
$ git log
```

Branching and merging

You can create a new branch and switch to this by issuing the following command:

```
$ git checkout -b <new_branch_name>
```

You can switch back to the master branch, and then to the new_branch like so:

```
$ git checkout master
$ git checkout <new_branch_name>
```

You can push and pull branches to and from a remote repo:

```
$ git push origin <branch_name>
$ git pull origin <branch_name>
```

When you attempt to push or pull content to or from a remote repo, you may discover merge conflicts—differences between your local copy of the codebase and the current state of the remote codebase—which need to be resolved. This often involves manually updating or editing your local copy of the codebase, or using an automated tool (often contained within modern IDEs) to perform the merge.

Because of the scope of this book, you will need to consult "Additional Resources" on page 206 to find additional information on merging. There are also many other useful Git practices to learn, such as rebasing your work against a repo that has had additional work committed since you last pulled a local copy, squashing commits to present more coarse-grained units of work, and cherrypicking individual commits from a complicated Git branch history.

Hub: An Essential Tool for Git and GitHub

Many public DVCS repositories exist online, such as Bitbucket and GitLab, but the one we find ourselves using the most is GitHub. Therefore, we are keen to share a few of the tools that have been useful to our teams. Hub is a command-line tool written by the GitHub team that wraps Git in order to extend it with extra features and commands that make working with GitHub easier. Hub can be downloaded from *github.com/github/hub*.

Once the tool is installed, cloning a repo from GitHub is then as simple as Example 9-2.

Example 9-2. Cloning a remote GitHub repo

```
$ hub clone <username_or_org>/<repo_name>
```

You can also easily browse the issues or wiki page within your default browser, as shown in Example 9-3.

Example 9-3. Loading the issues or wiki page within your default browser

```
$ hub browse <username_or_org>/<repo_name> issues
$ hub browse <username_or_org>/<repo_name> wiki
```

You can also issue pull requests (PRs) from the command line, as shown in Example 9-4.

Example 9-4. Issuing a pull request from the CLI

```
$ hub pull-request
→ (opens a text editor for your pull request message)
```

Because Hub simply wraps and extends the default Git CLI tool, Hub is best aliased as Git. You can type $ `git <command>` in the shell and get access to all of the usual Git commands, as well as the Hub features; see Example 9-5.

Example 9-5. Aliasing Hub to Git

```
$ alias git=hub
$ git version
git version 2.14.1
hub version 2.2.9
```

With the Git alias now in place, a typical workflow for contributing to a project looks similar to Example 9-6.

Example 9-6. Workflow with Hub aliased to Git

```
# Example workflow for contributing to a project:
$ git clone github/hub
$ cd hub
# create a topic branch
$ git checkout -b feature
  ( making changes ... )
$ git commit -m "done with feature"

# It's time to fork the repo!
$ git fork
→ (forking repo on GitHub...)
→ git remote add YOUR_USER git://github.com/YOUR_USER/hub.git

# push the changes to your new remote
$ git push YOUR_USER feature
# open a pull request for the topic branch you've just pushed
$ git pull-request
→ (opens a text editor for your pull request message)
```

Working Effectively with DVCS

Like any tool, a DVCS requires learning and experience to use it effectively. In this section, you will learn more about the overarching development and collaboration workflows you can use when working with Git. Essentially, a *Git workflow* is a recipe or recommendation for how to use Git to get work done in a consistent and productive manner. This is especially important if you are working within a large team, as it is all too easy to "step on others' toes" and accidentally create a merge conflict or unwind someone's changes.

Given Git's focus on flexibility, there is no standardized process for interacting with the tool, although there are several publicized Git workflows that may be a good fit for your team. To ensure that the team is aligned on the collaboration strategy, we recommend agreeing upon a Git workflow when starting any project.

Learn More About Workflows with Atlassian

Although you will learn the essentials of the various strategic approaches to working with a DVCS in this chapter, if you would like to learn more, we highly recommend the Atlassian tutorials (*https://www.atlassian.com/git/tutorials/syncing*).

Trunk-based Development

The *trunk-based*, or *centralized*, workflow is an effective Git workflow for teams transitioning from older VCS such as Subversion or CVS. Like SVN, the centralized workflow uses a central repository to serve as the single point of entry for all changes to the project. Instead of the name *trunk*, the default development branch is called *master*, and all changes are committed to this branch. This workflow doesn't require any other branches to exist besides master. You begin the trunk-based development process by cloning the central repository, and within your own local copies of the project, you can edit files and commit changes as you would with SVN. However, these new commits are stored locally, and they are completely isolated from the central repository. This lets you defer synchronizing your changes with the remote master branch until you are in a position to merge code.

Once the repository is cloned locally, you can make changes by using the standard Git commit process: edit, stage, and commit. If you're not familiar with the staging area, it essentially provides a holding area that allows you to prepare a commit without having to include every change in the working directory. This also lets you create highly focused commits through the use of *squashing*, even if you've made a lot of local changes initially across multiple commits. To publish changes to the official project, you "push" your local master branch to the central repository's master branch. When attempting to push changes to the central repository, it is possible that updates from another developer have been previously pushed that contain code conflicting with the intended push updates. Git will output a message indicating this conflict. In this situation, you will need to `git pull` to get the other developer's changes locally and begin merging or *rebasing*.

Feature Branching

The core idea behind the *feature-branch workflow* is that all feature development should take place in a dedicated branch instead of the master branch. This encapsulation of changes makes it easy for multiple developers to work on a particular feature without disturbing the main codebase. It also means that your master branch will never contain broken code, which is an advantage if you are using continuous integration. Encapsulating feature development also makes it possible to use PRs, which are a way to initiate discussions around a branch. PRs provide other developers on your team with the opportunity to sign off on or *+1* a feature before it gets integrated into the codebase.

The feature branch workflow assumes a central repository, and the master branch here represents the official project history. You create a new branch every time you start work on a new feature, and feature branches should have descriptive names, like *cart-service*, *paypal-checkout-integration*, or *issue-#452*. The idea is to specify a clear purpose for each branch, and this makes reviewing and tidying up branches much easier at a later date. Git makes no technical distinction between the master branch and feature branches, so you can edit, stage, and commit changes to a feature branch, and feature branches can (and should) be pushed to the central repository. This not only provides a backup against losing locally stored code, but also makes it possible for you to share a work-in-progress feature with other developers without touching any of the code within the master branch. Because master is the only "special" branch, storing several feature branches on the central repository should not pose any problems.

The workflow with the feature branching approach is relatively straightforward: start with the master branch; create a new feature branch; update, commit, and push changes; push the feature branch to remote; issue a PR; start discussion (if necessary) and resolve any feedback; merge or rebase the pull request; and, finally, delete the feature branch in order to save storage space and prevent confusion with later work.

Gitflow

Gitflow is a Git workflow that was first published and made popular by Vincent Driessen at nvie. The Gitflow workflow defines a strict branching model designed around the project release, and this type of workflow can be useful for collaboration across a large team working on a single codebase. Gitflow is also ideally suited for projects that have a scheduled release cycle or want to deploy using a *release train* approach of queueing up features into batches.

This workflow doesn't add any new concepts or commands beyond what is required for the feature-branch workflow. Instead, it assigns well-defined roles to different branches and specifies how and when they should interact. In addition to the use of feature branches, it also makes use of individual branches for preparing, maintaining, and recording releases. You get all the benefits of the feature-branch workflow: pull requests, isolated experiments, and more efficient collaboration.

Instead of a single master branch, Gitflow uses two branches to record the history of the project. The *master branch* stores the official release history (ideally, each commit contains a release version number), and the *develop branch* serves as an integration branch for features and will contain the complete history of the project.

When starting work, you clone the central repository and create a tracking branch for develop. Each new feature should reside in its own branch, which can be pushed to the central repository for the purposes of collaboration or as a backup. However, instead of branching off master, feature branches use develop as their parent branch; features should never interact directly with master. When you're finished with the development work on the feature, you merge the feature branch into the remote copy of develop. Because other developers are also merging features to the develop branch, you often will have to merge or rebase your feature onto the updated content of the develop branch.

Once the develop branch has acquired enough features for a release (or an iteration release date is approaching), you fork a release branch off the develop branch. Creating this branch starts the next release cycle, which means that no new features can be added after this point—only bug fixes, documentation generation, and other release-oriented tasks should go in this branch. Once the release is ready to be deployed, the release branch gets merged into master and tagged with a version number. In addition, it should be merged back into develop, which may have progressed since the release was initiated. Using a dedicated branch to prepare releases makes it possible for one team to finalize the current release while another team continues working on features for the next release.

In addition to the abstract Gitflow workflow strategy described here, a git-flow (*https://github.com/nvie/gitflow*) toolset is available that integrates with Git to provide specialized Gitflow Git command-line tool extensions.

No One-Size Fits All: How to Choose a Branching Strategy

When evaluating a workflow for your team, it's most important that you consider your team's culture. You want the workflow to enhance the effectiveness of, and ability to collaborate within, your team, and not to be a burden that limits productivity.

The following are things to consider when evaluating a Git workflow:

Release cadence
> As stated by Jez Halford in a great article, Choosing a Git Branching Strategy (*http://bit.ly/2xFW5jD*), the more often you release, the nearer your commits or feature branches should be to the trunk or master. If you are releasing features every day (or planning to), trunk-based development can provide the least

friction to the developer experience. However, if you release once every two weeks, say, at the end of a sprint or development iteration, then it makes more sense to merge to a *holding* branch (like Gitflow's develop and release branches) before code is merged into the trunk or master.

Testing

Continuing from Halford's article, development teams often use one of two approaches with testing: early-stage QA or late-stage QA. The early approach means that a feature is tested before it is merged; the late means that a feature is typically tested afterward. If your QA occurs early, you should probably have your feature branch close to the mainline. If it's late, a release branch is probably where your QA should take place, so that failures can be rectified before they reach the master. This approach is further impacted by the integration tests if you are working with a distributed (microservice or FaaS-based) system, which often skews testing requirements to the late stage (although the use of contract tests can mitigate this, as you will learn in "Consumer-Driven Contracts" on page 305).

The size of your team

Generally speaking, the larger a team that is working on a single codebase is, the further away your feature branches should be from the master. This assumes that the team is working on a codebase that is somewhat coupled, which often results in merge conflicts occurring as many developers are working on the same area of code. If you are working on a small team, or the application has been divided into loosely coupled modules or services, then it may be more appropriate to embrace trunk-based or feature branch–driven development in order to increase velocity.

Workflow cognitive overhead

In regards to practicing Gitflow, there is definitely a learning overhead that comes with the strict and highly controlled coordination of feature implementation. Not every team will be happy with the cognitive overhead (and extra process) that comes with a more complicated feature-branching workflow. However, it is worth noting that some of this complication can be overcome through the use of tooling.

In summary, every branching strategy is a variation on the theme of keeping code out of your (releasable) master or trunk branch until you want it there, balanced against the friction caused by having lots of branches that can be in an unmerged (and potentially unmergable) state.

Long-Lived Branches Can Be Unproductive

Much of Jez Humble's work argues that using long-lived branches leads to a loss of productivity. In *The DevOps Handbook*, Humble quotes Jeff Atwood, founder of the Stack Overflow site, that although there are many branching strategies, they can be put on a spectrum, with "optimize for individual productivity" at one end, and "optimize for team productivity" at the other. Optimizing for individual productivity, where in the extreme everyone works in their own private branch, can lead to merge hell when it comes time to integrate work.

Nicole Forsgren and Jez Humble also state in their book *Accelerate* that their research has shown that (independent of team size and industry) optimizing for team productivity and developing off trunk was correlated with higher delivery performance.

Paraphrasing Halford's article one more time, if your instinct is to avoid merging until the last minute, think about why. Perhaps your team likes to work in isolation or team members don't trust each other to coordinate work within the codebase effectively. Therefore, you may need work to build trust, or to schedule development more carefully. Conversely, if you're having to undo merges and cherrypick things a lot, perhaps you and your team are too keen to merge. This often calls for a more structured workflow with steps for testing and review before release.

You Can Mix and Match Workflows (with Care!)

Although care should be taken not to create even more cognitive overhead, it is possible to use different workflows across distinct, logically separated, areas of a codebase such as services. We have seen this work on several microservice migration projects, where the rigor and structure of Gitflow was ideal for use by several product teams all working around the existing monolith, but as this workflow added a lot of overhead for work on the new (less complicated and coupled) microservices, the teams working here decided to use trunk-based development.

Code Reviews

Code reviews are the process of at least one developer (and potentially more) reviewing the code written by another developer, and can be extremely valuable. The obvious benefit to code reviews is that sometimes a fresh pair of eyes can catch issues or potential future issues that would be introduced into the codebase. The more subtle (and powerful) benefit of code reviews is that they promote the sharing of knowledge —not just idiomatic programming knowledge, but also information about the business domain. This can lead to improved conversations and collaboration between developers, and also helps limit the impact of vacation or sick days.

Much like pair programming, code reviews can be an excellent mechanism for mentoring new engineers, and can also promote better estimates. However, you also have to watch out for various negative patterns, such as not sharing the load fairly among the senior members of the team, getting stuck on esoteric or dogmatic style issues (e.g., tabs versus spaces), not reviewing before merging, and using reviews as an excuse to not get early feedback.

Pair Program for More-Efficient Reviews

One of the original practices of eXtreme Programming (XP) was *pair programming*, and the use of this can reduce or remove the need for other reviews. By ensuring that at least two people are writing all of the code and configuration together on one computer, you can get the benefits of reviewing in real time. The two roles of *driver* and *navigator* operate very differently during the coding process, and it is generally easier for one of the pair to identify an issue that a single programmer working on their own may not. For more information on this, and the benefits and principles of XP in general, please read Kent Beck's classic *Extreme Programming Explained: Embrace Change* (*http://bit.ly/2QcCQFe*) (Addison-Wesley).

What to Look For

Entire websites and books have been written on this topic, so we won't go into what you should look for when reviewing code in much detail. However, reviewing code doesn't come naturally to many developers, so this chapter contains a basic overview of key review patterns.

Learning More About Code Reviews

Robert Martin's *Clean Code* (Prentice-Hall) and *The Clean Coder* (Prentice-Hall) books both provide good insight into the code review process. Another useful book is *Best Kept Secrets of Peer Code Review* (Smart Bear) by Jason Cohen. Josh Bloch's *Effective Java* (Addison-Wesley Professional) should also be mandatory reading for any Java developer looking to conduct a code review. A portion of the review patterns within this chapter comes from the useful reference Java Code Review Checklist (*https://dzone.com/articles/java-code-review-checklist*) by Mahesh Chopker.

Understandability

Writing code that is understandable not only helps other developers on your team work with the code, but also often helps you in the future when you are revisiting a feature or bug. Unless you are working within a domain where performance is of the utmost importance (e.g., high-frequency trading), it is typically best practice to sacrifice performance for increased understandability. Example understandability issues to look out for in a code review include the following:

- Use solution/problem domain names.
- Use intention-revealing names.
- Minimize the accessibility of classes and members.
- Minimize the size of classes and methods.
- Minimize the scope of local variables.
- Don't Repeat Yourself (DRY) within a single logical component (a package, module, or service).
- Explain yourself in code.
- Use exceptions rather than esoteric error codes and don't return null.

Language-specific issues

Every language has idioms for accomplishing tasks that the majority of developers would expect to see, but often new developers are not aware of these. There are also specific antipatterns that developers would not expect to see in Java, so a good code review will look for these:

- Use checked exceptions for recoverable conditions and runtime exceptions for programming errors.
- Check parameters for validity as close to their specification or associated user input as possible.
- Indicate which parameters can be null.
- In public classes, use accessor methods, not public fields.
- Refer to objects by their interfaces.
- Use enums instead of int constants.
- Use marker interfaces to define types.
- Synchronize access to shared mutable data.
- Prefer executors to tasks and threads.
- Document thread safety.

Security

The issue of security is of vital importance. Several common mistakes can be searched for during a code review:

- Input into a system should be checked for valid data size and range, and always sanitize any input that will be supplied to a data store, middleware, or third-party system.
- Do not log highly sensitive information.
- Purge sensitive information from exceptions (e.g., do not expose file paths, internals of the system, or configuration).
- Consider purging highly sensitive data from memory after use.
- Follow the principle of least privilege (e.g., run an application with the least privilege mode required for the correct functioning).
- Document security-related information.

Performance

Code reviews can be a good tool for detecting obvious performance issues. Here are several example issues to be aware of:

- Watch for inefficient algorithms (e.g., unnecessary multiple loops).
- Avoid creating unnecessary objects.
- Beware of the performance penalty of string concatenation.
- Avoid excessive synchronization and keep synchonized blocks as small as practical.
- Watch for potential deadlocks or livelocks in algorithms.
- Ensure that thread-pool configuration and caching is configured correctly.

Automation: PMD, Checkstyle, and FindBugs

Much of the fundamentals of code reviewing can be automated by static code analysis tooling like PMD, Checkstyle, and FindBugs. Automation not only increases reliability in the detection of issues, but it also frees time for developers to conduct code reviews that focus on aspects of code that humans excel at, such as reviewing in the context of the bigger picture, or mentoring a fellow engineer with guidelines and maxims on best practice.

Watch for False Positives

All of the code-quality automation tools in this section can result in *false positives* when an issue or bug is flagged incorrectly. This often occurs when using some of the more esoteric dependencies within your Java application, or when you are optimizing code for performance reasons. All of the tools can be configured to minimize these false positives, so don't be discouraged if you add automated code-analysis tools to a project and nonissues are found. Usually, after a few runs, you can easily identify the false positives and adapt accordingly.

Maven Enforcer: Codifying Best Practice with the Build

Although not a static code scanner, the Maven Enforcer plugin (*http://bit.ly/2O6EPJC*) provides useful goals to control certain environmental constraints such as Maven version, JDK version, and OS family along with many more built-in rules; for example:

banDistributionManagement
: Enforces that the project doesn't have distributionManagement.

bannedDependencies
: Enforces that excluded dependencies aren't included.

requireActiveProfile
: Enforces one or more active profiles.

requireEnvironmentVariable
: Enforces the existence of an environment variable.

requireJavaVersion
: Enforces the JDK version.

requireNoRepositories
: Enforces not to include repositories.

requireOS
: Enforces the OS/CPU architecture.

requireReleaseDeps
: Enforces that no snapshots are included as dependencies.

requireReleaseVersion
: Enforces that the artifact is not a snapshot.

There are many more useful rules, and you can also create your own custom rules if you want to enforce something else. The Maven Enforcer plugin is perhaps at its most powerful when specified in a parent POM. Otherwise, it can be challenging to maintain consistency across projects, or sometimes even to ensure that the plugin is run on each project.

PMD: static code analyzer

PMD (*https://pmd.github.io/*) is a static source code analyzer. According to the project's website, it finds common programming flaws like unused variables, empty catch blocks, unnecessary object creation, unused private methods, and a host of other bad practices. PMD features many built-in checks, or *rules*, and an API is provided to allow you to build your own. PMD is most useful when integrated into your CI process, because it can then be used as a quality gate, to enforce a coding standard for your codebase. Example 9-7 illustrates utilizing a Maven plugin to run PMD automatically during the verify phase of the build.

Example 9-7. Running the maven-pmd-plugin within a build

```
<project>
  ...
  <build>
    <plugins>
      <plugin>
        <groupId>org.apache.maven.plugins</groupId>
        <artifactId>maven-pmd-plugin</artifactId>
        <configuration>
            <failOnViolation>true</failOnViolation>
            <printFailingErrors>true</printFailingErrors>
        </configuration>
        <executions>
          <execution>
            <goals>
              <goal>check</goal>
            </goals>
          </execution>
        </executions>
      </plugin>
    </plugins>
  </build>
  ...
</project>
```

In addition to running PMD as a build plugin, you can also configure it to be run during the reporting phase. The PMD website contains many configuration options, and we refer you to that site to learn more.

Checkstyle: coding standard enforcement

Checkstyle (*http://checkstyle.sourceforge.net/cmdline.html*) is a development tool to help you write Java code that adheres to a coding standard. It automates the process of checking Java code to spare humans of this boring (but important) task. Checkstyle is highly configurable and can be made to support almost any coding standard.

Please Don't Argue over Tabs or Spaces

Using a tool like Checkstyle to enforce coding standards is a great way to promote readability and understandability across a codebase, but the tool needs to be configured to a single style. Some developers are very opinionated about coding styles, which can lead to wasteful arguments over which style is best. Our advice is to have a quick discussion at the start of a project, choose a style, enforce this with Checkstyle, and then never debate about this again. Examples of good Java programming styles include Google's (*http://bit.ly/2zx0F5f*) and Sun's (*http://bit.ly/2OcQOJJ*) (now Oracle's).

Checkstyle can be run as a Maven plugin that will fail the build upon violations to the style defined; see Example 9-8.

Example 9-8. Running the maven-checkstyle-plugin within a build

```
<project>
  ...
  <build>
    <plugins>
      <plugin>
        <groupId>org.apache.maven.plugins</groupId>
        <artifactId>maven-checkstyle-plugin</artifactId>
        <executions>
          <execution>
            <goals>
              <goal>check</goal>
            </goals>
          </execution>
        </executions>
      </plugin>
      ...
    </plugins>
  </build>
  ...
</project>
```

Much like PMD, Checkstyle can be configured in a variety of ways, and the project's website is the best source of guidance.

FindBugs: Static analyzer for bugs

FindBugs (*http://findbugs.sourceforge.net/*) is another static code analyzer for Java applications, and this tool operates at the Java bytecode level. PMD and FindBugs share many similarities, but each has its own strengths and weakness due to the way they are implemented. FindBugs identifies issues in three categories: *correctness bugs*, an apparent coding mistake resulting in code that was probably not what you intended; *bad practice*, indicating violations of recommended and essential coding practice; and *dodgy*, code that is confusing, anomalous, or written in a way that lends itself to errors.

FindBugs May Be Superseded by SpotBugs

According to Wikipedia, the last stable release of FindBugs was in 2015, which is quite a long time in the world of software. A successor named SpotBugs (*https://spotbugs.github.io/*) has been created, which is being kept up-to-date via a community effort. For new projects, you may benefit from using this tool instead.

FindBugs is best run as part of your build process, and an example of configuring this via Maven is included in Example 9-9.

Example 9-9. Running the findbugs-maven-plugin within a build

```
<project>
  ...
  <build>
    <plugins>
      <plugin>
        <groupId>org.codehaus.mojo</groupId>
        <artifactId>findbugs-maven-plugin</artifactId>
        <executions>
          <execution>
            <goals>
              <goal>check</goal>
            </goals>
          </execution>
        </executions>
      </plugin>
      ...
    </plugins>
  </build>
  ...
</project>
```

FindBug also has extensive reporting capabilities and configuration options. The best reference to learn more about this is the project's website.

Reviewing Pull Requests

Modern self-hosted or SaaS-based DVCSs like GitHub and GitLab allow developers to not only create pull requests, but also facilitate discussion around these requests. An example of this is shown in Figure 9-1. These features allow developers to review changes asynchronously at their convenience, or when conversations about a change can't happen face-to-face. They also help to create a record of the conversation around a given change, which can provide a history of when a change was made and why. Metadata can also be added to a discussion manually or automatically via a CI tool through the use of labels, indicating, for example, that a discussion relates to a specific bug.

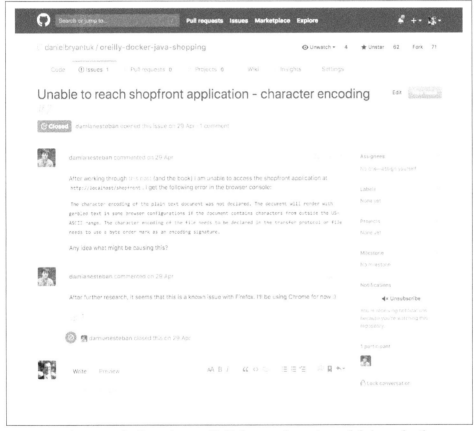

Figure 9-1. An example discussion on GitHub; note the assignee, labels, and milestones metadata that can be assigned to the issue

All of the rules you have learned about code reviews so far apply to this style of reviewing. Just because you may not be in the same office (building or country) does not mean you shouldn't seek to empathize with the developer who created the code.

Automating Builds

You will explore more about automating builds in the next chapter focused on deploying and releasing from the pipeline, but this is also a critical process within CI. Although build tooling like Maven and Gradle allow each developer to run the build process on their local machine, there still needs to be a centralized place in which all of the integrated code is built. This is typically achieved by using a build server, such as Jenkins or TeamCity, or a build service, such as CircleCI or Travis CI.

Jenkins

The code examples in the repository found at *https://github.com/danielbryantuk/oreilly-docker-java-shopping* include a directory that is called *ci-vagrant*. Within this directory is a Vagrant script for initializing a Jenkins build server VM. Providing you have Vagrant and a virtualization platform like Oracle VirtualBox installed, you can initialize the Jenkins instance by using the `vagrant up` command from this directory. After 5–10 minutes (depending on your internet connection speed and computer CPU speed), you will be presented with the Setup Wizard for a fresh Jenkins instance. You can accept the defaults and create an admin user for yourself. Once everything has been configured, you should see a screen similar to Figure 9-2.

Figure 9-2. Jenkins welcome page

You can then create a basic Java "freestyle project" build job for each of the services within the main oreilly-docker-java-shopping repository: stockmanager, productcatalogue, and shopfront. Figure 9-3 demonstrates the configuration parameters required for each job: the GitHub repository URL, the build triggers, and the Maven *pom.xml* location and build target.

Figure 9-3. An example Jenkins build job for the Shopfront services

The next chapter provides much more detail on creating build jobs, which also includes building Java applications that will be deployed within container images.

Other Build/CI Servers and Services

Many other free and commercial CI tools exist, some of which you can download and run on your own infrastructure, like TeamCity and GoCD, and some of which can be consumed as a service, such as Travis CI, CircleCI and Azure Pipelines. This book focuses on using Jenkins, because this is the tool that we have most encountered when working with organizations building and deploying Java code.

Getting Your Team Onboard

Continuous integration is a practice, not a tool, in and of itself. Therefore, everyone on your team must be on board with contributing to this way of working. Several practices in particular can make or break a team's success with implementing CI.

Merge Code Regularly

Code must be integrated into the trunk or master regularly—ideally, daily. It takes only one developer who is working on a critical feature and decides to create a long-lived branch to create havoc. Typically, the issues start during the merge process, and sometimes code already committed into the trunk can be accidentally lost.

If you are acting as a team lead, part of your job will be to regularly ensure that no branches are becoming long-lived within your VCS system. This is relatively easy if you are using a DVCS and associated service like GitHub, because a nice UI is provided that shows all branches currently not in sync with the trunk. But this does rely on all local branches being committed at least once.

"Stop the Line!": Managing Broken Builds

When many developers are integrating their code to a single trunk or master branch, there are bound to be merge conflicts and accidental breaking of the build or CI process. It is vital that fixing any breakage is top priority, even if this means reverted code is committed. It does not take long for a team to ignore the output from a build server if it is constantly broken, and then your development process effectively reverts to what it was before CI—everyone working on their own branches.

The simple rule to enforce among your team is that upon any build failure, the person or persons responsible should be notified (either via development dashboards or, ideally, via IM such as Slack), and they must immediately fix the issue. If they cannot fix the problem, they must escalate this or ask other teams involved for assistance.

Don't @Ignore Tests

Another temptation for teams is to mark failing tests within the trunk or master branch as ignore—not to be run (@Ignore in JUnit). Doing this is dangerous, as although the tests appear in the codebase, they are not providing any verification or value.

Much like the issues mentioned with a regularly broken build server, the ignoring of tests can quickly spread, as developers are happily marking any failing tests that they did not write as ignorable. The next, even more insidious, step is developers commenting out (or physically deleting) tests because the test code will no longer compile even though it is ignored at execution time.

The rule that must be enforced here is that anyone who checks in code to the trunk and causes a test failure is responsible for fixing this, even if it means communicating this to, or working with, another team.

Keep the Build Fast

The final piece of advice in this section is to keep the build fast. There are several reasons for doing this. First, having a slow build means that there is more time for things to change between the start of a build and its completion. This is especially an issue when the build fails. For example, other developers could have committed code to the trunk after the code you committed triggered the build. If the build takes too long, it is highly likely that you will have moved on to other work before you realize that the build has failed, so not only will you have to context switch, but you may also need to reconfigure your local development environment.

Second, having a long build process can become an issue when you need to quickly build and deploy a hot fix to production. The immediate need to address a customer facing issues often results in engineers not running the associated test suite or otherwise trying to shortcut the build process, which can lead to a slippery slope of more and more shortcuts being taken that result in a trade-off of time versus stability.

CI of the Platform (Infrastructure as Code)

The scope of this book prevents going into much detail about the continuous integration and delivery of infrastructure, but it goes almost without saying that CI and CD of infrastructure are vitally important. Kief Morris (*https://twitter.com/kief*) has discussed the concepts, practices, and importance of CD pipelines when creating platforms in his O'Reilly book, *Infrastructure as Code*. This is a highly recommended read, particularly if you are (or are an aspiring) technical lead or architect. You won't become a Terraform or Ansible expert after reading this book, but you will develop a good understanding of the principles, practices, and tooling required for the continuous delivery of platforms.

Simultaneous Continuous Delivery of Application and Infrastructure Code Can Cause Problems

We have worked on several projects with multiple application and infrastructure teams, where each team was responsible for either an application domain (or service) or components of the "platform" we were deploying onto. This can cause issues, particularly if the platform is evolving as rapidly as the application. Often when the engineering team is bootstrapping a product or project, the platform (such as Kubernetes and the associated infrastructure pieces like configuration management and service discovery) is still being assembled. The same can be said when migrating to a new platform.

This can cause headaches for the development team, because not only are the application components changing and causing friction between teams, but so is the underlying deployment fabric. This can lead to lots of "murder mystery" style debugging sessions, where a development team isn't sure who broke the build: was it them, a fellow development team, or the platform team? In our experience, this has to be managed carefully. Our recommendation is to have separate CI/CD pipelines and environments for the development and platform teams.

When a new release of the platform is ready, this should be gated for approval by the team leads within the development teams, and the platform team should present its new features and any breaking changes before deploying the latest platform code into a dev or QA environment.

Summary

In this chapter, you have learned about several core components to implementing continuous delivery, both from a technical and team perspective:

- The use of a distributed version-control systems (DVCS) such as Git is highly recommended for managing code within a modern continuous delivery pipeline. If you are still using a centralized VCS, we strongly recommend upgrading to a DVCS.

- Numerous DVCS workflows have been discussed and shared on the internet. Choose one that is appropriate based on your organization's requirements, your application architecture, and your team's skills.

- Utilize appropriate tooling for your DVCS workflow (e.g., use GitHub/Hub for branch-by-feature, and nvie/Gitflow for Gitflow).

- Automate all builds and ensure that the build process runs both locally and remotely on a centralized build server like Jenkins or TravisCI.

- When the build is broken, the highest priority of the team should be to fix the current issue. Never check in more code on a broken build. As soon as people believe the build server is unreliable, the adherence to the workflow and code quality will rapidly decline, ultimately causing big issues in the future.

- Any infrastructure (as code) that is required for the creation and operation of the deployment platform (e.g., cloud computing environments or a Kubernetes cluster) should be continuously delivered. Careful management of the collaboration and delivery of code between the development and infrastructure team is required, particularly for projects using a new platform or migrating onto a new platform.

So far, you have developed a firm foundation in the principles and practices of continuous integration. Let's now extend these skills with the implementation of a complete continuous delivery pipeline.

## CHAPTER 10

Deploying and Releasing from the Pipeline

With firm foundations in automating builds and continuously integrating code, we can now focus on the delivery of valuable software to various environments, including production. A key lesson that you will learn is that today's business requirements and popular software architecture practices strongly encourage you to separate the processes of deployment (a technical activity, as you will see) and release (a business activity); in fact, we will talk about *deploying* an application, but *releasing* a feature. This has ramifications for the way you design, test, and continuously deliver software.

One aspect of software development that becomes critical after you start to consider different environments is configuration. The need to track different configuration values depending on the environment that you are using (development, test, pre-production, production...) isn't new, but tracking all these has become much harder with the advent of cloud-based platforms, since you may not know a priori where your application might be running. On top of this, a continuous delivery process might require frequent changes in configuration, meaning configuration management has to be at the heart of your deployment and release strategies.

Deploying, releasing, and managing configuration are some of the most challenging aspects of continuous delivery, and there is a lot of ground to cover. To help you go through all of it, we have created the Extended Java Shop application, which will demonstrate many of the concepts outlined in this chapter.

Introducing the Extended Java Shop Application

The example application presented in "Introducing the "Docker Java Shop" Sample App" on page 173 was used to demonstrate how to work locally using Docker containers and Kubernetes. In this chapter and in Chapter 11, we will use an extended version of this application, called the Extended Java Shop (*https://github.com/*

continuous-delivery-in-java/extended-java-shop), together with a small external library known as java-utils (*https://github.com/quiram/java-utils*). The Extended Java Shop also includes three prebuilt Jenkins pipelines that demonstrate how the different phases of testing are linked together, and how deployments can be made to different platforms.

The particulars of each part of the Extended Java Shop and its supporting libraries are explained in detail in the relevant sections that follow, but a general overview is illustrated in Figure 10-1. Note that the purpose of this sample application is to demonstrate concepts related to deploying, releasing, testing, and managing configuration, but this is not necessarily a production-ready application. Shortcuts have been taken for simplicity; wherever possible, these shortcuts will be highlighted, indicating how a production-ready application would be constructed.

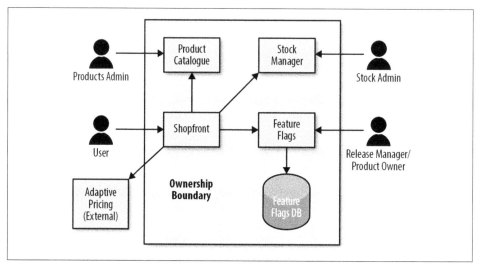

Figure 10-1. Architecture of the Extended Java Shop

The repository for the Extended Java Shop is a monorepo that includes the following:

Owned services
- Shopfront: The website that the user visits. This serves the same function as in the Docker Java Shop, with the exception that here it also communicates to a Feature Flags service and an Adaptive Pricing service.

- Product Catalogue: Holds information about each different product. It holds data in an in-memory database (in a real case scenario, the database would be real). Similar to its counterpart in the Docker Java Shop.

- Stock Manager: Holds available amounts for each product. It holds data in an in-memory database (in a real case scenario, the database would be real). Similar to its counterpart in the Docker Java Shop.

- Feature Flags: Holds information about the different feature flags and their activation levels. It stores its data in a real PostgreSQL database. New with regards to the Docker Java Shop.

"Third-party" services
- Adaptive Pricing: This is meant to represent a service provided by a third-party entity that the Shopfront service communicates with; in a real scenario, it wouldn't be part of our repository, nor would we have control over it. New with regards to the Docker Java Shop.
- Fake Adaptive Pricing: This is a "fake" Adaptive Pricing service, the sort a team would create to be able to test integration with a third party. This therefore would be part of our repository, and we'd have control over it. New with regards to the Docker Java Shop.

Databases
- Feature Flags DB: The production database used by the Feature Flags service. This is a PostgreSQL database running in a Docker container, although in a real-case scenario, the database wouldn't run in a container. New with regards to the Docker Java Shop.
- Test Feature Flags DB: The test database used by Feature Flags service, also a PostgreSQL database running in a Docker container, but using different credentials. New with regards to the Docker Java Shop.

Acceptance tests
A set of tests that puts all the owned services together and verifies that they work correctly. More on this in Chapter 11. New with regards to the Docker Java Shop.

Pipelines
- Jenkins Base: A prebuilt pipeline that automatically builds all the services and databases mentioned previously upon code changes, and then runs acceptance tests where needed. It includes a dummy deployment job (it doesn't really deploy anywhere). New with regards to the Docker Java Shop.
- Jenkins Kubernetes: An extension of Jenkins Base, where the deployment job has been overwritten to deploy services to a Kubernetes cluster. New with regards to the Docker Java Shop.
- Jenkins AWS ECS: A different extension of Jenkins Base, where the deployment job has been overwritten to deploy services to Amazon's Elastic Container Service. New with regards to the Docker Java Shop.

Exploring Deploy and Release for Serverless and IaaS

Because of the static nature and size limitations of a print book, this chapter focuses exclusively on the deployment and release of applications by using the technologies that appear to be the most popular at the time of writing: Docker, Kubernetes, and AWS ECS. The accompanying GitHub repository (*https://github.com/continuous-delivery-in-java*) contains more practical examples using serverless and IaaS technologies that have been talked about in previous chapters.

Separating Deployment and Release

Deployment and release are concepts that many people use as synonyms. However, in the context of continuous delivery, they mean different things:

Deployment
> A technical term that refers to the act of making a new binary package of a service available in production

Release
> A business term that refers to the act of making a particular functionality available to users

Deployments and releases many times happen at the same time—typically, when a new piece of functionality is implemented and then released into production as part of a deployment—but you can have one without the other. For instance, when a developer refactors a particular section of code without altering its functionality, and deploys this new version of code to production, we have a deployment without a release. You could also add new functionality but hide it away under a feature flag (see "Feature Flags" on page 274), in which case you also have a deployment without a release. On the other hand, if a feature is hidden behind a feature flag, and feature flags can be modified without deploying, then by altering the feature flag, you could be releasing a new functionality without the need of a deployment.

Understanding that deploying and releasing are two related but independent activities is crucial in order to create an environment for continuous delivery: it gives the development team the freedom to deploy new versions of the software as they need to, while it allows the product owners to keep full control over the features that are available to users. Because they are indeed different activities, they require different tools and techniques to make them happen in an effective manner; this is the focus of the next sections.

Deploying Applications

Although some aspects of the deployment will differ, depending on the platform that you are deploying services to, some concerns will be the same, regardless of said platform. In general, the deployment of an application will be influenced by the following activities:

Creating the releasable artifact

This is the binary file that will contain your application code (and potentially configuration—more on this in "Managing Configuration and Secrets" on page 285), and that will be sent to the machines where the application will be running. The releasable artifact can take many shapes (fat JAR, WAR, EAR, Buildpack, Docker container image, etc.), and the most suitable one will depend on the platform where your application is being deployed. In this book, we have decided to focus on Docker container images because of their flexibility and popularity, but you are free to try out others if you so wish.

Automating deployments

Years ago, when deployments happened only once a month, you could have a person manually copying your applications to the target server and restarting the application. With continuous delivery, you are potentially deploying a dozen times a day, and this is no longer practical.

Setting up health checks

An important drawback of the microservices architecture and cloud platforms is the increase in the number of moving parts. And more moving parts means a higher probability that something will go wrong. Your applications *will* fail, and you need to be able to detect it and fix it.

Choosing a deployment strategy

Whenever you need to make a new version of your application available to the public, there is the conundrum of how you are going to coordinate that with the removal of the existing version, especially if you run multiple parallel instances for reliability. A trade-off between complexity and functionality will need to be struck.

Implementing your deployment strategy

Latest cloud platforms can manage a cluster of machines and the deployment of your applications across them transparently, meaning you have to worry only about picking the strategy. However, if you are not in one of these platforms, you will have to implement the strategy yourself.

Working with databases

Continuous delivery affects everything, even databases, and changes will have to be brought about there, too. The process cannot be stopped for anything, so schema changes and data migrations will have to be executed from the pipeline as well.

Daunting as it may sound, managing the preceding factors is the key to unlocking the benefits of continuous delivery. Each activity has its own complexities and decision points; during the rest of this section, we will go through them and give you everything you need to set up your pipeline.

Creating a Container Image

Although packaging applications in a Docker image is certainly not the only way to deploy services into production, it is among the most popular ones. It is therefore useful to know how to create and publish a Docker image for your applications as part of the build pipeline, because then you will be able to use that image to deploy services. The image creation process is no different from the one outlined in "Creating Container Images with Docker" on page 151, although in the case of the build pipeline, you also have the option to wrap the command-line orders into a plugin.

This is the option that has been taken in the sample pipelines available in the Extended Java Shop repository, more particularly in folders *jenkins-base*, *jenkins-kubernetes*, and *jenkins-aws-ecs*. (See the relevant *README.md* files to execute these examples locally.) The creation and publication of the container image can then be performed with the following steps.

Installing the plugin

In this case, we are making use of the CloudBees Docker Build and Publish plugin (*https://plugins.jenkins.io/docker-build-publish*), which you can install either using the graphical interface (from the main page, choose Manage Jenkins and then Manage Plugins), or using the command line while logged into the Jenkins server:

```
/usr/local/bin/install-plugins.sh docker-build-publish
```

You need to restart Jenkins after this to activate the plugin.

Creating the DockerHub credentials

Unless you are publishing your Docker container images to a private repository that doesn't require authentication, you need to provide Jenkins with some kind of authentication mechanism when pushing each new container image. In fact, the CloudBees Docker Build and Publish plugin uses Docker Hub by default, so you need a Docker Hub account to proceed. Here are basic steps to do this in Jenkins:

1. Go to Credentials and then Add Credentials, as shown in Figure 10-2.

Figure 10-2. Creating new credentials in Jenkins

2. Select "Username with password" from the Kind drop-down menu.

3. Leave the scope as Global or restrict it to something more specifically aligned to your own security policies.

4. Give your credentials a meaningful name in the ID field, like **DockerHub**, and optionally a description.

5. Enter the username used to publish images.

6. Enter the password and then click OK. Figure 10-3 shows the selection of these options.

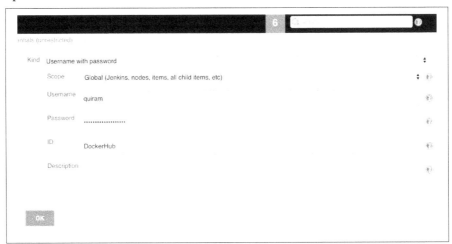

Figure 10-3. Adding new Docker Hub credential to Jenkins

Building and publishing

Finally, you can now create a step within your job definition to build the Docker container image and publish it into Docker Hub (or any other registry):

1. When adding the new step, select the type Docker Build and Publish to open the window shown in Figure 10-4.

2. Indicate the name that you want to give to the published image; this is equivalent to using the -t option in the command line when building the Docker image.

3. Indicate the credentials to use when pushing the image to Docker Hub.

Figure 10-4. Creating a new build step to build and publish a Docker image

4. If the necessary Dockerfile isn't in the root folder of your repository, indicate the folder where it is to be found, as shown in Figure 10-5.

Figure 10-5. Indicating the folder where the Dockerfile resides

With this, your build pipeline can now create Docker images for your applications in an automated manner, and you are ready to deploy them to your platform of choice.

Deployment Mechanisms

The first point to cover is the mechanism by which the service makes its way into production—in other words, the mechanism by which you communicate to the relevant platform and indicate that a new version is available. Once you know this, you can then configure your CD pipeline to do this automatically for you.

Most platforms out there, including Kubernetes, Amazon, and Cloud Foundry, have a RESTful API as their main means of communication that you can use to manage your deployments. However, this is not what most people use. In the same way that they provide a RESTful API, they also provide the following tools, built on top of this API, that make interaction easier:

A graphical interface

Usually in the form of a website, this is where deployments can be performed and managed. This is useful to get comfortable with the way a new platform works or to check the status of the platform at a quick glance, but not for deployment automation.

A command-line interface

Frequently including Bash completion, this interface acts as a wrapper for the RESTful API. The advantage of the CLI is that commands can easily be scripted, making it suitable for build automation.

On top of this, some platform providers, or sometimes even third parties, can develop plugins for different build automation tools that leverage either the RESTful API or the CLI to provide common use cases in a pipeline-friendly manner.

The plugin example: Kubernetes

As explained in Chapter 4, Kubernetes is an orchestrator platform for deploying immutable services encapsulated in containers. In Chapter 8, we already indicated how Docker and Kubernetes could be used to allow developers to work locally, mimicking a production environment. Now we will indicate how this deployment can be automated to deploy to the production Kubernetes cluster by using a plugin in Jenkins. A fully functional example is available at the Extended Java Shop repository—more precisely, at the *jenkins-kubernetes* folder. You can follow the instructions at the *README.md* file in that folder to run the example locally. (Incidentally, this example will also make use of a locally running minikube instance, but the process will be no different from a real-life Kubernetes cluster.)

Jenkins X: The Future?

As this book is going to print, the new open Jenkins X (*https://jenkins.io/projects/jenkins-x/*) subproject within the Jenkins Foundation is gaining momentum. Jenkins X is written by CloudBees, and many of the engineering team members have previously worked on the Red Hat fabric8 development tooling. The platform encompasses many of the recommended build and deployment practices they have encountered with customers deploying applications onto Kubernetes, such as declarative configuration, management of multiple environments, and GitOps (*https://www.weave.works/technologies/gitops/*) (automated synchronizing of config against environments).

Installing the plugin. First, you need to install the Kubernetes CD Jenkins plugin (*https://github.com/jenkinsci/kubernetes-cd-plugin*). Once again, this can be done using the graphical interface in Jenkins (from the main page, choose Manage Jenkins and then Manage Plugins) or via the command line at the Jenkins server:

```
/usr/local/bin/install-plugins.sh kubernetes-cd
```

You need to restart Jenkins after this to activate the plugin.

Kubernetes Plugin Versus Kubernetes CD Plugin

The Jenkins Plugin repository includes two similarly named but fundamentally different plugins: *Kubernetes* and *Kubernetes CD*. The former allows you to create additional Jenkins nodes in an existing Kubernetes cluster so as to assist on build execution, while the latter allows you to deploy your applications into a Kubernetes cluster. We are referring to the latter here.

Preparing the configuration files. Before diving into details, it's necessary to clarify some extra Kubernetes concepts:

Cluster

A cluster is a particular collection of nodes, driven by a single master, where Kubernetes can choose to deploy containers. You can have multiple clusters, for instance, if you want to completely separate test and production.

User

The Kubernetes cluster will expect some form of authentication to make sure that the requested operation (deploy, undeploy, rescale, etc.) is allowed for the specific actor; this is managed through users.

Namespace

A named subsection of the cluster, almost like a "virtual cluster." Users can have different permissions to execute operations, depending on the namespace. It's an optional parameter, and if unspecified, the default namespace will be used.

Context

A particular combination of cluster, user, and namespace.

Kubeconfig

A file indicating the cluster(s) that is available, the namespaces within it, the user(s) that can access it, and the known combinations of access named as contexts. The Kubeconfig file can also have information regarding how the user is to be authenticated.

With this, and assuming the creation and publication of Docker images is already set up as indicated in the previous section, you can configure an automatic step to deploy to a Kubernetes cluster by following these steps:

1. Ask the Kubernetes administrator to create a user specific for deployment. Users can be authenticated by providing username and password, or by means of certificates; for the deployment user, the second option will be preferred to facilitate automatic deployment.

2. Obtain the certificate and key files from the Kubernetes administrator for the deployment user; these will typically be *ca.crt*, *client.crt*, and *client.key*.

3. Copy these files into the Jenkins server and place them in a recognizable location; for instance, */var/jenkins_home/kubernetes/secrets*.

4. Prepare the *kubeconfig* file; the details may depend upon your particular installation, but the simplest form can be as follows:

```
apiVersion: v1
clusters:
- cluster:
    certificate-authority: %PATH_TO_SECRETS%/ca.crt
    server: https://%KUBERNETES_MASTER_IP%:8443
  name: %CLUSTER_NAME%
contexts:
- context:
    cluster: %CLUSTER_NAME%
    user: %DEPLOYMENT_USER%
  name: %CONTEXT_NAME%
current-context: %CONTEXT_NAME%
kind: Config
preferences: {}
users:
- name: %DEPLOYMENT_USER%
  user:
    client-certificate: %PATH_TO_SECRETS%/client.crt
    client-key: %PATH_TO_SECRETS%/client.key
```

5. Copy the *kubeconfig* file into the Jenkins server and place it in a recognizable location; for instance, */var/jenkins_home/kubernetes*.

Registering Kubernetes credentials.   Now that all the relevant configuration is available in the Jenkins server, it is important to let Jenkins know how to use it. For this, you will create a Kubernetes Credentials record, similar to the DockerHub credentials that you created previously:

1. Go to Credentials and then Add Credentials.

2. Select Kubernetes Configuration (Kubeconfig) from the drop-down menu.

3. Leave the scope as Global or restrict it to something more specifically aligned to your own security policies.

4. Give your credentials a meaningful name, like **kubernetes**, and optionally a description.

5. Indicate that the *kubeconfig* is in a file on the Jenkins master, and indicate the path where you previously saved the file; then click OK. Figure 10-6 illustrates these settings.

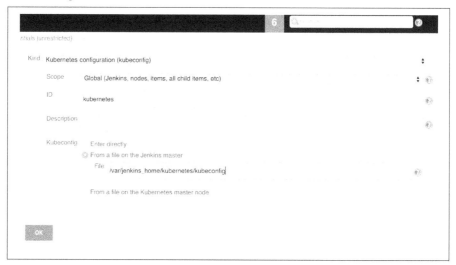

Figure 10-6. Adding new Kubernetes credentials to Jenkins

Creating service definitions.   You will need to create service definitions for all your services, much in the same way that you did in "Deploying into Kubernetes" on page 176 to deploy to the local Kubernetes; in fact, you can probably add those files to your version-control system and reuse them. As an example, the service definition file for the Feature Flags service in the Extended Java Shop is replicated in Example 10-1; further examples can be found in *jenkins-kubernetes/service-definitions*.

Example 10-1. Kubernetes service definition sample for Feature Flags service in Extended Java Shop

```
---
apiVersion: v1
kind: Service
metadata:
  name: featureflags
  labels:
    app: featureflags
```

```
spec:
  type: NodePort
  selector:
    app: featureflags
  ports:
  - protocol: TCP
    port: 8040
    name: http

---
apiVersion: apps/v1beta2
kind: Deployment
metadata:
  name: featureflags
  labels:
    app: featureflags
spec:
  replicas: 1
  selector:
    matchLabels:
      app: featureflags
  template:
    metadata:
      labels:
        app: featureflags
    spec:
      containers:
      - name: featureflags
        image: quiram/featureflags
        ports:
        - containerPort: 8040
        livenessProbe:
          httpGet:
            path: /health
            port: 8040
          initialDelaySeconds: 30
          timeoutSeconds: 1
```

Creating the deployment job.   Finally, your Jenkins server is ready to configure the deployment job. For this, you can create a new Freestyle element as indicated in "Jenkins" on page 224, configure the repository location, and add a build step of type Deploy to Kubernetes, as shown in Figure 10-7.

Figure 10-7. Adding a build step to deploy to Kubernetes

The configuration of the Deploy to Kubernetes step will need references to only two of the elements previously constructed: the Kubeconfig, for which you can select the Kubeconfig Credentials that was created previously ("kubernetes" in Figure 10-8), and the path to the service definition within the repository. You can now save this job, and you will have an automated way to deploy your services to Kubernetes.

Figure 10-8. Configuring the build step to deploy to Kubernetes

You can then repeat this step for each of the services, or you can tweak the existing one to take a parameter that indicates the service to deploy; this is the course that was chosen in the example available at the *jenkins-kubernetes* folder.

Helm Packaging for Kubernetes

If you are creating services or applications for Kubernetes that have complicated installation procedures or several external dependencies, it may be worth exploring the Helm package manager (*https://helm.sh/*). Helm allows you to create *charts* that are very much like traditional package manager artifacts such as RPMs or DEBs, and not only enable you to bundle all the required configuration, but also version the chart artifact for easy upgrading and auditing.

The CLI example: Amazon ECS

One of the advantages of using plugins in your build pipeline of choice is that they are usually nicer and more user-friendly to operate with. On the other side, one of the disadvantages is the lack of portability: if you ever want to change to a different auto-mated build platform, you'll probably have to start from scratch. This is one of the reasons that you may choose to leave plugins aside and use command-line tools instead.

This is the option that has been chosen in the second of our examples: deploying to Amazon Elastic Container Service (ECS). Amazon ECS is in many ways similar to Kubernetes, in the sense that Amazon provides a managed cluster of computers and orchestrates the deployment of containers across them; this way, you just need to provide Amazon ECS with the Docker image information, and the platform will do the rest. The main difference is that, in Kubernetes the nodes in the cluster can either be physical or virtual machines, but in Amazon ECS, the computers must be Amazon EC2 instances, keeping everything within the Amazon ecosystem. This means that adding or removing EC2 instances to an Amazon ECS cluster is a streamlined operation, although it adds the risk of vendor lock-in.

Combining Kubernetes and Amazon EC2

You can build a Kubernetes cluster by using Amazon EC2 instances as nodes, which might be a good middle step if you are already using one of these platforms and considering switching to the other one.

The setup and management of an Amazon ECS cluster is beyond the scope of this book (just as setting up and managing a Kubernetes cluster also is), so in this section we will assume the Amazon ECS cluster is already available and we will just focus on how to deploy services to it. The fully functional example available at the Extended Java Shop repository (more precisely, at the *jenkins-aws-ecs* folder) does include scripts to create and configure a minimal Amazon ECS cluster; readers can follow the instructions at the *README.md* to run the example locally and check the relevant scripts to know more.

Going Serverless with ECS

Although we have been talking about using ECS on top of EC2 instances, there is also the option to go serverless with ECS Fargate. This option eliminates the need to manage a cluster, choose computer instance characteristics, etc. The cluster will manage all of this, and you'll just need to provide the container images. There is a catch, though: as of the time of writing this book, ECS Fargate is still being rolled out and is available in only a handful of regions (Northern Virginia, Ohio, Oregon, and Ireland). Depending on when you are reading this, ECS Fargate may be an option to explore.

Installing and configuring the CLI.   Installing the AWS CLI is relatively straightforward, and can be done either by getting the packages from the official AWS CLI installation page (*https://amzn.to/2xVAGSG*), or by using a package manager of choice (`yum`, `apt-get`, `homebrew`, etc.). Configuring it requires a couple more steps, which are explained in detail at the AWS CLI configuration page (*https://amzn.to/2zx2SNN*), but essentially boils down to the following:

1. Create an AWS user to execute deployments.

2. Obtain an AWS Access Key and an AWS Secret Access Key for that user.

3. Log into your build server (Jenkins, for instance).

4. Execute `aws configure` and provide the previous details as requested.

After the preceding steps have been performed, every `aws` command that is introduced at the command line will run against your AWS environment.

Getting the Latest AWS CLI

Many package managers like `homebrew` or `yum` include AWS CLI in their repositories, making it easy to install. However, there will be a necessary lag between the latest existing version as provided by AWS and the latest available via these package managers. If you use only relatively established features, this will be fine, but if you need the latest, then you'll have to install AWS CLI from the official source.

Amazon ECS concepts.   At this point, we need to define some of the terms used in the Amazon ECS environment. These shouldn't be difficult to grasp, though, as they are quite similar to their Kubernetes counterparts:

Cluster
> The collection of all computers and the services that it runs.

Instance
> Each of the EC2 computers that have been included into a cluster.

Service
> An application that has been deployed to a cluster.

Task
> Each of the individual copies of the Docker containers of an application that are in execution. The same service may have multiple identical tasks across instances, typically with a limit of at most one per instance, although tasks of different services can share an instance.

Task definition
> The template from which a task is created; this includes details such as the location of the Docker image, but also the amount of memory or CPU that the task is allowed to use, the ports that it needs to expose, etc. Task definitions are referred to by using their *family* (a name) and their *version*.

There can be multiple task definitions for the same service, but a running service can be associated with only a single task definition at a time. This way, deploying a new version of an application will be done by creating a new task definition that refers to the new version, and then updating the service to associate it to it.

Note also that, while services and tasks run in a specific cluster, task definitions are cluster-independent, and can, in fact, be used across clusters. This allows you to have different clusters for test and production and make sure that the task definitions are consistent across environments.

Creating tasks, deploying services.   Now that you know the basic nomenclature of Amazon ECS, you can explore the minimum commands that will allow you to deploy services to a cluster. The AWS CLI reference documentation (*https://amzn.to/2N54KRB*) is the best place to investigate how to go further.

Before you can even create a service, you need to create a task definition. This can be done using the subcommand `register-task-definition`:

```
aws ecs register-task-definition \
    --family ${FAMILY} \ # The family of the task, i.e. the name
    --cli-input-json file://%PATH_TO_JSON_FILE% \ # File with the definition
    --region ${REGION} # Region for the task definition, default if omitted
```

The file at *file://%PATH_TO_JSON_FILE%* is what contains the actual definition, and may look like the one used for the Shopfront service in the Extended Java Shop application, displayed in Example 10-2.

Example 10-2. Amazon ECS task definition for Shopfront service in Extended Java Shop

```json
{
  "family": "shopfront",
  "containerDefinitions": [
    {
      "image": "quiram/shopfront",
      "name": "shopfront",
      "cpu": 10,
      "memory": 300,
      "essential": true,
      "portMappings": [
        {
          "containerPort": 8010,
          "hostPort": 8010
        }
      ],
      "healthCheck": {
        "command": [ "CMD-SHELL", "curl -f http://localhost:8010/health || exit 1" ],
        "interval": 10,
        "timeout": 2,
        "retries": 3,
        "startPeriod": 30
      }
    }
  ]
}
```

Once you have created the first task definition, you can then create your service by using the `create-service` subcommand:

```
aws ecs create-service \
    --service-name ${SERVICE_NAME} \ # Name for the service
    --desired-count 1 \ # Desired number of tasks when this service is running
    --task-definition ${FAMILY} \ # Family of the task definition to use
    --cluster ${CLUSTER_NAME} \ # Cluster where the service is to be created
    --region ${REGION} # The region where the cluster is, default if omitted
```

Finally, to deploy a new version, you can create a new task definition that points to the new version of the Docker image and then update the running service to use the new version of the task definition with the subcommand `update-service`; note that, since you can have multiple versions of a task definition, this has to be specified using both family and version:

```
aws ecs update-service \
    --service ${SERVICE_NAME} \ # Name of the service to update
    --task-definition ${FAMILY}:${VERSION} \ # Task definition to use
    --cluster ${CLUSTER_NAME} \ # Cluster where the service currently runs
    --region ${REGION} # The region where the cluster is, default if omitted
```

Once your scripts are clear, you can create a job in your automated build platform of choice that simply runs them. Ideally, you will also store this script in your version-control system, so you can track changes as your needs evolve. A full example, including some conditional logic to decide when to create and when to update a service, is available at the Extended Java Shop repository, located at *jenkins-aws-ecs/ deploy-to-aws-ecs.sh*.

It All Starts (and Ends) with Health Checks

Before continuous delivery became a standardized practice, when organizations still deployed their applications to production manually, there was a clear way to check that everything was working correctly after deployment: a manual check. But now, with automated deployments that happen typically several times a day, and each service being deployed to potentially multiple instances to provide horizontal scalability, checking services manually is not an option.

What's more, in a world of autoscaling, deployments may be happening at any time without our awareness: a peak in demand might signal the orchestrating platform of the need of additional resources, which the platform may respond to by deploying new copies of a particular service. Once again, you cannot be expected to manually check that these newly deployed services are working as expected.

Finally, there is another reason for an automated means to check that your services are running correctly. Modern microservices architectures provide you with unprecedented levels of flexibility, but at the cost of having to manage additional moving parts. With the increase in the number of components, the probability of a failure occurring anywhere in the system increases until it becomes an inevitability: a hardware failure, a lost communication link, a deadlock in a kernel, etc., are just some events that could bring a node down, and with it, all the services that are running within. You could be losing services at any point, and you need to detect when this happens and repair it.

This all leads to the concept of the health check. A *health check* is a purpose-built interface in a service, for instance a */health* endpoint in a RESTful API, that is used by the service to indicate its internal status. When invoked, this interface may run some quick checks to verify that everything is working fine, and then provide either a positive or negative response. The orchestrating platform can then be configured to regularly consult the health checks of all the different instances of a service and act accordingly:

- If the service responds with a positive outcome, the instance is healthy.

- If the service responds with a negative outcome, the instance is unhealthy.

- If the service doesn't even respond to the health check, the instance is unhealthy.

One needs to be careful with health checks, though. An instance appearing to be unhealthy at a particular moment in time is not necessarily indicative of an issue; after all, short glitches happen all the time. However, if an instance appears to be unhealthy too many times in a row, or too many times within a time window, the orchestrating platform can then deduce that the instance is faulty, bring it down, and re-create another one somewhere else. This self-healing mechanism adds resiliency to your platform, compensating for the added uncertainty of the continuous redeployments and the increased number of moving parts.

Providing health-check endpoints

Health-check endpoints have become so ubiquitous that multiple tools and frameworks can automatically attach them to your services, so you don't even need to create one yourself. This is the path that has been taken in the Extended Java Shop sample application, with two available variants.

Most of the web services in the Extended Java Shop are based in Spring Boot, which automatically adds a */health* endpoint to any service without further action. This can be noticed in the log as the application starts up, and can be verified by simply contacting */health* in the desired service after it has been deployed. For more details, see Example 10-3, an extract (edited and broken into multiple lines for readability) from the log of the Stock Manager service, where you can see that */health* and */health.json* have been automatically registered.

Example 10-3. Partial extract of the startup log for Stock Manager service

```
2018-05-02 11:49:37.487  INFO 56166 --- [main] o.s.b.a.e.mvc.EndpointHandlerMapping:
    Mapped "{[/health || /health.json],methods=[GET],
    produces=[application/vnd.spring-boot.actuator.v1+json || application/json]}"
    onto public java.lang.Object org.springframework.boot.actuate.endpoint.mvc.
    HealthMvcEndpoint.invoke(
    javax.servlet.http.HttpServletRequest,java.security.Principal
```

A different example is shown in the Product Catalogue service, which is a web service based in Dropwizard, as opposed to Spring Boot. Setting up a health check with Dropwizard requires a couple of steps, but it also comes with greater flexibility. The first step is to create a class that overrides `HealthCheck`, implementing the `check()` method; this is done in the `BasicHealthCheck` class, which is shown in Example 10-4. (In this case, the check simply returns the version number of the running application.)

Example 10-4. A basic health check in Dropwizard

```
public class BasicHealthCheck extends HealthCheck {
    private final String version;

    public BasicHealthCheck(String version) {
        this.version = version;
    }

    @Override
    protected Result check() throws Exception {
        return Result.healthy("Ok with version: " + version);
    }
}
```

Once the health check has been created, you need to register it in your application. This is shown in the `ProductServiceApplication` class, with the specific line required for registration copied next for reference:

```
final BasicHealthCheck healthCheck = new BasicHealthCheck(config.getVersion());
environment.healthChecks().register("healthCheck", healthCheck);
```

The advantage of this approach is that multiple health checks can be created and registered, all of them consulted when calling */healthcheck*.

Dropwizard Exposes Health Checks at a Different Port

Dropwizard differentiates between normal user traffic and what it considers admin traffic; health checks are registered as admin traffic. Endpoints for admin don't listen in the default port, but in what is called the admin port. By default, the admin port is the normal port +1 (e.g., if the application is listening on 8020, the admin port will by default be 8021), but this can be overridden. See *product-catalogue.yml* for an example on how to define your own admin port.

Needless to say, one doesn't need to be constrained to whatever framework is in use, and can choose to build health-check endpoints manually. At the end of the day, the health check is just an ordinary endpoint, which can be created just like any other endpoint in the application.

Consulting health-check endpoints

Creating health-check endpoints in your services is one side of the coin, and configuring the orchestrating platform to use them is the other one. This, again, is pretty straightforward with most orchestrating platforms.

Let's check our two examples: Kubernetes and Amazon ECS. With Kubernetes, the health check is configured at the very service definition. In fact, keen readers might have noticed the following section in Example 10-1:

```
livenessProbe:
  httpGet:
    path: /health
    port: 8040
  initialDelaySeconds: 30
  timeoutSeconds: 1
```

The parameters indicated here, together with others that have been omitted and for which default values are being used, tell Kubernetes the strategy to follow when checking the health of our service instances. Let's check these values in detail:

initialDelaySeconds

It is understood that services need time to become fully operational after they've been deployed. This value represents how long Kubernetes waits before it starts checking the health of a service instance.

timeoutSeconds

The maximum time we expect the health check to take.

periodSeconds

The time between two consecutive health checks (the default value is 10).

failureThreshold

The number of consecutive times a health check has to fail for Kubernetes to give up on the service instance and restart it (the default value is 3).

Configuring Amazon ECS to use health checks is similar. Let's look at the following extract from the task definition for the Stock Manager service (located at */jenkins-aws-ecs/task-definitions/stockmanager-task.json*):

```
"healthCheck": {
  "command": [ "CMD-SHELL", "curl -f http://localhost:8030/health || exit 1" ],
  "interval": 10,
  "timeout": 2,
  "retries": 3,
  "startPeriod": 30
}
```

Amazon ECS leverages the HEALTHCHECK command in Docker to verify whether the service instance is healthy (which is why the command parameter follows that particular syntax), but other than that, the parameters are analogous:

interval

The time between two consecutive health checks

`timeout`
    The maximum time a health check is expected to take

`retries`
    The number of consecutive times a health check has to file for ECS to consider the task unhealthy and restart it

`startPeriod`
    The wait time after the task has been deployed before it starts performing health checks

What these examples show is that, regardless of the technology in place, creating and configuring health checks is an easy and powerful task. Every orchestrating platform will offer the ability to perform health checks in one form or another and follow similar parameters, which means that you should always be able to count on them.

Keep Your Health Checks as Simple as Possible

Ideally, your health checks will have a simple, hardcoded answer. After all, they are just a way to check whether your service is fundamentally operational. You may consider doing some mild checks, but be careful not to overdo it.

Above all, *never* make a health-check endpoint call another health-check endpoint in another service; the health check applies to your service only, *not to dependencies*. Your infrastructure will be calling your health-check endpoints regularly; if the implementation of them calls for more health checks, you can have significant traffic dedicated to a "health-check storm." Moreover, if you ever happen to have a cyclical dependency among your services (which is not so uncommon), your health checks might enter into an infinite loop that can bring your entire system down, and you'll have to suffer the irony of having an unhealthy system because of badly designed health checks.

Deployment Strategies

Now that you know how to deploy services to production, and how to verify that those services are working as expected (or restarting them if they are not), it is time to decide how you coordinate the removal of an old version of a service and its replacement with a new version.

This is another of those concerns that didn't exist before continuous delivery. At the time when services were deployed manually, organizations chose a time when the application was meant to have the least active users, typically during the weekend or overnight, and informed everyone with sufficient time that the system would be unavailable due to maintenance during a particular time window. During this window, the operations team would bring down the old version, deploy the new one, and check that everything was working correctly.

Again, now that you are continuously deploying new versions into production, you cannot simply assume that a deployment will imply downtime, since this will leave you with a system that has one section or another down at almost any given time. You need to come up with new deployment strategies that take into account how much impact to the system you can tolerate during a deployment, and how many resources you are willing to dedicate to keep that impact at bay.

This section introduces six strategies to accomplish this in different ways. The philosophy behind each strategy is hinted by its name: single target, all-at-once, minimum in-service, rolling, blue/green, and canary. However, in order to describe them and compare them with ease, a common set of terms will be introduced first:

Desired number of instances
> This is the number of service replicas that are expected to be running whenever the service is fully operational. If you take this number to be n, this means that in any deployment, you will go from having n instances of an old version of a service, to having n instances of the new version of that service. We will refer to this simply as *desired*.

Minimum number of healthy instances
> As old service instances are taken down and new ones brought up, you may want to state that there is always a minimum number of them, either old or new, in a healthy state. This can be done to ensure a minimum level of service. We will refer to this as simply *minimum*, and it can usually be expressed as either a percentage of the total or an absolute number, depending on the platform.

Maximum number of instances
> Sometimes you may want to start the new service instances before taking out the old ones so you can limit the gap in the service. This implies a higher utilization of resources. By setting a hard limit on the maximum number of instances, you also set a maximum on the utilization of resources during a deployment. We will refer to this as simply *maximum*, and, again depending on the platform, it can also be expressed as either a percentage, indicating how many additional instances are allowed (e.g., if maximum was set to 100%, that would mean that you allow the number of instances to double during deployment), or an absolute number (this would indicate how many extra instances the platform is allowed to create).

Graphical representation
> For each strategy, we will show a diagram depicting the succession of events while the deployment is taking place. Light squares will represent old versions of the service instances, while dark ones will represent new ones; striped squares

indicate new version instances that are in the process of starting up, and therefore not available yet. Each row will represent a snapshot at a particular point in time, with older snapshots at the top and newer ones at the bottom.

Most orchestrating platforms provide some means to indicate these values in one way or another. In the case of Kubernetes, you can add an additional strategy section to the service definition, where replicas indicates *desired*, maxUnavailable indicates the opposite of *minimum* (minimum = 100% - maxUnavailable), and maxSurge indicates *maximum*:

```
spec:
  replicas: 5
  type: RollingUpdate
    rollingUpdate:
      maxUnavailable: 25%
      maxSurge: 25%
  [...]
```

In the case of Amazon ECS, you can specify this whenever you create or update a service that is based on a task definition:

```
# Creation
aws ecs create-service \
    --desired-count 5 \
    --deployment-configuration \
        'maximumPercent=25,minimumHealthyPercent=25' \
    # other parameters

# Update
aws ecs update-service \
    --desired-count 5 \
    --deployment-configuration \
        'maximumPercent=25,minimumHealthyPercent=25' \
    # other parameters
```

Regardless of your platform, once you know how you can set up the ergonomics of your deployment, you can then explore the different strategies and pick the one that suits you better. Let's go through all of them.

Single target deployment

This is the simplest of the strategies and the one that requires the fewest resources. In this case, you assume the service has only one running instance, and whenever you need to update it, you will have to take it down and then deploy the new one. This implies that there will be a gap in the service, but no additional resources will be needed. The values that define this strategy therefore are as follows:

- desired: 1
- minimum: 0%

- maximum: 0%

This is represented in Figure 10-9 with the following steps:

- Beginning: One instance of the previous version exists.
- Step 1: The one instance has been substituted by another of the new version; the service is effectively unavailable while this new instances starts up.
- End: The new instance is now up and running, available for requests.

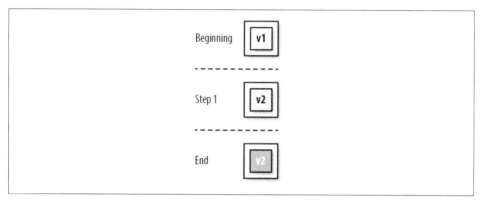

Figure 10-9. Single target deployment: the old instance is killed and replaced by a new one

All-at-once deployment

This strategy is similar to the single target deployment, with the only difference that, instead of having a single instance, you may have any fixed number of them. When a deployment is needed, all the current instances are taken down, and once they are down, all the new ones are brought up. As in the previous case, there is no additional need for resources during the upgrade, but there will also be a gap in the service. The parameters for this case are as follows:

- desired: n
- minimum: 0%
- maximum: 0%

This is represented in Figure 10-10 with the following steps:

- Beginning: Five instances of the previous version exist.
- Step 1: All five instances are taken down at the same time and substituted with five instances of the new version of the service; the service is effectively unavailable while the new instances start up.

- End: The new instances are now up and running.

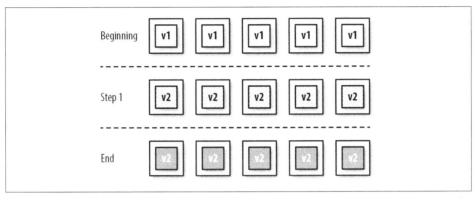

Figure 10-10. All-at-once deployment: all old instances are killed at the same time, and new ones are brought in as the old ones are gone

Minimum in-service deployment

The two previous instances have one major inconvenience: they both imply a service gap. You can improve this by tweaking your strategy and ensuring that there is always a minimum number of healthy instances. This way, instead of bringing down all the old instances at once, you bring down only a number of them and create new instances when they are gone. Once the new instances are up and running, you can remove another batch of old instances, substituting them with new ones. You can repeat this process until all old instances have been replaced by new ones.

This process prevents a gap in the service without the need of additional resources, but it does mean that the minimum in-service instances must take an additional hit of traffic to compensate for the fact that there are fewer of them; make sure not to set this limit too low, or the remaining instances may not be able to cope with the load.

For the case represented in Figure 10-11, the parameters are as follows:

- desired: 5
- minimum: 40% (or 2, if expressed as absolute number)
- maximum: 0%

The process can be described as follows:

- Beginning: Five instances of the previous version exists.
- Step 1: Since at least two instances have to be always operational, only three are taken down and substituted by new instances; deployment remains in the step while the new instances start up.

- Step 2: Once the new instances are operational, the remaining two old versions can be taken down and substituted with new versions.

- End: All the new instances are now operational.

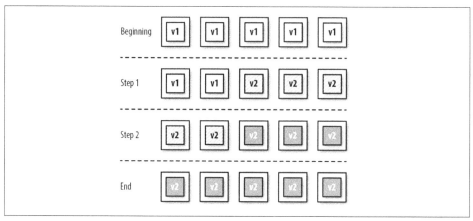

Figure 10-11. Minimum in-service deployment: at least two instances, either new ones or old ones, have to be operational at any given point

Rolling deployment

A rolling deployment can be seen as a different form of minimum in-service deployment: the focus isn't placed on the minimum number of healthy instances, but the maximum number of absent instances. The most typical case of a rolling deployment sets this maximum at one, meaning only one instance can be in the process of being updated at any given time. This means that one instance will be brought down, and then a new one brought up; and only when the new one is operational will we continue the process with the next one. In some cases, a rolling deployment may set higher limits, allowing for two, three, or more instances to be in transition at any given time.

As a variant of the minimum in-service deployment, the rolling deployment presents pretty much the same characteristics: it prevents service gaps without the need for additional resources. The main advantage with regards to minimum in-service is that, by limiting the number of absent instances, you limit the extra strain that the remaining instances may have to endure; the main disadvantage is that deployments will take longer and, depending on the number of instances, the startup time, and the rate of redeployment, the platform could end up with a batch of queued redeployments.

For the case of a rolling deployment, the defining parameters are as follows:

- desired: 5

- minimum: 80% (or 4, if expressed as an absolute number)

- maximum: 0%

Note that the rolling deployment is equivalent to a minimum in-service deployment where `minimum` = `desired` - `1`.

This process is shown step-by-step in Figure 10-12:

- Beginning: Five instances of the previous version exist.
- Step 1: One instance is taken down and substituted with a new one; deployment remains in the step while the new instance starts up.
- Step 2: After the new instance created in step 1 is operational, another old instance is taken down and substituted with a new one; deployment remains in the step while the new instance starts up.
- Steps 3, 4, and 5: The same process is repeated for the remaining old instances.
- End: All the new instances are now operational.

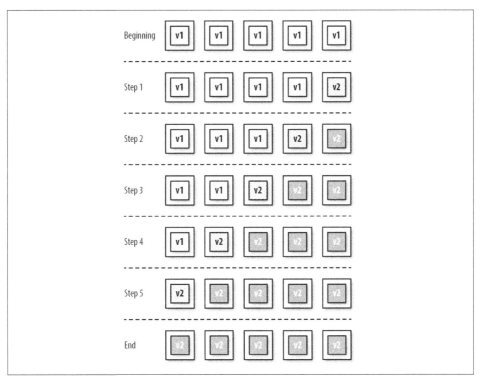

Figure 10-12. Rolling deployment, where the maximum number of absent instances is one.

Blue/green deployment

Blue/green deployment is one of the most popular strategies in the realm of microservices deployments, and perhaps for this reason is one whose meaning is not entirely set. The available literature seems to refer to two slightly different strategies under the same name, each solving a slightly different problem.

The first version of the blue/green deployment aims at fixing one of the disadvantages of both minimum in-service and rolling deployments: during the upgrade, there will be fewer healthy instances to share the total load, potentially causing a strain on them. To address this, blue/green deployments create new instances first, and only when these are available does it starts to take down the old ones. The number of healthy instances never goes below the desired total, but it does mean that we will need extra resources during the upgrade. Considering the standard parameters, a blue/green deployment described this way would have the following:

- desired: n
- minimum: 100%
- maximum: m% (where $0 < m \leq 100$)

Setting m to a higher value will exacerbate the peak use of resources, but will also shorten the length of the deployment.

The second version of the blue/green deployment goes beyond this, though, and cannot simply be obtained by a combination of the desired/minimum/maximum parameters. There is another disadvantage in the previous strategies: during the deployment, there will be a mix of old and new versions of the application in production. This might be OK in many scenarios, particularly if one is being careful with the release of functionality (see "Releasing Functionality" on page 273). However, when this mix is to be avoided, the second version of blue/green deployment adds a twist: no new instances will be available to the users until all of them are ready, and at that moment all old instances will be made immediately unavailable.

The way to achieve this is by manipulating the routing of requests, in addition to the orchestration of services; this is displayed graphically in Figure 10-13 via the following steps:

- Beginning: A number of instances of the previous version exists (two in this example). The load balancer/router, represented in the graph by a cylinder, is configured to send incoming requests to the old versions of the service.
- Step 1: New instances are created, aside from the old ones. These instances are not visible to the public, and the load balancer/router still sends all incoming traffic to the old instances. Deployment remains in this step while the new instances start up.

- Step 2: The new instances have finished starting up and are now operational, but no traffic is being directed to them yet.
- Step 3: The load balancer/router is reconfigured so all incoming traffic is directed to the new versions of the service. This switch is meant to be almost instantaneous. No new requests are sent to the old versions, although existing ones are allowed to finish.
- End: After the old instances are no longer useful, they are taken down.

As can be deduced, the second version of the blue/green deployment provides the best user experience, but at the cost of added complexity and high resource utilization.

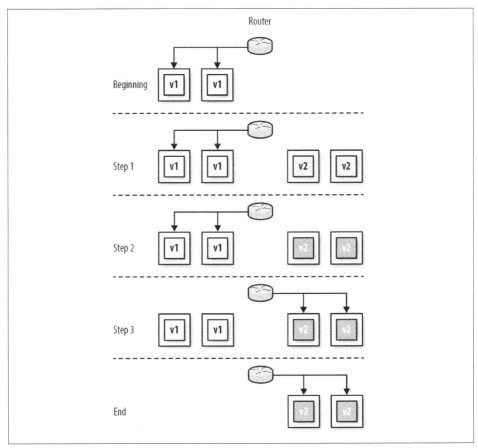

Figure 10-13. A blue/green deployment: new instances are not visible by the user until all of them are ready; at that moment, the router changes to point to the new instances, making the old ones inaccessible to users

Canary deployment

Canary deployment is another case that cannot be achieved by tweaking the combination of desired/minimum/maximum parameters. The idea of the canary deployment is to try out a new version of the service without fully committing to it. This way, instead of completely replacing the old version of an application with the new one, you simply add an instance to the mix with the new version. The load balancer placed on top of the service instances can divert some traffic to the canary instance, and by inspecting logs, metrics, etc., you can understand how this behaves. If the result is satisfactory, you can then perform a full deployment of the new version. A canary deployment is performed in two steps, as shown in Figure 10-14:

- Beginning: Multiple instances of the previous version exist (four in this example).
- Step 1: An instance of the new version is created, without removing any of the old ones.
- End: The new instance is now up and running and can serve requests together with the old ones.

Canary deployments involve a number of challenges when it comes to orchestration. For instance, when the platform is checking the health status of the different instances, it needs to treat the canary one differently from the rest: if the canary instance is unhealthy, it needs to replace it with another canary instance, but if any of the other instances is unhealthy, then it needs to be replaced with a noncanary version. Also, canary instances sometimes need to run for relatively long periods to properly understand the effects of the change under study, during which time you are probably making new versions of the normal instance, triggering redeployments that need to update the normal instances while leaving the canary one intact.

Fortunately, the use case for canary deployments is rather slim. If you just want to expose a new functionality to a subset of users, you can do this by using feature flags (see "Feature Flags" on page 274). The added value of a canary deployment is testing out deeper changes that cannot be hidden via feature flags, like a change in the logging or metrics framework, an alteration of the garbage-collection parameters, or the trial of a newer version of the JVM.

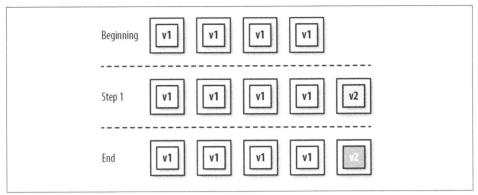

Figure 10-14. Canary deployment, where a new instance is simply added to the group of current-version instances without replacing any

---

The Future of Canary Testing

Currently, the majority of canary testing is conducted via the deployment platform. However, increasingly we are seeing open source API gateways like Ambassador (*https://www.getambassador.io/*) support the dynamic routing of traffic to differing backends, as well as service mesh control planes such as Istio (*https://istio.io/*) offering the ability to canary test interservice traffic. The Netflix team has also talked about how it performs automated canary analysis with Spinnaker and Kayenta (*http://bit.ly/2Q5UV7I*). We recommend keeping up-to-date with these developments.

Which deployment type should I choose?

As has been shown, the different deployment strategies provide solutions to different problems at the cost of additional resources and/or complexity, meaning each of them will be better suited for different scenarios. Teams will have to analyze what their needs are and the investments they are willing to make. Table 10-1 provides a quick look at the different things that may need to be taken into account to aide in this decision.

Table 10-1. Summary of the characteristics and costs of the deployment strategies

	Single Target	All-at-Once	Minimum in-Service	Rolling	Blue/Green	Canary
Overall complexity	Low	Low	Medium	Medium	Medium	High
Service downtime	Yes	Yes	No	No	No	No
Mix of old and new versions	No	No	Yes	Yes	No	Yes

	Single Target	All-at-Once	Minimum in-Service	Rolling	Blue/Green	Canary
Rollback procedure	Redeploy previous version	Redeploy previous version	Halt rollout, redeploy previous version	Halt rollout, redeploy previous version	Switch traffic back to previous version	Kill canary instance
Infrastructure support during deployment	Health checks	Health checks	Routing alteration, health checks	Routing alteration, health checks	Routing alteration, health checks	Routing alteration, weighted routing, health checks
Monitoring requirements	Basic	Basic	Simple	Simple	Simple	Advanced

Beware of Longer Warm-up Times

Java technology has evolved for many years under the paradigm of the big monolithic application, and the performance of the JVM has adapted to it: sections of code that run frequently are detected and compiled to native code from bytecode by the JIT (just-in-time) compiler, object creation and destruction patterns are recognized and the ergonomics of the garbage collector adjusted accordingly, etc. However, this can work only when the application has been running for a certain period of time and the JVM has had the chance to gather statistics and make calculations.

After adopting continuous delivery, you will deploy your applications much more often, and any statistical information that the JVM may have gathered during previous executions will be lost. Upon each new deployment, the JVM will have to start from scratch, which might affect the overall performance behavior of your application.

Moreover, if you have too many instances running in parallel, each of them will receive only a small portion of the total traffic, which means it will take longer to have run enough cycles so as to detect patterns. If you combine this with the frequent redeployments, you might have applications that never get to peak performance. If warm-up time is a problem for you, consider using some advanced features like CDS (Class Data Sharing) or AOT (ahead-of-time) compilation; Matthew Gilliard has written a good article about it (*https://mjg123.github.io/2017/10/02/JVM-startup.html*).

Working with Unmanaged Clusters

So far, we have assumed that we are working with a managed cluster—a cloud platform that keeps track of the totality of servers where our applications run, as well as the different instances of our applications within those servers. This is certainly the recommended approach, for it removes all the burden from the team, allowing it to focus on building useful functionality; unfortunately, teams don't always have this option.

If your cloud platform doesn't manage the cluster for you, or if you don't have a cloud platform as such but rather a set of machines, virtual or physical, that you can use for your production environment, then you need to keep track of what application is running where. The mechanism to do this will be different depending on the technology at hand and on the deployment strategy of your choice, but some general guidelines can be applied.

First, you will need a dedicated database to record what is running where. This database will have at least the following tables:

Servers
> Indicating the actual machines (virtual or physical) that exist, together with available resources in each of them (memory, CPU share, etc.).

Applications
> Details of all the different applications, together with the parameters that indicate their running configuration (number of instances, memory to be allocated to each instance, CPU share per instance, etc.).

Instances
> Details of each single running instance, including the application it belongs to, the server where it is deployed, its health status (deploying, running, failed, etc.), and the parameters used when it was deployed, as these might be different from the new parameters for the application (memory, CPU share, etc.).

Accounting for Resources Once

You might be able to specify only the total resources in the servers table, and deduce the available resources by adding up the resources used by all the instances in that server. Whether you want to have that value precalculated or calculate it on the fly every time is up to you.

Second, you need control over the routing logic. It doesn't matter which mechanism you use for this, whether you have a configurable load balancer, or edit DNS entries on the fly, or anything else. What matters is that you can decide, whenever an external request comes for your application, the actual instance or instances that the request can be directed to.

Finally, you will need to write your own application to manage deployments. Ideally, this will take the form of one or more command-line scripts, where you just need to indicate the application to be deployed, a pointer to the new version (a version number, for instance), and the new parameters for deployment (if any):

```
deploy <application-id> <application-version> [deployment-params]
```

Designing your deployment application this way will allow you to hide the complexity from the CI/CD pipeline and from the development activity itself, while also letting you create more and more sophisticated deployment strategies over time.

Deployment Scripts Are Code

Because the deployment scripts aren't part of the core of the business functionality that your team is providing, it may be easy to forget that these scripts are also code, and that they need to be treated like that. Make sure changes to deployment scripts are appropriately recorded in your CVS, apply the same coding standards (like pair programming or peer review), prioritize changes through your backlog, and, above all, test your changes! Consider having an entirely different cloud environment where you can try out new versions of your scripts without impacting production.

A generic strategy

Regardless of your deployment strategy, a deployment will be composed of a combination of three types of action, each potentially executed more than once and not necessarily in this order:

- Deploying new instances
- Bringing down old instances
- Rerouting

For instance, the "Rolling deployment" on page 258 strategy will imply a succession of the following:

1. Update routing to exclude one of the existing instances.
2. Bring down that instance.
3. Deploy the new instance.
4. Update routing to include the new instance.
5. Repeat for all other existing instances.

Similarly, the "Blue/green deployment" on page 260 strategy will imply the following:

1. Deploy all the new instances.
2. Update routing to point to the new instances.

3. Bring down all the old instances.

By breaking down the deployment logic into these three types of action, you can focus on each of them separately, knowing that you just need to combine them in different ways to achieve the different deployment strategies. Let's now cover the three actions in detail.

Deploying a single instance. Deploying a single instance is the act of having a new service up and running at a particular location; it doesn't concern itself with other instances that may or may not need to be deployed or taken down, and it doesn't concern itself with making this particular instance available to the world. It's just a matter of having a new instance up and running and ready to serve requests.

The actual process may be different, depending on your specific needs, but these general steps can work:

1. Check the resources that are needed for this instance by looking up the relevant application details in the Applications table.

2. Locate a server with the capacity to run this instance (and ideally one that is not already running another instance of the application) by looking in the Servers table; if none is available, the deployment fails.

3. Update the entry for the server to account for the resources to be used by this instance.

4. Create a new record in the Instances table to account for the new instance; mark its health status as Deploying.

5. Copy the application to the server and start it.

6. Poll the health endpoint of the new instance regularly until it provides a healthy status; this will let us know that the application is ready to serve requests.

   a. If the health endpoint doesn't return a healthy status within a configured period of time, abort the deployment. Update the record in the Instances table to Failed (or just delete it) and restore the available resources in the appropriate record of the Servers table.

   b. *(Optionally)* Retry deploying the instance into a new server up to a maximum number of times.

7. Update the record in the Instances table to mark the health status as Running.

8. The deployment is finished.

Bringing down a single instance. Analogously to the previous section, here we will just cover the generic steps to bring down a particular instance. Again, your particular needs might vary, but this can be a good base:

1. Update the relevant record in the Instances table to mark its health status as Undeploying.

2. Send a signal to the application to gracefully close (most frameworks support this). This will make the application stop accepting new requests, but will wait until existing ones have finished.

3. Poll the health endpoint until it no longer provides a healthy response; this will indicate that it has successfully closed down.

   a. If the health endpoint continues to provide a healthy response past a configurable time-out, abort the removal and mark the instance in the Instances table as Failed-to-undeploy.

4. Remove the application binary from the server to avoid clutter building up.

5. Look up the relevant record in the Instances table to gather how many resources were being used by this particular instance.

6. Update the relevant record in the Servers table to indicate the extra resources that are now available.

7. Update the relevant record in the Instances table to mark it as Undeployed (or simply delete it).

Transactions and Data Constraints in Your Deployments Database

We can't emphasize this enough: your deployment application is a production tool, and it needs to be treated as such. In the previous steps, we've described multiple changes to the database; make sure these are executed within a single database transaction. Also, consider adding data constraints to make sure you never over-allocate resources to any server or that you don't allocate two instances of the same application to the same server.

Rerouting. This action is the most dependent on your particular routing technology, and therefore the one that we can say the least about. The key thing to keep in mind is that the configuration change to move from the old to the new routing details needs to be atomic: after you provide a new routing configuration, no request can be directed using the old details. Make sure your load balancer or routing technology of choice can support this.

Changing Databases

Even though services seem to attract most of the attention when talking about continuous delivery, the fact is that information usually ends up being stored in a database. Therefore, if continuous delivery requires the ability to change services at a constant pace to keep up with business needs, it also requires the ability to change your databases accordingly.

If you are working with a NoSQL database, like MongoDB, there isn't much to worry about: the database isn't restricted by a data schema as such, and therefore any changes to the data structure or to data itself can be performed in the application code. If, on the other hand, you are working with a standard SQL database, there are a few things that you need to look after.

Managing database deployments

Changing a database needs to be seen under the same light as changing an application: like an automated and tested process within a CI/CD strategy. This implies that things like a schema modification or a data migration cannot be done manually or in isolation, but rather must be done as part of a CVS-registered change that triggers a build in our CI/CD pipeline. Moreover, you need to recognize that, as the needs of the business evolve, so does the optimum data schema. Therefore, you need to be comfortable with the idea of refactoring databases, just as you refactor application code.

Multiple tools can help with this, and DBDeploy (*https://github.com/tackley/dbdeploy*), probably the first tool designed to ease database changes as part of a CI/CD pipeline, is worth highlighting. Although DBDeploy still does its job, it's fair to say that development has been somewhat abandoned (the last commit in the DBDeploy repository as of the time of writing this book dates to 2011), so new adopters should probably look at more recent alternatives like Flyway (*https://flywaydb.org/*) or Liquibase (*https://www.liquibase.org/*). In either case, all these tools work in a similar way:

- Changes to the database, either structure or data, are performed via *migration scripts*. These scripts are standard SQL files.
- Each migration script must have a unique name and sequence number.
- The migration tool keeps a table for itself in which it keeps track of which migration scripts have been run in the database and which ones haven't.
- Whenever the migration tool is invoked, it will scan the totality of available migration scripts, compare it with the ones that have already been run against a particular database, identify the ones that *haven't* been run, and then run those.

This process allows you to keep track of changes across multiple environments, so you can try out a database schema change in test without affecting production. It also gives you a history of changes, and lets you jump to any particular version of the database at any point in time: you just need a blank database and then run the migration scripts up to your desired point.

Undoing or amending changes is a bit tricky, though. It may be tempting to think that, if you identify a bug after testing a particular migration script in the test environment, you can just amend that particular migration script and rerun it. The truth is that the migration tools don't usually understand *changes* in a migration script, they consider them only as either "already run" or "not yet run"; if a particular script has already been run against a database (for instance, staging), then an amendment to the script won't trigger a rerun: the tool considers it has already processed it, and therefore skips it. In these situations, the best option is to wipe out the database every time so that all the scripts are always run (definitely not a good idea for production), or simply add further migration scripts that undo or amend the previous ones.

Dealing with Long-Running Migrations: Abraham's Experience

The beauty of young projects is that they rarely have truly large amounts of data to deal with, which means database migrations run quickly and nicely. Fast-forward five or ten years, and the story will be quite different. Try adding a new column to a table that has hundreds of millions of records; even the best databases can take a good 30 minutes to cope—not the sort of time span that you have in mind when you use the phrase "tight feedback loop."

This is not the worst that I have seen, though. The main problem with these long-running migrations is that the migration tool itself, or the CI build invoking the migration tool, might time out halfway during the migration. This leads to a catastrophic outcome: the order sent to the database will eventually succeed, performing the migration, but the migration tool will not record it on its script-keeping table. In other words, the migration has been run (or at least partially run), but the migration tool hasn't acknowledged it, which means it will try to run it again the next time it's invoked.

I have had the (mis)fortune of dealing with my fair share of database migrations, and have learned a few tricks along the way. To overcome these limitations, you need to play dirty with the migration tool.

First, you have to understand how these tools work internally. For each migration script, the tool will analyze how many individual statements it has and will prepare to run them in sequence. After all of them have been run successfully, the tool will add a record on its script-keeping table to flag it as installed. Therefore, if one of these statements takes long enough to cause a time-out, I know that all statements up to and including the offending one will (eventually) run successfully, but any statements after it won't. So here is the trick:

1. Whenever I suspect a statement *might* take too long, I create an individual migration script for that statement alone. If multiple statements can cause trouble, I create an individual migration script for each of them.

2. I prepend each long-running statement with a data update statement that will add a record to the script-keeping table, marking this script as completed.

3. I then append after the long-running statement another data update statement that *removes* the record that I just added to the script-keeping table.

Depending on the actual data schema of your tool of choice, the final migration script will look something like this:

```
INSERT INTO SCHEMA_VERSION (SCRIPT_NAME, SCRIPT_NUMBER)
    VALUES ("23_long_running_change", 23)

-- long-running change

DELETE FROM SCHEMA_VERSION WHERE SCRIPT_NUMBER = 23
```

Now, if the long-running change does cause a time-out, the last DELETE statement won't be executed, and the migration tool won't attempt to record this migration script as installed. However, I already did that myself with the first INSERT statement, meaning my database will remain in a consistent status. The build in the CI/CD pipeline may appear as failed once, but the next time it runs, it will work with no problem.

If, on the other hand, the long-running change does *not* cause a time-out, then the DELETE statement *will* be executed, leaving the script-keeping table clean and letting the migration tool itself update it. Either way, writing the migration scripts this way will ensure that the database is in a consistent state at all times.

Separating database and application deployments

One of the requirements for a continuous delivery process is minimizing the impact of potential failures so as to allow for continuous changes. This is why you should always try to avoid multi-application deployments: each application should be deployable independently of others. The same is true for database and application deployments.

Whenever you prepare a migration script, you should make it so it can be deployed without breaking any compatibility with any running applications, for the following reasons:

- If multiple applications use your database, there is no guarantee that all of them will be deployed at the same time (an individual deployment may fail at any time); if this were to happen, the applications that haven't been upgraded to the next version will fail to communicate with the database from now on.

- Even if only one application uses your database, you could have a mix of old and new instances of your application, depending on your deployment strategy (e.g., rolling deployment); the new instances will work while the old ones won't, defeating the purpose of a deployment with zero downtime.

- Finally, even in the extreme case where only one application uses your database and you don't use a deployment strategy that mixes old and new instances (e.g., all-at-once deployment), there is no guarantee that database and application will be deployed at exactly the same time, providing a window of failure.

Regardless of your case, you need to acknowledge that your database is an independent component that has its own deployment cycle, and respect the relationship with connecting applications. For changes that can potentially break compatibility, take a look at "Multiple-Phase Upgrades" on page 283.

A different matter is whether the migration scripts need to be on their own repository. This is a debating point, and different individuals may lean toward different solutions. In general, if a database is used by multiple applications, and each of these applications has its own repository, then it is advisable that the migration scripts have their own space, too. If, on the other hand, the database is used by only a single application, or it is used by a set of applications that are all managed together in the same repository (a monorepo), then it is OK to include the migration scripts in the same repository.

Communicating via stored procedures: turning the database into just another service

Stored procedures have somehow grown out of fashion over the last few years. Many developers today tend to associate them with bureaucratic organizations in which everything that is database-related is managed by DBAs, and developers are allowed to access data only via a set of rigidly designed stored procedures. This has the unfortunate effect of blaming the messenger: if appropriately managed, stored procedures can be a great ally to provide a faster development environment, and can even let you look at your databases in a new, imaginative way.

The main reason a microservices architecture works is that it provides the right balance between exposure and encapsulation. Each service will hide its internal workings to others, and will allow communication only via a number of known endpoints. In the same way, you can look at your database as just another microservice where the stored procedures are the known endpoints, and where communication is performed via SQL as opposed to HTTP. Knowing that connecting applications access the database only via stored procedures, and assuming that you keep the behavior of the stored procedures constant, you can perform as many refactorings to the internals of the database as you want without affecting any applications.

This, of course, requires that your stored procedures are appropriately tested, just as you test the endpoints of your services. Testing databases is out of the scope of this book, but from a Java point of view, the best tools to consider are DbUnit (*http://dbunit.org*) and Unitils (*http://unitils.sourceforge.net/*).

Releasing Functionality

The previous section covered the mechanisms and strategies that allow code changes to make the journey from the pipeline to production. However, as we said before, that's only one side of the story. The fact that you are now able to continuously push new changes to production doesn't mean that you should expose your users to a constant stream of changes; users tend to like a rather stable and predictable experience, and there is only so much change they can tolerate. On the other hand, some changes may make sense only when grouped together with others, but you don't want to revert back to an old-style big-bang deployment where all these changes are introduced in one go. You need a mechanism to decide which features you expose to users that is orthogonal to the deployment mechanism.

On the other hand, you must not forget that it's not just users that you provide functionality to. In the world of microservices, there is a lot of service-to-service communication in the form of RESTful API calls, and sometimes you may need to make changes to these APIs to enable new functionalities. This is another instance where change cannot be brought about without further thought, since modifying the way an endpoint works may impact some of the client applications using it, and this, in turn, could create cascading effects onto ulterior services.

It is therefore essential that you adopt a set of practices, independent from the ritual of deploying services, that allow you to control the way in which changes that might affect other entities are introduced, so you can communicate with the teams or organizations responsible for those entities and make the necessary arrangements. That's what we will cover in this section.

Service Meshes: The Future of Releasing Functionality?

Since late 2016, there has been increasing interest in *service meshes*, a dedicated infrastructure layer for making service-to-service communication reliable, secure, and fast. Open source projects and commercial products have emerged in this space, such as Linkerd, Envoy/Istio, Cilium, and Consul Connect. As we go to print, the practices around working with a service mesh are still being developed, so we won't offer guidance here. However, we encourage you to keep up-to-date with this interesting space, particularly if you are working with containers. Thought leaders in this space who also have an interest in Java include Christian Posta and Burr Sutter from Red Hat. Both blog extensively, and have also published an O'Reilly report, *Introducing Istio Service Mesh for Microservices*, that is well worth reading.

Feature Flags

Feature flags are essentially configuration options that determine whether a particular functionality or feature should be exposed to the user during a given request. Since they are just configuration options, they can have different values in different environments, meaning you can give access to all the new features in the test environment while hiding them in the production environment until you are ready for full rollout. Also, like any other configuration option, you can construct them so they can be modified without redeploying the service (see "Managing Configuration and Secrets" on page 285).

There are several ways to implement feature flags, but they mostly come in one of three flavors:

Binary flags

> The flag can have a value of true or false, effectively enabling or disabling the functionality. This is the simplest of flags.

Throttle flags

> The flag represents the percentage of requests that should use the new feature, with 0% being equivalent to a disabled binary flag, and 100% equivalent to an enabled binary flag. For values in the middle, you can generate a random number between 0 and 100 for every request, and provide access to only those where the generated number is below the flag value. Implementing throttle flags carries a little more complexity than binary flags but allows for the new feature to be released gradually.

Category flags

> While throttle flags give control over the number of users exposed to the new feature, they don't give control over which particular population is exposed; this can be achieved with category flags. Given a particular property attached to each incoming request, a category flag includes the subset of possible values for that property that should grant access. In other words, access to the feature is provided if the value of the target property in the incoming request is within the configured set of values of the category flag, and rejected otherwise. Category flags are a bit harder to implement but provide the finest form of control. For example, if you are offering some kind of commercial deal for which you need legal approval, you could be opening the feature only to visitors from countries where approval has already been obtained. Similarly, if you have some kind of beta-tester user program, you could open experimental features only to affiliated users.

The Extended Java Shop includes a fully implemented example of feature flags. As mentioned before, this application represents a digital shop where different mechanical parts can be purchased. Prices are set and managed statically at the Product Catalogue service.

Let's assume that we want to trial a new Adaptive Pricing service, provided by a third party. This Adaptive Pricing service promises to calculate in real time the optimum price for a product, taking into account overall stocks in different providers, demand, etc. The idea is that, by using the Adaptive Pricing service, we might be able to automatically adjust the price of our products and increase profit margins. The third party charges us a fee for every single time they successfully provide a price in response to one of our requests, so we'd like to limit the number of calls that we make until we are sure that this service is worthy. Also, we are unsure of how users will react to these variable prices, so we want to limit any potential discontent.

The best way to tackle this dilemma is with a throttle flag. The Product Catalogue service provides to the Shopfront service the static prices as managed in our inventory, and then the Shopfront service decides whether to use that price or query the Adaptive Pricing service for a new one. In our case, we have created a service to manage feature flags, so the Shopfront service has to query the Feature Flags service on every request to get the current value of the flag, and then needs to decide whether the current request fits.

The Feature Flags service can be found under the folder */featureflags* of the Extended Java Shop repository. The section within Shopfront that uses this flag to determine the price to use can be found in the `ProductService` class, although the most relevant parts are displayed in Examples 10-5 and 10-6 for convenience.

Example 10-5. Using a feature flag to decide on-the-fly whether an adaptive price should be used instead of the original one

```
// Check value of flag, if it applies, attempt to get adaptive price
private BigDecimal getPrice(ProductDTO productDTO) {
    Optional<BigDecimal> maybeAdaptivePrice = Optional.empty();
    if (featureFlagsService.shouldApplyFeatureWithFlag(ADAPTIVE_PRICING_FLAG_ID))
        maybeAdaptivePrice = adaptivePricingRepo.getPriceFor(productDTO.getName());
    return maybeAdaptivePrice.orElse(productDTO.getPrice());
}
```

Example 10-6. Mechanism to decide whether a given throttle feature flag should be applied

```
// Get value of flag and check if a randomly generated value falls within
public boolean shouldApplyFeatureWithFlag(long flagId) {
    final Optional<FlagDTO> flag = featureFlagsRepo.getFlag(flagId);
    return flag.map(FlagDTO::getPortionIn).map(this::randomWithinPortion)
        .orElse(false);
}
```

```
private boolean randomWithinPortion(int portionIn) {
    return random.nextInt(100) < portionIn;
}
```

For Your Everyday Rump-Up: Smart Throttles

If you use throttle feature flags often, and you are in the habit of increasing the value of your throttle at a gradual pace until you reach 100%, you might find it tedious having to update the value of the flag every day. If that is the case, you can try with a *smart throttle*, which is just a fancy name for a throttle flag that automatically increases its value on a daily basis (or any other frequency that suits you). Your exact needs might vary, but something like this can do the trick:

```
public class SmartThrottleFlag {
    private int initialPortionIn;
    private LocalDate startDate;
    private int dailyIncrement;

    /* Constructor goes here */

    public int getPortionIn() {
        final LocalDate now = LocalDate.now();
        if (startDate.isAfter(now)) {
            return 0;
        }

        long daysPast = DAYS.between(startDate, now);
        long totalIncrement = daysPast * dailyIncrement;
        long currentPortionIn = initialPortionIn + totalIncrement;
        return Math.min((int) currentPortionIn, 100);
    }
}
```

Semantic Versioning (semver)

In the current world of microservices, the most common way to make shared functionality available across codebases is quickly becoming the creation of a new service for that functionality. Sometimes, however, you still might find it useful to create libraries of shared functionality, especially for syntactic sugar constructs, and you need to be careful about how these libraries evolve.

As introduced in Chapter 5, Semantic Versioning, or semver, is a set of rules that let you know the extent of a change in a library just by checking its version number. In its simpler form, version numbers that follow semver have three numbers separated by dots: MAJOR.MINOR.PATCH. When a new version of a library, framework, or

---

tool is released, only one of these three numbers is allowed to increase, typically by a single unit. The number that is increasing will tell you the scope of the change:

MAJOR
> The new version introduces backward-incompatible changes; using the new version might break client code at compilation and/or runtime. When the MAJOR is updated, MINOR and PATCH are commonly set to zero.

MINOR
> The new version introduces some new, backward-compatible features; existing clients should be able to adopt the new version without any impact. When the MINOR is updated, PATCH is commonly set to zero.

PATCH
> No new functionality has been added; this new version corrects an existing bug.

Semver allows clients to decide when they are ready to adopt a new version, or even whether they want to adopt new versions automatically. For instance, Maven allows you to provide dependency information indicating a fixed-value version or a range of versions. If you know that the maintainers of a particular library use semver, and you are currently using version v5.0.0 of their library, it would be advisable to write your dependency like this:

```
<dependency>
    <groupId>com.github.quiram</groupId>
    <artifactId>java-utils</artifactId>
    <!-- square bracket includes the value, curved bracket excludes it -->
    <!-- this is equivalent to v5.0.x -->
    <version>[v5.0.0,v5.1.0)</version>
</dependency>
```

If you feel adventurous enough, you could even register your dependency to automatically update to the latest minor version by using [v5.0.0,v6.0.0). This shouldn't ever break your client code (barring mistakes) and would always give you the latest available features. It is not a good idea to automatically upgrade to new major versions, though.

An example of semantic versioning in action can be seen in the external library java-utils (*https://github.com/quiram/java-utils*). If you take java-utils and explore versions v4.0.0 through to v4.6.0, you'll notice that each new version simply adds methods to helper classes, which are evidently backward-compatible changes. The next version after v4.6.0 is version v5.0.0, which represents a backward-incompatible change. If you inspect the changes in this new version, you we will see that the meaning of the method `ArgumentChecks.ensure(Callable<Boolean>, String)` has changed: in version v4.6.0, this method expected a fail condition as the first argument, but in version v5.0.0 it expects a pass condition—it's exactly the opposite!

The next version after v5.0.0 is v5.0.1, which indicates a bug fix. Indeed, if you inspect the changes, you will see that v5.0.0 inverted the meaning of the aforementioned ensure method, although it didn't update all the locations within the library where this method was called, breaking some functionality; v5.0.1 fixed this.

> **What's with the v?**
>
> Sometimes different organizations will push for different sets of best practices for slightly different but often interchangeable aspects of programming; versioning is one of them. While semver advocates for a purely numerical version number, GitHub advocates for prepending versions with the letter v. Both approaches aren't incompatible, since technically GitHub's style refers to a *tag* that points to a specific version, not to the version itself. So in GitHub speak, v1.2.3 is a tag that refers to version 1.2.3 of the code. As a matter of fact, even the semver repository uses the v prefix in its releases (*https://github.com/semver/semver/releases*).
>
> Some systems and tools may not make a distinction between the two styles, and treat either of them as a version number. This is usually OK, but depending on the build system that you use, this might have the effect of confusing the build tool when using ranges for the MAJOR component of the version (e.g., it might consider that version v10.x.y is *earlier* than v2.x.y). This is just another reason not to use ranges for the MAJOR component of the version.

Backward Compatibility and Versions in APIs

Semver is an incredibly powerful and yet simple paradigm that can reduce friction between producers and consumers. However, it doesn't easily apply to APIs. The consumption of libraries and frameworks has a history of using specific version numbers to record snapshots of code, and tools have been adapted to it. As we have shown, you can instruct your dependency management system (for instance, Maven) to grab the latest available version from within a range pattern, but this should not be done trivially when consuming a web service's API.

The first thing to realize is that, whereas the version number of a library refers to the *implementation* of the code within the library, the version number of a service refers to the *interface*. Therefore, a new versioning paradigm is needed, one that doesn't take into account changes in implementation, but changes in behavior.

Now, the topic of versioning APIs is a rather controversial one, and the development community hasn't yet agreed on a single best practice. Several options exist, and different people will defend their position passionately. The only thing that can be categorically stated is that *some* solution is needed. In this section, we present some of the most common options and indicate their pros and cons so that you can make your own informed decision.

Avoid versioning

The first approach to manage versioning in an API is simply to avoid it: if your team needs to make a particular change to the API, make it in a way that keeps backward compatibility. In practice, this means keeping the endpoint URL as it is, and changing the structure of the returned object only to add new fields. Existing clients can continue to use the API, oblivious to the change, while clients who need the new feature have it there available for them.

An example of this approach can be found in the Extended Java Shop—more precisely, in the Feature Flags service. The story goes as follows. The Feature Flags service was initially designed as a throttle flag with three parameters: the flag ID, the flag name, and the rate of requests that should be granted access to the feature (the "portion in"). At some point, the business realized there was a downside to the current way feature flags were managed: since each request was independent from the others, it could happen that the same user was granted access to the feature in one request and rejected in another one, potentially providing an inconsistent experience. Depending on the feature, this might be an acceptable situation, or it may not. To address this, a new functionality was to be added to the Feature Flags service: flags should include a "sticky" parameter, which indicated whether the behavior across requests would be the same for a given user or whether it was allowed to change.

The implementation of the sticky parameter has been done in a backward-compatible way to avoid the need for a new version: a new field has been added to the response. Existing consumers of feature flags, like the shopfront service, can simply ignore this new field until they are ready and/or willing to make use of it.

Ignoring New Fields May Not Be the Default Behavior

Backward-compatible changes implemented this way work only if the client application that is consuming the service ignores any new or unknown fields, which is not necessarily the default. For instance, in the case of acceptance tests in the Extended Java Shop, which uses Jackson to deserialize JSON objects, this has to be explicitly requested by using @JsonIgnoreProperties(ignoreUn known = true); see the Flag class in the folder /acceptance-tests for details.

A similar approach can be used when you need to modify an existing field: instead of modifying it, you can choose to add a new one with the new meaning. This, of course, can work for only so long, and eventually your API will be littered with a mixed bag of old and new fields. If you get to this point, or if you need to make changes that cannot be implemented by simply adding new fields, then you need to create a new version of the API as indicated next.

Version the endpoint

A simple and effective way to create a new version for a backward-incompatible change in the API is to include the version number as part of the endpoint itself. This way, if the current version of the resources is located under /resource, the new version can be located at /v2/resource. This is a common approach, used in well-known services like AWS, and it's one that is simple to implement and communicate. You can easily switch from one version to the other by quickly editing the URL. You can give someone a link to easily try out the new version. The pragmatism under this approach is its main advantage.

The Extended Java Shop includes a case of versioning through endpoints in the Product Catalogue service. Let's say that, in our example, the business has decided to have two different prices for the products: the single price, when the item is purchased in small amounts, and the bulk price, with an implicit discount for large purchases. The Product Catalogue would then also indicate, for each product, the number of units that need to be purchased at the same time to qualify for the bulk price. Developers decide that it would be too messy to implement this new feature simply by adding new fields to the response, and decide to create a new version of the API. Version 1 of the Product Catalogue returns a `Product` object like this:

```
GET /stocks/1

200 OK
{
  "id": "1",
  "name": "Widget",
  "description": "Premium ACME Widgets",
  "price": 1.20
}
```

Version 2 returns a modified object with extra information:

```
GET /v2/stocks/1

200 OK
{
  "id": "1",
  "name": "Widget",
  "description": "Premium ACME Widgets",
  "price": {
    "single": {
      "value": 1.20
    },
    "bulkPrice": {
      "unit": {
```

```
        "value": 1.00
      },
      "min": 5
    }
  }
}
```

You can see how this has been implemented by looking at the two versions of the `ProductResource` class in the Product Catalogue service.

This is a backward-incompatible change that has been implemented using the version-endpoint pattern. This way, requests to */products* would return the first version, while requests to */v2/products* would return the second version. Clients using the first version of the API can continue to operate as normal, but those who want to use the new features can make the necessary arrangements to use the second version. Note that, in our sample application, the Shopfront service is still using version 1 of the API.

Version the content

Detractors of the version-in-endpoint approach usually point out how it breaks the semantics of the RESTful principles: in a pure RESTful API, an endpoint is meant to represent a resource, not a version of a resource, so version numbers should not be included in the URL. Instead of versioning the endpoint, you can version the content by means of the `Content-Type` header.

Let's assume your service provides a response in JSON format. The value of the `Content-Type` header in this situation will most typically be `application/json`. You can, however, provide a *versioned* content type using the pattern `application/vnd.<resource-name>.<version>+json`, where *<resource-name>* is the name of the resource that this type refers to, and *<version>* is the version of the resource format. Clients can then indicate the version that they want to be provided by using the `Accept` header. This way, the same endpoint can serve different versions of the same resource.

An example of this can be found in the Stock Manager service of the Extended Java Shop. In this case, we can say that the business realized that some of the pieces on sale were particularly heavy, and they wanted to impose a limit on the number of them that a customer could buy in a single purchase to ease the packaging and delivery. (Whether it is credible that any business would willingly limit the number of products that they sell is something that we will not debate here—just roll with it.) For this, the development team decided that stocks should include both the total number of available units, and the number of units that could be purchased at the same time. Once again, the developers decided that it would be better to do a new version of the API than try to add the changes to the existing one in a backward-compatible manner, and decided to implement this change by using the version-in-content approach. This way, the old API still worked in the following way:

```
Accept: application/json
GET /stocks/1

200 OK
Content-Type: application/json
{
  "productId": "1",
  "sku": "12345678",
  "amountAvailable": 5
}
```

The new API is available by changing the header:

```
Accept: application/vnd.stock.v2+json
GET /stocks/1

200 OK
Content-Type: application/vnd.stock.v2+json
{
    "productId": "1",
    "sku": "12345678",
    "amountAvailable": {
        "total": 5,
        "perPurchase": 2
    }
}
```

Details of this implementation can be found in the `StockResource` class in the Stock Manager service. Note that, in our example, the Shopfront service is still using version 1 of the API.

Don't Mix Your API Versioning Strategies

Either of the API versioning strategies mentioned here can work, but we advise you to pick one and stick to it. Having *both* versioning strategies in the same application or system will make it harder to manage and will confuse your consumers. As Troy Hunt said (*https://www.troyhunt.com/your-api-versioning-is-wrong-which-is/*), the whole point of an API is to provide predictable, stable contracts.

Advanced change management

On the far end of the spectrum lies the argument that the mere fact that a RESTful API needs to be versioned is an antipattern, since it doesn't strictly follow the rules of hypermedia communication. The URIs of our resources should be immutable, and the provided content should use a language that is parsable upon a definite set of rules; this way, changes in the content can just be reinterpreted by the consumer, and no coordination between provider and consumer is needed.

Although strictly true, most people find this approach harder than it's worth, and revert back to one of the approaches outlined previously. For this reason, we have decided not to cover it in this book, although readers who want to investigate further are encouraged to check Roy Fielding's work (*https://roy.gbiv.com*).

You Don't Need API Versioning Until You Do

After reading this section, you might be compelled to pre-ppend /v1 to any new endpoint that you create, or even to the endpoints that you already have (or, if you have opted for versioning via content type, then change the content type of all your endpoints). The truth is that, even though you need to be ready to deal with API changes, you might not need to deal with them right from the outset: if you're creating a new service, and you have a lot of decisions to make, the versioning scheme is one that you might be able to delay. Simply assume that a lack of version means version 1, and when (and if) you need to deal with a change, then you can choose a versioning scheme.

Multiple-Phase Upgrades

In the previous examples, we presented some use cases in which a service is to offer a new piece of functionality *before* clients are ready to consume it, meaning backward-compatibility has to be preserved in some way: either by making a backward-compatible change, or by creating a new version of the API. You may be tempted to think that if you control both the provider and the consumer of the API, you can skip this trouble and simply change both at the same time, but you would be wrong.

Even if you do change both at the same time, there is no guarantee that those changes will be made available in production also at the same time. On one side, your deployment strategy may imply that both the old and the new version of the provider coexist in production during some time; if your client can cope with only the new version, it will experience significant disruption during deployment. On the other hand, and as you will see in Chapter 11, your changes will have to go through multiple test phases, and there is always the chance that those tests pass for the provider but not for the consumer (or vice versa), meaning you'll have in production mismatching versions of provider and consumer.

The moral of the story is that, regardless of whether you control both sides of the interaction or only one, you will need to perform your actions in numerous steps to make sure both sides don't fall out of sync. This is sometimes referred to as Expand

and Contract (*https://www.martinfowler.com/bliki/ParallelChange.html*), and usually boils down to the following steps:

1. Create a new version of your API or library, and push the changes.

2. Let the change make its way through the pipeline. If you are changing an API, make sure the deployment is completely finished and that the new API is available in all the running instances.

3. Change your consumer(s) to use the new API or library.

4. If you're updating an API, and once every consumer has been updated to use the new version, you can consider deprecating the old one.

Deprecating old APIs

Keeping every historical version of an API would be a maintenance nightmare. That's why, even though you want to make it easier for consumers to adopt new APIs at their own pace, you also want to make sure they do move on.

You can track the number of people using each version of your APIs (if at all) by keeping usage metrics of each of your versioned interfaces (see Chapter 13 for information about metrics). Once you are confident that nobody is using the old versions, either because you know or control all the potential consumers, or because you can see in the metrics reports that there is no usage, you can confidently delete the old versions.

Sometimes you won't feel in a position to remove the old endpoints straightaway, either because you know there is some usage but you can't track the owner, or because yours is a public API and you can't assert with confidence that nobody is using the old API anymore. If this is the case, you might be able to nudge the slow movers by keeping the old interface but removing the implementation: requests to the old API can be replied to with an HTTP redirect instruction:

```
GET /v1/resource

301 MOVED PERMANENTLY
Location: /v2/resource
Content-Type: text/plain
This version of the API is no longer supported, please use /v2/resource
```

Chances are, the consumer will still be broken by this, since the request will be redirected to the new version, for which the consumer is probably not ready. However, at least they will be notified of what they need to do to fix the situation.

Managing Configuration and Secrets

In previous sections, we correctly identified how to best manage application deployments and functionality releases as part of a continuous delivery process. There is, however, one last responsibility to be taken care of whenever we consider the evolution of applications onto newer versions: configuration.

In the past, configuration used to be something managed aside from code. Applications would be deployed to servers, assuming that they would be able to find a file at a particular location and that they would contain the different configuration options needed by the application. Changes to the configuration would be controlled by a separate process and different tools, typically known as Software Configuration Management (or SCM). Quite frequently, it would even be different people who handled code and configuration.

However, the dynamic environment that we have showcased in this chapter makes managing configuration in this way impractical. New computer instances might be created and added to your environment at any time, and configuration files would have to be copied there as part of the instantiation. A change in configuration would have to be spread across a large number of computers. And the fact that multiple services could be sharing the same computer instance presents us with the real possibility of a configuration clash. A different way is needed.

This section indicates the most common ways to manage configuration in the world of microservices and continuous delivery, indicating the pros and cons of each approach.

"Baked-In" Configuration

The simplest way to configure an application is to pack the configuration file with the application itself. What's more, you can keep the configuration file in the same repository as the code, which allows you to keep track of changes to configuration. Operating this way means you don't need to do anything special to ensure your application is configured when deployed into production, which makes it a convenient and appealing option. All the services in the Extended Java Shop make use of baked-in configuration; the Spring Boot-based ones use the file *applications.properties*, while the Dropwizard-based one (Product Catalogue service) uses *product-catalogue.yml*.

It might seem that, by following this baked-in configuration approach, you can have only one set of values for the configuration, meaning that you cannot have different configurations for different environments (e.g., test and production). However, your baked-in configuration can include several options or profiles, and then your application can decide to pick one or the other, based on a parameter or variable that the environment in question is making available. An example of this can be seen in the

Feature Flags service, which uses Spring Boot's concept of profiles to keep two sets of configuration values; this is achieved with three baked-in configuration files:

application.properties
>   Indicates which profile is used by default

application-test.properties
>   Indicates the configuration values to use according to the test profile

application-prod.properties
>   Indicates the configuration values to use according to the prod profile

The first file sets the property `spring.profiles.active` to prod, indicating that Spring Boot should use the contents of `application-prod.properties` to configure the application. However, this property can be overridden by an environment variable of the same name. This is done in the Acceptance Tests (folder */acceptance-tests*). If you inspect the *docker-compose.yml* file in the Acceptance Tests module, you will notice the following:

```
featureflags:
  image: quiram/featureflags
  ports:
   - "8040:8040"
  depends_on:
   - test-featureflags-db
  links:
   - test-featureflags-db
  environment:
    - spring.profiles.active=test
```

The last element, `environment`, sets the environment variable `spring.profiles.active` to `test`. This will override the setting in the file *application.properties*, and will signal Spring Boot to use the file *application-test.properties* when bringing up and configuring the Feature Flags service. This way, you can use the baked-in configuration pattern and still keep different configuration sets for different environments.

Externalized Configuration

One of the consequences of baked-in configuration is that, since you are tracking it as just another file (or set of files) within your code, any change to configuration will be treated by the build pipeline like a change in code. This will sometimes be desirable, because a change in configuration might require the execution of your test suite, but in many other cases it will just trigger unnecessary work: for instance, a change in a flag for the test environment will not only trigger the entire suite of sets, but also result in a new deployment to production for something that doesn't affect the production environment at all.

There is another disadvantage to baked-in configuration: since it is managed as another file in the code repository, only developers can make changes to it. Again, this might be appropriate for some configuration options (like the connection pooling parameters for a database connection). For some other cases, you might want to give that power to different members of the organization. For instance, for the case of managing feature flags, you may want to let the business decide when and how these are tweaked. Another case might be if the infrastructure team provides some resources for your application—for instance, log pools (see Chapter 13): maybe you want certain details to be managed by the infrastructure team, so they can manage and change details of the infrastructure with flexibility, and your application simply reads the configuration from them. Either way, they will be instances in which you don't want the configuration to live within your own application, but to be provided from outside.

The solution for externalizing configuration will depend on the reason by which you want this to be externalized; you might even want to have multiple solutions for different cases. In the Extended Java Shop, we opted for externalized configuration for the case of feature flags. We could have kept feature flags just as another parameter in the *application.properties* file of Shopfront service, but we decided to go through the trouble of creating an independent service to make that configuration editable without code changes. If business members are tech-savvy enough, they can make HTTP requests to the Feature Flags service to edit the flags as they need to; if not, you can always create a little GUI that wraps the calls to the service.

Other forms of externalizing configuration could be setting up environment variables in the computer instances where services will run, or creating files in special locations for the application to pick them up.

Remember: You Lose Control of What You Externalize

With baked-in configuration, you can be fairly confident that any configuration item that you need is exactly where you expect it; if not, you can just call it a bug and fix it. However, when you decide to externalize your configuration items, you're dependent on what other people or teams might decide to do. Feature flags could be deleted without notice; other configuration items may have invalid or unexpected values in them. Make sure your application can cope with all these scenarios.

Handling Secrets

Some configuration items are especially sensitive. We are talking, of course, about secrets of different kinds: database passwords, private keys, OAuth tokens, etc. We obviously can't include these in the baked-in configuration, but even the externalized configuration may need special treatment to make sure the values are secure.

Keeping secrets private while still making them available where they are needed is a surprisingly difficult task. Our best advice is that you don't try to create your own solution, at least not from the outset. All orchestrating platforms offer some kind of secret management with different degrees of privacy, depending on how hard your needs are.

For instance, you might not mind if everyone in your team or organization knows the values for these secrets; you just don't want to record them as plain text anywhere (least of all in your code repository). In this case, you can use tools like Kubernetes Secrets (*https://kubernetes.io/docs/concepts/configuration/secret*). Kubernetes allows you to create secret keys and give them a name to identify them. These keys are then stored safely by Kubernetes. You can configure your applications to consume these keys, and Kubernetes can make them available to them as either files or environment variables. When your application tries to read these files and/or environment variables, the keys will already have been decoded, and your application will be able to use them normally.

AWS provides a similar way to handle secrets via Parameter Store, which is part of Systems Manager (*https://aws.amazon.com/systems-manager/features/*). Parameter Store is integrated with Amazon ECS, meaning your applications can use it easily. Other platforms will have other similar features; check out the relevant configuration to know more.

Summary

In this chapter, we covered the aspects surrounding the last section of our continuous delivery pipeline: automated delivery. As it usually happens, the last mile is the hardest one, and extra challenges appear when you want to set up an environment where you deliver changes at a constant pace:

- Deployments and releases are two different concepts. The former is the *technical* activity of bringing a new version of an application to production, while the latter is the *business* activity of allowing users access to functionalities.

- Different deployment strategies are available, each with a different profile of advantages, resources needs, and complexity. There is no right or wrong strategy, but strategies that are more or less adequate to your needs.

- You may need to choose when and how to make new features available to your consumers, either end users or other teams. Feature flags allow you to gradually open features to the public, while versioning schemes for libraries (like semver) and for APIs (like version-in-endpoint or version-in-content) allow your consumers to adopt new features at their own pace.

- With the increase in the number of moving parts, configuration needs to become a first-class citizen. Baked-in configuration is easy to handle and track, but accessible only to developers. Externalized configuration allows other people to manage configuration details, but it can become less reliable. Secrets, like passwords or keys, need special support from the orchestrating platforms or sophisticated purposed-built solutions.

Thanks to the last two chapters, you can now build an end-to-end automated pipeline that can bridge the gap from the development station to production. In the next chapter, we will explore what you need to add to that pipeline to ensure that your changes don't introduce any regressions or unintended consequences.

## CHAPTER 11

Functional Testing: Correctness and Acceptance

Testing is vitally important to confirm that the delivery of software provides value to the business, is easy to maintain, and performs within specified constraints. In this chapter, you will learn about functional testing, which is focused on asserting that the system provides the specified functionality, both from the business perspective and the technical perspective.

Why Test Software?

Why should you test software? The answer that first jumps to mind is to ensure that you are delivering the functionality required, but the complete answer is more complex. You obviously need to ensure that software that you are creating is functionality capable of doing what was intended—delivering business value—but you also need to test for the presence of bugs, to ensure that the system is reliable and scalable, and in some cases cost-effective.

Traditionally, validating the quality of a software system has been divided into testing functional requirements and testing nonfunctional requirements—also referred to as *cross-functional* or *system quality attributes*. Before exploring the process of testing functional requirements within a CD pipeline, you first need to understand the various types and perspectives of testing.

What to Test? Introducing Agile Testing Quadrants

It is important that you are clear about the types of testing that must be performed on a system that you are building, and you also need to understand how much of this can be automated. A useful introduction to the types and goals of testing can be found in *Agile Testing: A Practical Guide for Testers and Agile Teams* (Addison-Wesley) by Lisa Crispin and Janet Gregory.

The entire book is well worth reading, but the most important concept for us in this chapter is the Agile Testing Quadrants, based on original work by Brian Marick. The Agile Testing Quadrants, depicted in Figure 11-1, is a 2 × 2 box diagram with the x-axis representing the purpose of the tests (from supporting the team to critiquing the product) and the y-axis representing whom the test is targeting (from technology facing to business facing). The resulting quadrants within the diagram are labeled Q1 to Q4, and no ordering is implied with this numbering system; this is purely for reference.

Quadrant 1 is located in the position that is strongly supporting the team and technology facing, so the tests falling within this quadrant are unit and component tests. These types of tests can act as scaffolding around which the development team creates the software. They can also shape the design and the architecture. For example, by using TDD, you can ensure that there are also two consumers of functionality: the original consumer component within the application and a test.

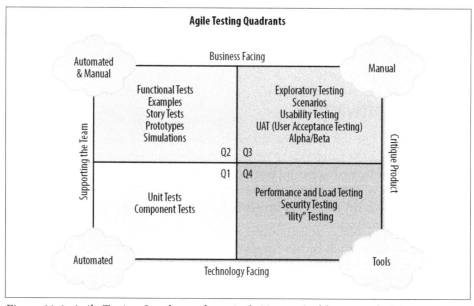

Figure 11-1. Agile Testing Quadrants from Agile Testing (Addison-Wesley) by Lisa Crispin and Janet Gregory

Tests falling in Quadrant 1 are highly automatable. You should be running these tests not only within a build pipeline, but also as part of minute-by-minute local builds and, ideally, through an automated process that watches for code changes and runs appropriate tests. Infinitest (*https://infinitest.github.io/*) is one such example of a continuous testing tool that operates as a plugin for Eclipse and IntelliJ.

Quadrant 2 is also strongly supporting the team, but is oriented toward being business- or customer-facing. Tests that fall into this category include functional tests, examples, and story tests. Tests within this quadrant are often referred to as acceptance tests, and are a focus of Specification by Example or BDD.

Quadrant 3, at the top right-corner, is also business facing, but switches the purpose toward critiquing the product. In this quadrant, you try to explore how the end user will feel when using the product. Is it appealing? Is it intuitive? Is it accessible by all types of users and devices? This kind of test cannot be easily automated, since the expected right answer is not always known before the test. However, this does not mean that the tests aren't important, since failing to address these questions can lead to the product's failure.

Finally, Quadrant 4 deals with critiquing the product from a technical point of view. These tests are usually difficult to write and tend to require special tools. Also, although their execution can be automated, their evaluation is a little more subjective. For instance, let's say you write a performance test that ensures that a particular transaction can be executed within 3 seconds. If after a change you see the transaction time jumping from 1 second to 2 seconds, should you worry about it? 2 seconds still falls within the 3-second allowance, but you have suddenly doubled the transaction time.

Quadrants 1 and 2 cover functional requirements, and they will be thoroughly explored within this chapter. Quadrant 4 covers nonfunctional requirements (also referred to as *operational requirements*), which will be dealt with in Chapter 12. Quadrant 3 goes beyond what can be achieved in a continuous delivery pipeline and is therefore out of scope for this book. However, you can take a look at resources like *Explore It!* (Pragmatic Bookshelf) by Elisabeth Hendrickson to learn more about this concept.

Continuous Testing

To be able to create new functionality and deliver value at a sustainable pace, you need to have a high level of confidence in your pipeline and practices. Every team makes mistakes, but it is a well-accepted maxim within software delivery that the earlier an issue is found, the less it costs to fix. No amount of testing (outside mathematical formal verification) can guarantee the absence of issues, but your testing approach must be able to highlight problems as early as possible in your development practice.

To achieve this, you need to establish a culture of testing your software thoroughly and continuously, from the moment the first line of code is written to when the associated feature is deployed. In his blog post, "End-to-End Testing Considered Harmful" (*http://bit.ly/2IjDf5U*), Steve Smith explores these ideas in depth and talks about the practice of *continuous testing*. The idea behind this is that software needs to be tested at all times. This can be a challenge, with things such as the choice of test tooling and the skills available across the team impacting how you implement this.

The entire article by Smith is well worth reading. The core ideas to remember are that although a unit test or acceptance test may appear to offer a low degree of coverage (compared with, say, an end-to-end test), a unit test will validate intent against implementation, and an acceptance test will check the implementation against the requirements. This means that both the code's behavior and its interaction with other parts of the system can be verified, and this can also be done in a small amount of time and with a minimum of coordination. For example, trying to verify a series of input edge cases within a part of an application by using only end-to-end tests can be ineffective, as a lot of orchestration has to be undertaken with the associated data stores, and each run of a test takes a long time to stand up the system, run the test, and tear everything down.

Building the Right Feedback Loop

Tests create a feedback loop that informs the developer whether the product is working. The ideal feedback loop has several properties:

It's fast
> No developer wants to wait hours or days to find out whether their change works. Sometimes the change does not work—nobody is perfect—and the feedback loop needs to run multiple times. A faster feedback loop leads to faster fixes. If the loop is fast enough, developers may even run tests before checking in a change.

It's reliable
> No developer wants to spend hours debugging a test, only to find out it was a flaky test. Flaky tests reduce the developer's trust in the test, and as a result, flaky tests are often ignored, even when they find real product issues. Flaky tests also add unnecessary delays: when a developer suspects a test failure might be spurious, their first reaction will be to simply run it again instead of investigating.

It isolates failures
> To fix a bug, developers need to find the specific lines of code causing the bug. When a product contains millions of lines of code, and the bug could be anywhere, it's like trying to find a needle in a haystack.

Turtles All the Way Down

There is an old expression—"turtles all the way down"—that refers to the mythological idea that a giant World Turtle supports Earth on its back. This World Turtle is supported by an even bigger turtle, and that bigger turtle is, in turn, supported by a yet bigger one. There is meant to be an infinite succession of increasingly bigger turtles, each supporting the previous one, therefore concluding that Earth is ultimately supported by "turtles all the way down."

This expression comes in handy when you think of how tests support your microservices. At the smallest level, you have unit tests, which can assert that all the individual smaller pieces of code are working as intended. This level of testing is obviously not enough, for you need to verify that those pieces can work with each other, which means unit tests need to be supported by a bigger level of tests: component tests. Component tests can check that all subparts of the service can work together to form a cohesive whole, but this is not enough; you also need to verify that your service can work with the rest of your owned components, like databases. This gives rise to acceptance tests. And then, to support this level of testing, you need to verify that your owned components can work as expected with the unowned ones, building end-to-end tests. This way, you can see that your test strategy includes "turtles all the way down."

The analogy isn't perfect, though. There are other types of tests that are useful but don't fit into this idea of *scope progression*. We are referring to *contract tests*, which verify that the *interaction* with an external component works as expected (without the need to include the full service on it), and integration tests, which test all the different communication patterns against components like databases (again, without including the full service).

This idea was effectively put into a graph by Toby Clemson in his presentation "Testing Strategies in a Microservice Architecture," an extract of which appears in Figure 11-2.

However, all the testing in the world cannot guarantee that your application will work in production for one simple reason: your tests didn't run in production. Needless to say, we're not trying to imply that you should run your tests in production. We're just highlighting the fact that there is a score of reasons for which your application could fail in production even though it passed all the tests prior to deployment: production configuration might be wrong, networking setup might prevent services from talking to each other, database keys may not have the right permissions, etc.

In the end, the only way of truly knowing that your application works in production is exercising it in production. This leads to the highest level of testing: *synthetic transactions*, or actions that you execute in the production environment as if you were a real user using the application.

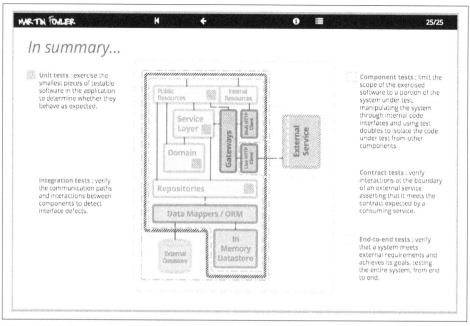

Figure 11-2. A microservice, adjacent components, external services, and the boundaries that all the different types of testing will cover. Image taken from Toby Clemson's online deck on Testing Strategies in a Microservice Architecture (https://martinfowler.com/arti cles/microservice-testing/).

In the rest of the chapter, we will explore all these types of tests, understand when to use them, and indicate examples of how to build them effectively. We will start with the outermost ones, the ones closer to "the real thing" (synthetic transactions), and we will progressively make our way in to the innermost ones, unit tests.

Synthetic Transactions

Synthetic transactions are real transactions exercised against a production system, but by fake users. This activity can be seen as the highest form of testing, since it is performed on the actual production environment with all the real components, and not just a test environment that is meant to represent production.

Synthetic transactions can also supplement typical monitoring techniques to provide more insight into production health, since you can monitor exactly what the user will experience. This way, they can detect when key business metrics fall outside acceptable norms and assist in identifying production issues fast. Some teams decide to have a bunch of key synthetic transactions scheduled to run on a daily basis, as a way to make sure that everything is working OK.

Remove Fingerprints from Synthetic Transactions

Although we are referring to these transactions in a way that somehow makes them look not real, they are very much so. Bear in mind that this is still your production environment, and any transactions that you execute will form the corpus of reports that might be generated by or presented to the business. Wherever possible, remove the effects of synthetic transactions after running them; you don't want the CEO to congratulate the company on the steady increase of new users when your synthetic transactions are responsible for a large number of them.

End-to-End Testing

The next level down from Synthetic Transactions is end-to-end testing. *End-to-end tests* only differ from synthetic transactions in the target environment: like synthetic transactions, end-to-end tests exercise the entire system, including unowned components; however, unlike synthetic transactions, end-to-end tests are run against a purpose-built test environment, as opposed to the real, user-facing production environment. Given that end-to-end tests don't impact real users, you can be more aggressive with them, performing more operations and manipulating the environment at any point to suit your testing needs.

As a microservice architecture includes more moving parts for the same behavior (compared to a monolithic architecture), end-to-end tests provide value by adding coverage of the gaps between the services. This gives additional confidence in the correctness of messages passing between the services, but it also ensures that any extra network infrastructure such as firewalls, proxies, or load-balancers is correctly configured (especially if the deployment and set-up of these have been automated). End-to-end tests also allow a microservice architecture to evolve over time: as more is learned about the problem domain, services are likely to split or merge, and end-to-end tests give confidence that the business functions provided by the system remain intact during such large scale architectural refactorings.

Writing and maintaining end-to-end tests can be difficult, though. Since end-to-end tests involve many more moving parts than the other strategies discussed in this chapter, they have more reasons to fail. End-to-end tests may also have to account for asynchrony in the system, whether in the GUI or due to asynchronous backend processes between the services. But, most importantly, since end-to-end tests include coverage of unowned components, the team won't be fully in control of the environment, limiting their capacity to adapt and react to circumstances. These factors can result in flakiness, excessive test runtime, and additional cost of maintenance of the test suite. Mastering the art of end-to-end tests takes time and practice.

Given all these caveats, and given that a high level of confidence can be achieved through lower levels of testing, the role of end-to-end tests must be just making sure everything ties together and that there are no high-level disagreements between the microservices. As such, comprehensively testing business requirements at this level is wasteful, especially given the expense of end-to-end tests in time and maintenance.

Once you take into account all the many drawbacks, it is fair to question whether you need end-to-end tests at all. The right answer is, it depends. The key thing to note at this point is that it is dangerous to over-rely on end-to-end tests, but that doesn't mean you cannot benefit from them. One of the things to bear in mind is that the difference between end-to-end and acceptance tests is that the former include external services and components, while the latter don't. The tools, the stakeholders, and the strategies are all the same. If your system doesn't interact with external entities, or if you trust that interaction, or if you think that automating the test of that interaction isn't worth the effort, you might be OK with just acceptance tests.

If you do decide to write end-to-end tests, one strategy that works well in keeping an end-to-end test suite small is to apply a time budget, an amount of time the team is happy to wait for the test suite to run. As the suite grows, if the runtime begins to exceed the time budget, the least valuable tests are deleted (or re-written as lower-level tests) to keep the build within the allotted time. The time budget should be in the order of minutes, not hours.

Also, to ensure that all tests in an end-to-end suite are valuable, you should model them around personas of users of the system and the journeys those users make through the system (e.g., "A customer that buys a product for the first time" or "An accountant that needs to review the tax balance for the last quarter"). This provides confidence in the parts of the system that users value the most and leaves coverage of anything else to other types of testing. Tools, such as Gauge and Concordion, exist to help in expressing journeys via business-readable DSLs.

You may have noticed that we have talked about the philosophy and recommended approaches of end-to-end tests, but we haven't delved into any tools or practices to do this. This is because the tools and practices are the same for end-to-end and acceptance tests; since you are likely to spend more time writing acceptance than end-to-end tests, we will cover the details of tools and practices in the next section.

End-to-End Testing May Be Considered Harmful!

As noted by Steve Smith in "End-to-End Testing Considered Harmful" (*http://bit.ly/2IjDf5U*), end-to-end testing often seems attractive because of its perceived benefits: an end-to-end test maximizes its system under test, suggesting a high degree of test coverage; and an end-to-end test uses the system itself as a test client, suggesting a low investment in test infrastructure. However, the end-to-end testing value proposition is fatally flawed, as both assumptions are incorrect:

- The idea that testing a whole system will simultaneously test its constituent parts is a decomposition fallacy. Checking implementation against requirements is not the same as checking intent against implementation, which means an end-to-end test will check the interactions between code pathways but not the behaviors within those pathways.

- The idea that testing a whole system will be cheaper than testing its constituent parts is a cheap investment fallacy. Test execution time and nondeterminism are directly proportional to system under test scope, which means an end-to-end test will be slow and prone to nondeterminism.

End-to-end testing is an uncomprehensive, high-cost testing strategy. An end-to-end test will not check behaviors, will take time to execute, and will intermittently fail, so a test suite largely composed of end-to-end tests will result in poor test coverage, slow execution times, and nondeterministic results.

Acceptance Testing

As previously mentioned, *acceptance tests* and end-to-end tests vary solely in scope: acceptance tests exclude unowned dependent services. If, for instance, you are responsible for a Company Accounts system that uses an external Payments service, and you want to write acceptance tests for it, your system under test would comprise the latest Company Accounts code and a Payments Stub.

Acceptance tests can be written just like any other tests: as a set of automated actions with some prior setup and a number of assertions at the end. However, their position gives you an opportunity to treat them slightly differently. Acceptance testing is the highest form of automated testing in which everything is fully under your control: you can create and delete data, take services up and down, inspect internal status, etc. This means that acceptance tests can be designed as a form of rewriting the business requirements, up to the point that tests and test results can be easily inspected by nontechnical people.

This idea is encapsulated in the term *behavior-driven development* which has become almost a synonym of acceptance testing. In the rest of this section, we will assume that you have chosen to use BDD to implement acceptance tests, and we will go over both the practice and the main tools that facilitate it.

Behavior-Driven Development

Behavior-driven development (BDD) is a technique to develop systems that appeared as a generalization of TDD. The idea is that, for each use case or scenario, you list the behavior that should be perceived when a user is exercising the system, express that behavior as a set of steps, and then turn those steps into executable actions. Those executable actions can then be run against the system, and if all of them succeed, the scenario can be considered to be successfully implemented. The art of BDD is a wide topic that would require a book on its own, and indeed there are some great resources (for example, *BDD in Action* [Manning] by John Ferguson Smart), so we'll only cover the surface here.

Now, whether the BDD tests need to be written before or after the feature is implemented is a matter of debate (see "Testing Outside-In Versus Testing Inside-Out" on page 327), but that's not the main point of BDD. The key advantage of BDD compared to other forms of tests is that BDD is expressed in a high-level language that business people can understand, and the test execution and reports are formatted in a way that nontechnical people can consume. In some teams, the business people write the steps, and then the developers implement them and make them pass.

There isn't a single tool that makes BDD possible. It could be said that in few areas has the combination of different tools designed to address different problems created such a powerful combined effect as in the realm of acceptance testing. There are essentially three problems that need to be addressed when designing acceptance tests in a BDD manner:

- The definition, execution, and reporting of scenarios and steps, using tools like SerenityBDD.
- The interaction with the system mimicking user interaction and experience, using tools like Selenium WebDriver.
- The enablement of such interaction in environments that are radically different from users' devices, using tools like HtmlUnit.

Let's go through them one by one.

Defining steps

Multiple tools can be used to define steps in a BDD interaction, all of which are similar. Some of the most popular ones that are available for Java are Cucumber, JBehave, and SerenityBDD.

The pattern in all of them is simple. You start by indicating a particular feature or story. (The terminology might be different, depending on the tool.) For each feature or story, you indicate various scenarios, or use cases, that describe how the feature is supposed to work. Each scenario is described by multiple steps, each of them tagged with one of these keywords:

Given

> Steps that start with "Given" are supposed to indicate the state of the system at the time of initiating the action; for instance, "Given that the user has an account...".

When

> Steps that start with "When" indicate the actions that the user runs against the system; it's a prelude of the conclusion that will happen next. For instance, "When the user enters her username and password and hits Enter...".

Then

> Steps that start with "Then" indicate the consequence of the previous steps, and they are essentially BDD's version of assertions. For instance, "Then the user is logged in."

It's important to note that these keywords are just syntactic sugar for the reader: they don't mean anything from the execution point of view. You could write all the steps with "Given," or with "Then," and the tests would run the same. Some tools even forgo the idea of Given/When/Then and simply call everything just a "Step."

One of these tools is SerenityBDD, which is also the one we have chosen to demonstrate acceptance tests in the Extended Java Shop. SerenityBDD integrates with JUnit and other tests' frameworks seamlessly, meaning you have to worry only about the definition of steps. Although full details can be found at the documentation page (*http://www.thucydides.info/docs/serenity/*), the basic working of SerenityBDD is as follows.

First, you need to create one or more classes that will hold your steps. Each step will be a different method, and will be tagged with the annotation @Step:

```
@Step
public void user_obtains_the_list_of_products() {
    productNames = page.getProductNames();
}

@Step
```

```
public void shopfront_service_is_ready() {
    page.load();
}

// ... //
```

These steps can then be used in normal tests:

```
@Test
public void numberOfProductsAsExpected() {
    // GIVEN
    shopfrontSteps.shopfront_service_is_ready();

    // WHEN
    shopfrontSteps.user_obtains_the_list_of_products();

    // ... //
}
```

You may think that annotating the methods with @Step seems redundant, since those methods can be called anyway from the test, but then you would be missing one of the most important features of this kind of tools: the reports. By tagging these methods as steps, SerenityBDD can then create appropriate, high-level reports that show which steps worked and which ones didn't, like the one in Figure 11-3.

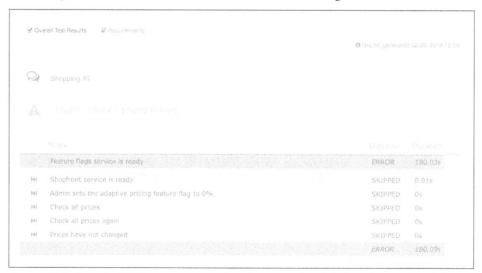

Figure 11-3. SerenityBDD's error report, showing steps that failed and steps that didn't run

Mimicking user action

Because you are testing at the highest possible level, you want your actions to be as close as possible to those of a real user. Despite all the microservices that may be present in your system, chances are that, eventually, your users are going to interact with you via a website. Therefore, what you want is a way to mimic the way in which a user interacts with your website. This is achieved with tools like Selenium Web-Driver (or just Selenium).

Selenium can bring up a browser and allows you to interact with it in an automated manner. Through Selenium, you can tell the browser to visit a page, fill in text boxes, click buttons, etc. Selenium also allows you to programmatically inspect the page, querying whether a particular object is present or whether it has certain text. What's more, since the action is driven through a real browser, any JavaScript code will also be executed, bringing it closer to a user's experience. Selenium lets you focus on what the user does, feels, and sees.

It's important to note that, even though Selenium can help in writing tests, it is not a test tool in itself. It's just a tool to interact with a web browser programmatically.

Making build instances work like a user device

The first time that you use Selenium, you will probably stumble upon one major hurdle: you can use Selenium in your developer machine with no problem, because your browser of choice is locally installed and Selenium can bring it up, but the browser is not available in the machine running your tests as part of the automated build pipeline, and it will fail. You may think that you just need to install the browser in the build nodes, but chances are that will fail, too: even if the browser is available, your nodes are most likely machines designed for running tests, and won't have a graphical environment. If you try to start up a browser, it will fail, because it won't have a graphical subsystem where it can open a window.

To be able to run Selenium in your automated build pipeline, you either need build nodes that include a graphical interface (which would consume significant resources), or a browser without the need for one. And that's exactly what HtmlUnit is.

HtmlUnit can communicate with a server and obtain websites like a user. It can process HTML and run JavaScript. It can even mimic the input of data and actions like clicking or selecting. And it can do all this without the need to create a graphical window, making it perfectly suitable for running Selenium actions in a windowless environment.

Visual Regression/Comparison Testing

Some organizations like to ensure that web-based user interfaces do not change in a meaningful way unless specifically updated. Visual regression and comparison test tooling allow you to automate the comparison of a "before and after" image of a web page. Popular visual regression testing tools to include in your CD pipeline include PhantomCSS (*https://github.com/HuddleEng/PhantomCSS*), Gemini (*https://*

---

github.com/gemini-testing/gemini), and Pix-Diff (*https://github.com/koola/pix-diff*). This is an area of testing that is in flux and beyond the scope of this book, and we recommend that if you're interested, you experiment with several of the tools, and potentially consider commercial offerings, before deciding on which to rely on within a build pipeline.

Stubbing or Virtualizing Third-Party Services

Although some systems are small enough that a single team has ownership of all the composite components, in many cases, systems grow to have dependencies on one or more externally managed services. As previously stated, you are not supposed to include these external services in your acceptance tests, but your application will still have to contact something that looks like them. The best thing to do at this point is to either stub or create a fake service that behaves like the external service, and include that in the mix when you are running your acceptance tests.

You could write a web service from scratch, or you could use tools like WireMock or Hoverfly (as you saw in "Virtualizing Services with Hoverfly" on page 165). Wire-Mock is a stubbing framework for web applications that can create a service that listens on a specified port, and that can respond to requests in any way you configure it. This then becomes the third-party service that your application communicates with during acceptance tests. More on WireMock in "Component Testing" on page 311.

Bringing It All Together

The Extended Java Shop includes a fully working example of acceptance tests that includes all the items mentioned in this section, and then some more. It can be found in the folder */acceptance-tests* of the Extended Java Shop repository, and is mainly characterized by the following items:

- A *docker-compose.yml* file that will bring all the owned services up so they can be tested together.

- To substitute the Adaptive Pricing service (which in our setup is meant to be a third-party system), we have decided to opt for a virtualized service called `fake-adaptive-pricing`. This is brought up also using `docker-compose` (in practice, you'll notice that the Fake Adaptive Pricing is simply a wrapper for the real one, but that's just to make the sample application simpler; the key thing is that, from the acceptance tests' point of view, we're not using the real one).

- Maven has been complemented with a docker-compose plugin to be able to start up and bring down all the necessary Docker containers for testing. See *pom.xml* for details.

- SerenityBDD is in use in the main test class, `ShoppingAT`, and in the steps classes in the `steps` package.

- Selenium WebDriver is in use in the `ShopfrontHomePage` class, where high-level ways to interact with the Shopfront home page are recorded.

- HtmlUnit is specified when we instantiate the Selenium WebDriver object in `ShoppingAT` (near the top of the class).

Consumer-Driven Contracts

Whenever a consumer couples to the interface of a component to make use of its behavior, an implicit contract is formed between them. This contract consists of expectations of input and output data structures, side effects and performance, and concurrency characteristics. The idea of *consumer-driven contracts* (sometimes called simply *contract tests*) is to make that contract explicit in the form of executable tests that will verify whenever either side is deviating from the agreement.

Tests based on consumer-driven contracts can be used in two different scenarios:

- Both parts, consumer and provider, agree on the need to have a contract that ties down the interaction. This could either be because your team owns both consumer and provider, and you just want to make sure the interaction is correct, or because even though consumer and provider are owned by different teams, they have agreed on having close communication to ensure that the interaction is fluid and flawless.

- Only the consumer is willing to create contract tests, maybe because the provider doesn't want to go through that trouble, or because the provider has so many consumers that they can't afford to share contract tests with all of them. The second case is more common that it would seem. For instance, if one writes a client to consume the Twitter API, it is very unlikely that they'll be able to share the burden of contract tests, even if they are willing—imagine if they had to do that with all consumers!

Being confronted with one case or the other will affect not just the type of tests that you write, but also the technologies that you use to write those tests, and even the frequency at which you run them. Let's begin with the latter case. If the provider is not willing or able to participate in the interface verification, you're just writing one-sided contract tests. This means you're essentially treating the external service as a black box and you're writing tests to verify that behavior doesn't change unexpectedly, which is no different from what you would do to test your own service (see "Component Testing" on page 311). Given this, you don't need any special tool to write these contract tests; normal testing libraries will do, but you do need to be careful about scheduling.

Is This Really a Contract?

You might be wondering whether a contract that exists for only one side of the interaction is really a contract. The technical response would be that what you are writing isn't the contract, but the *test* that verifies the contract. The contract is the implicit understanding that an API wouldn't change without notice. However, if the name troubles you, just call it something else.

Ideally, you would run your contract tests whenever the client component in the consumer or the interface component in the provider are modified. However, if the provider is not participating in the contract verification, you aren't likely to know when the provider has changed. You'll have to configure your pipeline to execute the contract tests whenever your client component changes, and then, depending on how often you do change your client component, you'll have to consider also scheduling a regular test execution (e.g., daily or weekly) to try to detect any changes that may have happened on the provider side.

Test What You Need, but No Further

If you remember from "Backward Compatibility and Versions in APIs" on page 278, one of the ways to handle changes in an API is to allow responses to be modified in a backward-compatible manner. This means that the provider might add new fields at any point without that being considered a violation of the contract. Given this, avoid testing that the entire response from the provider is as you expect. Instead, simply test that you can obtain whatever fields you need. That will save you a lot of time handling false-positives.

The story changes when both provider and consumer are willing to participate in the verification of the interaction. Here we can talk about proper contract-based testing, and use technologies aimed specifically at the specification and verification of contracts. Let's see them in detail.

RESTful API Contracts

Once provider and consumer have agreed to share the burden of contract testing, several things need to happen. On one side, the provider has to write tests that verify that the API doesn't change (at least, not inadvertently). On the other side, each consumer has to write tests that verify that their application works with the responses provided by the consumer. There are several issues with this approach. On one hand, there is a significant communication overhead whenever the provider changes the API. On the other hand, there is a non-negligible amount of duplicated effort by all the different consumers to test the same thing from the provider.

It is for this reason that contract tests shouldn't be written using typical testing tools, but specialized ones. The contract itself should be represented by an independent physical entity that both providers and consumers subscribe to: the provider verifies that the contract is a fair representation of what they produce, while the consumers verify that they can cope with responses from the provider as specified by the contract. Whenever a change in the API is needed, the contract is updated, and everybody reruns their tests against the updated version.

There are different tools to specify contracts, each following different approaches that try to align with different team dynamics and social interactions. We can roughly categorize these tools into two groups, depending on what is considered to be the source of truth. This way, you have contract-first tools, where an independent entity (the contract) is the source of truth, and interaction-first tools, where the consumer is the source of truth. As you will see in detail, in contract-first tools, either consumer or provider may be seen as aligning with or deviating from the contract, while for interaction-first tools, only the provider can be seen as abiding by or violating the contract.

Contract first, interaction second

Contract-first tools work by beginning with the definition of a contract in the form of a set of interactions. Each interaction will specify an example of a request followed by an example of a response. The tools usually provide options to include random values within the requests and/or responses to avoid falling into hardcoded value traps. This, together with many other variants, allows the configuration of the contracts to be as realistic as possible. The tool can then generate two types of artifacts for consumers and providers:

For providers
> The tool turns each interaction into a test; the sample request is sent to the service, and then it checks that the response from the service matches the sample response.

For consumers
> The tool creates a preconfigured, stubbed service that you can use when testing the consumer application. For each request that the consumer application makes to the stub, the stub will check whether it matches one of the sample requests and, if so, it will respond with the corresponding sample response.

The asymmetry in the artifacts created for consumers and providers reflects the difference in responsibilities: while the provider needs to abide by *all* the use cases specified in the contract, a given consumer may need to use only some of them. This is why the contract becomes a set of *enforced* rules for the provider, but a set of *available* rules for the consumer.

In the Extended Java Shop, we have chosen to demonstrate contract-first tools with the use of Spring Cloud Contract. In this example, we are using Spring Cloud Contract to verify the interaction between the Stock Manager service and the Shopfront service. The contracts themselves live in the Stock Manager project as a set of Groovy files in the package `contracts.stockmanager` (in the folder */stockmanager/src/test/ resources/contracts/stockmanager*); they should be easy to interpret, although full details about the syntax can be found at the Spring Cloud Contract documentation (*http://bit.ly/2Oa6BZZ*). These contracts are then used by both the Stock Manager service build, and the Shopfront service build.

The Stock Manager service build uses the contracts rather transparently, thanks to the inclusion of a specific Spring Cloud Contract Maven plugin. The only code that is needed is the creation of a base class for the generated tests to extend and where any setup will be performed; in our example, this will be `StockManagerCDCBase`.

The Shopfront service needs some extra setup, though. The job definition in Jenkins needs to be modified to make sure it is triggered whenever the contract is modified, and a step needs to be added to generate the artifact that contains the stubbed service. Check the job definition for the Shopfront service in either of the three prebuilt Jenkins instances in the Extended Java Shop repository. (You can do this by looking at the file */jenkins-base/jobs/shopfront/config.xml*, or by running any of the prebuilt Jenkins instances locally as specified in the relevant *README.md* files and looking at the job definition.) After this, a specific test that uses the generated stubbed service can be written; see `StockManagerCDC` in Shopfront service for details.

Interaction first, contract second

Interaction-first is a different breed of contract testing tools that take the idea of consumer-driven contracts to the extreme. In this kind of tool, the consumer starts by writing a set of tests that indicate how it expects to interact with the provider. By running these tests against a stub, the tool can make a record of the requests sent by the consumer and the responses that it expects, and call such record the *contract*. This contract is then sent to the provider, where it will be run against it as a form of component tests that the provider is expected to comply with. Interaction-first tools are therefore a way to run TDD against the definition of an API.

Despite being more faithful to the concept of CDC, interaction-first tools have shortcomings when compared to contract-first tools, at least under some scenarios. If the same team owns both the consumer and the provider, interaction-first tools are ideal, because they ensure that the provider is doing exactly what the consumer needs it to do and nothing else. However, if consumer(s) and provider belong to different teams, these tools can be a source of significant friction.

A provider's build might be broken because a consumer might have misunderstood the way the API is supposed to work and have written their tests wrong. (Remember, it is the contract that is written from the test, not the other way around.) A rogue consumer might "bully" the provider into developing new features by simply writing some tests for the interaction that they desire, breaking the provider's build until these are done. And a provider who wants to develop a new version of the API will have no contract tests to validate it until a consumer starts to use it, unless the provider's team writes a consumer themselves. These, of course, aren't faults attributable to the tool, but to a flawed organizational culture and misguided social interaction, but one needs to be aware that interaction-first tools enable this sort of behavior.

But remember: there aren't right or wrong tools, just tools that are more or less adequate for a particular scenario. Despite the aforementioned disadvantages, an interaction-first tool might be exactly what your team needs.

The Extended Java Shop doesn't include any examples of interaction-first tools, but we encourage you to check out Pact (*https://docs.pact.io*) and Pact Broker (*https://github.com/pact-foundation/pact_broker*).

Unvilifying Contract Tests

Contract testing has a bad reputation for being brittle, slow, and a source of friction across teams. The truth is that whenever these attributes are present, it is mostly due to a flawed approach.

Brittleness tends to come from overzealous contract tests that test way more than needed. For instance, and as we explained in the Test What You Need, but No Further, if you check full responses in your contract, you'll lock yourself against harmless, backward-compatible changes.

Slowness usually appears because a lot of business logic seeps into contracts, bloating them unnecessarily. Your business logic should be tested mostly elsewhere—for instance, in unit and component testing, while your interaction checks should be addressed in integration testing. The contract is there basically to check that the format of the resources hasn't changed.

Friction emerges when contract testing is used as a surrogate for real communication. For instance, if instead of engaging with consumers to negotiate an API change, you simply push it, assuming that "contract failures will let them know," you are asking for trouble.

The truth is that contracts can bring you a lot of benefit—if you use them wisely.

Message Contracts

When it comes to RESTful interfaces, services communicate with each other by using HTTP (barring some odd exceptions). Therefore, regardless of the technology used for the client and/or server side (Dropwizard, Play, Jetty, etc.), when it comes to contract testing, you can use anything that communicates via HTTP to mimic the client and/or server and verify your contracts. Unfortunately, the situation isn't quite as standardized for the case of messaging platforms, and we won't be able to provide a single solution for testing message contracts.

It is important to highlight that the objective of this section isn't to help you choose a messaging technology, but rather to assist in how to test it. For this reason, we will go through the most popular options when it comes to messaging platforms, and indicate how each of them can be tested most effectively. Because of the array of options, we won't cover each of them in detail, but we'll include references so you can explore further if needed.

Contract testing at the protocol layer

Testing at the protocol level is useful when the different services that send messages to each other do so using different technologies, but abiding by the same protocol. This is an analogous situation to RESTful services, where different services may use different web technologies, but they all communicate using HTTP. Among the different message queue protocols available, the most popular one is AMQP (*https://www.amqp.org*), with implementations including RabbitMQ, Apache Qpid, and Apache ActiveMQ, among others.

If you are using AMQP as your communication protocol, you can easily execute contract tests by using Pact (*https://docs.pact.io*) and Pact Broker (*https://github.com/pact-foundation/pact_broker*). The way the tests are executed is no different from the case of web services described previously. The only difference is that, instead of mimicking the HTTP interaction of server/client, you mimic the AMQP interaction of producer/consumer. Specifics can be found in the documentation, but to give a sense of how similar both approaches are with Pact, suffice it to say that the test setup will differ only in that it uses an `AmqpTarget` object instead of an `HttpTarget` object for the mimicked service.

Contract testing at the serialization layer

In some cases, you won't want to or be able to run your contract tests at the protocol layer. For instance, you might be using a message queue protocol for which there is no easy testing framework. Or you might be using exactly the same technology in all your services, meaning you can afford to move the actual protocol out of the equation. Regardless of the reason, you can assume that messages are going to be correctly delivered to the right recipient, and focus only on the messages themselves. In other words, you can focus on the *production and interpretation* of the messages.

The best strategy in this scenario is to define schemas for all your messages, including different versions of the same message. This is particularly easy to do if you use Apache Avro (*https://avro.apache.org*) to serialize your messages, because then you can leverage the Confluent Schema Registry (*http://bit.ly/2Q5Xyq6*) to store and retrieve your schemas during testing. Gwen Shapira's excellent talk, "Streaming Microservices: Contracts & Compatibility" (*http://bit.ly/2DzcSu4*), shows in detail how this can be achieved.

Even if you don't use Avro or the Confluent Schema Registry, you can still use Gwen's ideas to hone your serialization-based contract tests, especially if you need to support several versions of the same message schema:

- You can contract-test your producers to ensure that they generate messages using *all* versions of a schema, placing each copy in a different queue. You can then contract-test your consumers to ensure that they interpret messages of *at least one* version of a schema, taking it from the relevant queue.

- Similarly, you can contract-test your producers to ensure that they generate messages matching *at least one* version of a schema. You can then contract-test your consumers to ensure that they can interpret messages matching *any* version of the schema, again ensuring producer/consumer communication.

- Finally, you can contract-test both producers and consumers to ensure that they can produce/consume messages matching *at least one* version of schema, and then create a number of message transformers that you can contract-test to ensure that they can convert from any given version to any other version of a schema.

In some ways, serialization-based contract testing is a more natural form of contracts, because it takes the *schema* of the message as the contract to abide by. This way, you can leave aside the actual exchange mechanism and focus on the message itself.

Component Testing

A *component* is any well-encapsulated, coherent, and independently replaceable part of a larger system. Testing such components in isolation provides multiple benefits. By limiting the scope to a single component, it is possible to thoroughly test the behavior encapsulated by that component while maintaining tests that execute more quickly than broad stack equivalents. In the context of microservices, you can identify a component as one microservice.

Now, there are challenges and questions that need to be addressed when considering component tests. To begin with, your microservice is likely to have external dependencies that you want to exclude when testing your component, so you need an effective and efficient way to replace those. On the other hand, you may need to check some internal behaviors when testing your component, but you need to do this while still treating your service as a black box. Finally, you need to be careful with the very mechanism through which you run the component tests, since this may affect how much of your component you are actually testing. Let's go through all of this.

Testcontainers: Manage Containers for Testing

If you are building and deploying Java applications with containers, or are encountering challenges with (potentially non JVM based) reproducible test environments, then we recommend you take a look at the Testcontainers (*https://www.testcontainers.org/*), written by Richard North. Testcontainers makes it easy to launch useful Docker containers for the duration of JUnit tests; for example, when executing an integration test you can run throwaway instances of common databases, headless Selenium web browsers, or anything else that can run self-contained in a Docker container. We would like to thank Asaf Mesika, Chief Architect at Logz.io, for reminding us of this useful tool.

Embedded Data Stores

If your service uses a database, you will want to exclude that from your component tests. First, because the database is not really part of the service, it's a different component that your service communicates with (even if database and service are tightly coupled). Second, and maybe more important, including the database in your component tests would add complexity and slow it down. Besides, you are already including a real database in your acceptance tests, so you can part with it at this level.

What you need, therefore, is something that can look like a database to your service, but without all the added complexity. You need an embedded data store, which is typically implemented by an in-memory database. An in-memory database will offer the same interface as a normal database, but will run entirely in memory, removing the delays of network and disk access. There are multiple options for this, but the most common ones are H2 (*http://www.h2database.com/html/main.html*) for standard SQL databases and Fongo (*https://github.com/fakemongo/fongo*) for MongoDB.

The Extended Java Shop includes an example of component tests supported by an H2 in-memory database in the Feature Flags service, although this may not be entirely obvious at first. The component tests of the Feature Flags service (folder */feature-flags*), located in the `FeatureFlagsApplicationCT` class, make some heavy usage of "Spring Boot magic," so if you're looking to understand how H2 is used, you should look at the following:

- The *test/resources* folder includes an *application.properties* file that will override any matching files in *main/resources*. This file is empty, effectively removing all the configuration items provided in *main/resources*. In a situation like this, Spring Boot will try to guess the parameters from whatever it can find in the classpath.

- The *pom.xml* file has added an H2 dependency for testing.

- When running the tests, Spring Boot will notice the H2 driver in the classpath and, without any other parameters related to database, assume this is what it needs to use. Because H2 works in memory, no connection details such as URL or username are needed, and our application will be autowired to use H2.

For applications based on frameworks other than Spring Boot, you may need to explicitly indicate that H2 is to be used; this is usually accomplished by configuring the connection URL to something like `jdbc:h2:mem:`. For other H2 connection options, you can check the H2 documentation (*http://www.h2database.com/html/features.html#database_url*).

In-Memory Message Queues

The same arguments apply when running component tests for services that communicate to a message queue: for control and speed, you will want to run the message queue server in-memory. However, as we discussed when we talked about "Consumer-Driven Contracts" on page 305, the world of message queues is not as standardized as other disciplines, and while you can use an in-memory database that understands SQL to mimic any other database solution, there isn't a single tool that can help with message queue technologies. But you still have options.

First, many message queue brokers have the option to run without persistence, effectively turning them into in-memory technologies. If your message queue of choice does support this option, you can just start an instance locally before your component tests start and then stop it when you're done.

Sometimes you won't be able to do this for a variety of reasons: maybe the message broker doesn't support running without persistence, or maybe you can't run an instance locally because of license or resource constraints. In these cases, you can try the following:

AMQP-based queues
    All message queue brokers that implement AMQP are interchangeable at the functional level, meaning you can just pick a different technology for testing. ActiveMQ (*http://bit.ly/2R2zENK*) can easily be set up to run in-memory as part of your tests, with the drawback that it supports only AMQP 1.0; for earlier versions, you can use Qpid (*http://bit.ly/2Og50BR*).

Kafka

Apache Kafka is so popular that we consider it worth its own mention. Kafka runs on top of ZooKeeper, meaning you can effectively have an in-memory Kafka instance if you run it using the in-process `TestingServer` (*https://cura tor.apache.org/curator-test/*) for ZooKeeper. Alternatively, if you're using Spring Boot, you can just use `EmbeddedKafka` (*http://bit.ly/2zwPIR0*), which essentially runs the in-memory Kafka and ZooKeeper instances for you.

If none of the previous options apply to your case, you can still try some ad hoc options. You can consider creating a Docker image that will start up an instance of your message queue broker, and spin up a container for that image before your component tests; this won't be exactly in-memory, but at least it will keep things locally. Alternatively, if the protocol is simple enough, you can consider creating your own in-memory message queue implementation.

Finally, if no option fits you, maybe you need to take a step back and remove the message queue from the equation: instead of using an in-memory version of the message queue broker, you can use an in-memory version of the code that communicates with the message queue—your message queue client. It's true that this will avoid testing the connection to the message queue, but you can try to bridge that gap through acceptance and integration tests.

Test Doubles

In the same way that your service may make use of a database that you want to exclude in your component tests, it may communicate with other services that you also want to exclude. You can replace these dependencies with *test doubles*, owned entities that mimic the external behavior of your dependencies, but without the real internal logic.

The development community has a longstanding debate about the different types of test doubles and the names that each type should have, with terms like *stubs*, *mocks*, *fakes*, *dummies*, *spies*, and some others being constantly thrown in and out. In recent times, it has also added *virtualized services* to the mix. This is still a slightly contentious topic, and some readers might disagree with what we are going to expose next, but in our case, we have decided to adopt the view of Wojciech Bulaty (*http://bit.ly/2zwaiRm*) and define the following:

Stub

The simplest of test doubles, a static resource that has fixed values configured for each possible call. It doesn't keep a state, and it's not configurable.

Mock

An evolution of the previous; it can be configured to return different values according to different patterns, or it can be reconfigured before each test. It keeps a state, and it can be queried after the test has run to verify whether specific functions have been invoked and how.

Virtualized service

Similar to a mock, but long-lived and hosted at a remote server. Virtualized services can typically be shared between developers and testers.

Any of these types can be useful when replacing real dependencies in component tests, but because of their characteristics, mocks tend to be the most common option. Stubs are sometimes too simplistic to cover some of the cases of a component test, while virtualized services add the delay and uncertainty of a remote network connection.

Stubs can usually be implemented manually, but mocks and virtual services benefit from some tooling. In the realm of component testing, the most common of these tools is WireMock (*http://wiremock.org*). WireMock can be used as a mock or as a virtualized service in the following ways:

WireMock as a mock

You can start and configure a WireMock instance at any point during your tests; a good example of this can be found in `ShopfrontApplicationCT`, where we have used WireMock to replace the service dependencies of the Shopfront service.

WireMock as virtualized service

Once configured, WireMock can be started up as a standalone service and deployed into a server, making it permanently available for anyone who needs it. Alternatively, there is also the option of MockLab (*https://get.mocklab.io*), a service built on top of WireMock that allows the creation of virtualized services in the cloud.

Regardless of your choice, the important thing to take into account when writing component tests is that you make them independent from the real services your component has to communicate with. This will reduce the probability of false-positives and will allow you to run your tests with confidence.

Creating Internal Resources/Interfaces

As previously mentioned, there are situations in which you want to verify certain internal behaviors as part of your component tests, but you can't test them directly because that would break the encapsulation that component tests are meant to provide. The best option in this situation is to create internal resources or interfaces—endpoints in your web service that are not meant to be available to the general public. These internal resources can expose the details that you need to verify in your test, and you can use them to check whether the service is behaving as expected.

Perhaps the easiest way to expose this is with an example, which you can find in the Extended Java Shop—more precisely, in the Shopfront service (folder /shopfront). As we have mentioned before, the Shopfront service can talk to an external Adaptive Pricing service to try to override the price of our products to obtain a higher revenue. Let's say that this Adaptive Pricing service is still rather experimental and not reliable, and it's frequently down. To minimize the impact of this to our Shopfront service, we want to add a circuit breaker to the connection to the Adaptive Pricing service, for which we will use Netflix's Hystrix (*https://github.com/Netflix/Hystrix*) library; details of this can be seen in the `AdaptivePricingRepo` class.

Now, as part of our component tests, we want to verify that when the Adaptive Pricing service is down, the circuit breaker trips and we stop making calls to it, providing a default value instead. We also want to test that after the Adaptive Pricing service is restored, the circuit breaker closes and we continue to make calls to the external service. We could test this by keeping a count of the number of requests we are making to the Shopfront service and comparing it to the number of requests that our Adaptive Pricing service mock is receiving, but this would be a rather cumbersome test. What we have decided to do instead is create a new internal endpoint, called */internal/circuit-breakers*, and then use the `InternalResource` class to obtain information about all the circuit breakers within the Shopfront service and their status. This way, tests can easily query the status of the circuit breakers and verify that behavior is as expected. What's more, if you ever change the way circuit breakers are implemented, the component tests will be unaffected.

Internal resources can be restricted to tests (for instance, via feature flags), or they can be packaged with the application and deployed to production. The latter can be useful, because a quick way to assess the internal status of your service can assist in the investigation of production issues.

Control Access to Internal Resources in Production

Internal resources provide useful information for investigations, but may contain sensitive details that shouldn't be leaked to outsiders. If you do release your internal resources to production, make sure that access is restricted to authorized parties. You can do this by configuring your services so that a specific token is needed to access the resource, or by placing all your internal resources under a common path like */internal* and then adding a traffic rule so requests to that path can be performed only from within the organization's network.

In-Process Versus Out-Of-Process

The last concern to take into account when designing your component tests is perhaps one of the easiest to miss. The thing is, we have been talking about testing your entire service in isolation, but where does the service really end? Is it just the set of classes that you have written? Or does it also include whatever web framework that you have based your application on and that will be ultimately responsible for listening to requests and dispatching responses?

Depending on your answers to these questions, you will be implicitly choosing from two options: in-process testing or out-of-process testing. The names derive from the mechanics used to run the tests. With in-process testing, the service and the tests are running under the same OS process, and the communication between the two is largely done in-memory. However, with out-of-process testing, the service and the tests are running under *different* OS processes, and the communication between the two is performed over a communication protocol like TCP/IP (even though this will still be contained within the running machine). Let's analyze the pros and cons of each approach.

Assume that your answer to the previous questions was that you consider your service to comprise only the code that your team has written, and that the underlying web framework has already been thoroughly tested by its creators and by other parties. In this case, you probably don't want to include the web framework in your component test, because that will only slow it down unnecessarily. Most frameworks will include test utilities that allow you to bypass all the scaffolding and hook into the service at the point where your code starts. This will obviously need the tests and your service to run under the same process, because the machinery for over-the-wire communication might not even be available. You can find an example of this kind of test in the Product Catalogue service (folder */productcatalogue*)—more precisely, in the `ProductServiceApplicationCT` class. The Product Catalogue service is a Dropwizard-based application, and the test uses `DropwizardAppRule` to instantiate the server automatically before the test starts, and then brings it down after the test is finished.

Similarly, assume now that your answers to the preceding questions were the opposite: you consider that the web framework is, like any other dependency, part of your service, and therefore needs to be tested when you treat your application as a black box. In this case, you want to start up your application independently from your tests to keep them entirely separate, and then use a normal HTTP client (or whatever communication technology that you are using) to exercise your service from the tests. An example of this can be found in the Stock Manager service (folder */stockmanager*)—more precisely, in `StockManagerApplicationCT`. The Stock Manager service is a Spring Boot–based application. However, you won't see any references to Spring Boot in these tests; compare this with `ShopfrontApplicationCT` in the Shopfront service (folder */shopfront*), where we are using Spring Boot testing facilities. In the Stock Manager service, the component tests are contacting the application by using RestAssured, a library to execute actions over HTTP with a BDD-style syntax. The application itself is being started by Maven through the Spring Boot Maven plugin before tests are executed, and stopped also by this plugin after the tests are done; check the *pom.xml* file for details.

As usual, neither approach is intrinsically better than the other, and your choice will be based on the needs and values of your team. To assist in this decision, we have included a summary in Table 11-1 with the main pros and cons of each approach.

Table 11-1. Comparison of in-process and out-of-process approaches for component tests

	In-process	Out-of-process
Service execution	Startup and shutdown are automatically managed during test execution and performed transparently; tests can be run within an IDE without any manual steps.	Startup and shutdown of the application need to be managed independently from tests; the developer will have to start the service manually to be able to run component tests within an IDE.
Communication pattern	Depending on the framework, communication will be performed in-memory or via the chosen protocol (e.g., TCP/IP).	Communication needs to be done using whatever protocol the application will use in production; e.g., TCP/IP.
Scope	Framework may not be included in tests.	Framework will be included in tests.
Test coupling	Tests will depend on the framework used to develop the application; if the framework is changed, tests will have to be amended.	Tests are independent from the framework used to develop the application; if the framework is changed, tests remain unaffected.
Speed	Potentially faster, as parts of the stack are being bypassed.	Slower, because everything is being executed.
Running tests independently (e.g., manually and one by one from the IDE)	Slow, because the application will be started and stopped after each test.	Fast, because the application will remain active across test runs.
Bringing changes in	Automatic; because the application is autostarted at each test, any changes will be detected.	Manual; you'll have to restart the application yourself if you have changed the code.

Remember: Out-of-Process Testing Implies Manual Reload!

One of the most frustrating, baffling, and disheartening experiences comes when you're trying to fix a failing test: you keep changing the code of your application and, when you run it again, the test is still failing. You try ever more esoteric and drastic measures, but still no, the test is broken. And then it hits you: you have changed the code, but you haven't restarted the service! You can get so used to all the automatic actions by IDEs and tools that sometimes you forget that *you* need to press that pesky button. You've been warned!

Integration Testing

Integration testing is another of those terms that mean different things to different people. Some people consider that a system is "integrated" when all the components are fit together, and therefore understand that "integration testing" should involve all the existing components. That's what we have called *end-to-end* testing in this book. Here, when we use the term *integration testing*, we are referring to the test of a particular integration point; for instance, when your service talks to a database, the hard drive, or another service. James Shore and Shane Warden tried to solve this dilemma in their book *The Art of Agile Development* (O'Reilly) by calling this *focused integration testing*, emphasising that that you're *focusing* on a particular integration point. Although the name is certainly apt, we have chosen to avoid references to the word "integration" anywhere else in this chapter so as to make clear that, when we talk about integration testing, we mean individual points of integration and not the entire system.

At this point, it may seem difficult to ascertain what there could be about the connection between your service and other elements that hasn't been tested already by either end-to-end, acceptance, or contract tests. However, end-to-end and acceptance tests don't go into the details of the integration points; they just check that the pieces roughly fall in place. Contract tests verify that the *logic* of the interaction is correct, but they don't test the interaction itself.

There are several things that you may need to consider when you test interactions in detail, and we will go through them in the next couple of subsections. The most important thing is this: in order to test the integration with an external component, you don't need to test your entire application, only the bit that connects with the external component. This will not only give you greater control over the test, but will also result in smaller, faster tests.

Verifying External Interactions

Verifying *in detail* the interactions with an external component is one of the main reasons to do this kind of test. Moreover, because you're not bringing up your entire application, but only the bit that contacts the external component, you can afford to run your test against a real external component (or at least something that looks very much like that). Let's take the example of a database.

When you're running your component tests, you'll probably use an in-memory database to speed things up. When you run your acceptance tests or your end-to-end tests, you'll use the real components, but your tests will cover only a handful of the possible operations against the database. You need to make sure that *all* the operations against the database are going to work, so you can get the specific class that encapsulates database access, connect it to a real database, and try out all the operations that you may ever need to execute in production. This will give you the confidence that the integration between your service and the database is correct, and will remove the deep tests at acceptance or end-to-end levels.

The mechanism to do this will depend on the technology that you are using and on the type of component that you are connecting to. The Feature Flags service includes an example of this in the `FlagRepositoryIT` class. In the Feature Flags service (folder */featureflags*), all the communication with the database is encapsulated in the `FlagRepository` class, which provides a high-level interface for the persistence layer. By instantiating this class on its own and connecting it to a real database, we can verify all the operations. Bringing up a real database is also easier than it sounds: thanks to Docker, most database vendors now provide a container with a readily installed database. This, in combination with the Docker Maven plugin, allows you to create and start up a real database before running integration tests, and then dispose of it when you're done; check the *pom.xml* file in Feature Flags service for details.

Testing Fault Tolerance

The other reason to run integration tests is to verify that your application is going to respond correctly to multiple error scenarios. This might be impossible to do at the end-to-end test level, because you don't have control over the external components. You might be able to try this at the component- or acceptance-test level, because here you're operating with test doubles that you can control. However, given the many moving parts present in these kinds of tests, you may have trouble assessing whether the system did what you expected.

If you, however, isolate the class in the code that is in contact with the external component, and you expose it to different kinds of failures, you can assert exactly what that class is going to do, and then reason from there about how the rest of the service will behave.

Testing fault tolerance is different from verifying external interactions: to test the external interactions, you want to use a real component (or something as real as possible), in order to legitimate the transaction being tested, while to test fault tolerance, you will want to use a fake component, so you can generate all the different error scenarios. The technologies needed for this have been mentioned already. Typical mocking frameworks will provide options to respond with errors; it's only the *approach* that is different in this kind of test.

The Extended Java Shop includes an example of fault-tolerance testing in the Shop-front service. The Shopfront service verifies the integration with the Feature Flags service in `FeatureFlagsRepoIT`, and does this by mocking the Feature Flags service with WireMock and then forcing it to respond with multiple error conditions, among them empty responses, an HTTP status of `500 INTERNAL SERVER ERROR`, and a scenario in which the service takes too long to reply. These tests will make the class in contact with Feature Flags, `FeatureFlagsRepo`, experience exceptions that represent the different error scenarios, which we can now catch and handle appropriately. As you can see in the sample application, from where the code in Example 11-1 has been extracted, in this case we have opted to log the situation and simply indicate to the rest of the application that there is no flag available.

Example 11-1. Handling several error conditions when retrieving a feature flag

```
public Optional<FlagDTO> getFlag(long flagId) {
    try {
        final String flagUrl = featureFlagsUri + "/flags/" + flagId;
        LOGGER.info("Fetching flag from {}", flagUrl);
        final FlagDTO flag = restTemplate.getForObject(flagUrl, FlagDTO.class);
        return Optional.ofNullable(flag);
            } catch (HttpClientErrorException | HttpServerErrorException |
                ResourceAccessException | HttpMessageNotReadableException e) {
        final String msg = "Failed to retrieve flag %s; falling back to no flag";
        LOGGER.info(format(msg, flagId), e);
        return Optional.empty();
    }
}
```

Be Aware of How Much of the Stack Is Being Tested

When performing fault tolerance tests, it is easy to end up mocking more of the technology stack than you initially realize. This makes tests fragile.

Unit Testing

Unit testing is rather ubiquitous these days, and you probably don't need a primer on it. Countless resources out there explain unit testing and TDD and the main tools for it: frameworks like JUnit, TestNG, or Spock for text execution, and libraries like Mockito, JMock, or PowerMock for mocking dependencies. Also worth mentioning are libraries that help writing more expressive assertions, like Hamcrest or Fest-Assert. But none of this is news.

There is something, however, that we have only recently begun to understand. Over the years, a lot of debate has ensued about what is the "correct" way to write unit tests —more particularly, about how much a unit test should cover. Traditionally, a unit test should cover only the target class being tested, and any dependencies of the class should be abstracted away using test doubles of some sort. However, in some cases, pragmatism leads you to include some of the dependencies of the target class, effectively treating a set of classes as a single "unit."

Instead of debating about which way is more correct, what the industry is now leaning toward is admitting that both approaches can be correct, depending on the case. In fact, Toby Clemson has gone to the point of giving a name to each of these approaches so we can discuss them in detail: these are sociable unit testing and solitary unit testing. As you will see, some cases obviously call for either approach, and in others the decision won't be that clear.

New to Unit Testing? No Need to Fret!

Even though we are assuming that the majority of readers know about unit testing and TDD, we are aware that this assumption won't be true for everyone. If you are within this group, the following resources will lead you to the right place:

- For a primer with easy-to-follow examples, take a look at Kent Beck's *Test Driven Development: By Example* (Addison-Wesley).

- If you want something more Java-focused, Jeff Langr has you covered with *Agile Java: Crafting Code with Test-Driven Development* (Prentice Hall) and *Pragmatic Unit Testing in Java 8 with JUnit* (Pragmatic Bookshelf), the last one cowritten with Andy Hunt and Dave Thomas.

- If you are working with an existing codebase that doesn't have unit tests, and need to find a way to refactor it into more testable code, Michael Feathers's *Working Effectively with Legacy Code* (Prentice Hall) is the way to go.

- Once you have built a comprehensive unit test suite, keep it up to scratch by applying the teachings of *xUnit Test Patterns: Refactoring Test Code* (Addison-Wesley) by Gerard Meszaros.

- Finally, *Practical Unit Testing with JUnit and Mockito* by Tomek Kaczanowski is a great reference for applying these frameworks effectively.

Of course, this is just a small subset of the many good resources available, including some really good blog posts and videos. If you fancy learning together with someone else, Ping-Pong TDD (*http://bit.ly/2xEFQn1*) is a great way to apply TDD while pair programming.

Sociable Unit Testing

Sociable unit testing considers a group of two or more classes a *society* that performs a discernible function when brought together, but that doesn't have a clear goal when considered separately. In these cases, you can consider the whole group a *unit*, and you will test them together when writing unit tests.

We can see an example of this in the Product Catalogue service (folder */productcatalogue*)—more precisely, in `PriceTest`, which tests the `Price` class. As you can see in

---

the code, a `Price` object accepts two parameters: a `UnitPrice`, indicating the price of a single unit, and a `BulkPrice`, indicating the price of the item when bought in bulk (together with the minimum number of items that need to be bought together for the purchase to be considered "bulk"). One of the rules that needs to be verified in `PriceTest` is that the price of an element bought in bulk must be lower than the price of the element bought individually.

If you were strict about your unit testing, when testing `Price` in `PriceTest`, you wouldn't pass in real implementations of `UnitPrice` and `BulkPrice`. Instead, you would pass in test doubles for them. You would create these test doubles so that when `Price` invokes their methods to check the single and bulk prices (so as to verify the previous rule), the appropriate values are returned by the test doubles. However, you probably agree that this would be overkill here: `Price` is not entirely independent of `UnitPrice` and `BulkPrice`. It's not like the latter offer some kind of interface to the former. We don't need to keep the implementations of these classes separate. The concepts of `UnitPrice` or `BulkPrice` don't have that much value beyond the scope of the concept of `Price`. We have created different classes for these just to avoid duplication of code and to manage tests more easily, but that's not enough to fully decouple them.

That should convince you that sociable unit testing is the right approach for testing the `Price` class. If you still need further arguments, try to rewrite those tests by using test doubles instead of real objects, and then compare. You might think that `Price Test` looks better with test doubles (and if so, that's OK), but we honestly doubt it.

Solitary Unit Testing

Solitary unit testing is closer to the traditional idea of unit testing. A class is identified as a unit, and all of its dependencies need to be abstracted away when unit testing, among other things because using real objects for dependencies would make unit testing harder. Although any test doubles might be used for solitary testing, mocks are usually the best suited ones.

Perhaps one of the best examples within the Extended Java App can be found in the Shopfront service (folder */shopfront*)—more particularly, in the tests for `Feature FlagsService`. The objective of this class is, given a particular flag ID (which may or may not exist in the Feature Flags service), decide whether the user should be allowed to access the feature. The class therefore has a few responsibilities: obtain the flag, read its *portion-in* value, and decide whether this particular request will fall within the value. As can be seen in the code, this class accepts two parameters: a `Feature FlagsRepo` object to communicate with the Feature Flags service, and a `Random` object to generate random numbers.

Passing in a real `FeatureFlagsRepo` object would make `FeatureFlagsServiceTest` unnecessarily complex. For instance, `FeatureFlagsRepo` could fail to deliver a flag for multiple reasons: it could be because the flag doesn't exist, or simply because the Feature Flags service is currently unavailable and data couldn't be retrieved. But, from the point of view of `FeatureFlagsService`, all this is irrelevant. The only thing that matters is whether a flag is provided, not the reason. This is already pointing us toward the usage of mocks.

However, the case becomes even more obvious if you consider passing in a real `Random` object. This would imply you don't have any control over the execution of your tests, because you wouldn't be able to tell which number is being provided to the `FeatureFlagsService` object. In this case, the use of mocks is not just convenient; it's necessary.

Chicago School Versus London School

Although the terms might not be as common, an alternative way to refer to these approaches is *Chicago* (or sometimes *Detroit*) *School* for sociable unit testing, and *London School* for solitary unit testing. As a matter of fact, Solitary (London School) unit testing relies heavily on the use of mocking frameworks, and many of the most popular mocking frameworks in Java (for example, Mockito, jMock, or WireMock) have deep roots in London (United Kingdom). If you're interested in the history of these approaches and their names, check Martin Fowler's "Mocks Aren't Stubs" (*http://bit.ly/2kuR98s*) or Jason Gorman's "Classic TDD or "London School"?" (*http://bit.ly/2OdRWwF*)

Dealing with Flaky Tests

As the number of moving parts increases, the number of things that could go wrong also increases. This sometimes makes tests of larger scope flaky, failing for no apparent reason and then recovering without remediation. And the larger the scope, the higher the likelihood of flakiness. This is a more dangerous thing than it would seem, because it will slowly lead developers toward not taking failing tests very seriously; soon you will develop the habit of rerunning a failing test a couple of times before you start investigating it, delaying necessary action.

The truth is, most brittleness can be addressed with the right measures, although the "right measures" will be different depending on the technology and the problem at hand. A comprehensive compendium of these would require a book of its own, but we can discuss some generic approaches.

Most brittleness comes from some form of indeterminism that hasn't been accounted for, some implicit assumption or expectation that the test execution didn't meet. So the general approach will be to identify these assumptions and address them. Let's look at some examples.

Data

Bad data is one of the most common causes of flaky tests. Data, especially in test/staging environments, tends to be quite volatile: people may delete, add, or modify underlying data without prior warning. Entire databases may be erased and reprovisioned. Live refreshes from production (hopefully, with the right anonymization) might be coming in at any point. If your tests rely on a particular piece of data being there, it is asking for trouble.

The best thing to do regarding data is to have your tests create it as part of the test setup. That way, you know you have exactly what you need. (Ideally, you'll also delete the data after you're done, but that is not strictly necessary.) If your test cannot create the data it needs for whatever reason, at the very least it should include a precheck to verify that necessary data is indeed there in the expected form, failing with a meaningful error message otherwise. The former is the best option, since all failures would be proper red flags, but the latter case can still be a time-saver: when you know that your data isn't there, you can take the necessary measures to add it, but at least you don't have to do all the prior investigation.

Resource That Is Not Available Yet

This issue can take many forms, from a UI test (for instance, based in Selenium) that is trying to assert on a particular section of the page that hasn't loaded yet, to a service that is trying to contact a test database that is still in the process of being provisioned. The most common solution is to add delays in the assertion execution so as to try to wait for the relevant resource to be available. Others keep retrying the assertion for a period of time. The problem with this approach is that genuine failures will take very long to fail, because the configured delay will have to pass fully before considering the test a failure, which slows the tests down:

```
// Both test success and failure will always take 1 minute
Thread.sleep(60 * 1000);
/* assertion */

// Test success will be as fast as possible,
// test failures will always take 1 minute
await().atMost(1, MINUTES).until(/* assertion */);
```

A better approach is *detecting* when your resource has become available, and only then performing the relevant assertions. For instance, in the case of a Selenium test, you can add a hidden element that is present in all the pages served by your website, and that becomes available only after the page has fully loaded. Your test can then wait on this element being available, and then you perform your assertion: this way, if your assertion finds that an expected element is not there, you know it's a genuine error, and not just a premature assertion. Similarly, for checking that external components are up and running, you can use simple utilities like wait-for-it (*https://github.com/vishnubob/wait-for-it*).

Nondeterministic Events

Sometimes unexpected events will affect the execution of your test, yielding a different result than the one you expected, and therefore causing your test to fail. Now, the important thing to realize here is that the fact that the obtained result is different from expected does not necessarily mean that it's wrong: if an event has affected execution, maybe the test expectation is no longer valid. An example of this is an acceptance test that expects a particular response from a service, but whose result is affected by an unexpected communication failure between the tested service and a dependency. If the server has been configured to react to the communication failure, it will produce a correct response (given the circumstances), but different from the expected.

The general solution to this kind of problem is to detect that an anomaly has happened and adjust the test expectation accordingly. For instance, the service under test could indicate that its result is impacted by a communication failure, and the test assertion could be simply skipped. It is important to signal this to the test execution framework, though, and categorize the test as "skipped" or "ignored," because categorizing it as either "success" or "failure" would be misleading. Knowing that a test hasn't run, developers can then decide what to do in this situation, whether repeating the test or simply accepting the risk that this particular run had a slightly slower test coverage.

If Nothing Else Works

In some rarer scenarios, there will be nothing you can do to address the brittleness of a test, for a variety of reasons. Maybe you have a dependency from a system or component that is managed by a different team, or even a different organization. Maybe the system under test is inherently indeterministic, and you can't adapt to unexpected events without reimplementing the business logic in the test. Whatever the reason, when a fix is not possible, it's time to consider mitigation.

If a fix is possible, just not on your hand, and someone else is going to work on it, consider temporarily ignoring the tests. You can simply flag it as ignored and then remember to unignore it at some point in the future (a reminder in a team-shared calendar can work). Or if you want something more automated, you can configure it so it will run only from a particular date onward, effectively ignoring it for the time being and unignoring it automatically at some point in the future.

If a fix is not possible, neither by you nor by someone else, you can try to reduce the scope of the test. Maybe what you are trying to achieve at acceptance-test level can be done by a combination of component and integration tests, which might prove more reliable. Moreover, this might even have the advantage of being faster (and it's the reason so many teams end up with builds that take up to one hour to run).

Finally, if and when you conclude that no possible fix exists, you must consider deleting the test. This might seem a drastic measure, but you need to remember that tests are there to give you valuable information as part of a tight feedback loop: if the information that they are giving you is misleading and wasteful, you need to reassess what the value of that test really is. Deleting the test might be, overall, better than having to deal with it.

Testing Outside-In Versus Testing Inside-Out

Now that you know all the levels of testing that you will need in your application, a different question pops up: where should you start? Should you begin by defining the overall end-to-end tests and then work your way in? Or should you begin with unit tests for the smallest elements and then build up from there? At the risk of sounding repetitive, the answer is, once again, that it depends.

Your technology, build pipeline, skillset, and even personal preference will determine whether you should favor an outside-in or an inside-out approach. We can only enumerate the characteristics of each case to help you make a decision.

"Outside-In Versus Inside-Out" Is a Different Question from "In-Process Versus Out-of-Process"

Admittedly, the title of this section is awfully similar to that of "In-Process Versus Out-Of-Process" on page 316, but they refer to very different things. In this section, we discuss the order in which tests at different levels are written. In an outside-in approach, you start by the outermost tests (acceptance tests, for instance) and make your way through by specifying newer tests at lower levels. In an inside-out approach, you start at the lower scale (unit tests) and progressively build up bigger and longer tests.

On the other hand, the question of in-process versus out-of-process refers to the mechanics used to design and run component tests. In-process will have the service and the tests running under the same OS process. In an out-of-process approach, service and tests run in different OS processes.

Fortunately, these decisions tend to be made once at the beginning of the project, and you won't have to talk about them (falling prey to the risk of confusion) very often.

Outside-In

Testing outside-in forces you to think of the user experience up front. You will need to determine end-to-end and acceptance tests first; you will have to analyze the needs and limitations in the interactions with other systems; and you will check firsthand whether the environment allows you to do what you intend to do. Also, it allows you to define the feature in a more iterative way: as you make your way in, and you start defining more and more detailed tests, when you go through component, contract, integration, and unit tests, you and your team can decide how to handle edge cases as they approach. Developing outside-in ensures than you don't build any more code than you strictly need, because everything you do is just the consequence of a higher-level need.

Not everything is rosy, though. To begin with, practitioners agree that building and testing software outside-in requires stronger development skills. When programmers are testing at a particular level, they need to identify the right moment to refactor and switch to a lower level; failing to do this could result in an unbalanced test suite that is too heavy on big, overarching tests. Also, there is the question of when end-to-end and acceptance tests need to go green. If you consider that these tests should be red until the feature is fully implemented, but you have to write these tests first thing, they are going to be failing for a while. If your build is configured to stop the pipeline upon failing tests, your pipeline will be blocked until your feature is fully implemented, which is the opposite of continuous delivery. If your failing end-to-end or acceptance tests don't block the pipeline, you may be delivering bugs to production—not a great idea either. And, if you decide to write the tests at the beginning but hold off committing them until the end, your uncommitted code could grow stale, also going against the idea of continuous delivery.

Some teams overcome these issues by deciding that end-to-end and acceptance tests may go green *before* the feature is fully implemented. The idea is that, because these tests are meant to be rather superficial, they could be made to pass by means of a simplistic, incomplete implementation of the feature. The feature can then be fully fledged out as lower-level tests are written and implemented. This certainly addresses the aforementioned issues, but it also creates another one: people need to be aware of the fact that a green end-to-end test doesn't imply that the feature is available to the public. The useful reports created by tools like SerenityBDD cannot be taken like gospel, and close communication between business and developers is needed to avoid misunderstandings.

Inside-Out

Inside-out testing is, in a way, easier to execute. You may not be able to visualize the big picture, or have an idea of how all the components are going to fit together, but you can grab what you do know and start from there. Maybe you feel pretty confident about a particular class needing extra responsibilities to implement this feature, so you can start there.

Achieving the right balance between types of tests is easier when you work inside-out. If you start with unit tests, you can keep on writing tests until you realize that you have exhausted all the possible scenarios. Once you realize you cannot test anymore at the unit-test level, you go up one level and continue from there. Once you get to the end-to-end or acceptance-test level, you'll realize that there is little left to test, if anything, and you may focus on writing just enough tests so as to produce the right BDD reports.

One of the downsides of inside-out testing is that you might end up writing at the lower levels more functionalities and checks than you need, maybe because some of the edge cases that you considered at the lower level are just not possible when you put them in the context of the higher level. If you're having troubling visualizing this, you can find a small example in the Extended Java Shop application—more precisely, in the Feature Flags service (folder */featureflags*). We added the ability to update flags by using an inside-out approach, meaning we added an `updateFlag(Flag)` method in the `FlagService` class before we added the relevant `PUT` operation in `FlagRe source`.

When we were writing `FlagService` and `FlagServiceTest`, we considered the scenario where we pass to the `updateFag(Flag)` method a `Flag` without a flag ID. We considered that an error condition, and created `FlagWithoutIdException` to signal it. Faithful to the idea of working in small increments, we implemented these changes, tested them, and committed them. When we then added a `PUT` method to `FlagRe source`, we associated this to the path pattern `/flags/{flagId}`, and we realized that we would never have a case of updating a flag without a flag ID. If a client tries to update a flag without indicating a flag ID, the request would have the form `PUT /flags/`, but this would be interpreted by the framework as performing the wrong operation upon the `/flags` resource, which would be automatically rejected as `405 METHOD NOT ALLOWED`. In the end, this was just an unnecessary precaution.

Different People Have Different Brains, and Different Brains Work Differently

It is not uncommon for a person to have a preference over outside-in or inside-out testing, and then change preferences to the other one at some point in their career. This is often perceived as "maturing" or "learning," and people assume that the latter choice must be better than the former. The reality is much more complex. Different people may be more comfortable with different thought processes; some will have a skill for managing abstractions and thinking about the big picture, and some will need to focus on the details to establish a foundation. Don't make assumptions about the skill level of a person just because they favor one approach or the other.

Additional Resources (Particularly for Testing Java EE Apps)

Because of the scope of this book, there is only so much information we can provide about each topic. Testing is one of the topics that deserves an entire book to be dedicated to it, especially to cover all of the nuances with testing Java EE and Spring applications. If you want to learn more, we recommend the following books:

- *Testing Java Microservices* (Manning) by Alex Soto Bueno et al. (which is relevant even if you are not creating microservices)

- *Continuous Enterprise Development* in Java (O'Reilly) by Andrew Lee Rubinger and Aslak Knutsen

- *Growing Object-Oriented Software, Guided by Tests* (Addison-Wesley Professional) by Steve Freeman and Nat Pryce

---

Putting It All Together Within the Pipeline

The right balance of tests at all the levels gives a comprehensive and reliable test coverage. Now it's time to tie it all together in an automated build pipeline. The mechanism used to achieve this will depend on the technology used for your build (Maven, Gradle, Ant, etc.) and the technology used for build automation (Jenkins, TeamCity, GoCD, etc.). However, a few general recommendations can be made:

- Ensure that each deliverable (i.e., each service or library) has its own job in the build software. This job should trigger whenever a code change is detected that affects the deliverable either directly or indirectly.

- Tests that refer to a single deliverable (unit, contract, integration, and component tests) should all run within the job that is specific to that deliverable. What's more, ideally they should run with a single command of the build technology of choice (e.g., Maven), which would take care of any necessary setup or teardown.

- After a successful build, the specific deliverable should be packaged and made available in some form of repository for later consumption (e.g., DockerHub, Artifactory, etc.).

- Tests that refer to a set of deliverables (like acceptance or end-to-end tests) should have their own job in the pipeline, and should be triggered after any given service is successfully rebuilt.

- After a successful run of the acceptance and end-to-end tests, the deliverable whose change triggered the run should be deployed to production (optionally, going through one or more test environments first).

A full example of this can be found in the Extended Java Shop. The three prebuilt Jenkins servers contain a preconfigured pipeline that works exactly as described here. You can follow the instructions in the *README.md* file to run Jenkins locally and observe the behavior.

Identifying Your Test Types

Most build tools have a set of default suffixes that denote classes that contain tests, like *Test or *Spec. However, most build tools allow you to define your own, which can be helpful to identify at a glance at what level you have encountered a test failure. In the case of the Extended Java Shop, we have used *AT for acceptance tests, *CDC for contract tests, *CT for component tests, *IT for integration tests, and *Test for unit tests. You don't need to use exactly the same suffixes, but it is highly encouraged that you identify your different test types somehow.

How Much Testing Is Enough?

If a testing strategy is to be compatible with continuous delivery, it must have an appropriate ratio of unit tests, acceptance tests, and end-to-end tests that balances the need for information discovery against the need for fast, deterministic feedback. If testing does not yield new information, defects will go undetected. If testing takes too long, delivery will be slow, and opportunity costs will be incurred.

Continuous delivery advocates continuous testing—a testing strategy in which a large number of automated unit and acceptance tests are complemented by a small number of automated end-to-end tests and focused exploratory testing. The continuous testing test ratio can be visualized as a test pyramid, illustrated in Figure 11-4.

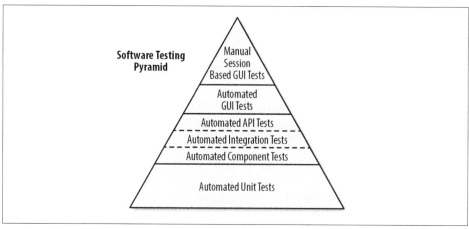

Figure 11-4. The test pyramid indicates that faster, localized tests should be the foundation for slower, broader ones

Finding this balance isn't easy, and nothing can tell you whether you have achieved it. There are, however, some heuristics that you can consider. Keep in mind that the real objective of your test suite is *not* to guarantee that your software is free of flaws; that is impossible. When you are constantly changing something, mistakes will happen and bugs will appear. The objective of the test suite is therefore to *detect* whenever these mistakes happen so as to limit the impact. When you start thinking about tests this way, you develop a sense to know whether you have too few or too many. If you can see parts of the code that, if broken, wouldn't cause a test to fail, you have too few. If you can identify tests that cannot be made to fail in isolation (i.e., make a change that will make that test and only that test fail), some of those tests are probably redundant.

Close inspection and awareness of your codebase are vital to achieve a test balance, but some tools can help. For instance, test coverage tools like JCov or JaCoCo can flag sections of code that are not covered by any test. Be careful, though, when interpreting the results of these tools: the fact that a line has been covered by a test doesn't necessarily mean that the right assertions about that line have been executed. Test coverage can warn you when something is *not* covered, but it cannot be used as a way to state that something *is* covered.

More advanced tools can flag when a particular section of code is not covered by a test, but they are slow and expensive to run. One of these tools is Jester. Jester will make a random change in your code and then run the tests, assuming something will fail; if it doesn't, then it flags this change as a test gap. After completing a cycle, it will revert the previous change, make another one somewhere else, and repeat the tests. It will continue until it considers it has tried all the possible combinations. You can easily see how Jester can take literally hours to complete a run, but that's the price that you pay for complete confidence.

In the end, the important thing is that you remain vigilant. The number of tests that you have will never be "just right." It will always be either too much or too little. But if you keep an eye on your system, and maybe get the help of some of the tools mentioned here, you'll be able to detect when you're deviating from the sweet spot and correct.

Summary

Tests are essential to building trust in your software; they give you the confidence to deliver a product. However, in a world of continuous delivery, you cannot rely on manual tests, for the pace of change is too fast, so you need an appropriate strategy for automated testing:

- Building a comprehensive test suite will ensure not just that the new features of the application work as expected, but also that you haven't broken any of the existing ones.

- Synthetic transactions are the ultimate test, for they replicate exactly what your users will do, but the fact that they run in the production environment adds a number of risks.

- Broad end-to-end tests are slow to run and often brittle, but they are the only ones that bring all the components together, and therefore the ones closer to the real user experience.

- Acceptance tests are also slow, but they verify that all the components that you own work well together, indicating whether you have done your job correctly.

- Consumer-driven contracts verify that the expectations between two services are appropriately met by both sides, without the overhead of loading entire applications.

- Component tests treat an entire service as a black box, ensuring that all the internal subsections fit in together.

- Integration tests look at the seams between components, verifying all the possible variants of the interaction.

- Unit tests are fast to run, so you can use them as your foundation to test as much of the logic of your software as possible.

- Tying all the tests together into an automated build pipeline will ensure that, upon any code change, your software is thoroughly tested and, if appropriate, released to production.

After this chapter, you have everything that you need to verify that the work you have done when building your software is correct, which is half of the user experience. The other half will be dependent on the nonfunctional requirements, and will be the objective of the next chapter: regardless of how "correct" your application is, users won't be pleased if the application is slow or unreliable.

## CHAPTER 12

System-Quality Attributes Testing: Validating Nonfunctional Requirements

You learned in the previous chapter that you must test software for correctness and the delivery of the required business functionality. However, it is equally important to ensure that the system is reliable and scalable, and that the software can be run in a cost-effective manner. Classically, validating the quality of a software system has been divided into testing functional requirements and testing nonfunctional requirements —sometimes referred to as *cross-functional requirements* or *system-quality attributes*. In this chapter, you will learn how to test the nonfunctional requirements.

Why Test Nonfunctional Requirements?

Testing nonfunctional requirements is often relegated to the end of a software delivery project, and sometimes completely ignored, particularly within small teams constrained by resources (and expertise). Enterprise development teams can fare somewhat better, partly through access to specialized skills and partly by understanding their customers and associated resource usage better.

Many enterprise organizations conduct capacity and security planning within the feasibility study of a large project. In reality, this is often fraught with uncertainty and danger, as business teams are unsure of the number of customers, usage patterns, and potential threats; and the engineering teams are unsure of the impact and capacity requirements of each unit of functionality offered by the software. The recent trend toward designing functionality within well-bounded services, deploying on flexible and programmatically defined infrastructure, and the embrace of the shared responsibility model (e.g., DevOps, SRE) has dramatically reduced the barrier to entry for this type of testing.

The terms *nonfunctional requirements*, *cross-functional requirements*, and *system-quality attributes* may be used interchangeably throughout this chapter. However, it should be stressed that although the term *nonfunctional requirements* is the most popular, it is also perhaps the most incorrect—and the potential cause of the lack of priority given to these types of quality attributes. The word "nonfunctional" could imply that not testing these requirements will not affect the functionality of the system. But this could not be further from the truth, especially in the current climate of Hacker-News or Twitter-driven customer-thundering herds, the potentially spectacular failure modes of underlying infrastructure platforms, and entire illicit organizations created (that are sometimes state sponsored) with the sole purpose of hacking software systems.

Launch Coordination and Production-Ready Checklists

Several large organizations, such as Google and Uber, have presented at conferences about how they require launch coordination checklists (*http://bit.ly/2OdU2g1*) or production-ready checklists to be completed by engineers before an application is deployed to users. There can be a lot of value in doing this, as a checklist forces you to think about all aspects of supporting your application after it is receiving traffic and becomes critical to the business. Many of the items within these checklists are focused on nonfunctional requirements.

The good news is that with current tooling, methodologies, and access to commodity programmable infrastructure, it is now easier than ever before to conduct this type of testing.

Code Quality

Writing code is an inherently creative act, so there are often many ways to implement each piece of functionality. Nearly every developer has their own personal style (often within each language they know), but when working as part of a team, you must all agree on a baseline for certain code qualities, such as code formatting and use of esoteric parts of the language.

The primary metric of code quality is whether the functionality created meets the requirements specified, and you learned how to verify this in the previous chapter, which focused on testing functional requirements. The "nonfunctional" perspective of code quality consists of reducing time-to-context (how readable is the code for another developer, and can someone else quickly understand the implementation logic) and being free of deficiencies (is the code written in a way that allows the application to scale effectively, or handle faults gracefully).

In Chapter 9, you explored how to implement automated code-style checking as part of the CI process with tooling like Checkstyle and PMD, and in this chapter you will learn how this can be augmented with automated architecture quality assessment.

Architectural Quality

The build pipeline should be the primary location where agreed-upon architectural qualities are codified and enforced. These quality assertions should not replace discussions with your team about agreed-upon standards and quality levels, and should definitely not be used to avoid intra- or inter-team communication. However, checking and publishing quality metrics within the build pipeline can prevent the gradual decay of quality that can otherwise be challenging to notice.

ArchUnit: Unit-Testing Architecture

ArchUnit (*https://www.archunit.org/*) is an open source, extensible library for checking the architecture of your Java code by using a Java unit-test framework like JUnit or TestNG. ArchUnit can check dependencies between packages and classes, layers and slices, check for cyclic dependencies, and more. It does this by analyzing Java bytecode and importing all classes into a Java code structure for analysis.

Why Test Your Architecture?

This is a fair question, and the ArchUnit Motivation web page has you covered! It starts by suggesting that most developers working in larger projects will know this story: once upon a time, an architect drew a series of nice architecture diagrams, showing the components the system should consist of, and how they should interact. Then the project got bigger, use cases became more complex, and new developers dropped in and old developers dropped out. In more and more cases, new features would be added in any way that fit. Suddenly, everything depended on everything and every change could have an unforeseeable effect on any other component. We're sure many of you will recognize this scenario.

You could fix this issue by having an experienced developer or architect look at the code once a week, identify violations, and correct them. Realistically, a more practical method is to define the components in code and rules for these components that can be automatically tested (for example, as part of your continuous integration build).

To use ArchUnit in combination with JUnit 4, include the dependency shown in Example 12-1 from Maven Central.

Example 12-1. Including ArchUnit within a Maven pom.xml

```
<dependency>
    <groupId>com.tngtech.archunit</groupId>
    <artifactId>archunit-junit</artifactId>
    <version>0.5.0</version>
    <scope>test</scope>
</dependency>
```

At its core, ArchUnit provides infrastructure to import Java bytecode into Java code structures. This can be done by using `ClassFileImporter`. Architectural rules such as "services should be accessed only by controllers" can be made by using a DSL-like fluent API, which can, in turn, be evaluated against imported classes; see Example 12-2.

Example 12-2. Using the ArchUnit DSL to assert that services should be accessed only by controllers

```
import static com.tngtech.archunit.lang.syntax.ArchRuleDefinition.classes;

// ...

@Test
public void Services_should_only_be_accessed_by_Controllers() {
    JavaClasses classes =
    new ClassFileImporter().importPackages("com.mycompany.myapp");

    ArchRule myRule = classes()
        .that().resideInAPackage("..service..")
        .should().onlyBeAccessed().byAnyPackage("..controller..", "..service..");

    myRule.check(classes);
}
```

A host of ArchUnit examples (*https://github.com/TNG/ArchUnit-Examples*) are available on GitHub, and we've included several next so that you are aware of the power of the framework. Extending the preceding example, you can enforce more layer-based access rules, as shown in Example 12-3.

Example 12-3. Enforcing additional layer-based access rules with ArchUnit

```
@ArchTest
public static final ArchRule layer_dependencies_are_respected = layeredArchitecture()
        .layer("Controllers").definedBy("com.tngtech.archunit.example.controller..")
        .layer("Services").definedBy("com.tngtech.archunit.example.service..")
        .layer("Persistence").definedBy("com.tngtech.archunit.example.persistence..")
        .whereLayer("Controllers").mayNotBeAccessedByAnyLayer()
        .whereLayer("Services").mayOnlyBeAccessedByLayers("Controllers")
        .whereLayer("Persistence").mayOnlyBeAccessedByLayers("Services");
```

You can also ensure naming conventions, such as prefixes, or specify that a class named a certain way must be in an appropriate package (this, for example, can prevent developers from putting controller classes outside controller packages); see Example 12-4.

Example 12-4. Enforcing naming conventions with ArchUnit

```
@ArchTest
public static ArchRule services_should_be_prefixed =
        classes()
                .that().resideInAPackage("..service..")
                .and().areAnnotatedWith(MyService.class)
                .should().haveSimpleNameStartingWith("Service");

@ArchTest
public static ArchRule classes_named_controller_should_be_in_a_controller_pkg =
        classes()
                .that().haveSimpleNameContaining("Controller")
                .should().resideInAPackage("..controller..");
```

Finally, you can also enforce that only specific classes can access other classes, fields; for example, only DAO classes can access an `EntityManager`, as shown in Example 12-5.

Example 12-5. Enforcing class-access patterns

```
@ArchTest
    public static final ArchRule only_DAOs_may_use_the_EntityManager =
            noClasses().that().resideOutsideOfPackage("..dao..")
                    .should().accessClassesThat()
                    .areAssignableTo(EntityManager.class)
                    .as("Only DAOs may use the " +
                    EntityManager.class.getSimpleName());
```

Generate Design-Quality Metrics with JDepend

JDepend has been around longer than ArchUnit, and although it potentially offers fewer features, the two frameworks can be complementary. JDepend traverses Java class file directories and generates design-quality metrics for each Java package. JDepend allows you to automatically measure the quality of a design in terms of its extensibility, reusability, and maintainability to manage package dependencies effectively.

JDepend Is Showing Its Age

The last official release of JDepend was in 2005, and in "tech years" (much like dog years), this is a long time. Someone else has forked the codebase and applied a series of bug fixes, but caution is warranted, especially in regards to support for new language features. Our preference is to use a combination of SonarQube for design-quality metrics, and ArchUnit for asserting architectural requirements. However, we have included JDepend here because we often bump into this framework on consulting engagements.

As specified on the JDepend website, the framework generates design-quality metrics for each Java package, including the following:

Number of classes and interfaces
> The number of concrete and abstract classes (and interfaces) in the package is an indicator of the extensibility of the package.

Afferent couplings (Ca)
> The number of other packages that depend upon classes within the package is an indicator of the package's responsibility.

Efferent couplings (Ce)
> The number of other packages that the classes in the package depend upon is an indicator of the package's independence.

Abstractness (A)
> The ratio of the number of abstract classes (and interfaces) in the analyzed package to the total number of classes in the analyzed package.

Instability (I)
> The ratio of efferent coupling (Ce) to total coupling (Ce + Ca) such that $I = Ce / (Ce + Ca)$. This metric is an indicator of the package's resilience to change.

Distance from the main sequence (D)
> The perpendicular distance of a package from the idealized line $A + I = 1$. This metric is an indicator of the package's balance between abstractness and stability.

Package dependency cycles
> Package dependency cycles are reported along with the hierarchical paths of packages participating in package dependency cycles.

Metrics Do Not Necessarily Indicate Good or Bad Designs

The JDepend documentation makes it clear that before using any design-quality analyzing framework like JDepend, it is important to understand that "good" design-quality metrics do not necessarily indicate good designs. Likewise, "bad" design-quality metrics do necessarily show bad designs. The design-quality metrics produced by JDepend are intended to be used by designers to measure the designs they create, understand those designs, and automatically check that the designs exhibit expected qualities while being enhanced or refactored.

JDepend can be used as a standalone tool, but it is more typical to implement the analysis via JUnit. You can include JDepend in your project as shown in Example 12-6. Note that the original JDepend is no longer maintained, and someone else has forked the codebase in order to apply bug fixes).

Example 12-6. Including JDepend within your Maven pom.xml

```
<dependency>
    <groupId>guru.nidi</groupId>
    <artifactId>jdepend</artifactId>
    <version>2.9.5</version>
</dependency>
```

Example 12-7 shows how to use JDepend to analyze a codebase and ensure that the dependencies asserted are valid.

Example 12-7. A constraint test with JDepend

```
public class ConstraintTest extends TestCase {
...
    protected void setUp() throws IOException {

        jdepend = new JDepend();

        jdepend.addDirectory("/path/to/project/util/classes");
        jdepend.addDirectory("/path/to/project/ejb/classes");
        jdepend.addDirectory("/path/to/project/web/classes");
    }

    /**
     * Tests that the package dependency constraint
     * is met for the analyzed packages.
     */
    public void testMatch() {

        DependencyConstraint constraint = new DependencyConstraint();
```

```
        JavaPackage ejb = constraint.addPackage("com.xyz.ejb");
        JavaPackage web = constraint.addPackage("com.xyz.web");
        JavaPackage util = constraint.addPackage("com.xyz.util");

        ejb.dependsUpon(util);
        web.dependsUpon(util);

        jdepend.analyze();

        assertEquals("Dependency mismatch",
                true, jdepend.dependencyMatch(constraint));
    }
...
}
```

Performance and Load Testing

Understanding the performance characteristics of your application and its individual service components is extremely invaluable. Accordingly, the practice of performance and load testing is a vital skill to master. Load tests can be run at an application level, covering the entire system, as well as at a modular level, covering an individual service or function. Combining the two approaches effectively will allow you to quickly spot performance trends within isolated components and in the overall user experience.

Additional Resources for Java Performance

If you want to learn more about writing performant Java code and applications, we recommend the following books:

- *Optimizing Java: Practical Techniques for Improving JVM Application Performance* (O'Reilly) by Benjamin J. Evans et al.
- *Java Performance: The Definitive Guide* (O'Reilly) by Scott Oaks

---

Basic Performance Testing with Apache Benchmark

The Apache Bench ab tool is an extremely easy-to-use performance benchmark tool. This CLI-driven tool works by generating a flood of requests to a given URL and returns performance-related metrics to the terminal. Although it is not a particularly flexible tool, the simplicity means that it is a great tool to reach for when you need to run quick performance tests. You can install this tool through your package manager. If you are using Windows, the alternative SuperBenchmarker (*https://github.com/aliostad/SuperBenchmarker*) can be installed via Chocolately. Once the tool is installed, you can simply type **ab** at the terminal to get a list of the available parameters. You

will find yourself most commonly specifying -n for the number of requests to perform for the benchmarking session, -c for the number of concurrent requests to perform at a time, and the target URL. For example, to benchmark Google with 10
requests that are executed 2 at a time, you can run Example 12-8.

*Example 12-8. Using Apache Bench ab to run a performance benchmark test against
Google*

```
$ ab -n 10 -c 2 http://www.google.com/
This is ApacheBench, Version 2.3 <$Revision: 1807734 $>
Copyright 1996 Adam Twiss, Zeus Technology Ltd, http://www.zeustech.net/
Licensed to The Apache Software Foundation, http://www.apache.org/

Benchmarking www.google.com (be patient).....done


Server Software:
Server Hostname:        www.google.com
Server Port:            80

Document Path:          /
Document Length:        271 bytes

Concurrency Level:      2
Time taken for tests:   0.344 seconds
Complete requests:      10
Failed requests:        0
Non-2xx responses:      10
Total transferred:      5230 bytes
HTML transferred:       2710 bytes
Requests per second:    29.11 [#/sec] (mean)
Time per request:       68.707 [ms] (mean)
Time per request:       34.354 [ms] (mean, across all concurrent requests)
Transfer rate:          14.87 [Kbytes/sec] received

Connection Times (ms)
              min  mean[+/-sd] median   max
Connect:       13   32   51.6     17     179
Processing:    14   18    3.5     16      23
Waiting:       13   17    3.1     16      23
Total:         28   50   50.4     35     193

Percentage of the requests served within a certain time (ms)
  50%     35
  66%     37
  75%     38
  80%     44
  90%    193
  95%    193
  98%    193
```

```
99%     193
100%    193 (longest request)
```

The Apache Bench tool is great for quick load tests, but its lack of configurability for ramping up virtual users (making the requests) and creating more-complex scenarios with assertion can be limiting. It can also be challenging to incorporate ab into a build pipeline and parse the output into a meaningful format. With this in mind, you can reach for alternative, more powerful, tools like Gatling

---

What Are Virtual Users?

When executing a load test, you simulate a certain number of users accessing your system concurrently. A *virtual user* (VU) is an application, or thread or process within an application, that acts just like a real user would when making requests to a web application. During a load test, requests from many virtual users can be generated from one compute instance—in this context, called a *driver machine*. This can either be your local machine, or a series of machines orchestrated via a build pipeline.

If you are looking for more information, "Determining Concurrent Users in Your Load Tests" (*http://bit.ly/2NEWFIi*), from Load Impact explains how to mine the relevant data from your Google Analytics data. The *webperformance.com* (*http://bit.ly/2DzridM*) website also has a useful VU calculator.

Load Testing with Gatling

Gatling is an open source load- and performance-testing tool based on Scala, Akka, and Netty. It is easy to run standalone or within a CD build pipeline, and the DSL ("performance tests as code") and request-recording mechanisms for generating interactions provide a lot of flexibility. Gatling really shines over a basic load-testing tool by providing a lot of configuration in regards to how you simulate the VU interaction with the site, in terms of quantity, concurrency, and ramp-up. The DSL also allows you to specify assertions, such as HTTP status codes, payload content, and acceptable latencies, which means that this is a powerful tool.

What Happened to JMeter?

The Apache JMeter load-test tool project is still very much alive and healthy. We personally still use this tool on projects. Because of space limitations in this book, and because the JMeter tool is starting to show its age, we decided to focus on the more flexible Gatling tool. JMeter can be a viable alternative to Gatling if you don't want to learn a new DSL. If you want to know more about JMeter, you can consult the home page (*https://jmeter.apache.org/*).

Gatling can be downloaded from the project's website (*https://gatling.io/download/*). Core concepts within Gatling include the following:

Simulation
> The simulation file includes the various scenarios of a test, its parametrization, and the injection profiles.

Scenario
> A scenario consists of a series of requests and can be thought of as a user journey.

Group
> Groups can be used to subdivide a scenario. You can also think of groups as a module that has a functional purpose (for instance, the login process).

Request
> A request is exactly what you think it is: a user request made against the system under test.

Injection profile
> An injection profile is the number of virtual users injected during the test in the system under test and how they are injected.

The O'Reilly Docker Java Shopping (*https://github.com/danielbryantuk/oreilly-docker-java-shopping*) example application contains a demonstration of how to run a Gatling-based load test against a Java application that is deployed via Docker Compose. The DSL allows you to write load-testing simulations as a Scala class, but don't worry, only minimal knowledge is required with this language.

If you look at the simulation in Example 12-9, you will see the protocol being specified, which is simply how the requests will be made. In this case, the protocol is HTTP, and you are running the simulation as if your users were using the Mozilla browser. Next, a scenario is specified and a request execution (exec) is defined against the API. The final part of the simulation specifies the number of virtual users the simulation will run alongside the ramp-up, as well as any assertions you require. In this example, you are asserting that the maximum global response time was less that 50 ms, and that no requests failed.

Example 12-9. DjShoppingBasicSimulation Gatling Scala load test

```
package uk.co.danielbryant.djshopping.performancee2etests

import io.gatling.core.Predef._
import io.gatling.http.Predef._

import scala.concurrent.duration._

class DjShoppingBasicSimulation extends Simulation {
```

```
  val httpProtocol = http
    .baseURL("http://localhost:8010")
    .acceptHeader("text/html,application/xhtml+xml,application/xml;q=0.9,*/*;q=0.8")
    .acceptEncodingHeader("gzip, deflate")
    .acceptLanguageHeader("en-US,en;q=0.5")
    .userAgentHeader("Mozilla/5.0 (Macintosh; Intel Mac OS X 10.8; rv:16.0)
                      Gecko/20100101 Firefox/16.0")

  val primaryScenario = scenario("DJShopping website and API performance test")
    .exec(http("website")
      .get("/")
      .check(
        status is 200,
        substring("Docker Java")))
    .pause(7)

    .exec(http("products API")
      .get("/products")
      .check(
        status is 200,
        jsonPath("$[0].id") is "1",
        jsonPath("$[0].sku") is "12345678"))

  setUp(primaryScenario.inject(
    constantUsersPerSec(30) during (30 seconds)
  ).protocols(httpProtocol))
    .assertions(global.responseTime.max.lessThan(50))
    .assertions(global.failedRequests.percent.is(0))
}
```

You can execute the simulation via the SBT build tool, which is shown in
Example 12-10.

Example 12-10. Run of Gatling to load-test the Docker Java Shop

```
$ git clone https://github.com/danielbryantuk/oreilly-docker-java-shopping
$ cd oreilly-docker-java-shopping
$ ./build_all.sh
$ [INFO] Scanning for projects...
[INFO]
[INFO] --------------< uk.co.danielbryant.djshopping:shopfront >---------------
[INFO] Building shopfront 0.0.1-SNAPSHOT
[INFO] ----------------------------[ jar ]----------------------------------
[INFO]
[INFO] --- maven-clean-plugin:2.6.1:clean (default-clean) @ shopfront ---

...

[INFO] --- maven-install-plugin:2.5.2:install (default-install) @ stockmanager ---
[INFO] Installing /Users/danielbryant/Documents/dev/daniel-bryant-uk/
```

```
                     tmp/oreilly-docker-java-shopping/
                     stockmanager/target/stockmanager-0.0.1-SNAPSHOT.jar to
                     /Users/danielbryant/.m2/repository/uk/co/danielbryant/
                     djshopping/stockmanager/0.0.1-SNAPSHOT/
                     stockmanager-0.0.1-SNAPSHOT.jar
[INFO] Installing /Users/danielbryant/Documents/dev/daniel-bryant-uk/
                     tmp/oreilly-docker-java-shopping/
                     stockmanager/pom.xml to
                     /Users/danielbryant/.m2/repository/uk/co/danielbryant/djshopping/
                     stockmanager/0.0.1-SNAPSHOT/stockmanager-0.0.1-SNAPSHOT.pom
[INFO] ------------------------------------------------------------------------
[INFO] BUILD SUCCESS
[INFO] ------------------------------------------------------------------------
[INFO] Total time: 12.653 s
[INFO] Finished at: 2018-04-07T12:12:55+01:00
[INFO] ------------------------------------------------------------------------
$
$ docker-compose -f docker-compose-build.yml up -d --build
Building productcatalogue
Step 1/5 : FROM openjdk:8-jre
 ---> 1b56aa0fd38c
...
Successfully tagged oreillydockerjavashopping_shopfront:latest
oreillydockerjavashopping_productcatalogue_1 is up-to-date
oreillydockerjavashopping_stockmanager_1 is up-to-date
oreillydockerjavashopping_shopfront_1 is up-to-date
$
$ sbt gatling:test

(master) performance-e2e-tests $ sbt gatling:test
[info] Loading project definition from /Users/danielbryant/Documents/dev/
                                  daniel-bryant-uk/tmp/
                                  oreilly-docker-java-shopping/
                                  performance-e2e-tests/project
[info] Set current project to performance-e2e-tests
       (in build file:/Users/danielbryant/Documents/dev/daniel-bryant-uk/tmp/
       oreilly-docker-java-shopping/performance-e2e-tests/)
Simulation uk.co.danielbryant.djshopping.performancee2etests
          .DjShoppingBasicSimulation started...


================================================================================
2018-04-07 14:49:00                                        5s elapsed
---- DJShopping website and API performance test -------------------------------
[----------                                                          ] 0%
          waiting: 768    / active: 132    / done:0
---- Requests ------------------------------------------------------------------
> Global                                              (OK=131      KO=0      )
> website                                             (OK=131      KO=0      )
================================================================================


================================================================================
```

```
2018-04-07 14:49:05                                          10s elapsed
---- DJShopping website and API performance test ------------------------------
[#####-----------------                                          ] 7%
        waiting: 618     / active: 211     / done:71
---- Requests -----------------------------------------------------------------
> Global                                         (OK=352    KO=0     )
> website                                        (OK=281    KO=0     )
> products API                                   (OK=71     KO=0     )
================================================================================

...


================================================================================
2018-04-07 14:49:33                                          37s elapsed
---- DJShopping website and API performance test ------------------------------
[###############################################################]100%
        waiting: 0       / active: 0       / done:900
---- Requests -----------------------------------------------------------------
> Global                                         (OK=1800   KO=0     )
> website                                        (OK=900    KO=0     )
> products API                                   (OK=900    KO=0     )
================================================================================

Simulation uk.co.danielbryant.djshopping.performancee2etests
         .DjShoppingBasicSimulation completed in 37 seconds
Parsing log file(s)...
Parsing log file(s) done
Generating reports...


================================================================================
---- Global Information -------------------------------------------------------
> request count                         1800 (OK=1800   KO=0     )
> min response time                        6 (OK=6      KO=-    )
> max response time                      163 (OK=163    KO=-    )
> mean response time                      11 (OK=11     KO=-    )
> std deviation                            8 (OK=8      KO=-    )
> response time 50th percentile           10 (OK=10     KO=-    )
> response time 75th percentile           12 (OK=11     KO=-    )
> response time 95th percentile           19 (OK=19     KO=-    )
> response time 99th percentile           36 (OK=36     KO=-    )
> mean requests/sec                   47.368 (OK=47.368 KO=-    )
---- Response Time Distribution -----------------------------------------------
> t < 800 ms                            1800 (100%)
> 800 ms < t < 1200 ms                     0 (  0%)
> t > 1200 ms                              0 (  0%)
> failed                                   0 (  0%)
================================================================================

Reports generated in 0s.
Please open the following file: /Users/danielbryant/Documents/dev/
                                daniel-bryant-uk/tmp/oreilly-docker-java-shopping/
                                performance-e2e-tests/target/gatling/
```

```
                    djshoppingbasicsimulation-1523108935957/index.html
Global: max of response time is less than 50 : false
Global: percentage of failed requests is 0 : true
[error] Simulation DjShoppingBasicSimulation failed.
[info] Simulation(s) execution ended.
[error] Failed tests:
[error]   uk.co.danielbryant.djshopping.performancee2etests.DjShoppingBasicSimulation
[error] (gatling:test) sbt.TestsFailedException: Tests unsuccessful
[error] Total time: 40 s, completed 07-Apr-2018 14:49:34
```

Gatling produces useful intermediate results when the tool is run via the CLI, and good summary information. When run via a build pipeline tool, it is also possible to generate HTML-based reports that are easy for an entire team to consume.

The Gatling Recorder Can Capture Interactions

The Gatling Recorder (*https://gatling.io/docs/2.3/http/recorder/*) helps you to quickly generate scenarios by either acting as an HTTP proxy between the browser and the HTTP server or converting HAR (HTTP Archive) files. Either way, the Recorder generates a simple simulation that mimics your recorded navigation. This can be an invaluable way to generate interaction scripts and tests.

Understanding the Dark Art of Performance Testing: Abraham's Experience

You've probably heard the phrase, "There are three kinds of lies: lies, damned lies, and statistics," or maybe the adapted version, "lies, damned lies, and benchmarks." It fits well in this context.

I have witnessed multiple teams who *think* that they have set up performance tests, only to realize upon closer inspection that their tests weren't really telling them what they thought they were telling them. The problem with benchmarks is that they are comparable only to other results obtained under *exactly* the same conditions—and guess what? Your performance test environment isn't the same as your production environment, which means that your performance tests are not running under the same conditions as your production application, which means that the results that you obtained during your performance tests are not really applicable to production.

I can tell you a dozen reasons why your tests are not a guarantee of performance, and I'm not a performance expert; an expert can probably tell you several dozens. Having a set of tests that can *guarantee* that your application can cope with a certain workload, or that transactions can run within a determined time limit, is surprisingly hard —so hard that it may not be worthy at all. Unless you are working on financial technology or another domain where bad performance truly means failure (and not just occasionally irritated customers), you don't need that kind of sophistication.

Most of the teams that I have seen benefiting from performance testing are not the ones worrying about hitting a particular value on a benchmark, but the ones who simply monitor the benchmark for unexpected changes. When your benchmark goes up or down for no apparent reason, that's when you have something to investigate.

Security, Vulnerabilities, and Threats

Modern criminals are becoming increasingly technically savvy. This, in combination with more and more valuable (and private) data being managed in publicly networked computers, makes for a potential security challenge. Therefore, it is everyone's job in a software delivery team to think about security, right from the beginning of the project. When attempting to implement continuous delivery, you need to be aware of and plan for many aspects of security. The CD build pipeline is often an effective location in which to codify and enforce security requirements. In this section, you will learn about code and dependency vulnerability checking, platform-specific security issues, and threat modeling.

Agile Application Security

Some organizations believe that the practice of agile methodologies and security are incompatible, which can lead to many arguments. If you are struggling with this, or discovering lots of security issues within your applications that require management buy-in to be fixed, then we recommend reading *Agile Application Security* (O'Reilly) by Laura Bell, Michael Brunton-Spall, et al.

Code-Level Security Verification

The go-to tool for checking Java code for known security issues is the Find Security Bugs (*http://find-sec-bugs.github.io/*) plugin for the FindBugs static analyzer (mentioned previously). It can detect 125 vulnerability types with over 787 unique API signatures. This tool integrates nicely with build tools like Maven and Gradle, and will produce an XML and HTML report based on the findings.

The Value of Commercial Code Scanning

Depending on your security requirements, it may be worth investing in commercial tools for security code scanning, such as those offered by Black Duck (*https://www.blackducksoftware.com/*) or Sonatype's (*https://www.sonatype.com/*) Nexus Software Supply Chain Management. These companies specialize in identifying and mitigating security issues, which is a rapidly shifting and evolving landscape. New attacks are created daily, and new vulnerabilities are found almost at the same pace. If the commercial security scanning tools look expensive, ask yourself (and the rest of your organization) if you can afford the cost of a security breach.

The Find Security Bugs plugin documentation is comprehensive. On the Bug Patterns (*http://find-sec-bugs.github.io/bugs.htm*) web page, you can find a full list of security issues that the plugin will find within your code. The following are some examples:

- Predictable pseudorandom number generator
- Untrusted servlet parameter or query string
- Potentially sensitive data in a cookie
- Potential path traversal (file read)
- Potential command injection
- TrustManager that accepts any certificates
- XML parsing vulnerable to XML external entity (XXE) attack via `Transformer Factory`
- Hardcoded passwords
- Database and AWS query injection
- Spring CSRF protection disabled

Example 12-11 is a simple Java application that is launched from a main method, and introduces several security bugs on purpose. The first is relatively easy to do, accidentally using *Random* in an attempt to generate cryptographically secure random numbers. The second is more obvious, and contains an unparsed argument value to a runtime execution (the same principle applies to SQL and other injection attacks)

Example 12-11. Simple Java application with obvious security issues

```
package uk.co.danielbryant.oreillyexamples.builddemo;

import org.slf4j.Logger;
import org.slf4j.LoggerFactory;

import java.io.IOException;
import java.util.Random;

public class LoggingDemo {

    public static final Logger LOGGER = LoggerFactory.getLogger(LoggingDemo.class);

    public static void main(String[] args) {
```

```
        LOGGER.info("Hello, (Logging) World!");
        Random random = new Random();
        String myBadRandomNumString = Long.toHexString(random.nextLong());

        Runtime runtime = Runtime.getRuntime();
        try {
            runtime.exec("/bin/sh -c some_tool" + args[1]);
        } catch (IOException iox) {
            LOGGER.error("Caught IOException with command", iox);
        }
    }
}
```

A snippet from the project's Maven POM is included in Example 12-12 that shows the inclusion of the Maven FindBugs plugin alongside the Find Security Bug plugin. You can see the Maven reporting that has been configured to include the generation of a Find Bugs HTML/site report.

Example 12-12. Including findbugs-maven-plugin with findsecbugs-plugin in a project

```xml
<?xml version="1.0" encoding="UTF-8"?>
<project xmlns="http://maven.apache.org/POM/4.0.0"
        xmlns:xsi="http://www.w3.org/2001/XMLSchema-instance"
        xsi:schemaLocation="http://maven.apache.org/POM/4.0.0
                            http://maven.apache.org/xsd/maven-4.0.0.xsd">
    <modelVersion>4.0.0</modelVersion>

...

    <build>
        <plugins>
...
            <plugin>
                <groupId>org.codehaus.mojo</groupId>
                <artifactId>findbugs-maven-plugin</artifactId>
                <version>3.0.5</version>
                <executions>
                    <execution>
                        <phase>verify</phase>
                        <goals>
                            <goal>check</goal>
                        </goals>
                    </execution>
                </executions>
                <configuration>
                    <effort>Max</effort>
                    <threshold>Low</threshold>
                    <failOnError>true</failOnError>
                    <plugins>
                        <plugin>
                            <groupId>com.h3xstream.findsecbugs</groupId>
```

```
                <artifactId>findsecbugs-plugin</artifactId>
                <version>LATEST</version>
                <!-- Auto-update to the latest stable -->
              </plugin>
            </plugins>
          </configuration>
        </plugin>
      </plugins>
    </build>
    <reporting>
      <plugins>
        <plugin>
          <groupId>org.codehaus.mojo</groupId>
          <artifactId>findbugs-maven-plugin</artifactId>
          <version>3.0.5</version>
        </plugin>
      </plugins>
    </reporting>

</project>
```

You can now execute this plugin as part of the verify life cycle hook: mvn verify, as shown in Example 12-13.

Example 12-13. Building the insecure project with the FindBugs plugin enabled

```
$ mvn verify
/Library/Java/JavaVirtualMachines/jdk1.8.0_151.jdk/Contents/Home/bin/java
    -Dmaven.multiModuleProjectDirectory=/Users/danielbryant/Documents/dev/
    daniel-bryant-uk/builddemo "-Dmaven.home=/Applications/IntelliJ IDEA.app/
    Contents/plugins/maven/lib/maven3" "-Dclassworlds.conf=/Applications/
    IntelliJ IDEA.app/Contents/plugins/maven/lib/maven3/bin/m2.conf" "-javaagent:/
    Applications/IntelliJ IDEA.app/Contents/lib/idea_rt.jar=50278:/
    Applications/IntelliJ IDEA.app/Contents/bin" -Dfile.encoding=UTF-8 -classpath
    "/Applications/IntelliJ IDEA.app/Contents/plugins/maven/lib/maven3/boot/
    plexus-classworlds-2.5.2.jar" org.codehaus.classworlds.Launcher
    -Didea.version=2017.2.6 verify
objc[12986]: Class JavaLaunchHelper is implemented in both
    /Library/Java/JavaVirtualMachines/jdk1.8.0_151.jdk/Contents/Home/bin/java
    (0x10f1044c0) and /Library/Java/JavaVirtualMachines/jdk1.8.0_151.jdk/
    Contents/Home/jre/lib/libinstrument.dylib
    (0x10f1904e0). One of the two will be used. Which one is undefined.
[INFO] Scanning for projects...
[INFO]
[INFO] ------------------------------------------------------------------------
[INFO] Building builddemo 0.1.0-SNAPSHOT
[INFO] ------------------------------------------------------------------------
...
[INFO] >>> findbugs-maven-plugin:3.0.5:check (default) > :findbugs @ builddemo >>>
[INFO]
[INFO] --- findbugs-maven-plugin:3.0.5:findbugs (findbugs) @ builddemo ---
```

```
[INFO] Fork Value is true
     [java] Warnings generated: 3
[INFO] Done FindBugs Analysis....
[INFO]
[INFO] <<< findbugs-maven-plugin:3.0.5:check (default) < :findbugs @ builddemo <<<
[INFO]
[INFO] --- findbugs-maven-plugin:3.0.5:check (default) @ builddemo ---
[INFO] BugInstance size is 3
[INFO] Error size is 0
[INFO] Total bugs: 3
[INFO] This usage of java/lang/Runtime.exec(Ljava/lang/String;)Ljava/lang/Process;
       can be vulnerable to Command Injection [uk.co.danielbryant.oreillyexamples
       .builddemo.LoggingDemo, uk.co.danielbryant.oreillyexamples.builddemo
       .LoggingDemo] At LoggingDemo.java:[line 20]At LoggingDemo.java:[line 20]
       COMMAND_INJECTION
[INFO] Dead store to myBadRandomNumString in uk.co.danielbryant.oreillyexamples
       .builddemo.LoggingDemo.main(String[]) [uk.co.danielbryant.oreillyexamples
       .builddemo.LoggingDemo] At LoggingDemo.java:[line 16] DLS_DEAD_LOCAL_STORE
[INFO] The use of java.util.Random is predictable [uk.co.danielbryant
       .oreillyexamples.builddemo.LoggingDemo] At LoggingDemo.java:[line 15]
       PREDICTABLE_RANDOM
[INFO]


To see bug detail using the Findbugs GUI, use the following command
"mvn findbugs:gui"



[INFO] ------------------------------------------------------------------------
[INFO] BUILD FAILURE
[INFO] ------------------------------------------------------------------------
[INFO] Total time: 6.337 s
[INFO] Finished at: 2018-01-09T11:45:42+00:00
[INFO] Final Memory: 31M/465M
[INFO] ------------------------------------------------------------------------
[ERROR] Failed to execute goal org.codehaus.mojo:findbugs-maven-plugin:3.0.5:check
        (default) on project builddemo: failed with 3 bugs and 0 errors -> [Help 1]
[ERROR]
[ERROR] To see the full stack trace of the errors, re-run Maven with the -e switch.
[ERROR] Re-run Maven using the -X switch to enable full debug logging.
[ERROR]
[ERROR] For more information about the errors and possible solutions,
        please read the following articles:
[ERROR] [Help 1] http://cwiki.apache.org/confluence/display/
                  MAVEN/MojoExecutionException

Process finished with exit code 1
```

Because the plugin threshold has been set to low, as well as to fail on error, you will
see that the build fails. This behavior can be fully configured—perhaps you want to

fail the build only on major issues. When you generate the Maven site, the FindBugs web page in Figure 12-1 will be created.

Figure 12-1. Output from the Maven FindBugs plugin with FindSecBugs enabled

Dependency Verification

It is important to verify the security properties of your code, but it is equally important to verify that the dependencies you are including within your project are equally secure. In a high-security environment (perhaps governmental or finance), this may involve scanning the codebases or binaries for all dependencies, and commercial tooling does exist to make this possible.

The Value of Commercial Dependency Scanning

Even if you believe your security requirements are quite minimal, it may be worth investing in commercial dependency scanning tooling, such as that offered by Snyk (*https://snyk.io/*) or Sonatype's Software Bill of Materials (*https://www.sonatype.com/software-bill-of-materials*). These companies specialize in identifying and mitigating security issues within common dependencies (across multiple languages). New vulnerabilities are found daily, so the build pipeline must be run at least this regularly, even if no code changes have been made. If the dependency scanning tools detect an issue, you must address this as soon as possible.

Depending on your security needs, a good first step (and perhaps solution) to this issue is to use the open source OWASP Maven Dependency Check plugin (*http://*

bit.ly/2xEGD7t). This plugin contacts the National Vulnerability Database (NVD) and downloads a list of Java dependencies with known Common Vulnerabilities and Exposures (CVEs), and then examines all of dependencies—and their transitive dependencies—within your project, looking for a match. If you have imported a dependency with a known issue, this will be highlighted for you, and the plugin allows configuration to warn during or to fail the build. A sample Maven POM file is included in Example 12-14 for a project that includes dependencies with several known vulnerabilities.

Example 12-14. Project POM that includes dependencies with known vulnerabilities

```xml
<?xml version="1.0" encoding="UTF-8"?>
<project xmlns="http://maven.apache.org/POM/4.0.0"
               xmlns:xsi="http://www.w3.org/2001/XMLSchema-instance"
          xsi:schemaLocation="http://maven.apache.org/POM/4.0.0
                               http://maven.apache.org/xsd/maven-4.0.0.xsd">
     <modelVersion>4.0.0</modelVersion>

     <groupId>uk.co.danielbryant.djshopping</groupId>
     <artifactId>shopfront</artifactId>
     <version>0.0.1-SNAPSHOT</version>
     <packaging>jar</packaging>

     <name>shopfront</name>
     <description>Docker Java application Shopfront</description>

     <parent>
         <groupId>org.springframework.boot</groupId>
         <artifactId>spring-boot-starter-parent</artifactId>
         <version>1.5.7.RELEASE</version>
     </parent>
...
     <dependencies>
         <!-- let's include a few old dependencies -->
     </dependencies>
...
     <build>
...
             <plugin>
                 <groupId>org.owasp</groupId>
                 <artifactId>dependency-check-maven</artifactId>
                 <version>3.0.1</version>
                 <configuration>
                     <centralAnalyzerEnabled>false</centralAnalyzerEnabled>
                     <failBuildOnCVSS>8</failBuildOnCVSS>
                 </configuration>
                 <executions>
                     <execution>
                         <goals>
                             <goal>check</goal>
```

```
          </goals>
        </execution>
      </executions>
    </plugin>
  </plugins>

  </build>
</project>
```

You can see the sample Maven verify output in Example 12-15.

Example 12-15. Build output when running verify against a project with known vulnerable dependencies

```
$ mvn verify
[INFO] Scanning for projects...
[INFO]
[INFO] ------------------------------------------------------------------------
[INFO] Building shopfront 0.0.1-SNAPSHOT
[INFO] ------------------------------------------------------------------------
...
[INFO]
[INFO] --- dependency-check-maven:3.0.1:check (default) @ shopfront ---
[INFO] Central analyzer disabled
[INFO] Checking for updates
[INFO] Skipping NVD check since last check was within 4 hours.
[INFO] Check for updates complete (16 ms)
[INFO] Analysis Started
[INFO] Finished Archive Analyzer (0 seconds)
[INFO] Finished File Name Analyzer (0 seconds)
[INFO] Finished Jar Analyzer (1 seconds)
[INFO] Finished Dependency Merging Analyzer (0 seconds)
[INFO] Finished Version Filter Analyzer (0 seconds)
[INFO] Finished Hint Analyzer (0 seconds)
[INFO] Created CPE Index (2 seconds)
[INFO] Finished CPE Analyzer (2 seconds)
[INFO] Finished False Positive Analyzer (0 seconds)
[INFO] Finished Cpe Suppression Analyzer (0 seconds)
[INFO] Finished NVD CVE Analyzer (0 seconds)
[INFO] Finished Vulnerability Suppression Analyzer (0 seconds)
[INFO] Finished Dependency Bundling Analyzer (0 seconds)
[INFO] Analysis Complete (6 seconds)
[WARNING]

One or more dependencies were identified with known vulnerabilities in shopfront:

jersey-apache-client4-1.19.1.jar (cpe:/a:oracle:oracle_client:1.19.1,
com.sun.jersey.contribs:jersey-apache-client4:1.19.1) : CVE-2006-0550
xstream-1.4.9.jar (cpe:/a:x-stream:xstream:1.4.9,
cpe:/a:xstream_project:xstream:1.4.9,
com.thoughtworks.xstream:xstream:1.4.9) : CVE-2017-7957
```

```
netty-codec-4.0.27.Final.jar (cpe:/a:netty_project:netty:4.0.27,
io.netty:netty-codec:4.0.27.Final) : CVE-2016-4970, CVE-2015-2156
ognl-3.0.8.jar (ognl:ognl:3.0.8,
cpe:/a:ognl_project:ognl:3.0.8) : CVE-2016-3093
maven-core-3.0.jar (org.apache.maven:maven-core:3.0,
cpe:/a:apache:maven:3.0.4) : CVE-2013-0253
tomcat-embed-core-8.5.20.jar (cpe:/a:apache_software_foundation:tomcat:8.5.20,
cpe:/a:apache:tomcat:8.5.20, cpe:/a:apache_tomcat:apache_tomcat:8.5.20,
org.apache.tomcat.embed:tomcat-embed-core:8.5.20) : CVE-2017-12617
bsh-2.0b4.jar (cpe:/a:beanshell_project:beanshell:2.0.b4,
org.beanshell:bsh:2.0b4) : CVE-2016-2510
groovy-2.4.12.jar (cpe:/a:apache:groovy:2.4.12,
org.codehaus.groovy:groovy:2.4.12) : CVE-2016-6497


See the dependency-check report for more details.


[INFO]
[INFO] --- maven-install-plugin:2.5.2:install (default-install) @ shopfront ---
[INFO] Installing /Users/danielbryant/Documents/dev/daniel-bryant-uk/
                oreilly-docker-java-shopping/shopfront/target/
                shopfront-0.0.1-SNAPSHOT.jar to /Users/danielbryant/.m2/
                repository/uk/co/danielbryant/djshopping/shopfront/
                0.0.1-SNAPSHOT/shopfront-0.0.1-SNAPSHOT.jar
[INFO] Installing /Users/danielbryant/Documents/dev/daniel-bryant-uk/
                oreilly-docker-java-shopping/shopfront/pom.xml to
                /Users/danielbryant/.m2/repository/uk/co/danielbryant/
                djshopping/shopfront/0.0.1-SNAPSHOT/shopfront-0.0.1-SNAPSHOT.pom
[INFO] ------------------------------------------------------------------------
[INFO] BUILD SUCCESS
[INFO] ------------------------------------------------------------------------
[INFO] Total time: 23.946 s
[INFO] Finished at: 2018-01-09T12:20:47Z
[INFO] Final Memory: 35M/120M
[INFO] ------------------------------------------------------------------------
```

In addition to the preceding build information, you can produce a report that contains more details, including links to more information on each CVE found; see Figure 12-2.

Once you have identified dependencies with known CVEs, it is up to you to resolve this issue. Often, a newer version of the plugin exists, and you can upgrade (and of course, run your comprehensive test suite to ensure that this upgrade causes no issues or regressions), but sometime it doesn't. Your alternative options are to find another dependency that offers similar functionality and modify your code to use this, or attempt to fix the vulnerability yourself, by forking the dependency and taking ownership of this codebase. Occasionally, neither of these alternatives is appropriate; perhaps you are maintaining very large legacy codebase that makes extensive use of the vulnerable dependency, or you don't have the skillset to fork and modify the dependency. This then leaves you with a difficult decision, because although doing nothing may seem appealing, it is also dangerous.

Figure 12-2. HTML report from the Maven Dependency Check plugin

You will need to conduct a thorough audit and analysis of the vulnerability, known exploits, and attack vector. You must communicate the risks within your organization and document the known vulnerability. You can also take steps to mitigate the risk—perhaps for a known vulnerability that requires OS-level access for an exploit to be undertaken, you may increase security around accessing the instances running your application. If there are no known exploits, or the attack vector is extremely obtuse, you may choose to do nothing more. But be warned: this is not simply a technical decision—the business must be consulted about this risk

Mitigating Risks Is a Business Decision: Be a Professional

We cannot stress enough the risks of ignoring security or vulnerability issues. You must inform and work closely with your business team if a problem is identified, because the decision of how to mitigate a risk is not just technical, it is also business related. Simply ignoring issues (or not checking for them in the first place) is at best case unprofessional—and at worst case, potentially criminally negligent.

Deployment Platform-Specific Security Issues

Each of the three deployment platforms you are learning about in this book has specific security properties and practices that it would be wise to learn more about.

Manual and Automated Penetration Testing

Regularly hiring professional penetration testers to inspect your systems can deliver much value, even if the domain you work in doesn't require this by regulation or compliance. In the same respects as good exploratory testers, many penetration testing experts think differently than other engineers, and accordingly can find potential security issues before they are exploited.

In addition to manual penetration testing, we also recommend automated scanning. One of the leading open source tools in this space is the OWASP Zed Attack Proxy (*http://bit.ly/1NIcfdT*), which can automatically find security vulnerabilities in your web applications. You can run this tool via the command line, and there is also a Jenkins ZAP plugin (*http://bit.ly/2zxbZy9*). A company named Continuum Security has also created the open source bdd-security tool, which provides a wrapper around ZAP that enables you to specify security tests in a BDD-style given/when/then syntax.

Cloud security

The core change in regards to security practices from on-premises infrastructure to public cloud is knowledge of the "shared responsibility model." Azure has created a short guide, "Shared Responsibilities for Cloud Computing" (*http://bit.ly/2xFNltC*), that introduces the shared responsibilities across the various service models. Figure 12-3 is taken from this guide, and clearly shows how your responsibilities for security differ as you move from on-premises to SaaS.

Amazon Web Services has also created a useful (although somewhat AWS-specific) whitepaper, "AWS Security Best Practices" (*https://amzn.to/2OhLjJR*), that explains the concept in depth, but in essence the model states that the cloud platform vendor is responsible for ensuring the security of certain parts of the platform, and you, the developer, are responsible for your code and configuration that is deployed onto the platform. Figure 12-4 shows IaaS offerings, such as EC2 compute and virtual private cloud (VPC) networking, and the shared responsibility.

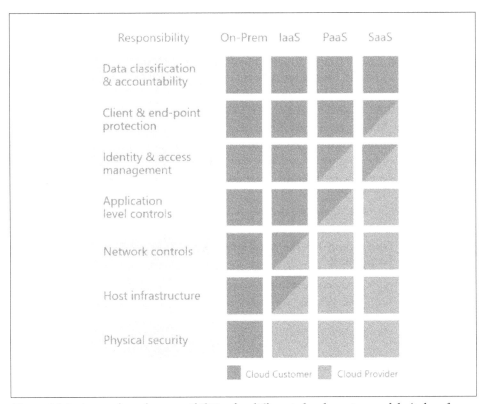

Figure 12-3. Azure shared responsibilities for different cloud service models (taken from the Azure Shared Responsibilities for Cloud Computing document)

Figure 12-4. Shared responsibility model for infrastructure services (taken from the AWS Security Best Practices (https://amzn.to/2OhLjJR) document)

We strongly encourage you to read the AWS and Azure shared responsibility guides and also the documentation from the other cloud vendors.

Other common "gotchas" for engineers moving to the public cloud include the importance of correctly managing API and SDK keys, which provide secured programmatic access to the cloud. It is all too easy for these keys to end up accidentally stored within code or committed to a DVCS. Once a key is exposed publicly, bad actors can use this to create infrastructure to perform illegal operations, such as DDoS attacks, or mine for cryptocurrency. Not only will you be charged money for the use of the cloud platform resources, but you could be legally liable for damage, too! These keys must be targeted to individual users; use the principle of least privilege (i.e., allow the smallest amount of access to accomplish the intended work); and be audited, well protected, and rotated regularly.

> **Cloud Security 101: The Shared Responsibility Model and Key Management**
>
> If you and your team are moving to a public cloud platform for the first time, the two core security concepts you must learn more about are the shared responsibility model and API/SDK access key management and security.

A public cloud platform often provides a higher level of security than an on-premises solution; after all, the cloud vendor has large, dedicated teams managing this. But you will have to play your part, too. In addition to managing API keys, you need to manage identity access management (IAM) users, group, and roles, as well as network security, often implemented by security groups (SGs) and network access control lists (NACLs). Core security concepts, such as securing data in rest and in transit, also change slightly with cloud usage. Finally, if you are managing your own VMs and operating systems, you will also be responsible for patching the software here.

As with any new technology, there is lots to learn, but there are many good cross-cloud resources like the online A Cloud Guru (*https://acloud.guru/*) learning platform. Each cloud vendor also typically offers a security review platform and associated automated tooling, as well as professional services.

Container security

The primary issue with container security is that "with great power, comes great responsibility," and in particular, this relates to the deployable artifact (the container image), as this now includes an operating system in addition to the Java application artifact. Container technology allows you to quickly deploy your applications and the supporting containerized infrastructure, such as queues and databases. However, the attack surface exposed by this is considerably larger than with traditional application artifacts and sysadmin-managed infrastructure. For this reason, we recommend the use of a static image vulnerability scanner as part of your continuous delivery pipeline.

The open source tool we recommend in this space is Clair from CoreOS. It can be challenging to get Clair working, especially when integrating within your build pipelines. Accordingly, Armin Coralic has created a Docker-based installation of Clair (*https://github.com/arminc/clair-scanner*) that is well worth exploring. There are also various commercial offerings in this space, and some container registry vendors, like Quay and Docker Enterprise, offer security scanning as part of this. There are also standalone image scanners like that offered by Aqua.

Static Container Image Scanning Is as Important as Code Scanning

Container technology allows convenient packaging of application artifacts, but you must not forget that you are typically including components (such as an operating system and associated tooling) in comparison with traditional artifacts. Accordingly, vulnerability scanning of images should be an essential part of any pipeline delivering applications as container images.

We also recommend learning more about operating systems, and building minimal images in order to minimize the attack surface. For example, instead of using a full Ubuntu distro for your OS, use Debian Jessie or Alpine, and instead of including a full JDK, include a JRE instead. Starting from Java 9, you could also investigate using the module system to build a smaller JRE. This is beyond the scope of a book this size, but we would recommend consulting *Java 9 Modularity* (O'Reilly) by Sander Mak and Paul Bakker for more information on this process and tooling such as jlink.

FaaS/Serverless security

The security issues for FaaS and serverless platforms are largely aligned with the issues discussed in Cloud Security. This is because the FaaS platforms are typically a subset of the larger cloud infrastructure offerings. Guy Podjarny, CEO of the Synk security company, has created a great InfoQ article that highlights key security issues with serverless technologies, "Serverless Security: What's Left to Protect" (*https:// www.infoq.com/articles/serverless-security*), and the primary issues discussed revolve around the importance of code and dependency vulnerability scanning and function provenance (tracking all of your functions)

Next Steps: Threat Modeling

Threat modeling is a structured approach that enables you to identify, quantify, and address the security risks associated with an application. The inclusion of threat modeling within the design and development process can help ensure that applications are being developed with security built in from the beginning. This is important, as even with modern, flexible architectures like microservices, it can still be difficult (or extremely costly) to retrofit security into a new system that is nearing completion. Baking in security from the start, in combination with the documentation produced as part of the threat-modeling process, can provide a reviewer with a greater understanding of the system, and allows for easier identification of entry points to the application and the associated threats with each entry point. The OWASP Application Threat modeling website states that the concept of threat modeling is not new, but a clear mindset change has occurred in recent years: modern threat modeling looks at a system from a potential attacker's perspective, as opposed to a defender's viewpoint.

Keen to Learn More About Threat Modeling?

The OWASP Application Threat Modeling (*http://bit.ly/1TQ0Qy3*) website is a fantastic free resource to learn more about threat modeling, and was also the inspiration for much of the content in this section of the chapter. If you want to learn even more, we strongly recommend *Threat Modeling: Designing for Security (https://threatmodeling book.com/)* (Wiley) by Adam Shostack. We have learned much from this book, and it often accompanies us on consulting engagements, where we bump up against security issues. Just to be clear, neither of us is a security expert, and because of the importance of this topic for some organizations, we often recommend calling in security specialists. Knowing when you are out of your league—and crucially, asking for help —is a key skill for all technical leaders.

The threat modeling process can be decomposed into three high-level steps, presented next.

Decompose the application

This involves creating use cases to understand how the application is used, identifying entry points to see where a potential attacker could interact with the application, identifying assets (i.e., items/areas that the attacker would be interested in), and identifying trust levels that represent the access rights that the application will grant to external entities. This information is documented and used to produce data flow diagrams (DFDs) for the application, as shown in Figure 12-5.

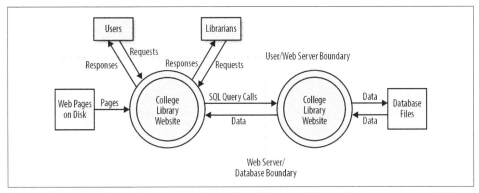

Figure 12-5. Data flow diagram for the College Library Website (image courtesy of the OWASP Application Threat Modeling website (http://bit.ly/1TQ0Qy3))

Determine and rank threats

Critical to the identification of threats is using a threat categorization methodology, such as STRIDE (an acronym for Spoofing, Tampering, Repudiation, Information disclosure, Denial of service, and Elevation of privilege). A threat categorization provides a set of threat categories with corresponding examples so that threats can be systematically identified in the application in a structured and repeatable manner. DFDs produced in step 1 help identify the potential threat targets from the attacker's perspective, such as data sources, processes, data flows, and interactions with users. Threats can be further analyzed by using a threat tree (shown in Figure 12-6) in order to explore the attack paths, the root causes (e.g., vulnerabilities) for the threat to be exploited, and the necessary mitigation controls (e.g., countermeasures, depicted as third-level leaf nodes).

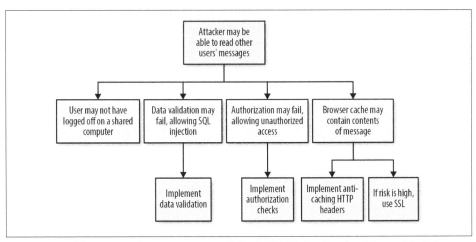

Figure 12-6. Threat tree (image courtesy of the OWASP Application Threat Modeling website (http://bit.ly/1TQ0Qy3))

Threats can be ranked from the perspective of various factors, all depending on the approach and methodology applied. A risk-centric threat model such as PASTA (Process for Attack Simulation & Threat Analysis) focuses on prioritization based on risks to the product, information owners, business, or other stakeholders. A security-centric approach may rank threats based on ease of exploitation or technical impact to the product or application. A software-centric approach may prioritize threats based on the adverse effects they may have against functional use cases and software features.

Microsoft's DREAD Model

Microsoft has been a strong advocate of threat modeling, and has made threat modeling a core component of its development process, which it claims to be one of the reasons for the increased security of Microsoft products in recent years. In the Microsoft DREAD threat-risk ranking model, the technical risk factors for impact are Damage and Affected Users, while the ease of exploitation factors are Reproducibility, Exploitability, and Discoverability. This risk factoring allows the assignment of values to the different influencing factors of a threat. To determine the ranking of a threat, the threat analyst has to answer basic questions for each factor of risk, for example:

For Damage
How big would the damage be if the attack succeeded?

For Reproducibility
How easy is it to reproduce an attack that works?

For Exploitability
How much time, effort, and expertise is needed to exploit the threat?

For Affected Users
If a threat were exploited, what percentage of users would be affected?

For Discoverability
How easy is it for an attacker to discover this threat?

Determine countermeasures and mitigation

A lack of protection against a threat might indicate a vulnerability whose risk exposure could be mitigated with the implementation of a countermeasure. The purpose of the countermeasure identification is to determine whether there is some kind of protective measure (e.g., security control, policy measures) in place that can prevent each threat previously identified via threat analysis from being realized. Vulnerabilities are then those threats that have no countermeasures. Risk management is used to reduce the impact that the exploitation of a threat can have to the application, and this can be done by responding to a threat with a risk mitigation strategy. In general, there are five options to mitigate threats:

- Do nothing (for example, hope for the best)
- Inform about the risk (for example, warn user population about the risk)
- Mitigate the risk (for example, by putting countermeasures in place)
- Accept the risk (for example, after evaluating the business impact of the exploitation)
- Transfer the risk (for example, through contractual agreements and insurance)
- Terminate the risk (for example, shut down, turn off, unplug, or decommission the asset)

The decision of which strategy is most appropriate depends on the impact an exploitation of a threat can have, the likelihood of its occurrence, and the costs for transferring (i.e., costs for insurance) or avoiding it (i.e., costs or losses due to redesign or reimplementation).

Chaos Testing

The concept of chaos engineering (*http://principlesofchaos.org/*) and resilience testing has become increasingly popular over the last year, even though pioneers such as Netflix (*http://bit.ly/2yukZU8*) have been talking about this for quite some time. One of the major concepts of working with infrastructure as code and with cloud and container environments is *designing for failure*. This is mentioned in nearly all the major cloud vendor best-practice documents, and the main idea behind designing for failure is accepting that things are going to go wrong, and making sure your application and infrastructure is set up to handle that.

However, it is one thing to say that your system is resilient; it is quite another to prove it by running chaos tooling attempts to tear your infrastructure apart and inject all manner of faults. Tooling such as Netflix's Chaos Monkey (*https://github.com/Netflix/chaosmonkey*) (and associated Simian Army (*https://github.com/Netflix/SimianArmy*) collection) are relatively mainstream, and many recent conference presentations (*http://bit.ly/2ObOwe5*) feature a mention of chaos (*http://bit.ly/2xNwK7B*). However, use of this technology often requires an advanced level of infrastructure and operational skill, the ability to design and execute experiments, and available resources to manually orchestrate the failure scenarios in a controlled manner.

Chaos engineering is fundamentally the discipline of experimenting on a distributed system in order to build confidence in the system's capability to withstand turbulent conditions in production, and is not simply about breaking things in production. According to the Principles of Chaos Engineering (*http://principlesofchaos.org/*) website, in order to specifically address the uncertainty of distributed systems at scale, chaos engineering can be thought of as the facilitation of experiments to uncover systemic weaknesses. These experiments follow four steps:

1. Start by defining *steady state* as some measurable output of a system that indicates normal behavior.

2. Hypothesize that this steady state will continue in both the control group and the experimental group.

3. Introduce variables that reflect real-world events such as servers that crash, hard drives that malfunction, network connections that are severed, etc.

4. Try to disprove the hypothesis by looking for a difference in steady state between the control group and the experimental group.

The harder it is to disrupt the steady state, the more confidence we have in the behavior of the system. If a weakness is uncovered, we now have a target for improvement before that behavior manifests in the system at large.

The Human Side of Chaos and Resilience

The human aspects of chaos and resilience testing should not be forgotten. Indeed, some thought leaders in this space—such as John Allspaw (*https://www.linkedin.com/in/jallspaw/*), cofounder at Adaptive Capacity Labs—are cautioning that the human side of resilience engineering (*http://bit.ly/2R2AdqS*) is, in fact, more important than the associated tooling. Tammy Butow has also argued that you must invest in processes for managing high-severity incidents (*http://bit.ly/2QVLo4x*). Testing these procedures through the running of game days (*http://bit.ly/2NIeeY4*) is also effective. Adrian Cockcroft refers to game days as the "fire drill for IT" (*http://bit.ly/2xGB48y*), because the idea is to simulate a failure in a controlled way, and watch how people respond to the incident. For example, is the problem detected, are the correct on-call engineers paged, and does everyone communicate effectively?

Causing Chaos in Production (Bring in the Monkeys)

Running chaos experiments in production is a relatively advanced pattern, so please apply caution before rushing off to try some of the tooling mentioned in this section! Arguably, chaos engineering began in 2011, with the publication of the Netflix blog post "The Netflix Simian Army" (*http://bit.ly/2yukZU8*), which properly introduced the Chaos Monkey and assorted friends to the world. Let's have a look at the various chaos engineering tools available for each platform.

Cloud chaos

If you are working with the AWS platform, the original Chaos Monkey (*https://github.com/netflix/chaosmonkey*) tool is still available as a standalone project on GitHub. You will have to install Golang on your local (or test) machine, but this is easily accomplished by using a package manager. The standalone Chaos Monkey should work with any backend that the Netflix/Google build tool Spinnaker supports (AWS, Google Compute Engine, Azure, Kubernetes, Cloud Foundry), and the documentation states it has been tested with AWS, GCE (*http://bit.ly/2IjXsZt*), and Kubernetes. If you are working with Azure, the Microsoft blog post Induce Controlled Chaos in Service Fabric Clusters (*http://bit.ly/2OSXE4j*) is the place to learn about the tooling offered for this platform, of which the primary offering is the Azure Fault Analysis Service (*http://bit.ly/2Q7aHiO*).

Container (and Kubernetes) chaos

PowerfulSeal (*https://github.com/bloomberg/powerfulseal*) a Kubernetes-specific chaos testing tool written by the Bloomberg engineering team, was inspired by the infamous Netflix Chaos Monkey. PowerfulSeal is written in Python, and is very much a work in progress at the time of writing. It has only "cloud drivers" for managing infrastructure failure for the OpenStack platform, although a Python `Abstract Driver` class has been specified in order to encourage the contribution of drivers for additional cloud platforms.

PowerfulSeal works in two modes—interactive and autonomous:

- *Interactive mode* is designed to allow an engineer to discover a cluster's components and manually cause failure to see what happens. It operates on nodes (*http://bit.ly/2y2yMjx*), pods (*http://bit.ly/2xFXGG1*), deployments (*http://bit.ly/2q7vR7Y*), and namespaces (*http://bit.ly/2r0wBc3*).

- *Autonomous mode* reads a policy file (*http://bit.ly/2xG6trJ*), which can contain any number of pod and node failure scenarios, and "breaks things" as specified.

Each scenario describes a list of matches, filters, and actions to execute on your cluster.

Each scenario can consist of matches and filters (target node names, IP addresses, Kubernetes namespaces and labels, times and dates) and actions (start, stop, and kill). A comprehensive JSON schema (*http://bit.ly/2Dx6Da9*) can be used to validate the policy files, and an example policy file listing most of the available options can be found within the project's tests.

PowerfulSeal can be installed via pip (*http://bit.ly/2N5J8nT*), and the command-line tool is initialized and configured against a Kubernetes cluster as follows:

1. Point PowerfulSeal at the target Kubernetes cluster by giving it a Kubernetes config file.

2. Point PowerfulSeal at the underlying cloud IaaS platform by specifying the appropriate cloud driver and credentials.

3. Ensure that PowerfulSeal can SSH into the nodes in order to execute commands.

4. Write the required policy files and load these into PowerfulSeal.

FaaS/Serverless chaos

As the FaaS paradigm is relatively new, there isn't much in the way of chaos testing tools for this platform. Yan Cui has written a series of Medium posts (*http://bit.ly/2R1DuXj*) on the topic, which demonstrate how to inject latency (*http://bit.ly/2xGCCz9*) into AWS Lambda innovations, and the Serverless framework team has built on Ben Kehoe's work on Monkeyless Chaos (*http://bit.ly/2zze6l4*). Although both of these sources are interesting, the accompanying work is still in an early stage and is predominantly conceptual.

Causing Chaos in Preproduction

Causing chaos in production may (quite rightly) be too risky for many organizations initially, but this is not to say that you can't benefit from the principles in a preproduction environment. Using service virtualization tooling like Hoverfly allows you to simulate service dependencies and inject middleware (*http://bit.ly/2xIcHqN*) into the tool, which can modify the response. The middleware can be written in any language, or be deployed as a binary, or target an HTTP endpoint. However, it is most common to write the middleware in a scripting language like Python or JavaScript, as these languages have great support for modifying JSON and HTTP headers, and they also execute fast. As shown in Figure 12-7, with middleware active in Hoverfly, each time a request/response is simulated, the middleware is started as a separate (forked) process that has full access to the associated request/response JSON.

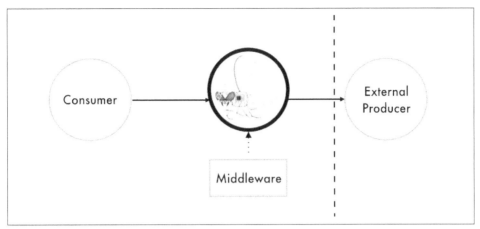

Figure 12-7. Causing chaos with Hoverfly middleware

Using middleware allows you to write simple scripts to modify the response and deterministically simulate the effects of increased latency, corrupted responses, and failures scenarios within the dependency.

This is a relatively low-risk approach to chaos testing, as you can simulate failure within your local development environment by using the Hoverfly JUnit rule, or a CD build pipeline or QA/staging environment by running Hoverfly as a standalone binary with the middleware configuration specified via the CLI parameters.

Deterministically Simulating Failure in a Dependency with Hoverfly: Daniel's Experience

On several projects I worked on, we used Hoverfly in combination with middleware to deterministically simulate and test failure scenarios. For example, in one project, my service was going to be integrated with an in-house legacy system. Fortunately, the legacy system had a REST API wrapper, and the legacy API was not changing over the life cycle of my project. However, I could get access to the staging version of the system only once every two weeks, and it was difficult to cause the system to fail deterministically in the way it had within production several times before.

I wanted to make sure my service (which was dependent on the legacy API) could handle the known failure scenarios, so when I was given access to the the system, I recorded a series of simulations using Hoverfly-Java, JUnit, and the REST Assured framework. I then modified the Hoverfly simulation request/response pair data to simulate the legacy system failures, and loaded this into a Hoverfly instance that was instantiated as part of my test. Success! I was not only able to test my service integration with the legacy API whenever needed by using the Hoverfly simulation, but also could reliably test the failure-handling code within my application.

How Much NFR Testing Is Enough?

Answering the question of how much nonfunctional requirement (NFR) testing is required for a product or project is nearly impossible, or very much like the answer to "How long is a piece of string?" How much effort you choose to invest in this will depend on the stage of your business and the resources and time you have available. If your business does not have product/market fit, experimenting to figure out what functionality to offer is most likely the highest priority. Likewise, if your leadership team has not dedicated (or allowed) any engineering time and energy to this type of testing, then the results will simply be best effort.

There are several "smells" to look for, though, which may indicate you would benefit from more nonfunctional testing:

- New team members have a difficult time understanding the design and code of the application.
- You are having difficulty extending the application; or every time you attempt to modify the architecture, everything breaks, and you don't know why.
- Your team is undertaking time-consuming manual performance and security verification.
- Worse, your customers are reporting performance and security issues.
- You are experiencing frequent production issues.
- All of your after-incident retrospectives point to the root causes as being very simple (e.g., the application ran out of disk space, the network experienced a small temporary amount of latency, or a user supplied bad data).

Balancing the correct amount of nonfunctional testing is, much like all jobs of a technical leader, about trade-offs. Here it is typically time/expense versus velocity/ stability.

Summary

In this chapter, you learned about the key concepts for testing what is commonly referred to as the *nonfunctional requirements* of a system:

- The nonfunctional perspective of code quality consists of reducing time-to-context (how readable is the code for another developer, and can someone else quickly understand the implementation logic?) and being free of deficiencies.
- Architecture quality can be maintained by having an experienced developer or architect look at the code once a week, identify violations, and correct them. Realistically, a more practical method is to define the rules and violations in code

and then automatically assert the properties as part of your continuous integration build.

- Understanding the performance characteristics of your application and its individual service components is extremely invaluable. Load tests can be run at an application level, covering the entire system, and at a modular level, covering an individual service or function.

- It is everyone's job in a software delivery team to think about security, right from the beginning of the project. The CD build pipeline is often an effective location in which to codify and enforce security requirements, from code and dependency issues to other threats.

- The concept of chaos engineering and resilience testing has become increasingly popular, primarily driven by pioneers such as Netflix. One of the major concepts of working with infrastructure as code and with cloud environments is designing for failure, and chaos engineering provides an approach to define a hypothesis, run experiments, and determine how failure is handled.

- Knowing how much NFR testing is enough is a difficult question to answer. However, there are several "smells" to look for, which may indicate you would benefit from more nonfunctional testing.

In the next chapter, you will learn about how to observe your systems through monitoring, logging, and tracing.

## CHAPTER 13

Observability: Monitoring, Logging, and Tracing

You have learned that testing is a vital skill to be mastered for the effective implementation of continuous delivery, but equally import is observability. Testing enables verification and promotes understanding at build and integration time, whereas observability allows verification and enables debugging at runtime. In this chapter, you will examine what you should observe and how, and you will learn about the implementation of monitoring, logging, tracing, and exception tracking. You will also explore several best practices for each of these implementations, and learn how to combine them with visualization to not only increase your understanding of your running systems, but also identify how to close the feedback loop and continuously enhance your applications.

Observability and Continuous Delivery

Continuous delivery does not end with the application being deployed into production. In fact, you could argue that deploying your application is really the beginning and that the process of continuous delivery stops only when an application or service is retired or decommissioned. Throughout the lifetime of an application, it is vital that you are able to understand what is occurring, and what has occurred, within the system. This is what observability is all about.

Why Observe?

An application is rarely deployed only once and never modified or updated again. A more typical pattern is that the business evolves or the organization changes, which generates new requirements, and, in turn, triggers the creation and deployment of multiple new versions of the application. Often, these new requirements are generated from insight into the application itself—for example, are key performance indicators (KPIs) being met, or is the application running at close to capacity? It is also common for a deployed application to crash or otherwise misbehave, so you may have to run tests and simulations locally in order to re-create the issues, or you may even have to log on to production systems to debug the application in situ.

Monitoring and Observability

The recent popularity of the term *observability* has driven some in the industry to question what exactly is meant by this term and how it relates to monitoring. An excellent blog post by Cindy Sridharan titled "Monitoring and Observability" (*http://bit.ly/2OiZpdU*) explores these topics in detail, and provides many useful references. Fundamentally, Sridharan argues that the goals of monitoring and observability are different but complementary:

> "Monitoring" is best suited to report the overall health of systems. Aiming to "monitor everything" can prove to be an antipattern. Monitoring, as such, is best limited to key business and systems metrics derived from time-series based instrumentation, known failure modes, as well as blackbox tests. "Observability," on the other hand, aims to provide highly granular insights into the behavior of systems along with rich context, perfect for debugging purposes. Since it's still not possible to predict every single failure mode a system could potentially run into or predict every possible way in which a system could misbehave, it becomes important that we build systems that can be debugged armed with evidence and not conjecture.

Observability may be a popular new term, but the chances are that you or your teammates have been creating "observable" Java applications for many years. If you have ever coded auditing, events logging, or exception tracking, then you have been attempting to observe the system behavior.

Monitoring, logging, and tracing help with all of these situations. These practices provide insight, often referred to an *observability*, into what is currently occurring or going wrong, as well as a record as to what the application has done. This allows you to "close the loop" on the continuous delivery process, as shown in Figure 13-1.

Once you understand the power that feedback provides, you will undoubtedly want to observe "all the things," but there is value in being systematic in focusing your efforts. Let's now look at what to observe.

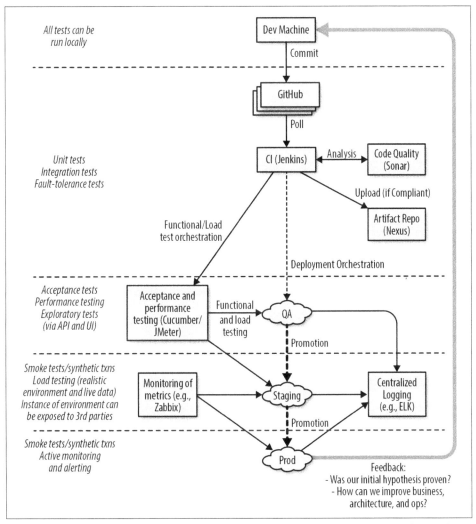

Figure 13-1. "Closing the loop" of continuous delivery—monitoring provides feedback

What to Observe: Application, Network, and Machine

In general, you will tend to monitor and observe your entire system at three levels: application, network, and machine. Application metrics are usually the most challenging to create and understand—yet they are the most important—and this is because they are very specific to your business and requirements. One perspective on monitoring is that it can be used to implement some form of testing in production; you know what a potential failure looks like, and you are asserting that everything is good. For example, you know that there will be trouble if a variety of scenarios occur:

- Your virtual machine runs out of block storage (disk) space.
- A network partition occurs.
- Your web application is returning a 404 HTTP status code for nearly all valid page requests.

For each of these scenarios, you can write a monitoring test. The first two will most likely be checked at the OS level. With the third, you could implement a counter or meter that outputs the number of 404s being generated, and create an alert based on this.

Monitoring and logging can also be used to provide data that is required to answer questions from the business in real time or at a later date. For example, your marketing team may want to know the average shopping basket checkout value during a promotion they are running, or your subscription retention team may want to mine activity logs to see whether they can identify behavior that suggests a customer will soon terminate their commercial contract. In order to implement effective monitoring, logging, and tracing, you have to design with observability in mind.

How to Observe: Monitoring, Logging, and Tracing

There are three primary approaches to observing modern software applications—monitoring, logging, and tracing:

Monitoring
> This is used to observe a system in near real-time, and typically involves the generation and capture of ephemeral metrics, values, and ranges. You generally have to know what data you want to observe in this approach. Because of the simplicity of the numbers captured, you cannot mine the data for additional insight later (other than producing aggregates or looking for trends).

Logging
> This is generally used to observe the system in the future, perhaps after a particular event (or failure) has occurred. Logs tend to be semantically richer and capture more data in comparison with metrics. Therefore, you can usually mine logs

in order to generate additional insight. Logs can also be analyzed to help you generate future questions.

Tracing

This captures the flow of a request as it traverses the (distributed) system, and captures metadata and timing at specific points you believe are interesting. Examples include traffic ingress to an API gateway, handling of the request by your application, and handling of a query against a database.

The outputs of these approaches will allow you to examine the behavior of your application and surrounding system and to reflect on how this can be improved. However, certain outputs demand immediate attention.

Alerting

Certain events that occur during the life of an application require human intervention; you want to be emailed, phoned, or paged when something bad is happening so that you can fix it. For this, you need to create alerts that are triggered based on specified thresholds or occurrences of data from monitoring and logging.

Many alerts can be designed and configured before an application is even deployed, although this does require some up-front planning. The *known unknowns* of running out of disk space or exceeding the JVM heap space are good examples that should generate alerts. You will want to be aware of impending failure, and ideally fix this before it impacts your users. In the examples provided, you will provision more disk space or reengineer the application to use less memory. Other scenarios that should generate alerts can be found only with the experience of running the system in production; these are the *unknowns unknowns*. This means it is necessary to continually iterate on creating and maintaining alerts.

Avoiding Alert Overload from Microservices at the Financial Times

Creating effective alerts is challenging, particularly when moving to a new infrastructure or working with a new architectural style. Daniel wrote an article based on a talk by Sarah Wells from *FT.com* "Observability and Avoiding Alert Overload from Microservices at the Financial Times" (*https://www.infoq.com/articles/observability-financial-times*), that explains how her team identified and overcame a series of challenges when embracing a microservice architecture. Three key takeaways from the article are as follows:

- A core goal of monitoring and alerting is to know about problems before clients do, so the practice of running synthetic requests that mimic user functionality behavior is vital.

- Creating alerts should be part of the normal development workflow: code, test, alerts. To ensure that the development team knows if an alert stops working, tests should be added to validate the alert.

- Alerts must continually be cultivated, and if an alert is received that doesn't make sense or does not require human interaction, it must be corrected or removed.

Alerts for metrics can be implemented using popular tooling such as the commercial PagerDuty (*http://bit.ly/2Ijp2pu*) and open source Bosun (*http://bosun.org/*). Basic metric alerting can even be implemented in Prometheus. Alerting based on log content can be implemented by commercial tools like Humio (*https://docs.humio.com/alerts/*) and Loggly (*https://www.loggly.com/docs/adding-alerts/*) and open source Graylog 2 (*https://www.graylog.org/overview*).

Rob Ewaschuk's Philosophy on Alerting

A comprehensive guide to alerting and being on-call is provided in a now famous shared Google doc by Rob Ewaschuk: "My Philosophy on Alerting" (*http://bit.ly/2zA4u9O*). If you are serious about learning more in this space, this is an essential read.

Designing Systems for Observability

Retrofitting monitoring, logging, and tracing into applications can be difficult, because often the required data is not easily available or is difficult to expose without impacting the application functionality. Therefore, it is important to design your system with monitoring in mind, specifically:

- Design your application to be capable of monitoring and logging from day one—include metrics and logging frameworks in your build dependencies (or, ideally, in the archetype of the project template).

- Ensure that any module (or microservice) boundaries that you create are capable of exposing data that an upstream system may require.

- Provide context data on downstream network calls (i.e., which service is calling, and on behalf on which application account).

- Ask yourself, the operations team, and your business what type of questions they are likely to ask in the future, and plan to expose the metrics and log data as the application is being designed and built. For example:

  — How effectively is a single instance of your application processing an event queue?

— How do you know if the application is fundamentally unhealthy?

— How many customers are currently logged into the application?

Design and Build Applications with Monitoring from Day One

As retrofitting monitoring, logging, and tracing into existing applications is difficult, you should include appropriate frameworks to support these practices from day one. This is especially true if building distributed applications like microservices and serverless functions, because not only will the applications need to support the frameworks, but so will the platform and infrastructure (e.g., collecting and presenting metrics for the system-level view of monitoring or implementing tooling for aggregated logging).

You will now learn how to implement each of the observability approaches with Java applications, but keep in mind the benefits of designing and implementing observability up front.

Metrics

Metrics are a numeric representation of some properties that your system has over intervals of time, such as maximum number of threads being used by your application, current heap memory available, or number of application users logged in during the last hour. Numbers are easily stored, processed, and compressed, and as such, metrics enable longer retention of data, as well as easier querying, which can, in turn, be used to build dashboards to reflect historical trends. Additionally, metrics better allow for gradual reduction of data resolution over time, so that after a certain period of time, data can be aggregated into daily or weekly frequency.

In this section, you will learn about the various types of metrics and the use cases for each. You will also be introduced to several of the most popular metrics libraries for Java—Dropwizard Metrics, Spring Boot Actuator, and Micrometer—and you will see examples of the various types of metrics demonstrated using these libraries.

Eclipse MicroProfile

We haven't covered Eclipse MicroProfile (*https://microprofile.io/*) in this chapter, purely for reasons of scope. The Metrics and OpenTracing projects within MicroProfile are excellent alternatives for the libraries discussed in this section, and the overall MicroProfile framework provides many great standards, implementations, and guidelines for building microservices with Java EE technology.

Type of Metrics

There are, generally speaking, five metric types:

Gauges

> The simplest metric type, a gauge simply returns a *value*. A gauge is useful for monitoring the eviction count in a cache or the average spending amount within a shopping basket that checks out.

Counters

> A simple incrementing and decrementing integer. A counter can be used to monitor the number of failed connections to the database, or the number of users logged in to the website.

Histograms

> This measures the distribution of values in a stream of data. A histogram is useful for monitoring the average response time of a downstream service or the number of results returned by a search.

Meters

> This measures the *rate* at which a set of events occur. A meter can be used to measure the rate in relation to total cache lookups as cache misses are occurring or the rate in relation to time that users are abandoning shopping baskets with a product still present.

Timers

> A histogram of the duration of a type of event and a meter of the rate of its occurrence. A timer can be used to monitor the time it takes to serve a web request or load a user's saved shopping basket.

All of these metric types can be useful for monitoring a system from an operational (application) perspective or business perspective.

Dropwizard Metrics

The popular Dropwizard Metrics (*http://metrics.dropwizard.io/4.0.0/*) library (formerly the Coda Hale Metrics library) started life as a personal project, alongside what is now called the Dropwizard Java application framework. This metrics library is extremely flexible, and principles from it have been copied in many other metric frameworks, even across other language platforms.

The Codahale Metrics library can be imported into your project via the following dependency (and Example 13-1 is shown using Maven).

Example 13-1. Importing the Dropwizard Metrics library into a Java project

```
<dependency>
    <groupId>com.codahale.metrics</groupId>
    <artifactId>metrics-core</artifactId>
    <version>${metrics-core.version}</version>
</dependency>
```

Metrics configuration and metadata

The starting point for metrics is the `MetricRegistry` class, which is a collection of all the metrics for your application (or a subset of your application). Generally, you need only one `MetricRegistry` instance per application, although you may choose to use more if you want to organize your metrics in particular reporting groups. Global named registries can also be shared through the static `SharedMetricRegistries` class. This allows the same registry to be used in different sections of code without explicitly passing a `MetricRegistry` instance around.

Each metric is associated with a `MetricRegistry` and has a unique name within that registry. This is a simple dotted name, like `uk.co.bigpicturetech.queue.size`. This flexibility allows you to encode a wide variety of context directly into a metric's name. If you have two instances of `com.example.Queue`, you can make them more specific: `uk.co.bigpicturetech.queue.size` versus `uk.co.bigpicture tech.inboundorders.queue.size`, for example.

`MetricRegistry` has a set of static helper methods for easily creating names:

```
MetricRegistry.name(Queue.class, "requests", "size")

MetricRegistry.name(Queue.class, "responses", "size")
```

Implementing a gauge

You can create a gauge with minimal effort by using Codahale Metrics. If, for example, your application has a value that is maintained by a third-party library, you can easily expose this by registering a `Gauge` instance that returns the corresponding value, as shown in Example 13-2.

Example 13-2. Gauge example using Codahale Metrics libary

```
registry.register(name(SessionStore.class, "cache-evictions"), new Gauge<Integer>() {
    @Override
    public Integer getValue() {
        return cache.getEvictionsCount();
    }
});
```

This creates a new gauge named `com.example.proj.auth.SessionStore.cache-evictions` that will return the number of evictions from the cache.

The Codahale Metrics library provides all of the common metrics mentioned earlier in this chapter, and the best way to learn more about how to implement them is to consult the documentation.

Spring Boot Actuator

Spring Boot Actuator (*http://bit.ly/2zzH0BE*) is a subproject of Spring Boot that provides several features to support production-readiness of your applications. After Actuator is configured in your Spring Boot application, you can interact and monitor your application by invoking different HTTP endpoints exposed, such as application health, bean details, version details, configurations, logger details, etc.

To enable Spring Boot Actuator, you need to include only the following dependency in your existing build script (Example 13-3 is using Maven).

Example 13-3. Enabling Actuator within a Spring Boot-based project

```
<dependency>
    <groupId>org.springframework.boot</groupId>
    <artifactId>spring-boot-starter-actuator</artifactId>
    <version>${actuator.version}</version>
</dependency>
```

Creating a counter

To generate your own metrics with Actuator, you simply inject a `CounterService` and/or `GaugeService` into your bean. `CounterService` exposes increment, decrement, and reset methods, and `GaugeService` provides a submit method. Example 13-4 provides a simple illustration.

Example 13-4. Creating a counter with Spring Boot Actuator metrics

```
import org.springframework.beans.factory.annotation.Autowired;
import org.springframework.boot.actuate.metrics.CounterService;
import org.springframework.stereotype.Service;

@Service
public class MyService {

    private final CounterService counterService;

    @Autowired
    public MyService(CounterService counterService) {
        this.counterService = counterService;
    }
```

```
public void exampleMethod() {
    this.counterService.increment("services.system.myservice.invoked");
}

}
```

Micrometer

Micrometer (*http://micrometer.io/*) provides a simple facade over the instrumentation clients for the most popular monitoring systems, allowing you to instrument your JVM-based application code without vendor lock-in. The tagline on the project's website is "Think SLF4J, but for application metrics!"

Micrometer can be imported into your Java application by using the following dependency (Example 13-5 is shown in Maven).

Example 13-5. Importing Micrometer into your Java project

```
<dependency>
  <groupId>io.micrometer</groupId>
  <artifactId>micrometer-registry-prometheus</artifactId>
  <version>${micrometer.version}</version>
</dependency>
```

Creating a timer

The metrics APIs exposed within the Micrometer framework are based on the fluent-DSL pattern, so creating a timer is relatively simple. The primary difficulty with initializing a timer typically revolves around how the timer is wrapped around the method to be invoked; see Example 13-6.

Example 13-6. Timers in Micrometer

```
Timer timer = Timer
    .builder("my.timer")
    .description("a description of what this timer does") // optional
    .tags("region", "test") // optional
    .register(registry);

timer.record(() -> dontCareAboutReturnValue());
timer.recordCallable(() -> returnValue());

Runnable r = timer.wrap(() -> dontCareAboutReturnValue()); (1)
Callable c = timer.wrap(() -> returnValue());
```

Best Practices with Metrics

There are many good practices in relation to generating and capturing metrics:

- Always expose core JVM internal metrics, such as: nonheap and heap memory usage; how often the garbage collector (GC) runs; and thread details, including the number of threads, current status, and CPU usage. The majority of modern metrics frameworks provide this as a bundled feature, so it is simply a matter of enabling this.

- Attempt to expose core application-specific technical details that will supplement the JVM internal details. For example, the queue depth of an internal processing queue, the cache statistics (size, hits, average entry age, etc.) of any internal caches, and throughput of core processing.

- Report on error and exception details. For example, the number of HTTP 5*xx* status codes returned when users call a REST API, the number of exceptions caught when calling a third-party dependency that is critical to your flow, and the number of exceptions that propagate through to the end user (which you should always attempt to minimize).

- Ensure that development and operation teams work together when designing and implementing infrastructure and platform metrics. Every layer of abstraction within a platform will need to be monitored, and developers and operators may have differing requirements. Example layers of abstraction include application framework (e.g., the Spring or Java EE framework), the runtime Java container (e.g., GlassFish or Tomcat), the JVM, the container implementation (e.g., Docker), the orchestration platform (e.g., Kubernetes), the virtualized cloud hardware (e.g., the VMs and software-defined networks [SDNs]), and physical infrastructure.

- Work closely with your business team in order to know what KPIs they want to track. Other systems might be best placed to provide this data, such as an associated data store or an ETL-based batch processing system. However, often a few well-chosen metrics can provide a lot of value in regards to real-time insight into the system. For example, when working with an e-commerce startup, it is common to expose metrics that indicated the number of users currently logged in, the average conversion from adding a product to the basket for purchasing, and the average basket value.

Now that you have developed a good understanding of metrics, it is equally valuable to learn about logging.

Logging

A *log* is an immutable append-only record of discrete events that happened over time, such as when the application initialized, when a disk read failed, or when an application user logged out.

Forms of Logging

Generally, logs are produced in one of three forms:

Plain text
A log record might take the form of free-form text. In the Java world, this is commonly seen within old applications that use `System.out.println` to log what is happening within an application. Unfortunately, this means that every log statement is uniquely formatted.

Structured
Here a log entry implements a defined structure, ranging from a simple JSON format entry to an XML format with a strict schema.

Binary
This type of log is generally intended for consumption by an application, where human readability is less of a concern. Examples include the MySQL binlog used for replication, and Protobuf or Avro logs of events that are used for point-in-time recovery.

Logs are useful when you need additional insight along with extra contextual information and other alerting and metrics do not provide enough. However, lots of logging information can be overwhelming, so you should also add metadata to log entries, such as the level of the entry and the cause (user, IP address, etc.) of the action. Many logging frameworks provide level categorization, such as `ERROR`, `WARN`, `INFO`, `DEBUG`, `TRACE`.

As with any new technology, there is a temptation to overuse logging when you first discover it. One method to help manage this is to understand and use the log levels. When you are writing a log statement, ponder to yourself whether this information that will be generated would be useful on a day-to-day basis. If it would be, it may well be an `INFO` statement. If the information is useful only to you, the developer, when trying to track down a bug, then `DEBUG` or `TRACE` is probably more appropriate. Any errors should, of course, be output using the `ERROR` level, but it is worth agreeing with the rest of the development team on where within the stack an error will be logged.

Our recommendation is to log an error at the highest possible level (closest to the call or user-initiated action). Attempting to log a single error multiple times within a call stack often just adds noise to the logs, and makes it even more challenging to track down the issue.

Guard Against "Overlogging"

The real power of log levels is that they allow the amount of logging to be modified at deployment or runtime. For example, if an application is not performing as expected, an operator can enable a more fine-grained logging level, such as DEBUG, in order to gain more insight. However, there will be a cost in performance for generating extra debug issues, and the irony is that many issues disappear when you start looking for them. This is often due to timing and memory usage patterns changing with the additional logging. On the contrary, we have also seen an application completely fall over when logging was enabled, as the memory requirements for generating log statements in a production environment were massive (and the associated TRACE statements had always been used in only tightly controlled development environments with minimal data).

There are several choices for logging frameworks with the Java ecosystem. You will now learn about the two most popular: SLF4J (with Logback) and Log4j 2.

Don't Invent Your Own Logger

Please don't attempt to implement your own logging framework, or almost as bad, simply use System.out.println. The modern Java logging frameworks are highly evolved, and offer much more flexibility compared with simply echoing details to the console output (which may or may not exist when running in a containerized environment).

SLF4J

The Simple Logging Facade for Java (SLF4J) (*https://www.slf4j.org/*) serves as a simple facade or abstraction for various logging frameworks (e.g., java.util.logging, Logback, Log4j), allowing you to plug in the desired logging framework at deployment time. You can include SLF4J (in this case, using Logback (*https://logback.qos.ch/*) under the hood) via Maven, as shown in Example 13-7.

Example 13-7. Including SLF4J with Logback, via Maven

```
<dependency>
  <groupId>org.slf4j</groupId>
  <artifactId>slf4j-jdk14</artifactId>
```

```
  <version>${slf4j.version}</version>
</dependency>
<dependency>
  <groupId>ch.qos.logback</groupId>
  <artifactId>logback-classic</artifactId>
  <version>${logbacl.version}</version>
</dependency>
```

The usage of SLF4J is simple, as you can see in Example 13-8, from the SLF4J user manual (*https://www.slf4j.org/manual.html*).

Example 13-8. Using the SLF4J APIs

```
import org.slf4j.Logger;
import org.slf4j.LoggerFactory;

public class HelloWorld {
  public static void main(String[] args) {
    Logger logger = LoggerFactory.getLogger(HelloWorld.class);
    logger.info("Hello World");
  }
}
```

SLF4J also supports Mapped Diagnostic Context (MDC), which allows you to add context-specific key-value data to a logger and can provide useful information for searching and filtering data from a system that is dealing with many user requests in a distributed system. If the underlying logging framework offers MDC functionality, SLF4J will delegate to the underlying framework's MDC. Currently, only Log4j and Logback offer MDC functionality.

Mapped Diagnostic Context

Mapped Diagnostic Context is essentially a map maintained by the logging framework; the application code provides key-value pairs that can then be inserted by the logging framework in log messages. MDC data can also be highly helpful in filtering messages or triggering certain actions. The chapter on MDC in the Logback user manual (*https://logback.qos.ch/manual/mdc.html*) provides useful information on this topic, and provides examples of the types and purpose of additional information within a log message, for example:

```
70984 [RMI TCP Connection(4)-192.168.1.6] INFO
      N:129 - Beginning to factor.
```

Log4j 2

Apache Log4j 2 (*https://logging.apache.org/log4j/2.x/*) is an upgrade to the original Log4j that provides significant improvements over the first (and very popular) version. The Log4j 2 website claims that it provides many of the improvements available in Logback while fixing some inherent problems in Logback's architecture. One of the key differences with version 2 of the logging framework is that the API for Log4j is separate from the implementation, making it clear for application developers which classes and methods they can use while ensuring forward compatibility. Applications coded to the Log4j 2 API always have the option to use any SLF4J-compliant library as their logger implementation with the Log4j-to-SLF4J adapter.

While the Log4j 2 API will provide the best performance, Log4j 2 provides support for the Log4j 1.2, SLF4J, Commons Logging, and java.util.logging (JUL) APIs. If performance is an especially important issue for you, you may be interested in the fact that Log4j 2 contains asynchronous loggers based on the LMAX Disruptor (*https://lmax-exchange.github.io/disruptor/*) inter-thread messaging library, which can provide higher throughput and orders of magnitude lower latency than Log4j 1.*x* and Logback.

You can include Log4j 2 in your Maven project with the dependencies shown in Example 13-9.

Example 13-9. Including Log4j 2 in your Maven-based application

```
<dependencies>
  <dependency>
    <groupId>org.apache.logging.log4j</groupId>
    <artifactId>log4j-api</artifactId>
    <version>${log4j.version}</version>
  </dependency>
  <dependency>
    <groupId>org.apache.logging.log4j</groupId>
    <artifactId>log4j-core</artifactId>
    <version>${log4j.version}</version>
  </dependency>
</dependencies>
```

The use of the Log4j 2 API is similar to that of SL4JF API, so if you are used to this framework, then you will feel right at home; see Example 13-10.

Example 13-10. Usage of Log4j 2

```
import org.apache.logging.log4j.LogManager;
import org.apache.logging.log4j.Logger;

public class HelloWorld {
```

```
    private static final Logger logger = LogManager.getLogger("HelloWorld");
    public static void main(String[] args) {
        logger.info("Hello, World!");
    }
}
```

Logging Best Practices

Lots of great articles online share logging best practices, and we've collated several of the recommendations here, combined with our own experience:

- Don't log every little detail. This not only can have a performance impact, but also adds a lot of noise to logs. Any future maintenance in the code will also potentially have to modify all of the logs.

- Conversely, do log important details, particularly around core flows or forks of processing within the overall application processing, as it is often a good idea to start at these places when debugging strange issues.

- Write meaningful logging information that will help you and others diagnose information in the future. Be sure to include relevant context—finding the phrase "Transaction failed" within a log without any other context is never helpful. Make the information machine parsable as well, which will also aid in searching for keywords.

- Log at the correct level: INFO for general information, DEBUG/TRACE for finer-grained diagnostic information, and WARN/ERROR for events that should require additional follow-up.

- Use a static modifier for your Logger object, as this means that the Logger will be created only once, reducing overhead.

- You can customize your layout in the logs (for example, with Log4j Pattern Layouts).

- Consider using a JSON layout for structured logging. This makes logs easier to parse into an external, centralized log aggregation platform.

- If you are working with SLF4J and you are running into issues with getting appenders configured correctly (or receiving no logging output), you can often resolve these issues after enabling the internal debugging by setting the log4j.debug system property in the configuration file or adding -Dlog4j.debug to the application/JRE startup command.

- Don't forget to rotate logs regularly to prevent the log files from growing too large, or the loss of data. Closely related to this topic is the recommendation that all logs should be asynchronously shipped off to a centralized log store, and a maximum number of rotated log files stored locally.

- Get in the habit of periodically scanning all logs, looking for unexpected WARNs, ERRORs, and exceptions. This can often be a great way to catch an issue before it becomes more significant.

Don't Log Sensitive Data

Although it may be tempting for debugging purposes, you should never log any sensitive information, such as confidential user or business data, personally identifiable information (PII), or any data that would fall under legal regulations, such as the EU's General Data Protection Regulation (GDPR). Not only can logging sensitive information lead to compliance violations and fines, but it is a potential security vulnerability. We have both seen logs that have recorded credit card information, passwords (and failed password attempts, which often contain passwords a user uses somewhere else), and answers to account reset questions.

One of our favorite logging articles is Brice Figureau's "The 10 Commandments of Logging" (*http://bit.ly/2zz8jvH*), and we recommend reading this for a more in-depth overview of logging practices.

Logging in the (Ephemeral) Cloud

When deploying Java applications on an IaaS or PaaS cloud platform, and especially on a FaaS serverless platform, don't forget that the underlying infrastructure will most likely be ephemeral, meaning that it could disappear at a moment's notice. You obviously have to code your application to be resilient to this, but you must also configure your logs appropriately. Primarily, you must ship your logs to a centralized collection or aggregation service, such as an ELK stack or commercial platform such as Humio, and it can also be beneficial to think about where you are storing your logs locally. For example, storing logs on a mounted persistent volume can help prevent data loss during an instance crash, but this will also have performance implications (i.e., less performance than writing log data to a locally attached volume).

Request Tracing

The basic idea behind request tracing is relatively straightforward: specific inflection points must be identified within a system, application, network, and middleware—or indeed any point on a path of a (typically, user-initiated) request—and instrumented. These points are of particular interest, as they typically represent forks in execution flow, such as the parallelization of processing using multiple threads, a computation being made asynchronously, or an out-of-process network call being made. All of the independently generated trace data must be collected, coordinated, and collated to provide a meaningful view of a request's flow through the system.

Traces, Spans, and Baggage

As defined by the Cloud Native Computing Foundation (*https://www.cncf.io/*) (CNCF) OpenTracing API (*http://opentracing.io/*) project, a trace (*http://opentracing.io/documentation/#what-is-a-trace*) tells the story of a transaction or workflow as it propagates through a system. In OpenTracing and Dapper, a trace is a directed acyclic graph (DAG) of *spans*, which are also called *segments* within some tools, such as AWS X-Ray (*https://aws.amazon.com/xray/*). Spans are named and timed operations that represent a contiguous segment of work in that trace. Additional contextual annotations (metadata, or baggage (*http://bit.ly/2DyAsXZ*)) can be added to a span by a component being instrumented—for example, an application developer may use a tracing SDK to add arbitrary key-value items to a current span. It should be noted that adding annotation data is inherently intrusive: the component making the annotations must be aware of the presence of a tracing framework.

Trace data is typically collected "out of band" by pulling locally written data files (generated via an agent or daemon) via a separate network process to a centralized store, in much the same fashion as currently occurs with log and metrics collection. Trace data is not added to the request itself, because this allows the size and semantics of the request to be left unchanged, and locally stored data can be pulled when it is convenient.

When a request is initiated, a *parent* span is generated, which, in turn, can have causal and temporal relationships with *child* spans. Figure 13-2, taken from the OpenTracing documentation, shows a common visualization of a series of spans and their relationship within a request flow.

This type of visualization adds the context of time, the hierarchy of the services involved, and the serial or parallel nature of the process/task execution. This view helps to highlight the system's critical path, and can provide a starting point for identifying bottlenecks or areas to improve. Many distributed tracing systems also provide an API or UI to allow further drill-down into the details of each span.

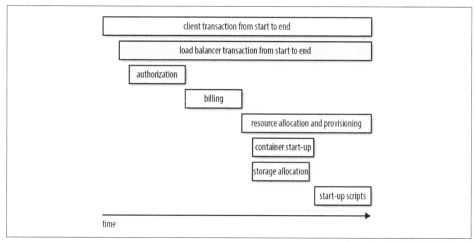

Figure 13-2. Decomposing a sample request trace, showing a parent and corresponding child spans that relate to specific actions conducted when processing the request

Java Tracing: OpenZipkin, Spring Sleuth, and OpenCensus

The world of distributed tracing is both fast evolving and becoming increasingly (cloud) platform specific. These facts, in combination with limitations of scope, mean that no implementation guide will be provided in this book. Interested readers are pointed to the popular open source frameworks OpenZipkin (*https://zipkin.io/*), Spring Cloud Sleuth (*https://cloud.spring.io/spring-cloud-sleuth/*), and OpenCensus (*https://opencensus.io/*) for more information, which all provide Java SDKs.

Commercial Distributed Tracing Solutions

Many of the large public cloud vendors offer their own tracing solutions, which can be well worth utilizing. If you are on AWS, the X-Ray (*https://aws.amazon.com/xray/*) service is useful, although it is a proprietary solution, and you will have to include the AWS SDKs within your application. Google Cloud Platform offers Stackdriver Trace (*https://cloud.google.com/trace/docs/zipkin*), which is OpenCensus and OpenZipkin compliant, and the GCP team offers a Maven JAR that performs all the integration. The Microsoft team has also created zipkin-azure (*https://github.com/openzipkin/zipkin-azure*), which integrates OpenZipkin into the Azure platform via Azure Event Hubs.

Closely related to distributed tracing, application performance management (APM) is also a useful tool for developers and operators to understand and debug a system. Historically, the commercial solutions have had much more functionality in comparison with open source tooling, but Naver's Pinpoint (*https://github.com/naver/*

pinpoint) is now offering much of the expected core functionality and provides distributed tracing features.

Recommended Practices for Tracing

Distributed tracing within the Java space is a relatively new practice, and therefore there are limited "best" practices. However, recommended practices include the following:

- You must remember to forward the tracing headers to all downstream services, middleware, and data stores; otherwise, part of the application will not be covered by the traces.

- In relation to the previous point, if you are working with a polyglot application stack, you should integrate Zipkin (or your tracing solution of choice) into the additional language frameworks. Zipkin is great for this purpose, as it is a language-agnostic tracing solution.

- Do not attempt to add a large amount of "baggage" metadata. Although this is collected out-of-band of the request itself, this can still result in noisy traces.

Finally, consider whether you want to run your own trace collection service, and whether you have the skills and resources available to make this a viable solution. Many of the cloud vendors offer excellent fully managed services.

Exception Tracking

Even if you have followed all of the advice within this chapter and implemented aggregated logging and centralized monitoring, you will still encounter scenarios within production systems where something goes wrong and you won't know about it. This is almost inevitable with the complexity of the systems being implemented today. Ideally, you always want to know about a problem before an end user sees this or (worse still) reports to you that your system is broken. Therefore, an additional tool in your issue management toolbox should be an exception-tracking system.

Commercial Exception-Tracking Tools

Because exception tracking can be valuable, in our opinion it is often worth paying for a commercial solution that not only hosts the service for you but also provides an SLA. Popular Java commercial exception- and error-tracking platforms include Airbrake (*https://airbrake.io/*), Sentry (*https://sentry.io/for/java/*), RayGun (*https://raygun.com/*), and OverOps (*https://www.overops.com*).

An exception-tracking system is typically provided by a SaaS vendor, although in-house solutions are also available (such as the open source Ruby on Rails Errbit (*https://github.com/errbit/errbit*) application, which is Airbrake compatible). A client SDK is added to your Java application, typically as a Maven or Gradle dependency, which captures any exceptions that are uncaught or have propagated to the view layer and reports the details to the exception-tracking service. Many tracking services have informative dashboards that help you in diagnosing and finding the associated issue, and they also typically alert you to the issue in near real time (or integrate with other services that provide this feature).

 Exposed Exceptions Can Provide Information to Hackers!

If an internal exception or error is propagated through to the end user, this is obviously a bad user experience, but the error may also leak sensitive or useful information to a hacker. Indeed, the hacker may have been trying to break your system, and even if they succeed, they should receive no information of the issue. For this reason, you should avoid including overly descriptive error messages, stack traces, or PII data with an error message that is displayed (intentional or otherwise).

In addition to utilizing an exception-tracking system, we also recommend implementing a catchall error-handling web page that is displayed by default on the event of an uncaught exception. This page can typically be configured within modern Java web frameworks, or alternatively by configuring a static error page within your web server or API gateway that is displayed when an error is indicated within the HTTP response (e.g., a $5xx$ HTTP status code). Any error page should apologize for the inconvenience, and suggest that the user contact the company help desk. If the error page is generated within the application server, it is acceptable to provide a UUID as a reference to the error.

 Don't Forget the Client Side

If you are working on an application that exposes a web-based interface, errors can also occur in the client-side code. These also need to be caught and tracked. Many of the commercial tooling mentioned can be integrated with frontend JavaScript to accomplish this, such as Sentry.

Airbrake

A popular cross-language exception tracker is Airbrake (*https://airbrake.io/*). To install the Airbrake client into your Java code, you can simply import the dependency via Maven, as shown in Example 13-11.

Example 13-11. Importing the Airbrake SDK into your Java project

```
<dependency>
    <groupId>io.airbrake</groupId>
    <artifactId>airbrake-java</artifactId>
    <version>${airbrake.version}</version>
</dependency>
```

As stated in the Airbrake Java client GitHub repository README (*https://github.com/airbrake/airbrake-java*), the easiest way to use Airbrake is by configuring a Log4j appender. Therefore, when an uncaught exception occurs, Airbrake will POST the relevant data to the Airbrake server specified in your environment. (Don't forget that you are still responsible for preventing or translating the display of this error to the end user.) You saw an example Log4j configuration in the preceding example, and Example 13-12 is a modified version configured to report errors to the external Airbrake service (which could be a self-hosted Errbit service).

Example 13-12. Log4j properties configuration file for reporting exceptions to an external Airbrake service

```
log4j.rootLogger=INFO, stdout, airbrake

log4j.appender.stdout=org.apache.log4j.ConsoleAppender
log4j.appender.stdout.layout=org.apache.log4j.PatternLayout
log4j.appender.stdout.layout.ConversionPattern=[%d,%p] [%c{1}.%M:%L] %m%n

log4j.appender.airbrake=airbrake.AirbrakeAppender
log4j.appender.airbrake.api_key=YOUR_AIRBRAKE_API_KEY
#log4j.appender.airbrake.env=development
#log4j.appender.airbrake.env=production
log4j.appender.airbrake.env=test
log4j.appender.airbrake.enabled=true
#log4j.appender.airbrake.url=http://api.airbrake.io/notifier_api/v2/notices
```

If you are not using Log4j, or want to send other exceptions to your exception-tracking service, you can call the Airbrake client directly, as shown in Example 13-13.

Example 13-13. Calling the Airbrake service directly via the SDK

```
try {
    doSomethingThatThrowsAnException();
}
catch(Throwable t) {
    AirbrakeNotice notice = new AirbrakeNoticeBuilder(
                        YOUR_AIRBRAKE_API_KEY, t, "env").newNotice();
    AirbrakeNotifier notifier = new AirbrakeNotifier();
    notifier.notify(notice);
}
```

System-Monitoring Tooling

You've seen how important it is to generate and collect metrics and logs from your Java applications within this chapter, and the same advice applies to the OS and infrastructure that your applications run on.

collectd

collectd (*https://collectd.org/*) gathers metrics from various sources (e.g., the operating system, applications, log files, and external devices) and stores this information or makes it available over the network. Those statistics can be used to monitor systems, find performance bottlenecks, and predict future system load. collectd runs as a daemon on each machine instance, and all of the functionality is provided as a series of plugins. collectd's configuration is kept as easy as possible—besides which modules to load, you don't need to configure anything else, but you can customize the daemon to your liking if you want. collectd utilizes a data push model: the data is collected and sent (pushed) to a multicast group or server. Thus, there is no central instance that queries any values.

Because of space limitations (and subtle differences between Linux distros), we won't cover how to install and set up a central collectd server. Usually, this would be done by a centralized operations team in a large organization, and for smaller teams using public cloud services, you can often transform collectd metric data into the vendor's proprietary centralized metrics collection framework (e.g., Amazon CloudWatch has a collectd plugin (*https://github.com/awslabs/collectd-cloudwatch*)). The client collectd daemon can be installed as a binary (available via the project's download page (*http://collectd.org/download.shtml*)), and the configuration is specified by modifying the */etc/collectd.conf* configuration file. More information can be found on the collectd website.

rsyslog

Modern Java applications involve lots of moving parts that are often distributed across multiple machines, and tracking what is happening and diagnosing issues at the OS level can be challenging. Therefore, centralizing your log output can be useful. Syslog is a standard developed in the 1980s for recording logging messages, and used widely, especially in Unix environments. All mainstream Linux distributions install a syslog implementation as part of the base system, which is a strong reason for adopting it in preference to other, less widely deployed systems. Rsyslog builds upon the basic syslog protocol, and extends it with content-based filtering, flexible configuration options, and a bunch of useful extensions, such as the support for ISO 8601 timestamps and the ability to log directly into various database engines.

Typically, this type of centralized log management will be implemented by a centralized operations team, but it is not difficult to run your own central receiving server. For the sake of brevity (and the subtle differences based on Linux distros), we won't cover the installation or configuration of a receiving server. For the client servers, all you need to do is tell syslog to forward all logs to the central server. This is typically achieved by adding the following to the base of the *etc/rsyslog.conf* config file:

```
*.* syslog.mycentralserver.com
```

This will send all log messages sent via syslog to the central receiving server.

Sensu

Sensu is an open source and commercial infrastructure and application-monitoring and telemetry solution that provides a framework for monitoring almost everything: from infrastructure to application health, and business KPIs. Sensu is designed to solve monitoring challenges introduced by the types of modern infrastructure platforms that we have talked about in this book (e.g., a mix of static, dynamic, and ephemeral infrastructure when using public, private, and hybrid clouds). Sensu is often deployed in place of existing infrastructure-monitoring solutions such as Nagios.

Sensu exposes all of its configuration as JSON files, so it is easy to automate and manage configuration via VCSs. Sensu also integrates well with alerting tools like PagerDuty, Slack, and email.

In general, Sensu can coexist with other tooling like Prometheus, and it is common to see both being utilized at an organization. Developers tend to gravitate toward Prometheus because of its user experience (UX) and extensive query features, and operators tend to embrace Sensu because of its extensive integration with infrastructure (including the ability to reuse existing Nagios health checks).

Collection and Storage

Any metric and logging data must be reliably captured and stored for later analysis. This section will explore a popular solution for each of these requirements.

> ## Commercial Metric and Log Collection Tooling
>
> All of the large cloud vendors offer their own metric and logging collection and analysis tooling, such as AWS CloudWatch, GCP StackDriver, and Azure Monitor. A number of startups are also exploring this space, as the challenges for collating and generating insight from all of this data is not trivial, and the value that can be added to organizations and engineers means that this is commercially interesting. If your cloud provider or in-house solution is not meeting your needs, it is worth exploring

commercial offerings such as Honeycomb (*https://www.honeycomb.io/*) and LightStep (*https://lightstep.com/*).

Prometheus

Prometheus (*https://prometheus.io/*) is an open source systems monitoring and alerting toolkit originally built at SoundCloud. It is now a standalone open source project (hosted by the CNCF) and maintained independently, and developers from many organizations now contribute. Prometheus fundamentally stores all data as time series: streams of timestamped values belonging to the same metric and the same set of labeled dimensions. Prometheus works well for recording any purely numeric time series. It fits both machine-centric monitoring as well as monitoring of highly dynamic service-oriented architectures. In a world of microservices, its support for multidimensional data collection and querying is a particular strength.

Prometheus provides its own Java SDK (*https://github.com/prometheus/client_java*) that provides all of the metrics types discussed previously. However, the Prometheus API is specific to this collection platform, and instead it is often advantageous to use a platform-agnostic library and integrate this with Prometheus. All of the main metrics libraries provide Prometheus integration, including Dropwizard/Codahale Metrics (*http://bit.ly/2OebIIr*), Micrometer (*http://bit.ly/2NMqZ3I*), and Spring Boot Actuator/Metrics (*http://bit.ly/2QeJxqp*). Metrics stored within Prometheus can easily be visualized via Grafana (*http://bit.ly/2Oi4YcA*).

Elastic-Logstash-Kibana

When discussing how to aggregate and store log data, you will often hear talk of the ELK stack. *ELK* is an acronym for three open source projects: Elasticsearch, Logstash, and Kibana (*https://www.elastic.co/elk-stack*). *Elasticsearch* is a search and analytics engine. *Logstash* is a server side data processing pipeline that ingests data from multiple sources simultaneously, transforms it, and then sends it to a "stash" like Elasticsearch. *Kibana* lets users visualize data with charts and graphs in Elasticsearch. Both SLF4J and Log4j 2 can be configured to format data into JSON that is ready for consumption by Logstash and Elasticsearch.

Beware of the Boiling Frog: Abraham's Experience

There is an old fable that states that if you put a frog in a pot of boiling water, it will immediately jump out, but if you put it in warm water and then gradually increase the temperature to a boil, the frog won't notice the increase and will boil alive. While the veracity of the story is probably questionable (and I'm most certainly not encouraging you to test it yourself), there is some knowledge that you can apply here.

A limiting factor of many metrics and visualization tools is the amount of resources that they require: storing data is expensive, and indexing it to quickly visualize it even more so. For this reason, I have frequently seen teams that will impose an age limit in their visualization tools, typically two weeks, but sometimes even less.

Most people don't mind that because they have configured their graphs with a rather short window, usually something between the last 30 minutes and the last day; I have rarely met teams that tend to be interested in checking what happened more than a day ago. I do like to check further, though, because I like to understand the long-term patterns: how much higher is traffic usually on weekdays compared to weekends? How many new users do we have in the summer months compared to the rest of the year? Is it normal that visits plummet like this during the holiday season, or are we having a bad year? Questions like these are the ones that bug me, and the ones that most monitoring tools cannot answer.

It is true that many problems tend to be sudden, and that these can be noticed with a short-term monitoring view. For the longer-term ones, I tend to maintain my own list of metrics that I keep in a rather unsophisticated way (typically, a spreadsheet with daily totals), and where I can observe patterns. It may sound like overkill, particularly if you have spent so much effort setting up a proper ELK stack or similar, but for me it has paid off: once I was able to identify one of these slowly cooking frogs, a performance issue that kept creeping up ever so slightly over the course of two months, but that was clearly growing at an exponential rate. Hopefully, we managed to catch it at the beginning, when it still wasn't too much of an issue, but imagine what could have happened if I hadn't kept an eye on the longer trends.

Visualization

Designing systems with observability in mind and collecting appropriate metric and logging data is a good first step toward understanding your application and system. However, an equally important step is converting this data to something that provides insight and drives actions and improvement. How you do this depends on your target audience: business, operations, or development. The goal of this section is to provide an overview of what is possible. Because of the scope of the book, you are invited to follow up with further reading and web searches.

Visualization for Business

The primary driver when creating visualizations for business use is to focus on the most important information and to minimize noise. A popular mechanism for displaying textual and numeric insight is a dashboard. The dashing.io framework, along with a more actively maintained fork, Smashing (*https://smashing.github.io/*) (shown in Figure 13-3) is a simple-to-use and effective dashboard tool. Dashboards are created using ERB Ruby scripts (much like JSPs), and data can be submitted to the tool via a REST-like API.

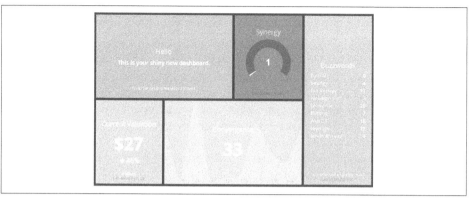

Figure 13-3. Smashing dashboard

Operational Visualization

Popular operations visualization tooling includes Graphite (*https://graphiteapp.org/*) and the more modern Grafana (*https://grafana.com/*), shown in Figure 13-4. These tools make it easy to create dashboards that focus on global system health and performance, as well as service- or infrastructure-specific properties. Core goals for visualization within this space include providing the ability for engineers to self-serve and create their own dashboards, and to create automated alerts on anything that should require an action to be taken.

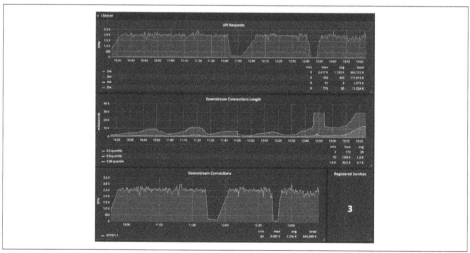

Figure 13-4. Grafana dashboard for the Kubernetes-native Ambassador API gateway

Another popular requirement from operators is the ability to understand the flow of requests and data across a system, and for this, the output of APM tooling can be valuable. Figure 13-5 demonstrates a request/response scatter chart from the user-generated request to the associated database query using the open source Pinpoint APM solution.

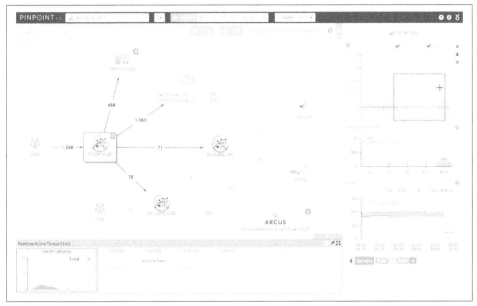

Figure 13-5. A request/response scatter chart generated by Pinpoint APM

Visualization for Developers

Developers are well catered to by visualization tooling like Kibana, which is often used as part of the ELK stack. Whereas Grafana is focused on metrics, Kibana, shown in Figure 13-6, is focused on logs, and enables full-text querying in addition to graphing. This functionality is invaluable for developers when debugging complex issues.

If you are utilizing distributed tracing, many of these tools provide a graphical interface that can be queried to show a single trace. As demonstrated in Figure 13-7, the benefit of this type of visualization is that it allows you to quickly identify the flow of the request/response and data across a single user-triggered action. Long spans allow you to locate a long-running process, and broken spans quickly highlight processes or services that are failing.

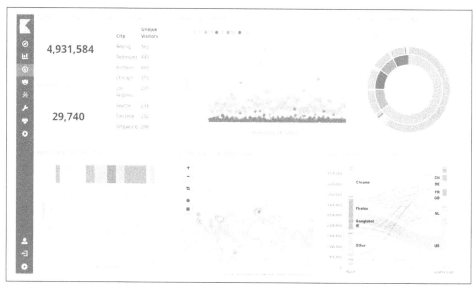

Figure 13-6. Kibana dashboard

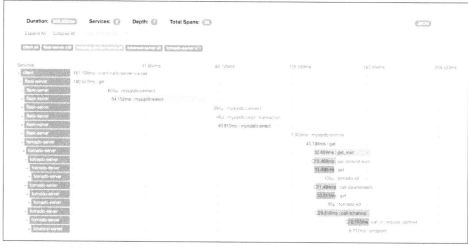

Figure 13-7. Zipkin trace

Although the lure of the command line can be tempting for many developers, you can also get a lot of value from the appropriate use of visualization. A core goal of visualization in this domain is to ensure that developers have self-service access to the tooling, and can create dashboards, charts, and trace queries with minimal overhead.

Summary

In this chapter, you have learned about the fundamentals of observability:

- Throughout the lifetime of an application, it is vital that you are able to understand what is occurring, and what has occurred, within the system. This is what observability is all about.

- In general, you will tend to monitor and observe your entire system at three levels: application, network, and machine.

- There are three primary approaches to observing modern software applications: monitoring, logging, and tracing.

- Monitoring is used to observe a system in near real-time, and typically involves the generation and capture of ephemeral metrics, values, and ranges.

- Logging is generally used to observe the system in the future, perhaps after an event (or failure) has occurred.

- Tracing captures the flow of a request as it traverses the (distributed) system, and captures metadata and timing at specific points you believe are interesting.

- Certain events that occur during the life of an application require human intervention. For this, you need to create alerts that are triggered based on specified thresholds or occurrences of data from monitoring and logging.

- Retrofitting monitoring, logging, and tracing to applications can be difficult. Therefore, it is important to design your system with monitoring in mind.

- You always want to know about a problem before an end user sees it. Therefore, an additional tool in your issue management toolbox should be an exception-tracking system.

- Using visualization tools and dashboards correctly can provide insight and reduce the amount of noise that is presented by raw metric and log data.

At this point in the book, you have learned about the technical details of implementing continuous delivery. The next chapter focuses on the challenges of migrating an existing organization or application to this way of working.

## CHAPTER 14

Migrating to Continuous Delivery

At this point in the book, you have learned many of the technical principles and practices associated with continuous delivery. In this chapter, you will learn about the challenges with migrating your organization and team to this way of working. You will also learn current good practices and approaches to make this easier.

Continuous Delivery Capabilities

If you have read the book chapter to chapter, you will have read several times about the continuous delivery capabilities that Nicole Forsgren, Gene Humble, and Gene Kim have identified in their book, *Accelerate*. Through their work with the State of DevOps Reports and by running the DevOps Enterprise conference series they have had a unique opportunity to identify what makes a high-performing organization. They have also developed insight into which approaches work and which don't, and developed scientifically validated models on best practices.

One of the key findings of their research is the uncovering of 24 key capabilities that drive improvement in software delivery performance in a statistically significant way. These capabilities have been classified into five categories: continuous delivery; architecture; product and process; lean manufacturing and monitoring; and cultural. You will note that continuous delivery is a category in and of itself; this is how significant the practice is for creating a high-performing organization.

Examining the continuous capabilities in more depth, you will see the following list:

- Use version control for all production artifacts.
- Automate your deployment process.
- Implement continuous integration.
- Use trunk-based development methods.

- Implement test automation.
- Support test data management.
- Shift left on security.
- Implement continuous delivery.

Forsgren, Humble, and Kim argue in their book that if you and your organization invest in these capabilities, your software delivery performance will increase. Throughout this book, you have learned the technical skills associated with these capabilities, and this is therefore a good checklist to reference when migrating a team within your organization to continuous delivery.

Implementing Continuous Delivery Can Be Challenging

So, you've worked your way through the book and are keen to start helping your organization move toward fully embracing continuous delivery. However, this is not as easy as it may initially appear. Maybe you have seen this when attempting to introduce new technologies or methodologies to your team in the past, or perhaps you are simply visualizing potential technical or organizational hurdles —you know, the ones that make your organizational working practices "special." (Spoiler alert: every organization is unique, but very few are particularly "special" when it comes to continuous delivery.) Don't be discouraged if your initial efforts appear fruitless; migrating to continuous delivery can take time.

The first question to ask, particularly if your organization consists of more than one software delivery team or product, is how do you pick which application to migrate first?

Picking Your Migration Project

The DevOps Handbook, a highly recommended read for any technical leader, contains an entire chapter dedicated to choosing which project, or more correctly, which "value stream" to start with when attempting a DevOps transformation. Whether you are looking to begin a full-scale transformation or simply to implement continuous delivery, the advice for choosing a target is very much the same. The first step in picking a migration process is to do some research on your organization. If you are a relatively small startup or medium-scale enterprise, this may be easy. If you are working in a large-scale multinational organization, this may be more challenging, and you may want to limit your research to only the geographic area in which you work.

Cataloguing the value streams, systems, and applications can provide you with an overview of which areas to tackle first. When doing your research, *The DevOps Handbook* authors recommend considering both brownfield and greenfield projects, as well as systems of record (resource planning and analytic systems) and systems of engagement (customer-facing applications). The advice continues by suggesting that you "start with the most sympathetic and innovative groups." The goal is to find the teams that already believe in the need for continuous delivery (and other DevOps principles), and teams that already possess a desire and demonstrated ability to innovate and be early adopters in new technologies and techniques.

The DevOps Handbook: An Essential Read

If you are a technical or team leader who is keen to embrace continuous delivery and spread this throughout your organization, we strongly recommend that you read *The DevOps Handbook*. The knowledge, models, and advice contained within are invaluable, and you will save yourself a lot of time and pain by reading this.

Once you have chosen your project or team to begin your continuous delivery journey, you must then take time to understand their situation in more depth.

Situational Awareness

Any large-scale change within a company or organization will take commitment of resources, time, and determination. An organization is a complex adaptive system and can appear at times to be much like a living creature itself. This is further compounded when the organization and the change involve the use of technology, as you are then dealing with a "socio-technical" system. The Cynefin framework is a conceptual framework used to help leaders and policy makers reach decisions. Developed in the early 2000s within IBM, it was described as a "sense-making device."

Cynefin offers five decision-making contexts or *domains*: simple, complicated, complex, chaotic, and disorder. The purpose of the framework is to enable leaders to indicate how they perceive situations, and to make sense of their own and other people's behavior and decide how to act in similar situations. Figure 14-1 shows that the domains on the right, simple and complicated, are *ordered*: cause and effect are known or can be discovered. The domains on the left, complex and chaotic, are *unordered*: cause and effect can be deduced only with hindsight or not at all.

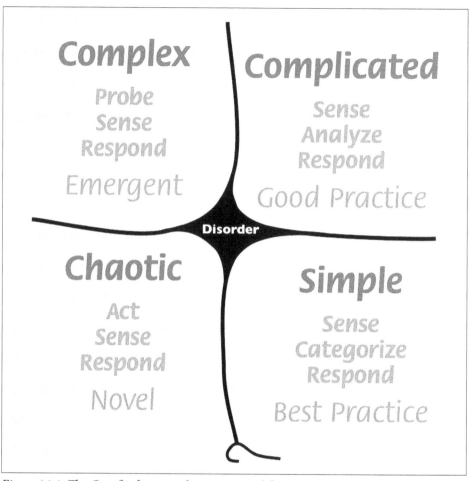

Figure 14-1. The Cynefin framework: a conceptual framework used to help leaders perceive and analyze situations, and decide how to act. (Image from Dave Snowden taken from Wikipedia (http://bit.ly/2DAXlde))

The Cynefin Framework and Continuous Delivery

The Cynefin framework can be a useful tool when implementing continuous delivery within an organization. Although nearly all organizations are in the Complex quadrant, many of the situations involved within a journey to embracing continuous delivery fall elsewhere in the framework.

Simple

The simple domain represents the *known knowns*. These are rules or best practices: the situation is stable, and the relationship between cause and effect is clear. The advice is to *sense–categorize–respond*: establish the facts (sense), categorize, and then respond by following the rule or applying a best practice. For example, one of the first situations encountered with a continuous delivery adoption journey is the storing, access, and management of source code. Here you can do the following:

Establish the facts
Application source code is stored in Git, config is stored only in a database, and infrastructure code is stored within scripts marked with version numbers.

Categorize it
Review the source code storage mechanisms.

Respond
The current best practice within this space is to utilize a version-control system (VCS) or distributed VCS (DVCS).

Complicated

The complicated domain consists of the *known unknowns*. The relationship between cause and effect requires analysis or expertise; there is a range of right answers. The framework recommends *sense–analyse–respond*:

Sense and assess the facts
Identify the steps required to take code from a local development machine to production.

Analyze
Examine and analyze each of the steps, and determine the techniques and tools required, along with the teams (and any challenges) that will need to be involved.

Respond
By applying the appropriate recommended practice.

You will often encounter the complicated domain when attempting to build your first continuous delivery pipeline. The steps within such a pipeline are known, but how to implement them for your specific use cases is not. Here it is possible to work rationally toward a decision, but doing so requires refined judgment and expertise.

Complex

The complex domain represents the *unknown unknowns*. Cause and effect can be deduced only in retrospect, and there are no right answers. Instructive patterns can emerge if experiments are conducted that are safe to fail (*http://bit.ly/2NIwTTz*). Cynefin calls this process *probe–sense–respond*. Complexity within continuous delivery is often encountered when attempting to increase adoption in an organization.

Chaotic

In the chaotic domain, cause and effect are unclear. Events in this domain are "too confusing to wait for a knowledge-based response," and action is the first and only way to respond appropriately. In this context, leaders *act–sense–respond*: act to establish order; sense where stability lies; respond to turn the chaotic into the complex. This is typically how external consultants operate when called in to implement continuous delivery pipelines or firefight operational issues.

Disorder

The dark disorder domain in the center represents situations where there is no clarity about which of the other domains apply. As noted by David Snowden and Mary Boone, by definition it is hard to see when this domain applies (*http://bit.ly/2NIwTTz*): "The way out of this realm is to break down the situation into constituent parts and assign each to one of the other four realms. Leaders can then make decisions and intervene in contextually appropriate ways."

All Models Are Wrong, Some Are Useful

Whenever your adoption of continuous delivery stalls or becomes stuck, it can often be a good idea to step back from the issue, look at the wider context, and attempt to classify where your issue sits within the Cynefin framework. This can allow you to use the best approach in resolving the issue. For example, if you are dealing with a simple issue (for example, whether to use a VCS), you don't need to conduct experiments—the widely accepted best practice suggests that this is beneficial.

However, if you are dealing with a complex problem, such as securing organizational funding to further roll out your build pipeline initiative to additional departments, then conducting experiments that are safe to fail can be highly beneficial. For example, you'd identify a team that has issues deploying software, collect baseline delivery metrics (build success, deployment throughput, etc.), and work with them on a time-boxes experiment to create a simple build pipeline to address their pain.

Bootstrapping Continuous Delivery

In an informative blog post by Steve Smith, "Resilience as a Continuous Delivery Enabler" (*http://bit.ly/2xTvRJD*), he presents a four-stage model for bootstrapping continuous delivery that complements the capabilities discussed at the start of this chapter (Figure 14-2).

The first stage to focus on is version controlling everything. This approach is echoed in the book *Accelerate*, as the research here shows that version controlling everything is correlated with higher performance in software delivery; "application code, system configuration, application configuration, and build and configuration scripts" should all be stored in version control. Not only can this provide increased performance, but deployment stability can also be improved.

Once this is achieved, Smith suggests that you should measure the stability and throughput of your delivery process; for example, how many deployments fail or result in near misses, and how fast can you get code committed to delivering value in production? The goal in this step is to improve delivery awareness and to provide baseline metrics that can be used for comparison later in your continuous delivery journey.

The third areas to focus on include adding production telemetry, which enables you to observe what is happening in the application both from a technical and business perspective, and moving to an adaptive (or "evolutionary") architecture, which promotes looser coupling between components and easier modifications. The goal here is to improve production reliability.

The final stage of Smith's model is to run parallel experiments with the goal of "improving all things." This is where continual improvement happens over a longer time period and sets the framework for ongoing iterative improvement. (You will learn more about this in the final chapter of this book.)

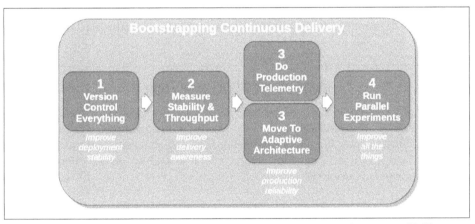

Figure 14-2. Bootstrapping continuous delivery (image courtesy of Steve Smith's blog post, "Resilience as a Continuous Delivery Enabler" (http://bit.ly/2xTvRJD))

You already learned about version controlling everything (stage 1) in Chapter 9. You also learned about increasing production telemetry, or observability, and cultivating an adaptive architecture (stage 3) in Chapters 13 and 3, respectively. In the next two sections, you will learn the fundamentals of how to measure continuous delivery (stage 2) and run parallel experiments (stage 4).

Measuring Continuous Delivery

In *Accelerate*, the authors state that software delivery performance can be measured effectively via four factors:

Lead time
> A measure of how fast work can be completed, from the ticket creation in a feature or bug tracker to the delivery into production.

Deployment frequency
> How often code or configuration is deployed into a production environment.

Mean time to restore (MTTR)
> The time taken to restore or fix a service when something goes wrong in production. This includes the time taken to identify and find the issues, as well as the time required for the implementation and deployment of the fix.

Change fail percentage
> A measure of how many changes that are deployed result in some form of failure.

Steve Smith builds on this work in his book, *Measuring Continuous Delivery*. He states that the sum of lead time and deployment frequency is the throughput of your CD process, and the sum of failure rate and failure recovery time (the MTTR) is the stability.

Measuring CD Is a Large Topic

Because of the scope of this book, we will cover only the fundamentals of the vitally important stage of measuring continuous delivery. We suggest that you commit to learning more by consulting the recommended reading of *Accelerate (https://itrevolu tion.com/book/accelerate/)* and *Measuring Continuous Delivery (https://leanpub.com/ measuringcontinuousdelivery)*.

All four of these metrics should be established from the start of your CD migration efforts, as this will provide a baseline for comparison later. Lead time and deployment frequency can typically easily be collected from your build pipeline tooling, such as Jenkins. The failure rate and failure recovery time can be more challenging to capture unless you use an issue-tracking system (which records discovery and remediation times), and these metrics may need to be collected manually by a responsible party.

Apply Maturity Models Cautiously

Many consulting companies and DevOps tool vendors are providing *maturity models* that promise to capture, measure, and analyze progress with a CD implementation. There can be some value in the structure that this provides, especially if an organization is in particular chaos, but, in general, they can present challenges. Often, maturity models present a static level of technical progress that relies on the measurement of the tool's *install-base* or technical proficiency, and they also assume that the steps in the model apply equally to all areas of the organization. Focusing on capabilities can account for context and variation across an organization, and drive focus on outcomes rather than obtaining a particularly qualitative measure that can be gamed.

Start Small, Experiment, Learn, Share, and Repeat

Adopting continuous delivery is a complex process, and therefore there are somewhat limited "best practices" that apply to all contexts. There are, however, many good experiments that can be run once you get to stage 4 in Steve Smith's model:

- If you are starting with a greenfield project, construct a basic but functional pipeline, and deploy a sample application to production as soon as possible. Dan North refers to this as creating a Dancing Skeleton (*http://bit.ly/2NIB6ql*). This will identify not only technical challenges such as deployments to production that must be conducted manually via a vendor portal, but also organizational issues such as the sysadmin team not giving you SFTP access to production for fear that you may damage other application configurations.

- Identify a piece of functionality that you can have end-to-end responsibility for delivery, and improve the stability and throughput of the associated application. Ideally, this will be non-business-critical (i.e., not the checkout process within an e-commerce system), but will clearly add business value, and the requirements must be well understood. A newsletter sign-up page or a promotional microsite are ideal candidates.

- Define one or two *metrics of success* that you will focus on improving with any component within your system. This could be something that is causing a particular challenge to your organization; for example, a high percentage of builds fail, or lead time for change is unacceptably high.

Once you have made progress, you must create a virtuous loop of feedback and learning across the organization:

- Demonstrate any positive results, benefits, and key learning to as big an audience as you can find. This must include at least one leader within your organization.

- Reflect on your approaches and technology choices. Make changes as appropriate and be sure to share this knowledge.

- Find a slightly bigger piece of functionality—ideally, something that uses a different technology stack, or that is owned by a different team or organization unit— and repeat the experimentation process.

- After two or three rounds of experimentation, you should have begun to identify common patterns and approaches to solve both technical and social issues within your organization. This is where you can once again elevate visibility of the program, perhaps taking the findings to the organization's VP of engineering or CTO, and campaign for a widespread rollout of continuous delivery.

- As soon as a senior engineering leader agrees to make the implementation of continuous delivery a priority, it's time to switch from experimentation to rollout.

Increasing adoption throughout an organization is challenging and depends a lot on the context in which you work, but several models and approaches can help.

Increase Adoption: Leading Change

Once your experiments with continuous delivery have proved successful, the next stage is planning a wider rollout to the entire organization. Although the full process for this is beyond the scope of this book, it is worth mentioning John Kotter's eight-step process for leading change. In his 1996 international bestseller *Leading Change* (Harvard Business Review Press), he defined the following steps:

1. Establishing a sense of urgency
2. Creating the guiding coalition
3. Developing a vision and strategy
4. Communicating the change vision
5. Empowering employees for broad-based action
6. Generating short-term wins
7. Consolidating gains and producing more change
8. Anchoring new approaches in the culture

These steps are relevant for any large-scale change within an organization, and implementing continuous delivery is very much a large-scale project for many companies. Figure 14-3 shows how the eight steps can be grouped into three stages, and the work you have undertaken so far falls into the first, "Creating the climate for change." The experiments you have run should enable you to create urgency, by providing you with data you can share that shows the benefits of adopting continuous delivery (perhaps in comparison with data associated with the issues the company is currently facing).

Finding like-minded individuals and teams within the organization allows the formation of a coalition and the creation of a vision for change. The next stages for engaging and enabling the organization and implementing and sustaining for change also build upon your success and CD implementation principles and practices learned in the journey so far.

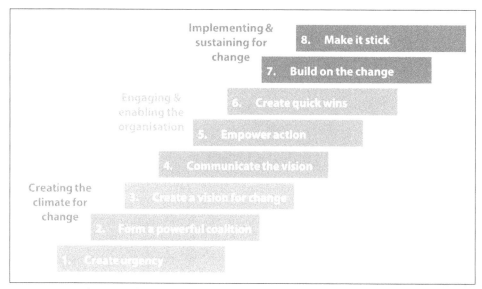

Figure 14-3. John Kotter's eight-step process for leading change

Driving adoption of continuous delivery within an organization can be challenging—particularly when the existing delivery processes have been in place for some time, or the organization is not yet feeling enough pain to drive change (think Blockbuster versus Netflix).

Leadership Is a Valuable Skill

Leading change, like implementing continuous delivery, requires a lot of skill, and skills that are different from that of software development. We have both been fortunate to have several mentors in our careers who have taught and guided us in developing these skills (and we recommend you find your own, too). We have also learned a lot from several books:

- *The Geek Leader's Handbook: Essential Leadership Insight for People with Technical Backgrounds* (Leading Geeks Press) by Paul Glen and Maria McManus
- *Talking with Tech Leads* (CreateSpace Independent Publishing Platform) by Pat Kua
- *The Manager's Path* (O'Reilly) by Camille Fournier

Additional Guidance and Tips

An entire book could be written on how to improve adoption of continuous delivery, but a few particular areas often provide challenges: common bad practices and dealing with ugly architecture.

Bad Practices and Common Antipatterns

You have read several times within this chapter that implementing continuous delivery within an organization is a complex process, and although many good practices are context-specific, there are also bad practices that are not. It is good to be aware of these so that you can avoid them:

- Overly ambitious choice (or scale) of functionality for continuous delivery proof-of-concept.

- Attempting to implement continuous delivery for a completely new and innovative piece of functionality. This can be a valid choice for experimenting with CD, but it can also lead to long delays if the new functionality is not well-defined or does not have political support within the organization.

- Introducing too much new technology into the stack—for example, going from deploying an EAR file for an application server hosted on in-house infrastructure to deploying Fat JAR applications within containers running on Kubernetes within the public cloud.

- Simultaneously modifying the architecture in a disruptive manner and attempting to create a build pipeline for the application—for example, going from deploying the application as a single monolithic WAR file to attempting to deploy and orchestrate the application as 10 microservices.

- Overreliance of external parties or vendors. Consultants and vendors can add a lot of value to a migration (and provide much needed expertise), but the migration process must ultimately be owned by an in-house team.

- Simply automating current manual practices. This can be a good starting point, but care must be taken to ensure that each manual practice is valid and necessary. Automating the wrong process simply means that you can do it faster and more often, which may cause even more damage than before!

- Not acknowledging the limitations or coupling imposed by a legacy application.

- Not understanding that the current organizational structure is not compatible with continuous delivery (e.g., the environment is heavily politicized or Conway's law (*http://bit.ly/2zzsSbs*) is not being respected).

- Not planning for migration or transformation of existing business data that is critical for the day-to-day operation of the organization.

- Overreliance on third-party integrations (which can be solved with mocking and service virtualization).

- Not providing access to self-service environments for development and testing.

This list is just some of the continuous delivery antipatterns that are seen in the wild. One of the most common issues deserves its own section within the chapter: the issue of "ugly" system architecture.

Ugly Architecture: To Fix, or Not to Fix

At some point within a continuous delivery implementation, the application's architecture may be a limiting factor. Several typical examples and potential solutions are explained in this section.

Conducting an Architecture Review

If you have just started working with a system or are unsure as to what state the current architecture is in, it can be worth conducting a formal architecture review. This process goes beyond simply drawing the (idealized) architecture on a whiteboard, and *Production-Ready Microservices* (O'Reilly) by Susan Fowler and *Software Architecture for Developers (https://leanpub.com/software-architecture-for-developers)* (Leanpub) by Simon Brown, contain useful practices and techniques to accomplish this.

Each end user/customer has separate codebase and database

It can be tempting to fork a single application codebase for individual customers, particularly if the applications share a similar core, but each customer wants customizations. This may scale when the business has only two or three customers, but soon becomes unmanageable, as a required security or critical bug patch has to be made on all the systems, and each fix may be subtly different because of the isolated evolution of each codebase.

Often an organization embracing continuous delivery with this style of application has to create as many build pipelines as there are customers, but this can also become unmanageable, particularly if the company has multiple products. A potential, but costly, solution to this issue is to attempt to consolidate all of the applications back into a single codebase that is deployed as a multitenant system, and any required custom functionality can be implemented via plugins or external modules.

Beware of the Big-Bang Fix

It can be tempting to try to fix all of your problems by throwing away (or retiring) an old application and deploying a new version as a "big bang." This can be dangerous for many reasons: the old application evolves while the new one is being built; the business team becomes nervous that no tangible value is being delivered by the team working on the new application; engineers working on the old application become unmotivated; and the complexity of deploying the new application means that something nearly always goes wrong.

One approach to overcoming big bang rewrites that has become popular, especially within microservice migrations, is the Strangler Pattern (*http://bit.ly/2OfQCpg*). This pattern promotes the incremental isolation and extraction of functionality from a monolith into a series of independently deployable services.

No well-defined interface between application and external integrations

In a quest to add increased functionality to a system, engineers often integrate external applications into their applications; for example, email sending or social media integration. Often, the interface between the system and the external applications is custom and tightly coupled to the specific implementation details. This often directly affects the release cadence of your application.

When these types of systems are put into a continuous delivery pipeline, the tight integration means that typically one of two issues is seen. First, developers have created mocks or stubs to allow testing against the external application, but frequently these mocks don't capture the true behavior of the application, or the external system constantly changes, which results in constant build failures and developers having to update the mocks. Second is that testing against the applications is conducted via external (test) sandbox implementations of the application, which are often flaky or lag behind the production implementation.

A solution to these types of issues is to introduce an anti-corruption layer (ACL)—or adapter—between the two systems. An ACL breaks the high coupling, and can facilitate the creation of a smaller, more nimble pipeline that tests the ACL adapter code against the real external (sandbox) service, and allows the company's application to be tested against the ACL running in a virtual/stubbed mode.

Infrastructure provides a single point of integration (and coupling and failure)

Existing systems that have been deployed into production for a long time, particularly within an enterprise organization, may communicate or integrate into a centralized communication mechanism like an ESB or heavyweight MQ system. Much like the preceding example, if these systems do not provide an embedded or mock mode of operation, then it can be advantageous to implement ACLs that reduce the coupling between the application and the communication mechanism.

The application is a "framework tapestry" and contains (too) many application frameworks or middleware

Many systems that are more than 10 years old will often contain multiple application frameworks, such as EJB, Struts, and Spring, and often multiple versions of these frameworks. This soon becomes a maintenance nightmare, and the frameworks often clash at runtime, both in regards to functionality and classpaths. It can be difficult to re-create the issues seen in production within a build pipeline, especially without executing the entire application and running end-to-end tests. The classic book *Working Effectively with Legacy Code* (Prentice Hall) provides several good patterns for dealing with this issue. Be aware, however, that this type of architectural modification typically requires a lot of investment, and it can be advantageous to rewrite or extract certain parts of the application if there is a business case for modifying the functionality.

Think: Incremental, Hard Problems, and Pilot Project

Any migration must incrementally demonstrate value; otherwise, it is likely to get cancelled midway through the implementation. Solving, or at least understanding, the hard problems first increases the chances of delivering value, and it also typically forces you to think globally rather than getting stuck on a local optimization problem. In addition, make sure that the pilot project you pick for a migration has a clear sponsor who has political support within the organization. There will be challenging times within the migration, and you will need someone to support you and stand up for the work being undertaken.

Summary

In this chapter, you learned about the challenges of migrating to continuous delivery. You also explored techniques that help mitigate some of these challenges:

- The research undertaken by Forsgren, Humble, and Kim shows that 24 key capabilities drive improvement in software delivery performance in a statistically significant way. Several of these capabilities have been grouped together and classified into the category of continuous delivery.

- The first step in picking a continuous delivery migration process is to do some research on your organization. The goal is to find the teams that already believe in the need for continuous delivery and already possess a desire and demonstrated ability to innovate and be early adopters in new technologies and techniques.

- Sense-making models, like Cynefin, can help you understand and classify some of the challenges you will encounter.
- Steve Smith's model for bootstrapping continuous delivery consists of: version controlling everything; measuring stability and throughput; adding production telemetry and moving to an adaptive architecture; and running parallel experiments.
- Continuous delivery can be measured by throughput—lead time and deployment frequency, and stability—the change fail rate and mean time to recovery.
- When you are learning how to implement continuous delivery effectively, you want to start with small hypotheses and ideas, experiment, learn, share locally and globally, and repeat.
- Leadership is a vital skill that you will need to cultivate when attempting to increase adoption throughout the organization.
- It is easy to fall into certain bad practices with CD, and there are potential challenges presented by "ugly" architectures.

With a good understanding of the technical practices of continuous delivery and the techniques required to roll this out across your team and organization, you are now in the perfect place to learn more about how to drive continual improvement in the final chapter.

## CHAPTER 15

Continuous Delivery and Continuous Improvement

In this concluding chapter, you will review what you've learned about how to implement continuous delivery, and focus once more on the core goals and challenges. Many of the practices associated with modern continuous delivery revolve around you, as a Java developer, to increase your knowledge, skills, and accountability throughout the software delivery and operation process. You will wrap up the book with a look at how the principles of continuous delivery can be expanded throughout the entire organization, and explore how continuous improvement should drive all the things that you do.

Start from Where You Are

Understanding the current situation you and your team are currently in is a vital skill. In Chapter 6, you learned about the evolution of the Java ecosystem, and the range of options modern developers now have to create applications. You built on this knowledge in Chapter 3 and Chapter 4 by learning how designing adaptive, or "evolutionary," architectures in combination with the use modern cloud and container technology can greatly increase both throughput and stability of the software delivery process.

A core requirement of modern software developers, especially technical leads, is keeping up-to-date with changes in technology, tooling, and practices. Learning from books, regularly reading blogs, watching online content, and attending conferences are all valuable uses of the essential portion of your time dedicated to continually improving. Only when you combine an understanding of the current situation you and your team are in with the potential possibilities can you most effectively decide on the best course of action to improve both the delivery of valuable software to users and the fun of building systems.

Build on Solid Technical Foundations

Chapters 5 and 6 provided you with foundational skills and tooling around building Java applications. Whereas in the early 2000s you could focus solely on coding Java, the reality is that now you also have to develop skills (or at least an understanding of those skills) that used to be purely within the domain of operations. The rise of the DevOps and SRE approaches to the delivery and running of software have crystallized this.

Chapter 7 built on many of the things you learned about packaging applications for the deployment onto available platforms you explored in Chapter 4. Packaging traditional Java deployment artifacts like the JAR and WAR for standalone execution adds new challenges, as does the use of VM, container, or FaaS technologies. Chapter 8 combined and extended many of the skills you learned over the previous chapters, and shared with you the importance of being able to develop and test locally as effectively as possible.

In Chapters 9 and 10, you began your journey into the early stages of the core of continuous delivery: continuous integration, and deploying and releasing functionality by using a build pipeline.

Continuously Deliver Value (Your Highest Priority)

The first of the 12 principles behind The Manifesto for Agile Software Development (*http://agilemanifesto.org/*) states the following:

> Our highest priority is to satisfy the customer
> through early and continuous delivery
> of valuable software.

Continuous delivery is not only the catalyst to enable early and continuous delivery of functionality to customers, but it is also the mechanism in which value (to a large degree) can be verified. Of course, you may not get the required functionality exactly right on the first try—probably far from it—but the framework provided by CD allows you to iterate fast.

Chapter 11 has shown you how to capture value hypotheses and codify user requirements, ideally through BDD-inspired collaboration and processes. With the emergence of container and FaaS technologies, and a whole host of testing harnesses and test double frameworks available to you, the Java ecosystem offers a compelling platform from which teams can deliver valuable software.

As you have seen in Chapter 12, an effective CD pipeline also enables the validation of system-quality attributes, or nonfunctional requirements, and these can be just as important to get right as their functional counterparts. It is vitally important that you take the time to implement these core validation steps within a CD pipeline, and equally crucial that you keep them up-to-date. In the previous chapter, your learned about the capability to "shift left on security," and the same value can be seen by "shifting" left many nonfunctional verifications, in both the pipeline itself and also in your thinking and designing process.

Once expectations have been codified within a CD pipeline, they can, of course, be automated and run multiple times. This not only provides more reliable results in comparison with the same operations carried out by humans (computers, after all, are great at carrying out repetitive and tedious tasks), but also frees up additional time for human engineers to do what they are good at: be creative, look for improvements, and empathize with the user requirements.

The effort to implement all of these validation steps should be shared throughout the team, as this is often the only way that enough time and energy will be available to work on the CD pipelines, and this is also typically the only way to get buy-in and shared responsibility across the organization. Every single person on the team should be focused on the continuous delivery of valuable software, and the practices on CD itself can often be a catalyst for organizational change.

Increase Shared Responsibility of Software

You have read about the importance of shared responsibility within several of the chapters of this book. The current market dictates that customer requirements change and shift faster than ever before. Technology also changes more rapidly today than ever before, as does the associated security threat landscape.

With the exception of the simplest website, it is clear that no one person can support all of these changes. When you are delivering software as part of a large enterprise, it would be impossible to even gather all of the scope into a single person's brain. Therefore, you have to embrace shared responsibility, and the CD pipeline is the perfect tool to rally around. As the pipeline captures a large part of the value stream, everyone involved can see the flow of business ideas, software, and functionality.

Two core concepts that you learned about in Chapters 13 and 14 are observability and measurements. Observability enables the monitoring of metrics from applications running in production to allow you to close the feedback loop and increase learning. Measuring continuous delivery outputs, such as lead time and the rate of failure, provide you with the ability to objectively evaluate the progress you are making through the use of continuous delivery as you increase throughput and stability.

Promote Fast Feedback and Experimentation

You learned in Chapter 14 that rapid feedback is vital when working with complex systems—and nearly all software applications are complex, adaptive systems. Continual, rapid, and high-quality feedback provides early opportunities to detect and correct errors. From a developer's point of view, one of the clear advantages of rapid feedback is the reduced cost in context switching and cognitive overhead of understanding a piece of functionality and the code and configuration that underlies.

The power of fast feedback and experimentation goes much deeper than this. Gene Kim, Kevin Behr, George Spafford, and Mike Orzen have talked extensively about the benefits of Three Ways of DevOps (*https://itrevolution.com/the-three-ways-principles-underpinning-devops/*): systems thinking, amplify feedback loops, and the culture of continual experimentation and learning. Figure 15-1 provides an illustration.

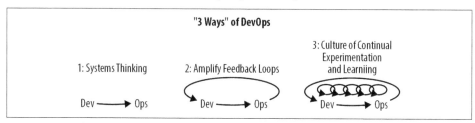

Figure 15-1. The Three Ways of DevOps (courtesy of The Phoenix Project by Gene Kim, et al.)

The First Way emphasizes the performance of the entire system, as opposed to the performance of a specific silo of work or department; you read about this previously in regards to increasing shared responsibility. The Second Way is about creating the right-to-left feedback loops, from operations to development, with the goal of shortening and amplifying feedback loops in order for corrections and improvements to be continually made. You've learned about this and the need to "shift left" many forms of testing and verification. The outcomes of the Second Way include understanding and responding to all customers, internal and external, shortening and amplifying all feedback loops, and embedding knowledge where we need it—both in teams and codified within the build pipeline itself.

The Third Way is about creating a culture that fosters two things: continual experimentation, taking risks and learning from failure; and understanding that repetition and practice is the prerequisite to mastery. Experimentation and taking risks ensure that you keep pushing to improve, and you need mastery of the skills that can help you recognize and course-correct when you have gone too far into the unknown. The outcomes of the Third Way include allocating time for the improvement of daily work (for example, focusing on improving the build pipeline and associated skills), creating rituals that reward the team for taking risks, and introducing chaos and disaster-recovery testing into the system and team in order to increase resilience.

Expand Continuous Delivery in an Organization

If you are keen to promote continuous delivery throughout your organization, there are two key approaches that you explored in Chapter 14: knowledge sharing and demonstration of benefits.

Knowledge sharing increases awareness of the principles, practices, and technologies associated with CD, such as those contained within *The DevOps Handbook* and *The Phoenix Project*. Many interesting presentation recordings from the DevOps Enterprise Summit (*http://bit.ly/2Ilj7QS*) YouTube playlists contain great stories and insights from thought leaders and practitioners across the industry, many of whom have focused on challenges in implementing the DevOps mindset and practices like CD within large enterprises. The culture in some organizations can be resistant to learning from resources like this, and therefore you may need to subtly introduce this type of knowledge sharing through the use of weekly book club sessions or "brown bag" lunchtimes, where anyone interested can join in and allocate dedicated time to learning.

The demonstration of benefits is also key to increasing adoption of CD principles throughout an organization, and for this to happen, you must become effective at capturing metrics, and at telling a story around these metrics. The starting point is often simply adding basic metrics capture to key processes within an organization, such as the time taken from idea to production, the number of failed deployments or production outages, or the number of bugs caught by automated testing. You can also add metrics to the systems running in production, and capture the number of user sessions, the average CPU and RAM requirements of an application, and the write performance of a data store.

Once you have these metrics in place, you can create a baseline from which you can (hopefully) demonstrate improvement. It is important to track how the metrics change with your attempts to implement CD, and also to attempt to fit a story to the changes. You may not always get this correct, but ideally you can frame the story as a hypothesis, and create tests to validate your ideas. Human beings have evolved alongside storytelling, and this is a powerful mechanism to create buy-in and understanding with people across the business.

Continuous Improvement

In conclusion, you should strive to continuously improve everything you do in creating software and delivery business value to customers. The principles of continuous delivery and the associated practices, like that of the build pipeline, are effective mechanisms for driving this improvement. The Continuous Improvement Kata (*http://bit.ly/1v73SSg*), taken from the Toyota Way and inspired by the martial arts kata approach to honing skills, is a great resource for helping to fully understand the approach, and codifies a lot of the practices you have learned from reading this book. Figure 15-2 illustrates the Continuous Improvement Kata.

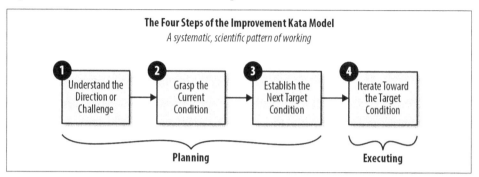

Figure 15-2. The Continuous Improvement Kata

It is key to first understand your challenges. Perhaps you are frequently slowed by failed releases, or you don't get appropriate requirements from the business. You must then grasp the current condition fully, and work with people across the organization and share responsibility for the potential improvements. After establishing the next target condition and planning with your team, you iterate toward this goal. Along the way, monitor for signs of success and failure, and continually reflect on and feed your learning forward into the process.

This book should act as your guide for implementing continuous delivery and ultimately drive continuous improvement within your organization. Although a book of this scope can never hope to cover every single topic (or every topic in the depth you may require), we are confident that this book can point you in the correct direction and provide a foundation to get started. When you have success and identify new techniques or areas of improvement, please do get in touch, or ideally write an article or book that expands on your idea.

Summary

In this concluding chapter, you have reviewed the core skills that you learned from this book so far, and explored the key ideas behind continuous delivery:

- Understanding the current situation that you and your team are currently in is a vital skill. This must be combined with continually developing your understanding of the possible practices and tooling in order to set goals for continual improvements.

- A core requirement of modern software developers, especially technical leads, is keeping up-to-date with changes in technology, tooling, and practices.
- Whereas in the early 2000s you could focus purely on coding Java, the reality is that now you also have to develop skills (or at least an understanding of those skills) that used to be purely within the domain of operations.
- Continuous delivery is not only the catalyst to enable early and continuous delivery of functionality to customers, but also the mechanism in which value (to a large degree) can be verified.
- Every single member of a software delivery team should be focused on the continuous delivery of valuable software, and the practices of CD itself can often be a catalyst for organizational change.
- Observability enables the monitoring of metrics from applications running in production and allows you to close the feedback loop and increase learning.
- Measuring continuous delivery outputs, such as lead time and the rate of failure, provide you with the ability to objectively evaluate the progress you are making.
- Gene Kim, Kevin Behr, George Spafford, and Mike Orzen have talked extensively about the benefits of Three Ways of DevOps: systems thinking, amplify feedback loops, and the culture of continual experimentation and learning.
- If you are keen to promote continuous delivery throughout your organization, there are two key approaches: knowledge sharing and demonstration of benefits.
- You should strive to continuously improve everything you do when creating software and delivering business value to customers. The Continuous Improvement Kata is a great resource for helping to fully understand the approach.

The end of this chapter also marks the end of this book, but this is the beginning of your journey. We wish you the best of fortune on this journey with continuous delivery!

Index

500 INTERNAL SERVER ERROR, 320
indicating errors, 396
HTTPie, 120-123
Hub tool for Git and GitHub, 209
hybrid cloud, 54
hypervisors, 169

I

IaaS (see infrastructure as a service)
IAM (Identity and Access Management), 362
IBM Bluemix, 62
IDEs (integrated development environments), 159
cloud-based, 173
immutable infrastructure, 58
enabled by containers, 66
improvement, continuous, 429
in-memory message queues, 313
in-process vs. out-of-proccess component testing, 316, 327
Independent Systems Architecture Principles, 37
INFO logging level, 387
infrastructure
cloud (Iaas) platforms, 54-59
benefits of, 58
challenges in, 56, 57
components, 54
continuous delivery into, 58
traditional platfoms
challenges with, 52
traditional platforms, 51-54
benefits of, 53
CI/CD on, 53
components, 51
infrastructure as a service (IaaS)
cloud (IaaS) platforms, 54-59
cloud platform security, 360
exploring deploy and release for, 234
infrastructure as code (IaC)
continuous integration of the platform, 227
tools, 184
working with, 74
inside-out testing, 328
(see also outside-in vs. inside-out testing)
instances (EC2), 247
integrated development environments (IDEs), 159
integration testing, 319-321

facilitation by good architecture, 32
testing fault tolerance, 320
verifying external interactions, 319
internal resources or interfaces, creating, 315
iostat utility, 115

J

JAR (Java Archive) files, 17
applications deployed via FaaS or serverless model, 21
building, 129-133
escaping JAR hell, 141
building a fat executable uber JAR, 133-137
using Maven Shade plugin, 134-137
using Maven Spring Boot plugin, 137
deploying Java applications as fat JARs running in a container, 19
executable fat JARs and twelve-factor apps, 18
skinny JARs instead of fat JARs, 138
Java
running within Docker, gotchas, 65
tracing with OpenZipkin, Spring Sleuth, and OpenCensus, 394
java (command-line utility), 78
java -jar command, 132
Java Development Kit (see JDK)
Java development, evolution of, 13-28
DevOps, SRE, and release engineering, 22-27
release engineering, 25
shared responsibility, metrics, and observability, 26
site reliability engineering (SRE), 23-25
Java deployment platforms, 17-21
requirements of modern Java applications, 13-17
impacts on continuous delivery, 17
need for business speed and stability, 14
opportunities and costs of the cloud, 15
rise of the API economy, 15
small services, 16
Java Runtime Environment (see JRE)
Java Shop application, extended (example), 231-233
Java Virtual Machines (see JVMs)
javac, 78
JAVA_HOME environment variable, 87, 90
JBehave, 301

About the Author

Daniel Bryant works as an independent technical consultant and product architect at Datawire. He specializes in enabling continuous delivery within organizations through the identification of value streams, creation of build pipelines, and implementation of effective testing strategies. Daniel's technical expertise focuses on DevOps tooling, cloud/container platforms, and microservice implementations. He is also a Java champion, contributes to several open source projects, writes for InfoQ, O'Reilly, and Voxxed, and regularly presents at international conferences such as OSCON, QCon, and JavaOne.

Abraham Marin-Perez is a Java and Scala developer with more than 10 years of experience in industries ranging from finance to publishing to the public sector. He also helps run the London Java Community, and provides career advice at the Meet a Mentor London group. Abraham likes sharing his experiences with other people, which has led him to speak at international events like JavaOne or Devoxx UK, and to write about Java news at InfoQ. He is also the author of *Real-World Maintainable Software* (O'Reilly). Currently based in London, Abraham likes going out on a hike whenever the English weather permits it, and cooking when it doesn't.

Colophon

The animals on the cover of *Continuous Delivery in Java* are lanternfish, a family of fish known as Myctophidae. Lanternfish get their name from their natural bioluminescence, which causes them to glow with blue, green, or yellow light. This light is produced by organs known as photophores, which are arranged along the body and head of the fish. It is theorized that bioluminescence plays a role in communication between lanternfish.

Small and slender, Lanternfish are covered in silvery scales. They live deep in the ocean, diving deeper by day and rising at night. They are a major food source for marine predators, such as whales, dolphins, tuna, and sharks, making them an important link in the oceanic food chain.

Lanternfish are extremely numerous, and are estimated to make up 65% of all deep sea fish biomass. They account for much of the deep sea scattering layer, a phenomenon where ships' sonar is scattered off the swim bladders found in deep sea fish, causing false depth readings. Although common in the wild, there is very little commercial fishing of lanternfish.

Many of the animals on O'Reilly covers are endangered; all of them are important to the world. To learn more about how you can help, go to *animals.oreilly.com*.

The cover image is from *Lydekker's Royal Natural History*. The cover fonts are URW Typewriter and Guardian Sans. The text font is Adobe Minion Pro; the heading font is Adobe Myriad Condensed; and the code font is Dalton Maag's Ubuntu Mono.

Learn from experts.
Find the answers you need.

Sign up for a **10-day free trial** to get **unlimited access** to all of the content on Safari, including Learning Paths, interactive tutorials, and curated playlists that draw from thousands of ebooks and training videos on a wide range of topics, including data, design, DevOps, management, business—and much more.

Start your free trial at:

oreilly.com/safari

(No credit card required.)

Lightning Source UK Ltd.
Milton Keynes UK
UKHW031205071221
395200UK00005B/15